Springer Series

FOCUS ON MEN

Daniel Jay Sonkin, Ph.D., Series Editor
James H. Hennessy, Ph.D., Founding Editor

Focus on Men provides a wide range of books on the major psychological, medical, and social issues confronting men today.

Jerrold Lee Shapiro, PhD, is a clinical psychologist in private practice. He is the author of *The Measure of a Man: Becoming the Father You Wish Your Father Had Been, When Men Are Pregnant,* and *Methods of Group Psychology and Encounter.* He is co-author with Alan Scheflin of *Trance on Trial,* (winner of the 1991 Manfred S. Guttmacher award from the American Psychiatric Association) and *Classic Readings in Educational Psychology* with Harold Ayabe. He received his Ph.D. from the University of Waterloo and he has taught at the University of Hawaii, St. Bonaventure University and the University of California at Santa Cruz prior to his current position (since 1982) as Professor of Counseling Psychology at Santa Clara University. He is also Managing Partner of Ohana Family Therapy Institute and Family Business Solutions and guest SYSOP of the Men's Conference on the Shrinktank BBS. Dr. Shapiro frequently appears in electronic and print media. He lives in Los Altos, CA with his wife, Susan, and two children.

Michael J. Diamond, PhD, is in the private practice of psychotherapy and psychoanalysis in Los Angeles. He received his doctorate from Stanford University and completed his psychoanalytic training at The Los Angeles Institute for Psychoanalytic Studies. He is a Diplomate in Clinical Psychology of the American Board of Professional Psychology and a Fellow of the American Psychological Association. Dr. Diamond is currently an Associate Clinical Professor in the Department of Psychiatry at UCLA, a Member of the Teaching and Supervisory Faculty at the Wright Institute, Los Angeles, and is on the Faculty of the Los Angeles Institute for Psychoanalytic Studies. He is on the editorial boards of several journals and has published over 70 articles and chapters in the areas of psychotherapy, psychoanalysis, hypnosis, group process, and cross-cultural psychology as well as fathering, gender, and men's issues. He is the recipient of numerous honors and awards for his teaching and writing. His current scholarly interests include explorations into "good enough" fathering for both sons and daughters and its neglected implications for psychoanalytic developmental theory and treatment, and the efficacy of psychoanalytic treatment for adults who were sexually abused in childhood. He lives in Los Angeles with his wife and two children.

Martin Greenberg, MD, was born in New York City. He did his undergraduate study at U.C.L.A. and attended medical school, did his pediatric internship, and psychiatric training at the University of California School of Medicine in San Francisco. Dr. Greenberg also did research in Sweden at the Karolinska Institute. Dr. Greenberg is the author of The *Birth Of A Father* and contributing author to *Experts Advise Parents.* He was special projects editor for *Nurturing News* (later known as *Nurturing Today,* one of the first fathering quarterlies that was published on a regular basis). He is also on the parenting panel for *USA Today.* He was scientific advisory editor for *Preparent Advisor* and *New Parent Advisor* annuals. Currently Dr. Greenberg is medical director at the Venture Adolescent Day Treatment Center as well as consulting psychiatrist for the county juvenile forensic service in San Diego, CA. He is also in private practice. Dr. Greenberg lives with his wife and two children.

BECOMING A FATHER

Contemporary, Social, Developmental, and Clinical Perspectives

Jerrold Lee Shapiro, PhD

Michael J. Diamond, PhD

Martin Greenberg, MD

Editors

Springer Publishing Company

Springer Publishing Company, Inc.
536 Broadway
New York, NY 10012-3955

Cover design by Tom Yabut
Production Editor: Pam Lankas

Cover photo of Hannah and Matt Fenton by Judith Fenton

95 96 97 98 99 / 5 4 3 2 1

Library of Congress Cataloging-in-Publication Data
Becoming a father: contemporary social, developmental, and clinical
    perspectives / Jerrold Lee Shapiro, Michael J. Diamond, Martin
    Greenberg, editors.
        p. cm.— (Springer series, focus on men)
    Includes bibliographical references and index.
    ISBN 0-8261-8400-6
    1. Fathers. 2. Fathers—Psychology. I. Shapiro, Jerrold Lee 1943–
II. Diamond, Michael J., 1944– . III. Greenberg, Martin, 1941–
    IV. Series.
HQ756.B39   1995
306.874'2—dc20   94-39952
                                                                          CIP

Printed in the United States of America

oclc 31610148

To our treasured children

Natasha and Gabriel
Maya and Alex
Jonathan and Jacob

Our beloved wives

Susan Bernadett-Shapiro
Linda Feldsott Diamond
Claudia Law-Greenberg

And our loving parents

Myer and Beatrice Shapiro
Moses and Elaine Diamond
Samuel and Rachel Greenberg

Contents

Part I: The Social Perspective

Sociocultural Dimensions

Part II: The Developmental Perspective

Personal Experience

Psychological Issues

Part III: The Clinical Perspective

Psychodynamic Dimensions

Treatment Issues

Contributors

Alan P. Bader, PhD, received his doctorate in Counseling Psychology from Lehigh University. As a student he completed research on fathers' engrossment with their newborns and fathers' abilities to recognize their newborns by touch, smell, or sight. His newborn recognition study is being submitted for future publication. Dr. Bader is a licensed psychologist and child and family therapist in a group private practice, Growth Opportunity Center, located in suburban Philadelphia, Pennsylvania. He coordinates services for fathers and children. Dr. Bader runs play/discussion groups for fathers and their children and gives lectures and workshops promoting the active role of fathering.

Charles A. Ballard, MSW, was born in Underwood, Alabama in 1936. At age 17 he became a young father, joined the Army and became a Paratrooper with the former 101 Screaming Eagles' Division. He returned to Alabama in 1959 and adopted his 5 1/2-year-old son. In 1963, he moved to Oakwood College, a Seventh Day Adventist Institution designed to prepare Christian African Americans for service to their fellow men. He received his B.A. from Oakwood in 1970 and his M.A. in Social Work from Case Western Reserve University in 1972. In 1976 he began research on the impact of fathers' presence on mothers and children. By 1978 he started the Teen Father Unit at Cleveland Community Health Services. This program is now The Institute for Responsible Fatherhood and Family Revitalization. To fulfill his mission of building bridges between generations, Mr. Ballard creates environments that are father friendly, child friendly and family friendly.

Henry B. Biller, PhD, has five children, ranging in age from 10 to 30, and a 3-year-old grandson. He is Professor of Psychology at the University of Rhode Island, where he has taught since 1970. He is a consulting editor to *Archives* of *Sexual Behavior and Sex Roles* and is a fellow of the American Psychological Association and the American Psychological Society. He has contributed to *Annual Progress in Child Psychiatry and Child-Development* and *The Handbook of Developmental Psychology*. Dr. Biller is the author or co-author of nine books including *Father Power, Child Maltreatment and Paternal Deprivation, Fathers and Families,* and *The Father Factor*. A developmental-clinical psychologist, he has worked with a variety of human service organizations serving parents and children.

Henry Brown, BA, completed his Bachelors at San Diego State University and received his teaching credential through that University as well as USIU. He worked as a football, basketball, and baseball coach at Lincoln High School in San Diego, and later, worked for several years with handicapped individuals at the vocational rehabilitation program of Grossmont Unified School District. Subsequently, he was employed at San Diego State University in the counseling program focusing on rehabilitation with ex-offenders. Currently, Mr. Brown is a teacher at The Sarah Anthony School where he teaches and works with delinquent youth. His focus in his life's work is to motivate youngsters to have self-worth.

David DeBus, PhD, is a licensed psychologist practicing in La Jolla, California. He specializes in therapy with religiously-oriented and artistic people. In addition to his professional psychological training, he has degrees in literature and religion and training in music. His daughter continues to delight him.

Diane Ehrensaft, PhD, is a professor of psychology at The Wright Institute, Berkeley, California and a practicing clinical psychologist in Oakland, California. She has done extensive research and writing in the area of family, parenting, gender, and child development. She is the author of *Parenting Together: Men and Women Sharing the Care of their Children* and *Parenting Against All Odds: Raising Children for the Twenty-First Century.* Dr. Ehrensaft is presently co-director of the Center for the Changing Family with Dr. Anne Bernstein and is involved in a project editing a book series on Disassembling and Reassembling the Family. Much of her clinical work involves consultation to mothers and fathers about "parenting together" and she herself has been a participant observer for the past twenty two years as a mother in a shared parenting family.

W. Ernest Freud, D. Phil., himself a near miss "premature father," received his academic education in London where he studied psychology, trained as adult- and child-psychoanalyst and became a training analyst at the London Institute of Psychoanalysis and at the Hampstead Child Therapy Clinic. At both institutions he taught infact observation for several years. He got hooked by the prematures and became interested in the emotional impact of what he observed in many NICU's in the United States, England and Central Europe. The psychosocial side of neonatal intensive care, on which he has written and lectured widely, has become his primary focus of interest.

Geoffrey L. Greif, DSW, is associate professor at the School of Social Work, University of Maryland at Baltimore. He is the author of over 50 articles and four books, including *Single Fathers* and *The Daddy Track and the Single Father.*

Alan R. Gurwitt, MD, is currently on the faculties of the Boston Psychoanalytic Society and Institute (BPSI), and the Division of Child and Adolescent Psychiatry of The Cambridge Hospital (Harvard University). At BPSI he is co-chair of the Parenthood Study Group. Dr. Gurwitt has three children and one grandchild. He is co-editor of two books on fatherhood, *Father and Child: Developmental and Clinical Perspectives* (1982, with Stanley Cath and John Ross) and *Fathers and Their Families* (1989, with Stanley Cath and Linda Gunsberg) as well as many articles on various fatherhood topics.

Judith Partnow Hyman, PhD, MSW, is on the faculty of the California Graduate Institute (CGI) Psychoanalytic Department and is a Supervisor at Wright Institute of Los Angeles. She is an Associate Member of the Los Angeles Institute for Psychoanalytic Studies. She has been Staff/Consultant in the Early Childhood Department of Thalians at Cedars/ Sinai Hospital. Her private practice is in Encino, CA.

Pamela L. Jordan, PhD, RN, is an Associate Professor in the Department of Parent and Child Nursing at the University of Washington in Seattle. Her program of research focuses on the transition to fatherhood, both enhancing understanding of this major life transition and developing and evaluating interventions to promote and support paternal behavior.

Lawrence Kutner, PhD, is a clinical psychologist who trained at the Mayo Clinic and teaches at Harvard Medical School. He's best known, however, as a journalist and author. From 1987 through 1994 he wrote the "Parent & Child" column for the *New York Times,* which also ran in several hundred other newspapers throughout the United States and Canada. He currently writes a monthly column for *Parents* magazine and has just published the third book of his five-book series on child development and parent-child communication. He lives with his wife and son in New York City.

Michael E. Lamb, PhD, has been Head of the Section on Social and Emotional Development at the National Institute of Child Health and Human

Development. He was formerly a Professor of Psychology, Pediatrics, and Psychiatry at the University of Utah, the University of Wisconsin, University of Michigan, Hokkaido University (Japan), and the University of Haifa (Israel). He is co-author of *Development in Infancy, Socialization and Personality Development, Infant Mother Attachment,* and *Child Psychology Today.* He has edited several books on the role of the father in child development, founded and co-edited the *Advances in Developmental Psychology* series, and has edited about two dozen other books on various aspects of child development, including *Infant Development: Perspectives from German-speaking countries* (1991); *Child care in context: Cross-cultural perspectives* (1992); *Adolescent problem behavior* (1994) and *Images of Childhood* (in press). Dr. Lamb has also published widely in all major journals and currently serves on the editorial board of nine journals. He is on the advisory boards of research, academic, and service agencies in Germany, Israel, and the United States. He is the recipient of two national awards from the American Psychological Association and two awards for research excellence from the University of Utah. He received his Ph.D. from Yale University.

Ronald F. Levant, EdD, earned his doctorate in Clinical Psychology and Public Practice from Harvard in 1973, and for 13 years was on the faculty of the Counseling Psychology Program at Boston University, where he served as the founder and Director of the nationally prominent Fatherhood Project. He is now on the faculty at Cambridge Hospital/Harvard Medical School, and is in Independent Practice in Brookline, MA. Dr. Levant's research interests are in the fields of family and gender psychology. He has authored, co-authored, or edited seven books and over 40 articles and book chapters in the areas of family psychology and the psychology of men. In addition, he serves as Editor for the *Journal of Family Psychology* and is President of the Division of Family Psychology of The American Psychological Association.

Katharyn A. May, PhD, RN, received her BSN from Duke University, and her graduate degrees from the University of California, San Francisco. Prior to her current position at the University of British Columbia, she was on faculty at UCSF School of Nursing from 1978 to 1987 and Vanderbilt University until 1994. Dr. May has focused her research on psychosocial adaptation in the childbearing family, beginning with her dissertation research on the social psychological experience of first-time expectant fatherhood. This and other studies related to fatherhood, including an exploratory study of fathers' responses to unexpected cesarean birth, have gained media attention. From 1984–1987, Dr. May was a co-investigator on a NIH-funded study of the impact of antenatal stress on maternal, paternal, infant and family outcomes in the first year after birth. At present, she is directing a three-year project funded by NIH to examine the impact of prescribed home-Management of preterm labor on families. She is recognized as an expert in grounded theory method, and serves as a methodological consultant on several research projects. Dr. May has published a major textbook on maternity nursing which has been selected twice as an American Journal of Nursing Book of the Year, numerous original articles in journals within and outside nursing, has served on the editorial boards of several journals, and currently is Associate Editor of *Qualitative Health Research.*

Brian Neville, PhD, received his doctorate in Clinical/Community Psychology from the University of Illinois at Urbana-Champaign in 1992. He is currently the Project coordinator for Michael J. Guralnick's Children's Friendships and Families Project at the University of Washington. His interests are in the developmental outcomes of parent-child relationships, the contextual factors which influence those relationships, and clinical work with families.

Sam Osherson, PhD, is the author of *Finding Our Fathers: How a Man's Life is Shaped by His Relationship with His Father* and *Wrestling with Love: How Men Struggle with Intimacy.* He is a psychotherapist in practice in Cambridge, MA and a research psychologist at the Harvard University Health Services as well as on the faculty of the Fielding Institute. He is married, with two children.

Ross D. Parke, PhD, is Professor of Psychology and Director of the Center for Family Studies at the University of California, Riverside. He received his PhD in developmental psychology from the University of Waterloo in 1965 and previously taught and conducted research at the University of Wisconsin, the Fels Research Institute and the University of Illinois. Parke is author or editor of several volumes including *Fathers, Child Psychology: A Contemporary Viewpoint* (with M. Hetherington), *Family-Peer Relationships* (with G. Ladd) and *Children in Time and Place* (with G. Elder & J. Modell). He was previously editor of *Developmental Psychology* and president of the Division of Developmental Psychology, American Psychological Association. He has conducted research on fathers since the late 1960s and is currently interested in barriers to changing men's roles in the family, as well as family-peer relationships.

Lawrence Peltz, PhD, is a Marriage, Family and Child Therapist dedicated to the value of the client-therapist relationship as the indispensible foundation for psychological development. He has maintained a full-time private practice in San Rafael, CA since 1984. His training includes graduate degrees from the University of Southern California (Systems Management), University of Hawaii (Counseling Psychology) and the California Graduate School of Marital and Familly Therapy. He frequently consults to a broad range of clinical programs, business organizations and management teams.

Joseph H. Pleck, PhD, is an Associate Professor in the Division of Human Development and Family Studies at the University of Illinois at Urbana-Champaigne. Formerly Research Associate at the Wellesley College Center for Research on Women, he was a founder of the National Organization for Men Against Sexism. Dr. Pleck is the author of *Men and Masculinity* and *The Myth of Masculinity.* He is the proud father of Daniel Pleck.

William Shelley Pollack, PhD, is on the Faculty of the Harvard Medical School, on the staff of the Massachusetts General Hospital, and is Associate Psychologist at McLean Hospital where he serves as Director of Continuing Education in the Department of Psychology. He is a principal of the psychological consulting firm, Spectrum, O.E.D., Inc.; and Past President of the Massachusetts Psychological Association. With Dr. William Betcher he is the coauthor of *In A Time of Fallen Heroes: The Re-creation of Masculinity.* He has researched, written, and lectured widely on the psychology of men, and is a founding member of the Society for the Psychological Study of Men and Masculinity. With offices in Newton and Belmont, MA, Dr. Pollack resides in Newton with his wife and daughter.

Kyle D. Pruett, MD, is Clinical Professor of Psychiatry, Yale Child Study Center, New Haven, Connecticut. He is the author of *The Nurturing Father* and a host of research articles and contributions to the literature on fatherhood.

Brad Sachs, PhD, is a Psychologist specializing in clinical work with children, adults, couples and families and the Founder and Director of the Father Center in Columbia. He has written *Things Just Haven't Been the Same: The Transition from Marriage to Parenthood, If Only We Had Known: Transforming Marital Pain Into Marital Growth,* and *Blind Date: Poems of Expectant Fatherhood.* He also composed and performed the music for two recording projects, "Opening Day: Songs of Expectant Fatherhood" and "Love So Hard: Songs of Marriage." Dr. Sachs writes "Dad's Corner," an advice columan in *American Baby Magazine,* the only regular question and answer article that focuses on fatherhood. He is married to Karen Meckler, a psychiatrist, and is the father of three children, Josh, Matthew, and Jessica.

Peggy Shecket, MS, has been working with families of young children for over 20 years. In the early 1970s she was a co-author of a Piagetian-based infant stimulation curriculum that was disseminated nationally as a model for working with babies with developmental delay. She received her master's degree in family and child development at Ohio State University in 1973. She has worked in a variety of agency and hospital settings and has been, since 1986, at the Elizabeth Blackwell Center at Riverside Methodist Hospitals in Columbus, OH, where she helped to create a comprehensive, hospital-based parenting program to provide education and support to parents from preconception through the later parenting years. She was founder and co-facilitator of Dads' Group, a support group for fathers. Peggy often appears on local television and radio stations for her parenting expertise and has been quoted in *New Parents* magazine.

Peter Wolson, PhD, is a clinical psychologist and a Training and Supervising Analyst, as well as the current President of the Los Angeles Institute and Society for Psychoanalytic Studies (LAISPS). He is also on the faculty of LAISPS and the Wright Institute of Los Angeles. His private practice is in Beverly Hils, CA.

Foreword

Becoming a Father speaks eloquently about the critical contributions fathers make to the healthy development of children. This is sadly ironic, as the number of households headed by single women is soaring. Propelled by high divorce rates and out-of-wedlock births, father-absent families represent about 25% of all families. This poses a formidable challenge as we seek to strengthen the family. It is encouraging that the writers in *Becoming a Father* provide a broad perspective on this challenge from social, clinical, and developmental perspectives.

It is clear from the chapters included here that men should acquire as much knowledge as women about the nurturing of children. Many fathers will no longer be spared the mundane duties and pleasures of diapering their infants, bathing them, putting them to bed at night, and partaking of daily childcare tasks. No doubt many men will learn some of these responsibilities in parenting classes associated with the birth of their first child but many more will not, particularly unwed fathers.

Written for professionals, this text addresses the challenges we face in helping young men effectively learn about fathering when the pedagogy related to fatherhood has changed so dramatically over the past several decades. Many of the chapters highlight the knowledge that is sought by these men along with a substantive discussion of the normal dilemmas, fears, and developmental issues facing fathers. Both mental health professionals and birth educators must increasingly focus on, and deal with, the emotional clinical, and social issues of fatherhood and truly partnered parenting.

The father's importance in rearing children was downplayed until recently, and often totally neglected by child care experts. The general public, supported by the pronouncements of leading professionals about women's "natural instincts"—promulgated the belief that women were best-suited to raise children and supervise the related duties in the home. Because women carry and bear babies, and are physically equipped to breast feed, it seemed reasonable to assume that they possess innate "mothering" talents. The ability to nurture children was not only believed to be a woman's God-given *gift*, but her *duty* as well. The responsibility for most of the child's emotional and psychological development was placed on the mother while the father was relegated to the background. The father was not deemed responsible for his children's development, except when he was actively abusive or abandoning, an attribution that often amounted to a major distortion.

In the psychiatric literature, problems in the emotional growth of children were usually attributed to the mother, who was largely held accountable and "blamed" for the pathology of her children. For instance, we had the now outmoded theory of the "schizophrenogenic mother" but not the counterpart of the "schizophrenogenic father." This in-grown cultural bias has contributed to our ignorance and lack of study of the father's role in the family.

As chapters in this volume will outline, the father's role was traditionally described as remote from the children—an authority figure who disciplined and taught the children the ways of the outside world. Many famous clinicians and developmental theorists including Freud, argued that the mother–child bond was the most critical to the healthy development of children, and that men, even if they so desired, were not equipped to assume such an involved role with children. The old-fashioned, emotionally distant father is a misleading stereotype, however.

Historically, many fathers have been very close to their children and often provided the main sources of warmth and affection for them. This side of the story is seldom told. Fortunately, today those aspects of the traditional father's role that were interactive and responsive to the developmental needs of the child are being reemphasized and encouraged. This book is at the forefront in helping us to take a fresh look at these important functions of the early stages of fathering.

What is new about fathers' roles is the importance of their participation in the custodial care of their children. The current emphasis is on fathers appreciating the role they can play in their child's development by being interactive and nurturing, both in the process of doing the child care chores previously consigned to the mother, and in their specifically paternal roles requiring the active provision of necessary psycho-emotional "supplies" to their offspring. Fathers who have assumed more of these duties, including some who have become "house husbands," have found that these activities build the intimate, satisfying relationships with their children that mothers have experienced for centuries. Today, involved fathers need not see themselves as weak or maternal. In contrast to the standoffish image of the "strong father," today's nurturing father adds much more strength to the family than his old-style counterpart.

The women's movement certainly helped bring about these changes by questioning the legitimacy and health of fixed roles for parents. In turn, men questioned their place as mere financial providers and secondary parents. Concurrently, social and economic changes have forced fathers and mothers to modify their perspectives in order to meet the child rearing demands of changing family patterns. There are more divorced, single-parent, dual-career, blended, and same-sex-couple families than ever before. Though the main responsibility for child rearing still remains with women, more men have been drawn into active fathering roles.

As with most movements, there is support from a new generation of experts as exemplified in *Becoming a Father*. Scholars, aware of the previous neglect of the subject of fatherhood, are restoring balance to the literature on parenting. Recent evidence suggests that the ability of fathers to support their children's healthy growth is equivalent to that of mothers, though it may be different. Nonetheless, the modern father must relinquish old-fashioned ideas about "manliness" and what constitutes "women's work" vis-à-vis "men's work." There is perhaps no mystique of motherhood that a man cannot master except the physical acts of pregnancy, delivery, and breast feeding. All other notions about which gender makes the more natural parent are arguable. These changing attitudes, eliminating sexism in child-rearing practices, will ultimately maximize opportunities for both boys and girls.

Even though the women's movement in America has helped many men to become more involved in the parenting role, this has not been true around the world. We must be cautious in applying these contemporary family ideologies and changing roles to different class and ethnic groups. For example, gender roles in African-American, Latino, and Asian families may require specific study and evaluation. There is no doubt, however, that at least in America, the father as an involved parent is the wave of the future. By bringing together so many of the experts and writers in the field of fathering, *Becoming a Father* is invaluable in its contribution to the support of research, and under-standing of the often-unappreciated Daddy.

ALVIN F. POUSSAINT, MD
Clinical Professor of Psychiatry, Harvard Medical School
Senior Associate in Psychiatry, Judge Baker Children's Center

Preface

At the 1991 American Psychological Association meetings in San Francisco, several clinicians and researchers who had long been studying fatherhood came together under the auspices of several APA Divisions (Family Psychology, Independent Practice, Psychotherapy) as well as the Committee for the Scientific Study of Men and Masculinity. Prior to this convention and another (1994 APA Convention in Los Angeles), many of us in the field had labored in isolation. The 1991 San Francisco convention provided an opportunity for exposure of new work and synthesis between a host of workers in the field. One of the symposia entitled, "Becoming a Father," was chaired by the senior author. This unique presentation involved a combination of empirical research, clinical insights, and personal subjective reactions, which were communicated in a variety of ways including poetry and music.

Barbara Watkins, then of Springer Publishing Co., saw the possibilities for a greater collaboration. The editors of the volume proposed a wide-ranging look at the phenomenon of "becoming a father," keeping with the spirit of the San Francisco symposium and our own research and clinical findings over the past two decades. We believed that the scope of the book would have to include empirical research, developmental observation, clinical insight, pragmatic advice, and subjective experience.

We contacted each of the eminent writers and workers in the field, hoping that some percentage would agree to contribute to the edited work. To our great surprise and beyond our wildest hopes, virtually every person we contacted responded with a desire to be part of this volume: perhaps a tribute to the need for this book and the isolation in which many of us have labored. Unfortunately, several noteworthy contributions had to be eliminated due to space limitations. The resultant text, *Becoming a Father: Contemporary Social, Developmental, and Clinical Perspectives*, is a compilation and synthesis of the work of these experts. Most of the chapters are original for this volume. However, we have also included a few classic papers that remain contemporary in scope.

Because of the nature of the response to our invitation, page limitations, and the quality of the submissions, several difficult editing decisions had to be made. Most of these painful cuts were made to keep the focus of the book clearly on the father during the period from the decision to have a child through the child's first year of life. The text also maintains its primary focus on biological fathers in a coupled relationship. Some attention also has been paid to stepfathers and single fathers. Although these latter groups as well as gay fathers are worthy of similar treatment, space limitations made it impossible to adequately address their concerns. That we leave to future work.

It is our hope that this book will serve both as a reference source-book and as a guide to the complex transformation that men experience as they become fathers. We have endeavored to provide a clear understanding of this phenomenon from both objective, empirical observations and clinical, subjective perspectives. The beginning of the text provides a clear illustration. Following our introduction to the sections and chapters, the text opens with a poem by Brad Sachs followed by a scholarly review of the literature by Michael Lamb.

There are many people to acknowledge in the production of this work. Most of our authors have labored over the years to study their own personal transformations in response to parenting as well as the unique responses of thousands of other fathers. To all the men and women who contributed to the original research that is integrated into this text, we give our heartfelt thanks. We recognize the groundbreaking work by individuals in the field who produced the Fatherhood Projects at Bank Street College in New York and Boston University. Of course we extend our deepest gratitude to our own fathers and the many men who have "fathered us."

Finally we thank the many contributors to this book, who gave their time and their creativity without financial remuneration to make this book a reality. The submitted manuscripts to this text represent to us a true "Who's Who" in the field. We believe their work will be cherished for its heuristic, scholarly, and applied value for decades to come.

JERROLD LEE SHAPIRO, PHD
MICHAEL J. DIAMOND, PHD
MARTIN GREENBERG, MD

Becoming a Father

1

Introduction

Jerrold Lee Shapiro, Michael J. Diamond, and Martin Greenberg

Over the past 30 years, the father's role in childbirth and early parenting has shifted dramatically. The vast majority of fathers in the western world now have the opportunity to be present for the birth of their children. They may experience first hand the pains of labor, the agony of transition, and the incredible joy at the birth. Greenberg (1985), Shapiro (1987, 1993a), and other contributors to this book have shown that the experience is one of the most important events in men's lives.

Although fathers are increasingly involved in pregnancy, childbirth, and early parenting, we have, as a culture, all too often neglected to understand more about the positive and negative nuances of this experience for the father. The process of becoming a father often triggers tremendous turmoil for an individual father. It marks his entrance both into the world of parenthood and into a more empathic appreciation of his own father's experience. This further establishes his sense of adult masculinity, replete with cultural and social expectations.

BECOMING A FATHER: HISTORICAL CONSIDERATIONS

In the agrarian communities of the past, the demand that the father provide for his family resulted in his working long hours in the fields. Historically, his wife and children would join him in these efforts. The father was a presence and a force within the family. He could be seen,

3

heard, and fully experienced in an ongoing way. His work was mean-
ingfully integrated into the family fabric and larger social context. For
many sons, working alongside their fathers as an "apprentice," provided them with a model of manhood and a yardstick by which they
could measure themselves. Years later, many men would reminisce
joyfully about the fond, intimate feelings they experienced while
working beside their fathers. This active father–son connection served
both to initiate younger men into culturally sanctioned male roles and
orient them in relation to the world. Such shared experiences also
enabled them to feel close and connected to their fathers.

In these agrarian communities, the father was expected to play a
special role at the birth of his children. It was the expectant father who
boiled water, physically and emotionally supported his wife during
labor, and was the general support person for the midwife during the
frequent home births. Two major social revolutions served to move
fathers out of the picture and progressively diminish his importance.
These were *the movement of births from home to hospital* and *the
advent of the industrial revolution.*

The Shift of Births from Home to Hospital.   By the turn of
the twentieth century, births began to occur in hospitals in an attempt
to combat the rising tide of puerperal (childbirth) fever, which had
resulted in women dying in childbirth. The father, frequently viewed
as unsterile and thus potentially contaminated, was denied entrance
into the delivery room. Following the birth, his access to his newborn
was limited to peering through a wall of glass for 1 hour a day, during
special visiting hours.

The Industrial Revolution.   The Industrial Revolution provided additional impetus for separating the father from his child and
family. With the advent of the Industrial Revolution, a father's work
became less home-based as he labored in a distant work place for much
of his waking day (cf. Rotundo, 1993; Shapiro, 1993b). This increasing
separation of the workplace from the family home resulted in fathers
often feeling isolated and disconnected from their families as less time
was available to spend with their children.

Social and economic factors required the typical father to relinquish
much of his traditional role as a teacher, mentor, and spiritual guide
for his children. Mothers consequently expanded the scope of their

responsibility at home to include activities surrendered by the increasingly absent father. As external work demands multiplied, fathers' home-based influence and authority decreased. As fathers became less available, their families were required to adaptively coalesce without such fatherly presence.

Many men of the current generation have grown up with little of their father's influence and involvement. This has been well documented in the popular literature on the changing roles of men (e.g., Bly, 1990; Keen, 1991; Kipnis, 1991; Osherson, 1987; Pruett, 1993; Shapiro, 1993b). These writers (three of whom are contributors to this text) have sounded a clarion call to our society to bring the father out of exile and back into the family, where he may again serve as an important influence to his children and to future generations.

They are not alone. During the past three decades, a multitude of social, political, and economic factors have combined to alter dramatically the role expectations for fathers as well as mothers. Among the host of social conditions and changes that have set the stage for this more involved fatherhood, four stand out as most salient: the women's movement; fathers' presence in the birthplace; an increased understanding of the effects of father absence; and changing economic conditions.

The Women's Movement

Growing out of the civil rights movement of the early 1960s, the *women's movement* has been a powerful political and social force that has called into question many of the previous assumptions about relationships, work, and gender roles. A woman's "automatic" role as housewife and mother was challenged. As a result, and coincident with a declining economy, women have left the home to enter the marketplace in record numbers. Whether through economic necessity, freedom from rigid and demeaning gender-role expectations, a need for creative adult stimulation, or a drive for equality, the majority of western women are no longer *primarily* mothers and homemakers. As women increasingly leave the home empire, childrens' continuing needs for active parenting, in conjunction with the loss of the full-time homemaker, have allowed additional opportunities for fathers to become more involved in the home. As Pleck and others have indicated, many men have responded to the challenge by increasing time spent with their children and with household tasks.

Most fathers who take on a greater share of household and parenting duties must do so without relevant role models or examples from previous generations. They also do so with little acknowledgment, credit, or relief from their otherwise full-time work demands. Much like many mothers who work outside of the home, they often feel over-worked and under-appreciated.

Fathers in the Birthplace

As recently as the mid-1960s, only 15% of fathers in intact families expected to be present at the birth of their children. Today, fully 85% of North American fathers expect to be present. This represents a major revolution in both the birth process and parenting. A father who is involved during the pregnancy is far more likely to bond earlier and more intensely with his infant (Greenberg, 1985; Shapiro, 1993b). Being present at the birth of one's child is almost universally described by fathers as the most significant event in their lives. Greenberg and Morris (1974) coined the term "engrossment," to describe the father's reaction to the birth of his child while making the point that such early bonding has lifelong implications. Certainly, contemporary fathers are far more involved in the birthing process and early child care than their own fathers were. Fathers who are involved in the pregnancy and birth tend to desire a more active role with increasing closeness with their children, and a greater say in how the children are parented (Shapiro, 1993b).

Of greatest importance is a father's early bonding, connection, and pleasure in contact with his children. When this bonding or engrossment occurs in the context of a shared pregnancy and birth, with fathers supporting their mates throughout the process, a father's bonding with his child is more likely to become a family bonding experience as well. Woman whose husbands participated in this way described themselves as feeling closer to their mates due to the significance of their husband's presence (Greenberg, 1985). Furthermore, engrossed fathers who felt included early on were less likely to feel jealous of their wives' subsequent attentiveness toward their children (Greenberg 1985). Finally, Greenberg (1992) and Parker and Parker (1984) have argued that men who have experienced this engrossment will be far less likely to abuse their children.

Understanding the Impact of Absent Fathering

Over the past 10 years, a burgeoning literature has indicated the negative impact of absent fathers on both sons and daughters. In the current text, several contributions (Biller, Greenberg & Brown, Parke & Neville, and Pleck) underscore the importance of paternal deprivation and explore its ramifications.

A vast literature demonstrates that different forms of paternal deprivation are associated with later developmental problems in children, adolescents, and adults. On the other hand, this literature also indicates the powerful role that positively involved fathers can play in fostering their children's healthy long-term psychological adjustment (e.g., Biller, 1971; 1974; Biller & Soloman, 1986; Lamb, 1976, 1981a,b,c).

The father's absence takes its toll indirectly as well. There is an increased likelihood that mothers will maltreat their children when fathers are uninvolved in child rearing, whereas the father's presence and support can contribute to the mother's emotional health by reducing her stress level in the context of shared parenting responsibilities. (e.g., Biller & Soloman 1986; Ehrensaft; Jordan, this volume).

Fathers and Sons: Generational Effects. How does the father's absence affect his boys who in turn become the next generation of fathers? One outcome is that boys without fathers often grow up without an appropriate role model and object for identification (cf. Corneau, 1991). Instead, these sons are forced to create their own models. Some look to cultural icons such as sports figures, television stars or neighborhood "heroes" and try to emulate them. Sadly, these heroes must remain only images and caricatures rather than real men with responsibilities, pressures, and frustrations. Other sons of absent fathers turn to their peer group for paternal mentoring, although as William Golding (1962) so aptly depicts in *Lord of the Flies,* there is no guarantee that healthy models of masculinity can be transmitted by boys and adolescents.

The degree of pain and the wounded cry of fatherless young males have only recently been recognized. These boys, desperately awaiting their father's return, finally turn in rage toward other male support systems. It is not surprising then that gang membership is so closely related to a father's absence. These young teens repeat the cycle by unconsciously reenacting what was done to them. They too become fathers early in their own development and tend to replicate their own fathers' absence through idenfication. In spite of wanting desperately to change the pattern, they often lack an alternative path to follow (Greenberg & Brown; Ballard & Greenberg this volume).

Fathers and Daughters.   "Father hunger" is not exclusive to boy children—girls suffer as well (cf. Secunda, 1992; Shapiro, 1993b). Fathers play a key role with girls in validating their femininity and thereby enhancing their daughters' self-esteem and autonomous functioning (Benjamin, 1988, Biller & Weiss, 1970; Leonard, 1966). Girls with absent fathers seem to have greater difficulty with their later adult male relationships, often choosing men who have diminished educational and vocational success, more negative feelings toward their wives and children, problems with impulse control and maturity, and are more likely to have committed illegal acts (e.g., Hetherington & Parke, 1979). In their adult relationships, the daughters of unavailable fathers tend to experience the same sense of longing and dissatisfaction as they experienced in their primary relationship to their father— adult relationships that frequently replicate desertion and feelings of rejection or abandonment.

Economic Conditions

During the past decade, shifting family economics have necessitated dual incomes in order to maintain living standards that were once sustained by a single "breadwinner." With both parents working outside the home, the father's role has taken on increased importance as parenting and household responsibilities fall more heavily on *both* mothers and fathers. As mothers are less available, the opportunity has arisen for men to become more involved in the day-to-day child care. Children can consequently more fully experience the strength and uniqueness of *two* involved parents. Pruett's (1987) work with primary nurturing fathers demonstrates dramatically the joy and excitement of some fathers who move into this vast domain of involved parenting. Even when fathers feel they were caring for their children out of necessity, the opportunity for close contact with the child may bring its own potential reward to the father, to the child, to his spouse, and to the entire family.

When men take over more of the home and parenting responsibilities, they begin to parent in their own unique way. In this fashion mothers and fathers bring different and contrasting experiences to the child. Frequently, these experiences are not interchangeable. Although most mothers are delighted by their mate's participation with their children, they sometimes experience concern that their mates are not parenting in what they regard as the correct way—a mother's way. This creates an opportunity for the couple's creative discussion or for more contentious dissent. Atkins (1982) has written eloquently of the mother's ability to quietly give the message with subtle cues to the child that "Daddy" is not truly to be accepted by the child. He notes how this can have life-long ramifications.

The Women's Movement has come full circle with respect to encouraging women to provide a space available for fathers with their children. Nearly a decade ago, on NBC's *Today Show,* Gloria Steinem publically emphasized the importance of men's contact with their children (Giveans, 1986). Feminist intellectuals such as Dinnerstein (1976), Chodorow (1978) and Friedan (1991), have noted that women must allow men to enter the space of childcare and parenting, and that to do so they will have to give up, to some degree, total influence of this domain. This was a necessary complement to women moving increasingly into the world of work. Both Ehrensaft (this volume) and Jordan (this volume) have posited that this may be a challenge for some women. In every family in which this space is opened, men will be called on to face the challenge of relinquishing some of the substantive and typically more predictable rewards of the world of work in order to be available for the potential rewards and risks of closer parenting.

THE ISSUES IN BECOMING A FATHER

As we examine the changing socioeconomic realities and gender role expectations occurring over the past 25 years, it is apparent that contemporary mothers and fathers have few role models who afford a perspective on dual career, working parents. We tread awkwardly in an unfamiliar terrain as we acknowledge the different ways that mothers mother and fathers father. A father cannot, nor should he be asked to, parent as his wife does and conversely, a mother should not be expected to parent as her husband does. Children flourish best with *two* parents, each bringing their unique and complementary styles of parenting. In this book, we focus essentially on the earliest 21 months of a child's life; conception through the first year. As a way of better elucidating the major issues confronting an expectant or new father, we have divided the text into three sections: Social, Developmental, and Clinical Perspectives.

Part I: The Social Perspective

Among the social concerns for modern fathers are social roles, shifting expectations, an unsupportive political environment, the lack of effective role models, cultural instability, and seemingly unlimited demands on a father's time. To date there are few direct studies on what fathers actually give to children. Most of what we know is based on studies of absent fathers as well as theoretically grounded inferences as to what present, involved fathers need to provide (for example, Henry Biller in this text). However, Kyle Pruett (this volume) taking a more empirical approach, reviews what the father's presence brings to the child, the family, and also to the father himself.

In addition to more global social factors that affect most men becoming fathers, there are special concerns that impact large numbers of new fathers. For example, fathers who adopt children have to face unique situations that involve a lack of time to prepare for a new child and a fear of bonding with an infant who may be taken away. Similarly, new stepfathers face tremendous challenges in walking the fine line between being another adult in the home and parenting. How does one honor the absent parent and still take a paternal role in the household?

There are also special concerns for fathers of high-risk, premature, and disabled infants (Freud; May, this volume). Single fathers (Greif, this volume) also face special challenges with far less emotional support than single mothers. Although "family leave" is available officially for both mothers and fathers, few men have the financial wherewithal to be able to avail themselves of the opportunity. In addition, most men in the corporate world believe that taking the "daddy track" will be costly in terms of promotions and future opportunities.

Perhaps the largest universal concern for fathers is that of being a *provider for his children.* In modern society, this means being the financial provider. Few new fathers are unconcerned with the added fiscal responsibilities that accompany a new mouth to feed. Many men become sharply aware of the pressure of going from two incomes for two people to one income for three. Indeed, for most new fathers, financial providing and protection are closely intertwined with nurturing. Often, men describe wanting to work to provide financially for their child in the midst of talking about the spiritual/emotional high of the birth (Greenberg, 1985).

The chapters comprising this section reflect the wide range of the social aspects of fathering. Lamb, Jordan, and Parke & Neville examine paternal impact from a social perspective. Ehrensaft offers her thoughts on shared parenting. Ballard, Greenberg and Greenberg & Brown focus on specific sociocultural facets of prospective fathering. Finally, Levant and Shecket discuss their applied programs aimed at ameliorating the gaps that fathers experience in their multidimensional roles. The father has indeed emerged as a social force.

Part II: The Developmental Perspective

Despite an apparent desire for men to be more open and to share their feelings in their relationships, the pregnancy is still the last bastion of more traditional role expectations. Indeed during the pregnancy the expectant father is looked upon to be both the protector and provider for his understandably more needy partner. He is literally expected to be supportive, yet must suffer any personal discomfort, anxiety, or sadness in stoic isolation. The model is the strong silent husband doting on "the little woman."

Most expectant fathers do feel protective toward their partners. They provide for her and keep many of their negative personal feelings under wraps. That doesn't mean that they are without such emotions, however. Indeed, as Shapiro (1993b) has indicated, expectant fathers are quite emotional and suffer a host of fears, anxieties, and discomforts. Among these fears are worries about the health and safety of wife and child, concerns about being a successful protector and provider, anxiety about the effect of the baby on the marital and sexual relationship, and fears about personal autonomy and safety. These reflect the most basic of core insecurities that are felt, yet remain considerably unacknowledged.

Other feelings often come as surprises. Few men expect the outpouring of love that they will feel for their wives or babies. Few of them are prepared for the feelings of mortality that accompany the pregnancy and birth, or the sense of vulnerability that comes with children.

In this section, several authors describe the emotional side of their development as fathers during the pregnancy and early phases of fathering. some share their personal experiences in prose (Kutner, Osherson, Peltz, and Pleck) or poetry (Debus and Sachs). Others describe the salient psychological issues impacting the developing father from more theoretical and empirical perspectives (Bader, Freud, and Diamond).

Part III: The Clinical Perspective

The clinical section is divided into *psychodynamic dimensions* and *treatment*. For clinicians dealing with men, the advent of fatherhood is likely to bring up a host of pertinent issues. In addition to the normal developmental hurdles for fathers, clinicians must help clients address a number of issues that relate to unfinished psychological tasks, such as unresolved intrapsychic conflicts from the past. In addition, for some men, the advent of fatherhood elicits pathological reactions. For these reasons, effective treatment must include consideration of fatherhood.

One aspect of this section orients clinicians as to what is normal and what is truly pathological in the new father. Psychodynamic considerations become important as unconscious issues, concerns, and adaptations become central (Hyman, Diamond, and Wolson). Because there has been such little attention to fathering and the normal process of becoming a father, clinicians may be prone to view fathers' dysphoric reactions, occurring throughout the paternal developmental process, as pathological. Following a consideration of these *psychodynamic dimensions,* pertinent *treatment issues* pertaining to new fathers are examined (Gurwitt, Pollack, and Sachs).

Psychodynamic Dimensions.   What is the normal progression of feelings in becoming a father? When is the normal father's obsession with death during a pregnancy pathological, and when is it normal and appropriate? To what extent is the phallic pride common in new fathers seen as narcissism? Where is the line between a normal envy of the woman's reproductive capability and pathological jealousy? When is his desire to be a part of the mother/baby bond representing the outside world a healthy addition and when is it an interference? Chapters by Diamond, Pruett, and Hyman each address the development of an appropriate paternal identification, whereas Wolson explores healthy "adaptive" grandiosity.

During the pregnancy, the man is thrust into a secondary role; his pregnant partner is the star. Some men experience this as a great loss of status. At the same time, his wife may turn away from him as she bonds with the new life growing inside her. At such times, some expectant fathers experience a profound sense of abandonment or rejection. He may also experience a new distance from his friends; especially those who are not themselves fathers. The new father must integrate his envy of the primary maternal–infant bond (Hyman). Moreover, the culmination of the lost closeness with his wife and friends, and the diminishing status by comparison with his pregnant partner, may throw some fathers back into their emotional past. They reexperience many of the feelings they had as little boys. A man's view of himself may begin to change—seeing himself less as a son in relation to his own partents and more as a father of his own child. Psychologically, when a man's child is born, his replacement has arrived; he loses that psychological buffer against mortality; he becomes more aware of his limited life time. Diamond examines these and other psychodynamic issues as they emerge for a man becoming a father.

As he moves into prospective fatherhood, a father must develop a paternal identification (cf. Diamond, Pruett, this volume) and use his capacity for adaptive grandiosity (Wolson). He becomes the watchful protector of his family and develops a new sense of the vulnerabilities of all children. His child will carry his name and his "presence" forward into the next generation. This elicits both a great deal of pride and feelings of responsibility.

One of the changes that almost every man experiences at this time is an enhanced sense of protectiveness, whether it involves talking to life insurance salesmen, changing patterns of spending, shifting to safer or more secure jobs or hobbies, even purchasing weapons (Diamond, this volume). Men become more nurturing as their softer, more tender sides, begin to emerge (Shapiro, 1993a).

Treatment Issues. For many men, becoming a father creates an existential crisis. Being so close to the beginnings of life, they become increasingly aware of its ending. These men become acutely aware of their own mortality and of their place in the life cycle. Such cognizance also more deeply connects them to their own fathers and to their early years. In the course of this reflection, unfinished psychological tasks become salient. Gurwitt examines these aspects of prospective fatherhood as they arise for a patient in psychoanalysis, whereas Pollack explores how fatherhood opens new doors for insight and transformation.

Not all of the clinical attention must be on the patients. Indeed, there is a heretofore unexamined question about the impact of expectant and recent fatherhood on male therapists. In his chapter on countertransference, Sachs explores the internal psychological reactions for therapist-fathers.

The therapy focus often must go beyond the prospective father's issues. Many therapists will see expectant couples in their practices. There is often a strong pull for all therapists to lose objectivity and to side with the perspective of the pregnant woman in such scenarios. It is very important for fathers to be heard and for the couples work to remain balanced and couples oriented, rather than trying to fix the male to correspond to the female's desires or needs.

CONCLUSION: THE CIRCLE OF LIFE

As we become fathers we realize that part of experiencing closeness with our children is accompanied with the need to simultaneously let go. Changes in our children's development result in changes in our relationship with them. Each new maturational achievement made by our children forces us to let go in a deeper way. There is a sense of exultation in the accomplishment, but also a sense of loss. This experience of sadness and loss, and at the same time, joy in seeing our children's evolution is a repetitive theme throughout their development. It is part of the circle of life (Greenberg, 1985). In becoming fathers, images from our own childhood and of our own fathers will flash before our eyes.

The sense of this experience is captured in the following remembrance:

> When I was seven years old, I was living with my parents in Long Beach, California. My father was teaching me to ride a bicycle. He was breathing hard as he raced along beside me, pushing my bicycle down the alleyway, always holding on with one hand and stabilizing me as I struggled to keep the bike upright. There came a point when it seemed that his presence and my union and the bicycle had become one. I will never forget that. I thought he was still pushing me when all of a sudden I heard my father's voice from ten yards back. "You're riding, he shouted. "You did it." "But I'm scared," I shouted back as the bicycle surged forward. "You can do it!" he cried back. "You don't need me anymore. You can do it on your own." And his voice trailed off as I left him far behind. (Greenberg, 1985, p. 59)

These kinds of images enrich both parent and child. In this way the father's participation and his acts of closeness are not only an experience in the present but they can also become shared memories that are part of that child's and that parent's history. The recounting of these past memories is intensely pleasurable both for parent and child, because of the intensity of the sharing, and the acknowledgment of the reality they hold in common. Such shared reminiscence enhances both a *child's* feelings of closeness to his father, as he hears vivid stories of his father's life, and supports the *father's* sense of his importance in the lives of his children.

Becoming a father helps sets in motion the next chapter in each family's history. It is a potential link with eternity. Each new connection and letting go allows a father to make his mark and provide an essential gift to the next generation.

Part I
THE SOCIAL PERSPECTIVE

Sociocultural Dimensions

Applied Interventions

Warnings

Last night for 15 minutes
You did everything but
Bust through your mothers gut
And join us in bed.
We saw ripples, jumps, turns, and flips
What's your hurry? I joked
But, frankly, I was frightened
You better not be trying any funny business, kid
we're supposed to have four months left.
On you tumbled, though,
Belting the walls with your skinny limbs
Sloshing through your soaked home
Like a hunter in the marsh
I slept with one eye open, you know,
just in case you're planning
An early escape.

—Brad Sachs

In this abbreviated form of his classic paper, Michael Lamb, one of the premier writers in the area of fatherhood explores a number of issues pertaining to the current increasing interest in "The New Fatherhood." He underscores several variables that impact on paternal involvement including motivation, skills and self-confidence, support, and institutional factors.

Dr. Lamb also examines the research on both direct and indirect influences of paternal involvement on child development and on the family's emotional and social climate. He concludes that paternal involvement, whether of a high or low level, can be beneficial or harmful to child development, depending on the attitudes and values of the parents concerned. Because of this, the importance of intercultural and intracultural diversity on child development is stressed.

2

The Changing Roles of Fathers

Michael E. Lamb

Over the last decade and a half, professional and public interest in the roles played by fathers in their children's development has increased enormously. Early in this era of paternal rediscovery, psychologists believed that fathers might have an important role to play in child rearing, even if their involvement (relative to that of mothers) was severely limited. Specifically, psychologists questioned the implicit assumptions (1) that there is a direct correlation between extent of involvement and extent of influence, and (2) that if mothers are more influential than fathers, they must be exclusively influential (e.g., Lamb 1976, 1981c; Lynn 1974). Interest in fathers was subsequently accentuated by the popular and professional discovery of "the new fatherhood."

The new father, immortalized for many by Dustin Hoffman's performance in *Kramer vs. Kramer,* was an active, involved, nurturant participant in all aspects of child care and child rearing. Not surprisingly, belief in the existence and proliferation of such fathers led to further speculation about the importance of paternal influences on child development. As a result, rhetorical exchanges concerning the new father abounded; unfortunately, rhetoric continues to outpace serious analysis. This chapter attempts to redress that imbalance by

18

providing a brief integrative overview of research and theorizing concerning the role (or multiple roles) that fathers play.

The thesis advanced here is that we are currently witnessing the fourth of a series of changes in popular conceptualizations of the father's roles and responsibilities. Today's fathers are expected to be more actively involved in child care than in the past, and to a modest extent the average contemporary father is indeed more involved than was his predecessor. To assume that this increased involvement is necessarily beneficial in all family circumstances may be a mistake, however (Lamb, Pleck, & Levine, 1985). Rather, individual circumstances have to be considered to understand how children are affected by variations in paternal involvement.

In the recent debate about the changing roles of fathers, much of the discussion has focused on their increasing role in the direct care and rearing of their children. This new focus highlights a shift from a concern with fathers as persons primarily involved in the economic support of the family and perhaps in the discipline and control of older children (e.g., Benson, 1968; Bowlby, 1951) to a view that places increasing stress on the role that fathers play in the direct care of children of all ages.

To fully appreciate this shift, and to explain better the ways in which contemporary fathers are influential, it is helpful to examine historical changes in the conceptualization of paternal roles and responsibilities. Consequently, this chapter begins with a brief historical review designed to place contemporary paternal roles into perspective. In the second section, evidence concerning the nature and extent of paternal involvement today is discussed, as well as data concerning the extent to which father involvement has changed over the last several years. Paternal effects on child development are then considered, and finally, the findings generated by research of three different genres conducted over the last four decades is summarized.

FATHERS IN AMERICAN HISTORY

To understand the contemporary concern with and confusion about fatherhood, it may be helpful to step back historically and examine the changes in the conceptualization of paternal roles that have taken place. The available data are obviously limited, but social historians argue that much can be learned by examining letters (admittedly, few wrote letters and even fewer thought to preserve them for posterity) and literature written or popular during particular eras.

According to Pleck (1984), one can actually discern four phases or periods over the last two centuries of American social history. In each of these, a different dominant motif came into focus, making other aspects of a complex, multifaceted role seem much less important by comparison.

Moral Father

The earliest phase was one that extended from Puritan times through the Colonial period into early Republican times. During this lengthy period, the father's role was perceived as being dominated by responsibility for moral oversight and moral teaching. By popular consensus, fathers were primarily responsible for ensuring that their children grew up with an appropriate sense of values, acquired primarily from the study of religious materials like the Bible.

To the extent that a broader role was defined, fathers assumed responsibility for the education of children—not because education and literacy were valued in their own right, but because children had to be literate to read the Scriptures. Thus the father's responsibility for education was secondary; helping children become literate served to advance the father's role as moral guardian by ensuring that children were academically equipped to adopt and maintain Christian ways. In their reviews, Demos (1982) and Pleck (1984) pointed out that, during this era, good fathers were defined as men who provided a model of good Christian living and versed their children well in the Scriptures.

The Breadwinner

Around the time of centralized industrialization, a shift occurred in the dominant conceptualization of the father's role (Pleck, 1984). Instead of being defined in terms of moral teaching, his role came to be defined largely in terms of breadwinning, and this conceptualization of the father endured from the mid-nineteenth century through the Great Depression (Pleck, 1976). An analysis of the then-popular literature and of letters written between fathers and children during that period confirms the dominant conceptualization of fatherhood in terms of breadwinning.

This is not to say that other aspects of the father's role, such as the presumed responsibility for moral guardianship, had disappeared. Rather, breadwinning came into focus as the most important and defining characteristic of fatherhood and as the criterion by which "good fathers" could be appraised.

The Gender-Role Model

Perhaps as a result of the Great Depression, the New Deal, and the disruption and dislocation brought about by the Second World War, the end of this war brought a new conceptualization of fatherhood. Although breadwinning and moral guardianship remained important, focus now shifted to the father's function as a gender-role model, especially for his sons.

Many books and articles in the professional literature focused on the need for strong gender-role models, and many professionals concluded that fathers were clearly not doing a good job in this regard (e.g., Levy, 1943; Strecker, 1946). Their inadequacies were underscored in dramatic works such as *Rebel Without a Cause*, and were ridiculed in comedies and cartoons, for example, "Blondie" and "All in the Family" (Ehrenreich & English, 1979).

The New Nurturant Father

Around the mid-1970s, finally, a fourth stage was reached. For the first time there was widespread identification of fathers as active, nurturant, caretaking parents. Active parenting was defined as the central component of fatherhood and as the yardstick by which "good fathers" might be assessed. This redefining of the most noteworthy and laudable aspect of fatherhood occurred first in the popular media, where it was promulgated in works like *Kramer vs. Kramer* and *The World According to Garp*. Professional interest in the new fatherhood soon followed.

It is important to acknowledge the changing conceptualization of fathering, because all four of the images or functions just outlined remain important today, although the extent of their importance varies across groups. In a pluralistic society like ours, various conceptions of the father's role coexist, and it is important to bear in mind that although journalists and film makers here have been lauding active and nurturant fatherhood for the last 10 years, many citizens have a very different conception of fathering. In addition, one must recognize that fathers fill many roles, that the relative importance of each varies from one context to another, and that active fathering—the key focus here—must be viewed in the context of the various other things that fathers do for their children (e.g., breadwinning, gender-role modeling, moral guidance, emotional support of mothers).

Modes of Paternal Influence Today

If one thinks about fatherhood simply in terms of the ways in which fathers are likely to influence their children, one can discern at least four ways in which fathers can have a substantial impact on their children and their children's development. Clearly, breadwinning remains a key component of the father's role in most segments of society today (Benson, 1968; Cazenave, 1979; Pleck, 1983). Even in the vast majority of families in which there are two wage earners, the father is still seen as the primary breadwinner, if only because of continuing disparities between the salaries of male and female workers. Economic support of the family constitutes an indirect but important way in which fathers contribute to the rearing and emotional health of their children.

A second important but indirect source of influence stems from the father's role as a source of emotional support to the other people, principally the mother, involved in the direct care of children (Parke, Power, & Gottman. 1979). The father's functioning as a source of emotional support for the mother and others in the family tends to enhance the quality of the mother–child relationship and thus facilitates positive adjustment by the children: by contrast, when fathers are unsupportive, children may suffer (Rutter, 1973, 1979). Fathers can also affect the quality of family dynamics by being involved in child-related housework, thus easing the mother's workload (Pleck, 1983, 1985). (Paternal involvement in housework may also provide a good model for children.)

Fathers also influence their children by interacting with the children directly, and much of this chapter is concerned with paternal influences deriving from the caretaking, teaching, play, and one-on-one interaction with particular children (Lamb, 1981b). Most of the research on paternal influences is concerned with such direct patterns of influence, even though the father's role has multiple aspects and fathers can affect their children's development in many ways other than direct interaction.

QUANTIFYING THE NEW FATHERHOOD

Much attention has recently been paid to the changing roles of fathers, with particular focus on "the new father," who is, by definition, deeply involved in the day-to-day care and rearing of his children. Unfortunately, much of the evidence concerning the new fatherhood is journalistic in nature, and we do not know how representative the men featured in such accounts really are.

Before pursuing our topic further, therefore, we need to ask: What does the average American father do, and how has that changed over the last several years?

Components of Father Involvement

A large number of studies have been designed to determine both how much time fathers spend with their children and what sorts of activities occupy that time (Lamb, Pleck, Charnov, & Levine, 1985; Pleck, 1983). Many of these studies involve small and often unrepresentative samples—a perennial problem in developmental research. Fortunately, this area of research can boast of several studies involving nationally representative samples of individuals (both mothers and fathers) who are asked what fathers do and how much they do.

Given the availability of these data, it would seem easy to determine what contemporary fathers really do. Sadly, the task is not as easy as it sounds because the results of different surveys vary dramatically. One problem is that different researchers have invoked very different implicit definitions as parental involvement, using different activities as aspects of paternal involvement. Thus a comparison of results becomes very difficult. To make sense of the data, therefore, it is first necessary to group the studies in terms of their similarities in the implicit definitions of paternal involvement (Lamb, et al., 1985).

For purposes of analysis, one can distinguish three components of parental involvement. The first and most restrictive type is time spent in actual one-on-one interaction with the child (whether feeding her, helping him with homework, or playing catch in the garden). This time, which Lamb and coworkers labeled time of *engagement or interaction,* does not include time spent in child-related housework, or time spent sitting in one room while the child plays in the next room. Lamb and colleagues included these times in a second category comprised of activities involving less intense degrees of interaction. These activities imply *parental accessibility* to the child, rather than direct interaction. Cooking in the kitchen while the child plays in the next room, or even cooking in the kitchen while the child plays at the parent's feet, are examples.

The final type of involvement is the hardest to define but is perhaps the most important of all. It is the extent to which the parent takes ultimate *responsibility* for the child's welfare and care. It can be illustrated by the difference between being responsible for child care and being able and willing to "help out" when it is convenient. Responsibility involves knowing when the child needs to go to the pediatrician, making the appointment, and making sure that the child gets to it. Responsibility involves making child care and babysitting arrangements, ensuring that the child has clothes to wear, and making arrangements for supervision when the child is sick. Much of the time involved in being a responsible parent is not spent in direct interaction with the child. Consequently, survey researchers can easily overlook this type of involvement. It is hard to quantify the time involved, particularly because the anxiety, worry, and contingency planning that comprise parental responsibility often occur when the parent is ostensibly doing something else.

When the different components or types of parental involvement covered in various studies are differentiated, greater consistency is found from study to study than was apparent earlier, but a considerable degree of inconsistency remains. In part, this is because the recent distinction between the three types of involvement has been applied retrospectively to the results of independent investigations conducted years earlier, and thus there are still differences across studies in specific definitions of engagement, accessibility, and responsibility. For example, in one of the major national surveys, "watching TV together" was grouped with activities of the interaction type, whereas in another study, it was included as a component of accessibility.

To integrate and compare the findings of different studies, each researcher's idiosyncratic definition of involvement must be allowed to stand, but *relative* rather than *absolute* measures of paternal involvement must be used to compare results. Instead of comparing those figures purporting to measure the amount of time that fathers spend "interacting with" their children, proportional figures must first be computed (i.e., compared with the amount of time that mothers devote to interaction, how much time do fathers devote to it?) and these proportional figures be compared. The picture then becomes much clearer. Surprisingly similar results are obtained in the various studies, despite major differences in the methods used to assess time use (diary versus estimate), the size and regional representation of the samples employed, and the date when the studies were conducted.

Extent of Paternal Involvement

Consider, first, figures concerning the degree of involvement by fathers in two-parent families in which the mother is unemployed (Lamb, Pleck, Charnov, & Leviner, 1987; Pleck, 1983). In such families the data suggest that the father spends about 20%–25% as much time as the mother does in direct interaction or engagement with their children, and about a third as much time being accessible to their children. The largest discrepancy between paternal and maternal involvement is in the area of responsibility. Many studies show that fathers assume essentially no responsibility (as previously defined) for their children's care or rearing.

In two-parent families with an employed mother, the levels of paternal compared with maternal engagement and accessibility are both substantially higher than in families with an unemployed mother (Lamb et al., 1987; Pleck, 1983). The figures for direct interaction and accessibility average 33% and 65%, respectively. As far as responsibility is concerned, however, there is no evidence that maternal employment has any effect on the level of paternal involvement. Even when both mother and father are employed 30 or more hours per week, the amount of responsibility assumed by fathers appears as negligible as when mothers are unemployed.

In light of the controversies that have arisen on this score, it is worth noting that fathers do not spend more time interacting with their children when mothers are employed, but rather the proportions just cited go up only because mothers are doing less. Thus, fathers are proportionately more involved when mothers are employed, even though the depth of their involvement, in absolute terms, does not change to any meaningful extent. The unfortunate controversies in this area appear attributable to a confusion between proportional figures and absolute figures.

Child and Family Characteristics Affecting Paternal Involvement

Researchers have also explored changes in paternal involvement related to the age of the child (Pleck, 1983). Interestingly, the changes that take place are the same for mothers and fathers. Both parents spend more time in child care when the children are younger—a trend that, although understandable, contradicts the popular assumption that fathers become more involved as the children get older. Fathers may know more about older children than about younger children, they may feel more comfortable and competent, and they may appear more interested, but they apparently do not spend more time with their older children. In part, this may be because older children no longer want to interact with parents as much; they prefer to interact with peers and/or siblings.

Popular presumptions are correct, however, so far as the effects of the child's gender are concerned (Lamb, 1981b). Fathers are indeed more interested in and more involved with their sons than their daughters. They tend to spend more time with boys than with girls, regardless of the children's ages. Beyond these variations associated with age and gender, however, there are no consistent regional, ethnic, or religious variations in the amount of time that parents—mothers or fathers—spend with their children (Pleck, 1983).

Changes Over Time

The term "new fatherhood" implies that today's fathers differ from fathers of the past. Unfortunately, few data are available concerning changes over time in levels of paternal involvement.

The best data available come from a recent report by Juster (1989) who compared figures from a 1975 national survey with figures obtained in a follow-up survey undertaken 6 years later. In 1981, the average father spent much more time (26% more) in the most intensive type of child care (direct interaction) than in 1975. The percentage increase for mothers was substantially smaller (7%), at least in part because the changes for mothers took place relative to higher baseline levels. In any event, the discrepancy between the levels of maternal and paternal involvement remained substantial: Mothers in 1981 still engaged in substantially more interaction with their children than did fathers, despite the larger increase in paternal involvement. In both 1976 and 1981, paternal involvement was about a third that of mothers, rising from 29% in 1976 to 34% in 1981.

Behavioral Styles of Mothers and Fathers

Thus far we have considered only how much time parents spend with their children, ignoring the fact that there may be variations in terms of the content of their interactions. Both observational and survey data suggest that mothers and fathers engage in rather different types of interaction with their children (Goldman & Goldman, 1983; Lamb, 1981a, 1981b). Mothers' interactions with their children are dominated by caretaking, whereas fathers are behaviorally defined as playmates. Mothers actually play with their children much more than fathers do, but as a proportion of the total of child–parent interaction, play is a much more prominent component of father–child interaction and caretaking is more salient with mothers.

Although mothers are associated with caretaking and fathers with play, we cannot assume that fathers are less capable of child care. A number of researchers have attempted to investigate the relative competencies of mothers and fathers with respect to caretaking and parenting functions, and the results of these studies are fairly clear (Lamb, 1981a). First, they show that, in the newborn period, there are no differences in competence between mothers and fathers—both parents can do equally well (or equally poorly). Contrary to the notion of a maternal instinct, parenting skills are usually acquired "on the job" by both mothers and fathers.

Mothers are "on the job" more than fathers are, however; not surprisingly, mothers become more sensitive to their children, more in tune with them, and more aware of each child's characteristics and needs. By virtue of their lack of experience, fathers become correspondingly less sensitive and come to feel less confidence in their parenting abilities. Fathers thus continue to defer to and cede responsibility to mothers, whereas mothers increasingly assume responsibility, not only because they see it as their role, but also because their partners do not seem to be especially competent care providers. As a result, the differences between mothers and fathers become more marked over time.

These differences are not irreversible, however. When circumstances thrust fathers into the primary caretaking role, or when fathers choose to redefine their parental roles and their parent–child relationships, they are perfectly capable of acquiring the necessary skills (Hipgrave, 1982; Levine, 1976; Russell, 1983). In reality, of course, most fathers never get as involved in child care as their partner does, and so the differences between mothers and fathers tend to increase.

Summary

There have been increases over time in average degrees of paternal involvement, so the notion of a "new emergent nurturant father" is not entirely mythical. Mothers continue to spend more time in, and to take responsibility for, most of the day-to-day care of their children. The discrepancy between mothers and fathers is especially great in the area of what we have called responsibility; in this regard, few data are available concerning secular changes in paternal behavior. In other areas the changes, although significant, are still quite modest. In addition, the characteristics of mothers' and fathers' interactions with their children have for the most part remained remarkably consistent over time. Mothers are identified with caretaking, fathers with play.

PATERNAL INFLUENCES ON CHILD DEVELOPMENT

The focus of this chapter now switches from fathers' actions to fathers' influences on their children's development. Over the decades of research on this topic, three bodies of literature have emerged: (1) correlational studies, (2) studies concerned with the effects of father absence, and (3) studies concerned with the impact of high father involvement. All are important to an understanding of paternal influences on child development. The three approaches are described and their results summarized separately in this section. The summaries, however, are by no means exhaustive: indeed, in the first two subsections, discussion is limited to illustrative research involving fathers and sons. More detailed and comprehensive reviews are provided elsewhere (Adams, Milner, & Schrepf 1984; Lamb, 1981c; Lamb et al., 1985). The goal here is to illustrate the key features of empirical research that have prompted major changes in our conceptualization of paternal influence patterns.

The Correlational Approach

Let us first consider studies concerned with the search for correlations between paternal and filial characteristics. In such studies, researchers might try to measure the warmth, closeness, or hostility (for reviews see Biller, 1971; Lamb, 1976, 1981c) of father–child relationships, or the masculinity or authoritarianism of fathers, and then correlate measures of these paternal or relational constructs with measures of some theoretically related characteristics in the children. This strategy was adopted in many of the earliest studies of paternal influences, the vast majority of which focused on gender-role development, especially in sons. This is understandable, since many of these studies were done from the 1940s to the early 1960s when the father's role as a gender-role model was considered most important.

The design of these early studies was quite simple: The researchers assessed masculinity in fathers and in sons, and then determined how strongly the two sets of scores were correlated. To the researchers' great surprise, there was no consistent correlation between the two; a puzzling finding because it seemed to violate a guiding assumption about the crucial function served by fathers. If fathers did not make their boys into men, what role did they really serve?

It took a while for psychologists to realize that the guiding assumption might have been inappropriate. Researchers failed to ask: Why should boys *want to be like* their fathers? Presumably they should only want to resemble a father whom they like and respect, and with whom their relationship is warm or positive. In fact, the quality of father–son relationships was found to be an important mediating variable: When the relationship between masculine fathers and their sons was good, the boys were indeed more masculine. Subsequent research suggested that the quality of the relationship was actually the crucial variable so far as the development of filial masculinity was concerned (Mussen & Rutherford, 1963; Payne & Mussen, 1956; Sears, Maccoby, & Levin, 1957).

By contrast, the masculinity of the father was rather unimportant. In other words, boys seemed to conform to the gender-role standards of their culture when their relationships with their fathers were warm, regardless of how "masculine" the fathers were. Because of this we might expect that the effects of close father–son relationships have changed over the last 15 years, during which cultural preferences for, and expectations of, male behavior have changed also.

Today, for example, we might expect warm fathers who have close relationships with their children to have more androgynous sons than other fathers (since androgyny seems to be the contemporary goal), just as similarly close relationships formerly potentiated the development of masculine sons (Baruch & Barnett, 1983; Radin, 1978; Radin & Sagi, 1982).

As far as paternal influences on gender-role development are concerned then, the key finding is that characteristics of the father (such as masculinity) are much less important formatively than the father's warmth and the closeness and nature of his relationship with his son. This is an interesting and important finding because warmth and closeness have traditionally been seen as feminine characteristics.

Thus "feminine" characteristics of the father—his warmth and nurturance—seem to be associated with better adjustment in sons, at least to the extent that adjustment is defined in terms of sex role.[1]

Similar findings have been obtained in studies concerned with paternal influences on achievement (Radin, 1981). Initially, the assumption was that fathers would influence achievement motivation positively, because they were the family members who exemplified achievement in "the real world" and their sons would surely want to emulate them in this regard.

Once more, it soon became clear that the father's warmth, closeness, and involvement were most important; fathers with these characteristics tended to have competent and achievement-oriented sons (Radin, 1978, 1981, 1982). The same characteristics are important with regard to a mothers' influence on her child's achievement, again implying that fathers influence children not by virtue of "male" characteristics (like masculinity) but by virtue of nurturant personal and social characteristics.

A similar conclusion is suggested by research on psychosocial adjustment: Paternal warmth or closeness is advantageous, whereas paternal masculinity is irrelevant (Biller, 1971; Lamb, 1981b). Thus across these three areas of development—gender-role development, achievement, and psychosocial adjustment—children seem better off when their relationship with their father is close and warm. In general, the same is true in the case of mothers, and children who have close relationships with both parents benefit greatly. As far as influence on children is concerned, very little about the gender of the parent seems to be distinctly important. The characteristics of the father as a parent rather than the characteristics of the father as a man appear to influence child development.

Father Absence Research

Although the whole body of research that is here termed "correlational" was burgeoning in the 1950s, another body of literature was developing. This involved investigations in which researchers tried to understand the father's role by studying families without fathers. The

---

[1]This is a questionable assumption, particularly given the ways in which sex roles are usually operationalized in the research literature. Readers are referred to Pleck (1981) and Lamb et al. (1985) for further discussion of these issues, which are not critical to the argument being developed here.

assumption was that by comparing the behavior and personalities of children raised with and without fathers, one could—essentially by a process of subtraction—estimate what sort of influence fathers typically had. The chief father-absence and correlational studies were conducted in roughly the same era, not surprisingly, the outcomes studied were very similar and the results were in many ways similar.

In the case of father-absence studies, the results also appeared consistent with popular assumptions. Unfortunately, the literature on father absence is voluminous and controversial; readers are referred elsewhere for more detailed discussions (Adams et.al., 1984; Biller, 1974; Lamb, 1981a,b,c; Herzog & Sudia, 1973). In the present context, suffice it to say, that boys growing up without fathers seemed to have "problems" in the areas of gender-role and gender-identity development, school performance, psychosocial adjustment, and perhaps in the control of aggression.

Two related issues arising from father-absence research must be addressed, however. First, even if one agrees that there are differences between children raised in families with the father present and those raised in families with the father absent, one must ask *why* those differences exist and how to interpret them.

Second, it is important to remember that although there may be *group differences* between, say, 100 boys growing up without fathers and 100 boys growing up with fathers, this does not mean that every child growing up without a father has problems in some if not all of the areas just mentioned, or that all boys whose fathers live at home develop normatively. One cannot make inferences about individuals from data concerning groups simply because there is great within-group heterogeneity. This forces us to ask why such heterogeneity exists. Why do some boys appear to suffer deleterious consequences as a result of father absence, whereas others do not? More broadly, the question is: What is it about the father-absence context that makes for group differences between children in father-absent and father-present contexts, and what accounts for the impressive within-group variance?

Researchers and theorists first sought to explain the effects of father absence in terms of the absence of a male gender-role model. In the absence of a masculine parental model, it was assumed that boys could not acquire strong masculine identities or gender roles and would not have a model of achievement with which to identify (Biller, 1974). The problem with this interpretation is that many boys without fathers seem to develop quite normally so far as gender-role development and achievement are concerned. Clearly, an explanation that emphasizes the absence of a male gender-role model cannot be complete or inclusive. It has thus become increasingly clear that some other factors may be at least as important as (if not much more important than) the availability of a gender-role model in mediating the effects of father absence on child development.

First, there is the absence of a co-parent—someone to help out with child care, to be there when one parent needs a break, to supplement one parent's resources in relation to the demands of the child (Maccoby, 1977). Second, there is the economic stress that goes along with single parenthood, especially single motherhood. The median and mean incomes for single women heads of household are significantly lower than the average income in any other group, and the disparity is even larger when one considers per capita income rather than income per household (Glick & Norton, 1979). Third, the tremendous economic stress experienced by single mothers is accompanied by emotional stress occasioned by a degree of social isolation and the largely disapproving attitudes that society continues to hold with respect to single or divorced mothers and children (Hetherington, Cox, & Cox, 1982). Lastly, there is the predivorce (and postdivorce) marital conflict, an important issue because, of all the findings in the area of socialization, the best validated is the fact that children suffer when there is hostility or conflict in the family, (Rutter, 1973, 1979, Lamb, 1981b).

Since most single-parent families are produced by divorce and because divorce is often preceded by periods of overt and covert spouse hostility, predivorce conflict may play a major role in explaining the problems of fatherless children. By contrast, fatherless children who have good relationships with both parents before and after the divorce tend to be better adjusted than those who do not (Hess & Camara, 1979).

In sum, the evidence suggests that father absence may be harmful not necessarily because a gender-role model is absent, but because many aspect of the father's role—*economic, social, emotional*—go unfilled or inappropriately filled. Recognition of the father's multiple roles as breadwinner, parent, and emotional support for partner is essential in understanding how fathers influence children's development.

Studies of Increased Paternal Involvement

Finally we must consider more recent studies concerned with the effects on children of increased father involvement, as exemplified by fathers who either share in or take primary responsibility for child care (Lamb et al., 1985; Russell, 1983; Russell & Radin, 1983). This question has been addressed in three or four studies, and results have been remarkably consistent with respect to preschool-aged children whose fathers are responsible for at least 40% to 45% of the within-family child care. Children with highly involved fathers are characterized by increased cognitive competence, increased empathy, less gender-stereotyped beliefs and a more internal locus of control (Pruett, 1983b; Radin, 1982: Radin & Sagi, 1982; Sagi, 1982). Again the question that has to be asked is, *why* do these sorts of differences occur?"

Three factors are probably important in this regard (Lamb et al., 1985). First, when parents assume less gender-stereotyped roles their children have less gender-stereotyped attitudes themselves about male and female roles. Second, particularly in the area of cognitive competence, these children may benefit from having two highly involved parents rather than just one. This assures them the diversity of stimulation that comes from interacting with people who have different behavioral styles. A third important issue has to do with the family context in which these children are raised.

In every study reported thus far, a high degree of paternal involvement made it possible for both parents to do what was subjectively important to them. It allowed fathers to satisfy a desire to become close to their children and mothers to have adequately close relationships with their children while also pursuing career goals. In other words, increased paternal involvement may have made both parents feel much more fulfilled. As a result, the relationships were probably much warmer and richer than might otherwise have been the case.

One can speculate that the positive outcome obtained by children with a highly involved father is largely attributable to the fact that the father's involvement created a family context in which the parents felt good about their marriage and the arrangements they had been able to work out.

In all of these studies, fathers were involved because both they and their partners desired this. The results might be very different in cases with fathers forced to become involved, perhaps because of a layoff from work, whereas their partner could get and hold a job. In such circumstances the wife might resent the fact that her husband could not hold a job and support his family while the husband might resent having to do "woman's work" with the children when he really wanted to be "out there" earning a living and supporting his family (see Russell,

1983). This constellation of factors might well have adverse effects on children, just as the same degree of involvement has positive effects when the circumstances are more benign.

The key point is that the extent of paternal involvement may be much less significant (so far as the effects on children are concerned) than are the reasons for his involvement and his and his partner's evaluation of that involvement.

In sum, the effects may in many cases have more to do with the context of father involvement than with father involvement per se. What matters is not so much who is at home, but how that person feels about being at home, for the person's feelings will color the way he or she behaves with the children. Behavior is also influenced by the other partner's feelings about the arrangement: Both parents' emotional states affect the family dynamics.

SUMMARY

The three genres of research on paternal influences together paint a remarkably consistent picture. First, by and large fathers and mothers seem to influence their children in similar rather than dissimilar ways. The important dimensions of parental influence are those that have to do with parental characteristics rather than gender-related character-istics. Second, the nature of the effect may vary substantially, depending on individual and cultural values. A classic example of this can be found in the literature on gender-role development. As a result of cultural changes, the assumed gender-role goals for boys and girls have changed, and this has produced changes in the effect of father involve-ment on children.

In the 1950s gender-appropriate masculinity or femininity was the desired goal; today androgeny, or gender-role flexibility is desired. And whereas father involvement in the 1950s seemed to be associated with greater masculinity in boys, it is associated today with less gender-ste-reotyped gender-role standards in both sons and daughters. Third, influence patterns vary substantially, depending on social factors that define the meaning of father involvement for children in particular families in particular social milieus. Finally, the amount of time that fathers and children spend together is probably much less important than what they do with that time and how fathers, mothers, children, and other important people in their lives perceive and evaluate the father–child relationship.

All of this means that high paternal involvement may have positive effects in some circumstances and negative effects in others. The same is true of low paternal involvement. We must not lose sight, however, of recent historical changes in average levels of paternal involvement (Juster, 1994). If the trend continues, the number of families in which greater father involvement would be beneficial will increase.

Whatever the extent of their involvement, fathers do appear to influence their children's development both directly by means of interaction and indirectly by virtue of their impact (positive and negative) on the family's social and emotional climate. Attitudes concerning appropriate levels of paternal involvement vary widely. Thus paternal involvement, whether of a high or low level, can be beneficial or harmful to child development, depending on the attitudes and values of the parents concerned. It is thus critically important to recognize intercultural and intracultural diversity when exploring paternal influences on child development.

This chapter, which originally appeared in Families in Society: The Journal of Contemporary Human Services, discusses the distinct role fathers play in the life of their children and the impact that role has on the father, his children, and the family as a whole. The fathering, Dr. Pruett describes, different from mothering, allows men and their children to affect each other as profoundly as any relationship they may ever have. He calls for greater attention to the "paternal presence" in the lives of children.

3

The Paternal Presence

Kyle D. Pruett

Obviously, fathers are not mothers—they never will be and shouldn't try. Yet most men struggle with feeling an essential inadequacy when beginning life as a parent. Conversely, they often assume that the essential adequacy is inherent in their mate. They reason as follows: "Obviously, 'mothering' is the only way to approach children effectively; I'll copy what she is doing." Fathers often overlook the fact that the mother, too, is undergoing on-the-job training and feeling often enough inadequate to the task.

But the mother-mimic tactic soon falters. It feels wrong at all levels, because it is. The child does not expect it, and the father cannot do it. This lesson is his first on the journey to complete himself as a man-now-father: Fathering is not mothering any more than mothering is ever fathering.

If the father is not a mother, what is his nurturing role to be? This question has profound implications, for within it lies the surprise of his life. If he can get close enough to his baby for long enough, his love, physical caring, and concern for the well-being of his baby awakens his role as father.

This chapter is about the celebration of that discovery, the impact of that discovery on the life of the father, the child, and the family as a whole. That men and children can affect each other as profoundly as any relationship that they will ever have in their life is a truth many young fathers do not understand and many older fathers hold as canon. A paternal presence in the life of a child is essential to the child emotionally and physically. The following discussion attempts to close the gap between the problems that contemporary families face regarding the many changes in the fathering role and the family issues researchers have chosen to address.

The Nurturing Instinct

When men become fathers, the nurturing instinct is reawakened in them. I use the prefix because we know that preschool boys robustly explore the nurturing domain in their imaginary play. Before the end of the third year, both boys and girls share the conviction that the nurturing (or more common "maternal") role is open to them. Boys explore with a vigor equal to that of girls, the joys of domestic care, feeding, bathing, and nursing babies. It is not until approximately 5 years of age that most boys affirm their gender identity and consciously yield the gestational role and its physical differences to the female.

What happens to that nurturing instinct in boys varies from family to family. In Western cultures, the instinct to nurture is often repressed in boys, although it may attempt to reaffirm itself around the birth of siblings, the entrance of pets into the family, or through empathy and concern for the physically vulnerable. In adolescence, the instinct often is overwhelmed by sexual fascination and the need to establish control over genital performance and competence. When sex education classes address the procreative as well as the health aspects of intercourse, boys respond with questions, concern, and interest in the paternal ramifications of sexual activity. One of the most confused aspects of sex education in America, however, is that although girls are taught about sexually transmitted diseases, pregnancy, and mothering, boys are taught primarily about sexually transmitted diseases.

The nurturing instinct may make its most unalloyed, unconflicted appearance during grandfatherhood. By then the myths and trappings of male competence, such as work, sports, the celebration of physical and monetary assets, have paled or worn thin, allowing the third generation to reach directly into the hearts of these men, who are often surprised by the vigor with which they fall in love with their grandchildren.

Clearly, from the beginning of their wife's pregnancy, men are quite involved, even at a physical level. Toothaches are so common among men whose wives are pregnant that dentists and orthodontists are advised to ask men between the ages of 20 and 40 about possible pregnancies in the family, if no other cause of pain can be elicited in the differential diagnosis (Richman, 1982). Men also may crave unusual and exotic foods during the final trimester of the pregnancy. Stress, anxiety, and even depression occur in men as they become concerned about their capacity to protect and provide for their new family. When coupled with the commonplace exclusion from the adoration of extended families, even psychologically healthy and supportive men may find themselves rummaging through refrigerators and exotic food counters at the supermarket. In my research into the development of children raised primarily by fathers (Pruett, 1983a, 1985, 1987), significant quantities of ice cream, eggs, milk, and cheeses enter men's diets during the second trimester and often remain in the diet until well after the successful birth of the child. In the Yucatan, a woman's pregnancy is often considered confirmed when her mate has food cravings that he did not have before.

After the baby does arrive on the scene, it is clear from 25 years of research that fathers can nurture and rear their children quite competently. Parke and Sawin (1975) found that fathers were capable of feeding their babies formula appropriately and on time as efficiently as were their spouses, regardless of previous experience with infants. Despite the paucity of most men's infant-care experience, they seem to have more knowledge about the ways of stimulating and interacting with children than even they consciously realize. In delivery rooms and nurseries, fathers frequently address their children in a falsetto voice. Neonatal research indicates that newborn infants, even those born prematurely, attend better to a high-pitched verbal stimulus than to lower-pitched sounds.

In their studies of premature infants, Gaiter and Johnson (1984) and Yogman (1987) found that early paternal involvement has a significant mitigating effect on the long-term vulnerability of the infants. Clearly, the vulnerability and physical fragility of the preterm baby is an important factor in encouraging men to express themselves as provider and protector. The small, helpless, often sickly looking babies can draw their fathers into their lives precisely because their needs are so patent. As the wife may be anxious and guilty about the baby's troubles and may herself be ill after giving birth, fathers of preterm infants often take up the slack in caretaking responsibilities. Both Gaiter and Johnson (1984) and Yogman (1987) found that when fathers visited the hospital frequently, touched their babies, and spoke with the nurses about the baby during the hospitalization, fathers were significantly more involved with their infants up to a year after discharge from the hospital.

FEATURES OF FATHERING

If mothering is not a central feature of fathering, then what are its unique characteristics? Pedersen, Zaslow, Suwalsky, and Caine (1980), Parke (1981), and Biller and Meredith (1974) articulated innate paternal characteristics that are important to the well-being of children's development over time. Biller and Meredith (1974) found that fathers played with their children differently, using fewer toys, when mothers were not present. Men encouraged their children's curiosity in the solution of intellectual and physical challenges, supported the child's persistence in solving problems, and did not become overly solicitous with regard to their child's failures. These behaviors, according to Biller, illustrated important differences in the way fathers and mothers respond to their babies' exploration of the environment.

Parke (1981) found that if fathers were involved in the daily care of their infants during the first 8 weeks after childbirth, the babies were more socially responsive and able to withstand stressful circumstances later during their school years. Pedersen et al. (1980) found that 6 month-old babies who had been actively involved with their fathers had higher scores on the Bailey Test of Mental and Motor Development.

Maccoby and Jacklin (1974) found that men were more likely to clarify gender identity of their children both to themselves and to the outside world than were women. Men tend to use masculine-specific language with their sons and feminine-specific language with their daughters, which suggests that men play an important part in clarifying gender roles.

Obviously, fathers interact with their children in ways different from the way mothers do and the long-term effects of these interactions do not seem to be innately damaging to children. Moreover, these interactions affect the fathers as well as the children. Parker and Parker (1984) found that if a man is involved in the daily physical care of his child during a significant period before the child reaches the age of 36 months, the probability that the man will be involved in the sexual abuse of his own or any one else's children is dramatically reduced. The intimacy of infant care creates a strong barrier against later exploitation of that intimacy, whether physical or emotional.

In my longitudinal research into a small group of families in which the father served as a primary caregiver, I found that children raised primarily by men are often active, vital, and vigorous babies, toddlers, preschoolers, and school-age children (Pruett, 1987; Pruett & Litzenberger, 1992). These children are interested particularly in the external environment and are able to deal comfortably with the increased stimulation of such interactions. Moreover, the majority of infants functioned somewhat above expected norms on standardized developmental tests.

These findings may be the result of the following factors:

1. The benefit to the child arose from the presence of two parents who interacted well with the child and not necessarily from special cognitive stimulation from the father alone.
2. The fathers participated early in the transactional and reciprocal nurturing activities that stimulate the emotional attachment so vital in the development of personality in the early years.
3. The style and choice of caretaking behaviors are rooted deeply within the father's normal, self-involved wish to be nurtured and to nurture. This mechanism is important in mothers as well, although the mechanism is obviously different in that mothers are more physically intimate earlier with their children as a result of pregnancy.
4. The paternal caregiving style reflects the father's selected mirrorings and identifications with the important caregivers in his life. Thus nurturing capacities of men do not appear to be wholly determined by either genetic endowment or gender identity.

Interestingly, Maccoby and Jacklin's (1974) observations of fathers' propensity to clarify children's gender identities through the use of more stereotypic language and behaviors do not apply to this population. Apparently, gender stereotyping is less likely to occur if the relationship between the father and child is more intimate.

A gender-related issue that does not change when fathers assume primary caretaking responsibilities is gender difference in the management of same and opposite-sex children. Female children are generally more compliant with mothers, and male children are generally more compliant with fathers. Perhaps parents' capacity to more fully understand same-sex children and, conversely, their less immediate understanding of the opposite-sex child at essential moments in the caretaking process make the "no" of the opposite gender child to a management directive more cogent.

Erikson's (1968) observation that "mother love and father love" are essentially different was borne out in my longitudinal study. Erikson states that fathers "love more dangerously" because their love is more "expectant . . . more instrumental" (p. 106) and qualitatively less unconditional than that of mothers. Although I found these distinctions somewhat less obvious in fathers who were involved in primary caretaking activities, the essential truth of this observation prevails. Perhaps this "more dangerous" love is at the root of many fathers' reluctance to be involved with, or conversely, institutional exclusion from their children's schools, mental health clinics, and churches. With most activities in which children are involved (except for sports), the absence of the father is condoned, almost expected. I suspect the negative connotation of this more "expectant," "instrumental" love may be the culprit in this mutual avoidance pattern. The resulting absence is destructive to the development of children and to families as a whole.

As with motherhood, fatherhood is expressed at various levels of intensity and competence. Single custodial fathers, the number of whom has quadrupled since the 1980 census, as a group do a decent job with their children. DeFrain and Eirick (1981) describe single custodial fathers as a reasonably successful group, educated, usually in managerial positions, and earning incomes equal to or above the national average. As more children sink into poverty in this country, the economic benefits of placing children with fathers are difficult for judges to avoid when assigning custody in controversial divorce battles in which both parents seem equally competent (or equally incompetent). Philosophically, single custodial fathers tend to be supportive of the women's movement and are described as open-minded, flexible in their fathering, and responsive to their children's needs. These fathers are those who seek, not merely assent to, custody of their children, however. The children of the latter group tend to live out their lives in a kind of no-man's land, in which they essentially raise themselves because no one has sought to raise them.

Stepfathering, which is as prone to negative stereotypes as is stepmothering, is increasingly common and increasingly complex. Research suggests that stepfathers may be more attentive to the needs of their children and that they are less arbitrary in their parenting style than are fathers of many intact families, partly because their consciousness has been raised about the overriding significance of two parents in the lives of their children.

Teenage fathers are as uninformed about the needs of their children as are many teenage mothers. Surprisingly, however, most teen fathers feel close to their partners and to their babies. Many teen fathers wish to be included in the rearing of their children. For poor, inner-city, minority teenage mothers and fathers, the ability to find work is a critical factor in the young male's identity as a father. Levine (1992) and Greenberg and Brown (1992) point out the importance of job training in teenage fathering programs.

For all fathers, research in the United States, Australia, and Europe shows that involved fathers have better self-esteem, are less subject to physical illness, have marriages in which their spouses are more satisfied, and have children who are better able to adapt to life stresses.

The largest gap between paternal and maternal involvement and presence occurs in the area of emotional responsibility. When mothers are present, fathers tend to defer to their caretaking wishes. They tend to become assistants to, rather than partners of, mothers. Neither children nor marriages are well served in this regard. Grossman (1987) suggests that a mothers control of the father's access to their child can be rectified if the couple become conscious of its existence. Children need and appreciate having both parents involved in their lives.

CONCLUSION

Although progress is being made, much work remains in defining the meaning of fathers' presence in their children's lives. In recent years, economic and social forces have drawn fathers into the lives of their children, whether they want to be there or not. Once drawn into the child's domain, many men have discovered the pleasures and rewards of establishing intimate relationships with their children. Unlike women, men tend not to talk about their children's caretaking needs in social groups; rather, they "own" their experience privately, as if they have discovered a wonderful secret that can be preserved only by not calling attention to it. However one may feel about the impact of the paternal presence on children and their families, children clearly respond positively to close, meaningful relationships with their fathers.

The paternal presence is a vital, life-giving force in the lives of children and families. Although we have made some progress in understanding the impact of paternal absence on children, we must now begin to understand, define, and appreciate the meaning of paternal presence.

In this chapter, Dr. Ehrensaft combines interview research and feminist-influenced object relations theory to explore the gender based nature of co-parenting in shared parenting families. Focusing on the maternal "being" and the paternal "doing," she explains some of the important advantages of each gender-related style of active parenting. Dr. Ehrensaft concludes that mothers and fathers each offer much to their children as well as provide important models for connection and separation for the parents' relationships as well.

The research stands in direct opposition to cynics and critics of more involved fathering. It also leads to a strong recommendation that pervades this volume: fathering is different than mothering, yet equally valuable. This original article opens avenues for exploring what involved fathering is, and how it is appropriately different from mothering.

4

Bringing in Fathers: The Reconstruction of Mothering

Diane Ehrensaft

Rate Your Mate as a Father:

Gets child up and dressed in morning
Changes baby's diapers
Feeds baby
Picks child up from sitter, day care or school
Stays home if child is sick
Puts child to bed
Sets limits or disciplines child
Shops for child's clothes

Takes child to sitter, day care or school
Takes child to doctor, dentist, etc.
Fixes meals for child
Bathes child (or supervises bath)
Gets up with sick child at night
Attends day care or school functions
Helps child with homework

James Levine, *Working Mother,* February 1982

For the past decade there has been increasing scrutiny of the nature and extent of fathers' participation in child care. Today's fathers are both expected to and often personally desire to be more fully involved. Expectant fathers face challenges unlike those of their predecessors: being adequate providers and anchors to their wives will no longer suffice. Attendance at childbirth classes, in the delivery room, and at diaper changings have become required elements of fatherhood.

Over the last 25 years a new family form has evolved, the *shared parenting family,* where hearth and home are no longer mothers' sole domain and fathers participate as fully as mothers in the daily care of their sons and daughters. An increasing number of American fathers-to-be can anticipate involvement in such a family in which he will be called on to perform child-rearing tasks that may feel awkward or out of synch with his boyhood dreams of manhood and parenting.

Both changing gender norms and economic realities have been the moving force behind shared parenting. Women no longer want their lives solely dictated by an ascribed role of homemaker and full-time mother. Few two-parent families today can exist on one income. With the unattractive alternative of women now doing two jobs for the price of one—bringing in a paycheck and bringing up baby, a revolution in parenting roles has been in the making. This revolution demands that fathers pick up some of the load and many fathers, quite willing to become more involved in their children's "magic years," have responded to the call.

Within the context of contemporary social and economic realities, social-psychological theorists have urged gender equality in parenting. Both Dinnerstein (1976) and Chodorow (1978) have argued that we can no longer afford *not* to have fathers intimately involved in the care of their children if we want to raise future generations of children less restricted by gender roles and less riddled by antagonism toward members of the opposite sex.

As economic, social, and gender norms have shifted, some men and women have actually embarked on the ground-breaking experiment of fully sharing the primary tasks of parenting. Cynics and social scientists alike have argued that because of genetic programming or centuries of socialization, such experiments are doomed to fail. Women were "meant" to mother;[1] fathers lack the psychological skills or "instinctual drive" for primary caretaking, particularly of young babies (e.g., Rossi, 1977).

Yet contemporary social conditions dictate that more and more expectant fathers may be asked to be co-primary caretakers. It must be asked whether men can enter the child-rearing arena with women,

---

[1] "To mother" or "mothering," as used here, refers in genderless terms to all the tasks, both practical and relational, that are required to be the primary parent to a child.

equally share the responsibility with their female partners, and truly be primary caretakers along with their wives.

RECONSTRUCTING MOTHERING

Psychoanalysis has significantly shaped Western conceptions of parenting and child development. In almost every psychoanalytic and psychological formulation of development, it is taken as a given that the mother is the first primary attachment figure for the child in early life. Fathers hardly exist, except to offer support to their wives. Whole theories and paradigms are built from this premise: the oedipal drama; the stages of separation-individuation; the development of a self. In the past two decades feminists have questioned these formulations. To take as immutable or universal the female mother as *the* single significant other in the young child's life is erroneous. It is a socially constructed, not a biologically determined reality that does not necessarily foster the best interests of parent *or* child, and most significantly, ignores the role of fathers.

Culturally based problems, including sexual perversions (Gillespie, 1956; Stoller, 1975), masochistic romantic relationships in high achieving women (Schaefer, 1991), and confusion about gender identity in young boys (Green, 1987), have been attributed to overbearing, powerful mothers and physically or emotionally absent fathers. Given these trends, it is puzzling why so many American social scientists, mental health professionals, and policymakers alike adhere to a theory that supports child-rearing arrangements in which women in isolation rear their young, while fathers play no part.

Three feminist social theorists, Chodorow, Dinnerstein, and Benjamin, make a particularly strong argument against the acceptance of this parenting arrangement. As long as women care for children and men do not, the gender split between female as subjective, connected, and dependent and male as objective, rational, and autonomous will remain intact, resulting in domination of women by men (Benjamin, 1988), gender antagonism between the sexes (Dinnerstein, 1976), and an incomplete, unintegrated personality configuration within each of the sexes (Chodorow, 1978).

Chodorow argued that mothering is taken on by women from generation to generation not because of biology but because women keep taking the social position as the primary rearers of children. When women mother, they create female children who will also mother, and male children who will not, based on mothers' sense of similarity to their daughters and difference from their sons. This she labelled the "reproduction of mothering."

There are, however, a group of men and women today who have broken that cycle by equally sharing all the tasks of raising a child. They have challenged mothering as a gendered affair and have alerted us to the need for a new term that incorporates *all* the tasks of raising a child, "paternal" and "maternal," that can now be done by *any* primary parent, regardless of his or her gender. For our purposes, we will adopt "parenting" as that new term.

Shared parenting families create not the reproduction, but the *reconstruction* of mothering, as both male and female parent together. But what exactly is getting reconstructed?

MEN AND WOMEN PARENTING TOGETHER

In 1983 I embarked on a study of couples who attempt to fully share all the responsibilities of child-rearing (Ehrensaft, 1987). Eighty individual interviews were conducted with heterosexual mothers and fathers in intact families who agreed that they were both primary parents equally sharing the responsibilities of parenting. These families all *chose* a shared arrangement, rather than having it dictated by financial or logistic necessity. They believed this was the best way to raise a child and have a healthy relationship with one's partner. Subsequent to that study I have continued to follow some of these families and have also had the opportunity to observe many more families in shared parenting households. Some still do so by choice, but increasing numbers of fathers are pressured into service less by philosophy than necessity, such as parents' work schedules, lack of funds for paid child care, and a dearth of decent care outside the home.

The Study

In my shared parenting study, fathers and mothers, ranging in age from 21 to 47 and all engaged in professional careers or college or graduate training, were each interviewed separately. Twenty-three couples had two children, 17 couples had one child. The children ranged in age from 0 to 14; there were 33 boys and 30 girls. The families were recruited through a snowball technique, a referral technique I hoped would allow me to cast my net as far afield as possible from my own social and collegial network. Major metropolitan areas throughout the country were represented in the 80 people interviewed, although the San Francisco Bay Area was overrepresented.

A couple qualified for the study if they each reported in a screening interview that they considered themselves to be a primary caretaker of their child(ren) and had been so since the birth of their child. To confirm their subjective labelling against the actual realities of their parenting, each mother and father was then interviewed individually about the daily tasks of parenting, the relationship with their spouse, their relationship with their child(ren), their child(ren)'s development, their own family histories, and their internal experiences, conflicts, and fantasies related to their position as a sharing parent. Qualified couples had to have actual time arrangements for child rearing stay within a 60–40% band of time sharing between the two parents.

Just as the psychoanalyst D. W. Winnicott said there is no infant without a mother, in the shared parenting family there can be no infant without a mother *and* father. So if we are to understand if men are truly capable of sharing half the responsibilities of child rearing, we can only answer that question by looking not just at the father's experience, but also integrating it with the experience of the woman with whom he is sharing the intimacy and daily tasks of caring for a child.

At first glance it became very clear that fathers were indeed able to equitably share the *role* of primary parent with their wives, that is the behaviors, functions, and attitudes that are required in the day-to-day rearing of children. They were capable of managing daily tasks, such as feeding schedules and bathing; functioning as a socialization agent to their children, as in modelling nurturing behavior, setting limits, and introducing cognitive stimulation and establishing emotional bonds necessary for good-enough parenting. Role sharing involves taking full responsibility when "on duty."

Expectant fathers and their partners could not have easily predicted this outcome. Prior to the birth of their first child, all the parents had great hopes and visions of being a successful shared parenting couple. At the same time, they were riddled with doubts and misgivings. As one mother succinctly put it, "I had just figured that if I gave him about 90% of the responsibilities, we might just average out at a 50–50 arrangement." Women were skeptical about whether the men would actually come through. Men were nervous about whether they actually could. This dance of expectancies may sound familiar to mothers and fathers-to-be from all walks of life, not just the shared parenting family. The identifying feature of the shared parenting couples is that their hopes, rather than their fears, were fulfilled.

In fact, one element of the expectant and new father's experience may well serve as an accurate predictor of his ongoing involvement and commitment to primary parenting. The more a man expressed jealousy of his wife's pregnancy and breast-feeding, the more both parents emphasized what an involved father he had become over the months or years. So the more an expectant or recent father feels left out of the *biological* aspects of motherhood, the more he will find pleasure in being a father.

The reality of genuine role sharing in co-parenting families is eloquently portrayed in the interview statements of a couple married for 18 years and engaged in a shared parenting relationship for 11 of those years:

> Louise: *"I think there's been a consistency in terms of loving, caring, nurturing—the real primary basis of parenting. I've never felt that Jeff could not take care of Rachel. In terms of the emotional aspects of parenting, I feel we have divided it up very equally. I've never had any question of the sharing of the emotional responsibilities with Jeff. Again, the nurturing, the emotional, the psychological have been completely shared from the very beginning."*

> Jeff: *"Louise and I now have a real respect for the arena that we have evolved over time and what we're good at and what we are more comfortable with, rather than thinking we can be the all-around parent separately. And we have a tremendous amount of respect for each other's abilities to parent. Louise is a very, very good parent. I've learned a lot, and modeled on the way she has acted with Rachel. And I think that's true of her toward me.*

The key variables in accomplishing role equity were time, flexibility, and commitment. A fairly even distribution of time involvement, a willingness to be flexible and cover for each other, and a firm commitment to the identity and functions of primary parenting were the cornerstones of a successful shared parenting arrangement. Both mothers and fathers agreed in their separate interviews that fathers indeed qualified along each of these dimensions.

A closer examination revealed a more complicated picture, however. When it came to exploring the internal experience, psychic conflicts, and self-identity as a parent, distinct gender-related differences emerged. Feelings about being a parent and the emotions called into play in the child-rearing arena were very different for these fathers and mothers. Indeed, men and women parent very differently, based on a gender-specific set of inner conflicts and tensions.

First, I will summarize the differences as they met the observer's eye. Mothers are more involved in their children's wardrobes than fathers, both psychologically and practically, regardless of the gender of the child. Mothers buy their children's clothes, fathers rarely do, even when there is a commitment to equality.

Mothers spend more time thinking, indeed even obsessing, about their children, whether the children are present or not. They are more involved in what I have termed the "psychological management" of parenting. Beyond keeping track of doctors' appointments, gymnastics classes, and mentally logging developmental milestones, they worry more about the emotional health of their children while at work or away from the children; their "internal mothering switch" is permanently set to the "On" position.

Fathers, in contrast, have a more "nine-to-five" quality in their parenting involvement: "When I work, I work, and when I parent, I parent." They seem much more adept than mothers in integrating parenting and nonparenting activities: rocking baby while reading a book, practicing piano while overseeing homework. When they go to their jobs, they may rarely think about their child throughout the work day. They are not burdened with the excess mental baggage of parenting that the mothers complain about so consistently. When it comes to parenting, they definitely have access to an On-Off switch.

These observable, palpable differences between the shared parenting fathers and their female partners all fit into a gender-divided categorization: *Fathers possess a better sense of separateness with their children, an ability to create boundaries between self and baby. In contrast, the mothers demonstrate more of a sense of connectedness, a sense of fusion or extension with their sons and daughters.* The father–mother difference pertains regardless of the gender of the child. Even with sons, fathers feel less of a sense of fusion than mothers do. So a father reports, "When something goes wrong for Ben, our son, I figure 'That's him, not me and he'll get through it.'" Whereas, the mother reports, "When Ben's having a hard time, I feel like a part of me has been clobbered."

SEPARATE FATHERS AND CONNECTED MOTHERS

These mothers and fathers had entered parenthood with a mission. Prior to the birth of their first child they had already decided that they would establish egalitarian parenting relationships in which both would be actively involved in their child's daily upbringing. When I first asked each parent if he/she was aware of any major differences or inequities in their parenting arrangement, the first response was "No, none that I can think of."

It was only when the person was probed about specific areas, "What about clothes and dressing?," "What about worrying about the kids?," etc., that the gender differences surfaced. From the gender splits in wardrobe and psychological management, the interviews went on to reveal that fathers have an easier time than their wives with separations when away from the child and also a different mode of play with their children, more rough and tumble and "action-oriented" than the comparatively sedentary and quiet play of the mothers who "molded" with their children (Ehrensaft, 1987; Lewis, Feiring, and Weinraub, 1981)

A pattern emerged: *women were more connected, men more separate* in relationship to their children. Why? All of these mothers and fathers were themselves mother-raised children. According to Chodorow (1978), "the basic feminine sense of self is connected to the world, the basic masculine sense of self is separate" (p. 169). She believed this pattern, in a mother-reared culture, stemmed from the early experience of a like-sex primary parent (for girls) versus an opposite-sex primary parent (for boys).

The mother identifies with her daughter, on the basis of their shared gender, and keeps her close to her heart and close to the hearth. The little girl on her part takes note of this identity between self and female parent, and remains connected to her mother far longer than her brothers.

In the meantime, the mother views her son very much as an other, different than her, and encourages his autonomy and independence strivings. He becomes her little man, rather than a full extension of herself (Chodorow, 1978; Lawrence, 1985). For the little boy to find someone like himself, he must, in the mother-raised household, turn to a more distant father and extrapolate in a more abstract rather than intimate fashion how to be a male in the world.

The basic feminine sense of self as connected prepares females for the responsibilities and relationship of mothering, whereas the basic masculine sense of self as separate leaves males less prepared or predisposed toward the primary identification, empathy and connectedness that are the basic requirements of mothering. Therefore, women are drawn toward primary parenting, men are not.

Shared parenting fathers defy this construct by predisposing themselves toward the primary child-rearing tasks for which they are not expected to be prepared. Why? Every infant, both male and female, develops the basic capacities for human relatedness in its earliest relationship with its mothering figure, provided there is good-enough parenting. It is only later that the experience becomes gender-divided, at least in a female-raised culture. Boys, in separating from their mothers and conforming to cultural expectations, squelch their basic relational abilities, in their efforts to be more "objective," "rational," and independent. But the basic capacities are still within, merely repressed or suppressed throughout the male acculturation process. The presence of one's own child is the facilitator that releases these capacities in the men.

Nonetheless, both parents agree that fathers approach the experience of parenting very differently than mothers. Because they bring the weight of their own gendered personality to the parenting process, they demonstrate a separateness and sense of boundariedness in their parenting that was nowhere to be found in like fashion among the women.

For example, a mother of a toddler reports, *"Rick (father) can tolerate Matthew's crying and screaming much more than I can. It drives me crazy, I feel like I absolutely have to do something."*

As she witnesses her child's pain, it is as if her own heart is bleeding. Rick has a more relaxed and measured approach: *"Just let him cry."* Left to his own resources, Matthew will manage it. Why this difference? In the reconstruction of mothering through shared parenting, at least in its first generation, the feminine form of parenting highlights *connection*, the masculine form highlights *separateness*. Of course, each comes with its own pluses and minuses.

DOING VERSUS BEING

Fathers have a nine-to-five quality to their parenting. Their wives, in contrast, are very much immersed in a parenting-without-walls experience. Although both are strongly bonded to their children, men exhibit more separateness, women more connectedness. We can also cast it in different terms. Men *do* mothering whereas women *are* mothers.

D.W. Winnicott (1971) delineates two elements of personality: feminine and masculine. The female element, "being," occurs very early in human development. Parent and baby are felt as one. The simplest of all experiences, and the source of the true continuity of generations, Winnicott also chose to label it as "feminine."

"Doing," the male element in personality, follows "being" in development and presupposes a separateness between baby and parent. The infant begins to recognize that the person who takes care of him or her is "not me" and can then start to act on its environment. This requires an advancement in mental structure beyond that of birth, whereas being can begin immediately. Winnicott chose to label this more complicated process, doing, as "masculine."

Winnicott (1971) posits that each individual, whether woman or man, has both a female and a male element within: "The male element *does,* while the female element (in both males and females) *is.*" The male element, doing, has more to do with separateness, whereas the female element, being, is more about connectedness. The healthiest, most integrated individuals will be those who can strike a nice balance between "being" and "doing."

It seems likely that when women are the exclusive early figures in the child's life, however, the male element, which represents more separateness, will be enhanced in sons, whereas the female element, which is about connectedness, will be dominant in daughters. By adulthood, we would expect men more likely to "do," and women more likely to "be," and an extensive body of empirical evidence exists to support this (i.e., Chodorow, 1989).

There is no reason that the parenting arena should be exempt from this *being–doing* gender difference, even among men and women highly committed to gender equality in child-rearing. Pete is representative of all the parents as he differentiates the parenting experience for him and his wife, both of whom are academics and highly involved and loving parents: *"For me, out of sight is out of mind. At work, I might think about the kids for five seconds. For Stephanie, at work at 11:00, she'll start thinking, 'Are the kids O.K.?' At 1:00 she'll think, 'Did I pack Sandra with her clothes?' I have no more thoughts of the kids through the day. As for Stephanie, it's her funeral."*

Stephanie concurs with Pete's assessment of her, and admires his ability to do the "on and off stuff."

In the gender divisions revealed in the shared parenting relationship, the following parenting equation can now be made: *female = connected = being,* and *male = separate = doing.* Now let us go back into the shared parenting fathers and mothers' lives to investigate further whether the equation works in practice.

DOING VERSUS BEING IN ACTION

A father envies the ease with which his wife absorbs parenting into her way of being. A mother longs for the father's capacity to compartmentalize. Each has something of which the other wants more.

This could be no more evident than in the differential ability of the men and the women to draw boundaries between themselves and their children and between their parenting and nonparenting aspects of self. Fathers, for example, were much better at getting two things done at once and warding off intrusions from the children. Although there were exceptions to the rule, in the typical household, fathers were able to take care of baby and simultaneously do something else, while mothers looked on in awe.

If it came to the simultaneous management of *household* chores and child-tending, women were better able to cope than men. Men either got overwhelmed by too much going on at once or let the household tasks slide, giving full attention to the more engaging activity of child care. The "two things at once" that men could do better than women did not involve home-management tasks, "women's work," but rather the coordination of work or "doing things for myself" and parenting.

Within the family, women are highly tuned into their child's presence, and feel almost compelled to intervene. Men are better equipped to maintain some distance: Their child does not "penetrate" or get to them as much.

A woman has difficulty disengaging herself from her child, not just because she thinks she "ought to" do something for the child, but more deeply, because she has trouble not "being" a mother. The strongly internalized identification and "at-oneness" with her child become liabilities as soon as she attempts to pick up a coveted magazine article if her child is in the same room. To vacuum would be acceptable, because it is part of caretaking.

Structuring time for herself removes her from her child, and threatens that very relationship. It comes so "naturally" to her to remain connected, because of her personality structure, that she cannot understand why it is so hard for her to create boundaries between herself and her child, and yet so easy for the man with whom she lives. Her husband's better ability to establish a healthy separation between self and child has a great deal to teach her about a less tension-filled and saner way of parenting, where time for oneself can live in consort with connection with an other.

The "tuning out" that makes the father less of a psychological manager is the same "tuning out" that allows him to more easily work and tend to baby at the same time. Father is much clearer as to where he stops and baby starts. By contrast, mothers have a hard time sorting out their own needs from their children's: "I can't tell if I'm picking her up to make her feel better or to make me feel better."

This relative difficulty in intermingling nonparenting and child-rearing tasks is mild when compared to her more profound struggles to integrate parenting and nonparenting parts of herself. Living and breathing are things we just take for granted; so it is for many women in the case of mothering. It permeates her entire self, sometimes to the point that feels stifling, but most often with an inner propelling and rhythm that takes its own course whether the woman wills it or not. The expectation of the external world that she is *parent first* above all else (why else would we have only the term "working mother," but never the term "working father"?) both influences and mirrors her internal experience; not necessarily that she is mother *first,* but that she is mother all the time.

A man looks at what he experiences as his wife's obsessive preoccupation with the child, her complacency with this state of affairs, and feels neither envy nor guilt that he does not intermingle, but rather compartmentalizes his life. It comes "naturally" for men to be able to do this because they have something women do not: a capacity to maintain a distance between themselves and their child and also between different parts of themselves. The man understands full well that it leaves him less overburdened and facilitates a more relaxed relationship with the children, and he cannot fathom why his wife would not "choose" the same mode for herself. When he sees how much she overworks at parenting, he just shrugs his shoulders and sighs, "It's her funeral."

It has been documented that in families with two working parents men have an easier time blending work and family. Sociologically, there are two salient explanations. First, there are the pulls, both external and internal, that draw women toward their traditional "roles" of wife and mother and men toward the traditional "roles" of breadwinner and public participant for which they have been socialized.

Second, it is difficult for a woman to give up power in the arena that has traditionally been hers, the hearth, in exchange for participation in the public realm where power seldom comes her way.

There is yet a third psychological explanation for the gender difference in the psychological experience of integrating work and family roles in light of the "doing versus being" phenomenon in parenting. The "out of sight, out of mind" relationship to the children more common among men going off to work is not because work is more important to men than it is to women. These men and women talked with equal intensity about their work involvement and identities.

Instead, it is because men do different "balancing acts" than women within their psyches. As one mother said, "Sometimes I want to rush back to the day care center, scoop him up, and take him home. Other days I wish I could just barricade myself in my office." This mother, like many others, is continually plagued, in a way men *never* expressed, by the tensions between her familial and extra-familial identities. Marsha, an expectant mother, predicts that she will experience similar feelings: "I have nightmares about it. I want the work, I want myself, I want the kid." The question for her is, "How can I have all three?" It is an easier question for the man, because it seems more possible for him to *do* all three than it is for the woman to *be* all three.

When a father says, "If Aaron is not doing so well, I wouldn't take that as me. I would say that's in Aaron, and that's too bad," he is demonstrating the male balancing act. With that level of autonomy between himself and his child, this father is free to go to work and leave his parenting burdens behind. The inner capacity that allows him to remain a clear, separate person from his son is the same capacity that allows him to put up firm dividers between the part of himself that is parent and the part who is worker or some other nonparenting self. To be able to maintain a separateness between self and other is the prerequisite for the male element of doing. It is also a key factor in the development of healthy relationships. This element appears much more highly exercised in men and allows them to separate child from self and parent from worker because they are not hampered by the "merging," the "being" that is so much more fully developed in women. It allows sharing fathers to be freed of the "mother guilt" so pernicious in all of the sharing mothers' psyches.

If men feel more separate from their children and can more easily implement "out of sight, out of mind," the finding that any extended separations from the children will be easier on the fathers than on the mothers seems only logical. In every one of the families, both partners agreed that this was the case. Not that men breezed through extended separations from their child. Like their wives, they thought about their child, wondered if he or she was doing well, and looked forward to their reunion. But they did not report the same level of suffering that the mothers did.

At a very deep level separations were simply not as great a loss for the men and they found them much easier to negotiate. Not one man talked about his existence being at stake or about total confusion (What am I to do, who am I without her/him?) in response to separations. Several women did.

Some mothers felt so over-connected to their children that in fact their only haven was the actual separations from them, during which they reported relief and appreciation for the breathing space from parenting. Not one father reported that need to escape. Instead, a father was freer to experience sheer positive feelings during time away from his child. It gave him time to smell the flowers and attend to other facets of himself. When he leaves his child, there is no major threat to his core being. He is still intact, no part of him is missing.

BRINGING IN FATHERS

Cynics who doubt the capacity of men to become primary parents are wrong. Men can both take on that role and engage in the essential tasks that qualify for "good enough parenting." But when we go beyond role sharing and tasks to the identity and psychological experience of parenting, the sharing mothers and fathers do part ways, based on their own gender. At best we could call shared parenting a "separate but equal" phenomenon: *separate* because of the gender-specific upbringing, socialization, and internalization of their own childhood histories that the mothers and fathers bring to parenting, *equal* because fathers' "doing" has as much to offer as mothers' "being' in raising the children.

We need to bring the fathers in because the degree of separateness and the level of boundaries they are able to maintain between themselves and their sons and daughters are a great resource to both their children and to their wives. Women have often been accused of being over-involved, overbearing, or suffocating of their children, loathe to relinquish their attachments to give the children the autonomy they need. Although this is often an unfair aspersion cast on mothers' characters, it does speak to the virtue of fathers' boundedness as an antidote to women's struggles to avoid fusion with their offspring.

Fathers, in their "doing" mode of parenting, can both serve as role models to their wives and provide an alternative relationship with their children in which sons and daughters can experience intimacy with a degree of separateness that protects them from emotional smothering. Balanced by intimacy with mother that comes with a tad more connectedness or psychological merging, children can experience expanded forms of love. Fathers, who may find it easier to love without engulfing, can free their children to develop their own selves rather than being extensions or reflections of their parents.

Exempt from mother guilt, the male balancing act can also produce a more conflict-free, relaxed state of parenthood, a nice complement to the mother's wall-to-wall emotionally intense mode of parenting. In a modern world, which demands both full-time work and family responsibilities from women and men alike, fathers, falling on the doing/separate side of the parenting equation, have something critical to show mothers about how to accomplish both.

Relative to women, men will remain doers. Even in a population in which the "feminine" being element is relatively highly developed in men, as it was in these men who chose to become intimately involved with their children, it will still not be as dominant as it is in a woman or operate in the same way.

At the same time, the doing versus being gender difference does not remain static over the course of the shared parenting experience. On becoming a sharing parent, the woman begins to experience a "thirst for autonomy," whereas the man finds himself with a "hunger for intimacy." Women drawn to a co-parenting relationship are opting out of being the sole and primary caretaker in their child's life. They typically do not want to be burdened with the full responsibility of their child. Yet they find themselves constantly in a bind: between self and child; between child and work. They long for and work toward a bit less connectedness and are engaged in a continual balancing act between autonomy and attachment. They envy the facility with which their husbands can achieve that balance. Fathers present a very different picture. The dynamic for the men does not involve a constant balancing act between autonomy and attachment, as it does for the women, but instead a powerful longing for connectedness and openness with their children, a move toward "being."

This was the most unexpected finding in the study of the shared parenting couples. As one mother in the study exclaimed, "The men have gone ga-ga over the children." As I heard the men speak of their children, they spoke in the terms of a love affair, regardless of whether their child was female or male. They basked in the new-found opportunity to open up to another human being, to be childlike and playful with no self-consciousness, to feel they could totally "be" themselves. They had discovered intimacy.

Men who embark on shared parenting are a unique sector of the male population. Just in the act of actively parenting a child they are propelled by a desire to have a close relationship with a child that has traditionally been the domain of women and children. Many of these men admitted to being dissatisfied or uncomfortable with traditional gender roles, but they do not fully shed their gendered personality when they choose to become a shared parenting father.

In that sense, the experience of the shared parenting father gives us a window into the phenomenon of fatherhood per se. Any man awaiting the birth of his first child can expect to feel longings from his earliest experiences, yearnings for closeness, cuddling, protection, and playfulness. Whether or not he has ever picked up a doll or rocked a cradle, if he himself received adequate maternal care in his own life, he will be able to call up capacities for primary care from within himself. He may feel nervous that the task is beyond him, but it is not. His potential as a good-enough parent can become activated by the birth of his own child, facilitating an unfolding of even previously dormant talents for empathy, connection, and nurturance.

In his reveries he may find himself reaching toward his awaited child as the safest arena in which to explore and express his desires for intimacy. Whereas he might be equally as involved and as excited as his wife about their joint venture, it is likely, at this point in history, that parenthood will not be as deeply embedded in his core psyche as it is in his wife's. Neither he nor his wife should lose sleep over this—it is just the being versus doing phenomenon in motion. If he wishes to become a shared parenting father, he can now respond to dubious relatives and acquaintances, with research to back him, that men can and do take care of the children, they just do it in their own male way. He can also gently remind his wife not to become agitated if he does not always do it her way. Her way is not the only way, and the separate/doing mode of parenting has its own merits, for *a child needs a combination of both separateness and connection.*

A father raising his children typically finds himself on the "doing" end of the spectrum in relation to his wife. He has some things he can teach her: how not to get over-involved or smothering, how to create some healthy separateness between her own life and her child's. In turn, his wife can teach him how to stay connected: how to lower the walls of autonomy, open up, and establish a close intimate relationship with his child. The more both mother and father can find a better balance between being and doing within themselves, the better parents they will be. It is the blend of the two that facilitates the healthiest human relationships. Every day that fathers and mothers parent together their emotional quest for a healthier balance comes closer to fruition. If men embarking on parenthood wish to play their hand in the reshaping of history, they can now know that by bringing in father, mothering will indeed be reconstructed.

Breadwinner

I can loaf no longer
But must soon labor for bread alone
Since my wife will be a mother.
I have sought this for years, it seems,
I will be Stanley Kowalski
Broad and drenched
Heaving hunks of meat up to my nursing honey
With a bellow of love.
I will be Ward Cleaver
Home for lunch and lectures
To my strapping boys.
I will be my father
Hot, irritable, untalkable-to
Until an hour
After two drinks and a shower.
I will be confused
Proud of my doughy wallet
Sore about my daily eviction
From the cave I will
Cautiously re-enter each evening
This curious victory
Slung like a club
Across my stalwart back.

—Brad Sachs

In this empirically oriented article, the significance of the mother in promoting fatherhood during the perinatal and postnatal period is explored. Dr. Jordan observes that in the well documented changes in parental division of labor, mothers are often reluctant to share control over the determination of parental and household roles. Instead there is a tendency for mothers to be "chief among equals."

Fathers may unconsciously reinforce mothers' dominance in the home realm by assuming that their wives are the more knowledgeable or competent parent. They may also "freeload" by subtly supporting the mothers' adoption of the extra work load. Using interview data and quotes from participants in her investigations, Dr. Jordan advocates the need to alter the mother's mind set as well as the father's in order to effect changes in paternal involvement.

5

The Mother's Role in Promoting Fathering Behavior[1]

Pamela L. Jordan

Parenting and occupational roles are the primary roles of adulthood. The late 1960s women's movement led to major changes in the traditional female gender-role. The traditional male role subsequently underwent scrutiny and change, as male and female gender-roles are defined vis-á-vis each other. Resultant changing societal beliefs about gender-roles and an altered economic climate that accelerated women's paid employment outside the home, have prompted greater sharing of domestic responsibilities, including parenting. Despite the multiple role demands on women and their frequent plea for greater sharing of responsibilities in the home, the mother remains the primary parent in the vast majority of households. If there is to be greater sharing of domestic responsibilities, a better understanding of factors influencing men's involvement at home is necessary. This chapter

[1]Data presented in this chapter come from the studies, "The Male Experience of Expectant and New Fatherhood: grant #R23-NRO1480, and, "Expectant/New Fathers at Risk," grant #KO7-NROO030, National Institute of Nursing Research, Pamela L. Jordan, Principal Investigator.

61

focuses on the mother's role in promoting or impeding paternal involvement and behavior during the perinatal period.

Few studies address the influence of the mother's beliefs, actions, and expectations on the father's role enactment. Reiber (1976) reported that first-time fathers demonstrated interest and competence in nurturing their children but were involved in child care activities *only to the extent* the mothers wanted them to be. Shared parenting could only become a reality when the barriers set up by *women* as well as men were broken down. Mothers' antepartum expectations of their mates' parenting involvement predicted the fathers' actual level of involvement even more strongly than did the fathers' expectations (Fein, 1976; Humenick & Bugen, 1987). Greater ambivalence about paternal involvement on the part of the mother was reported by Tomlinson (1987) to be associated with lower levels of paternal involvement. Despite the documented heavier role burden for women and unequal division of labor (e.g. Hochschild, 1989; Pleck, 1985), *women do not necessarily want or appreciate* greater male participation in family work (Barnett & Baruch, 1987, 1988; Kimball, 1988).

THROUGH THE FATHERS' EYES

Four studies, including two longitudinal studies have been conducted by this investigator over the last 15 years. The first two studies discussed in this chapter were cross-sectional descriptive studies of the experiences of men becoming parents for the first time. Although not a primary focus of the initial longitudinal study, fathers discussed aspects of the mothers' behaviors that impacted their own behaviors as fathers. They characteristically viewed women as innately or instinctively superior parents. Lurking in the fathers' comments were hints that mothers controlled parenting and the extent to which fathers were able to be involved. These perspectives seemed significant and were examined more closely to better appreciate what was seen through the fathers' eyes. The mother's role in promoting fathering behavior was a serendipitous finding.

In the first longitudinal study, 56 expectant and recent first-time English-speaking fathers living with their mates were recruited through obstetrical care providers, word-of-mouth, and media publicity. Twenty-eight participants chose longitudinal participation and 28 comprised the cross-sectional group. Ages ranged from 20 to 41 years with mean and median ages of 30. Participants had from 11 to 21 years of formal education (M=16 years). Four participants were unemployed and 13 were students. A broad variety of occupations were represented and the median annual household income was $26,000. This figure is inflated as demographic data were gathered at the initial interview for longitudinal participants when the majority enjoyed dual household incomes. Interviews lasting from 30 minutes to 2½ hours were conducted six to seven times over the perinatal period: After conception, mid-pregnancy, late pregnancy, after birth, and at 6 weeks, 6 months, and 1 year post birth.

Each interview began with the broad question, "What can you tell me about your experience of being an expectant/new father?" Additional questions included, "At this point in time, what are people saying or doing that is helpful or supportive to you as an expectant/new father?' and "What do you wish people would say or do to be helpful or supportive to you?"

The major finding indicated *the fathers' lack of essential resources to assume the position of chief parent.* The paucity of biological and social resources was salient. Findings related to the desire for parenthood and the control of conception suggested that it was usually the woman who was responsible for contraception, though the measures she was likely to employ were often unnoticed by her mate. A woman can independently decide to conceive and can keep knowledge of conception to herself. The vast majority of these fathers stated the pregnancy was unplanned. They and their mates had discussed having a child someday, but *someday* was not now. It was not ascertained if the mothers also would have characterized the pregnancies as unplanned.

Fathers' reactions were quite revealing when asked, "As far as you know, have you ever fathered a child before?" Many were astounded by this question, realizing for the first time, given their sexual activity, they might have conceived a child about whom they knew nothing. This finding suggests further the extent of the woman's control. For example, one woman *faked her period* so she could tell her mate about the pregnancy as a Christmas present the next month. Women may be aware of their control over conception and childbearing, and potentially take full advantage of their control. As one interviewed father put it: *"The actual pregnancy and birth and everything is happening to the female and not the male. The husband is a third party . . . You feel the kicking on the outside of the body whereas [she] feels the kicking on the inside. . . . Women go through the pregnancy. Men experience it vicariously."*

As this father suggests, mothers are deemed biologically advantaged as parents. Mothers are pregnant, give birth, and lactate. Fathers are outside the physical experience. Most fathers subscribed to the *hormonal advantage theory,* whereby females were perceived as innately competent and superior parents because of their monthly cycles and the physiologic capabilities of the uterus and breasts. One such father said: "It's instinctive for women to take care of babies, whether it's a baby human or a baby anything."

Participant fathers believed that as a result of biology and socialization it continued to be the natural role of adult women to care for their children. These men attributed innate and instinctual parenting capabilities to their mates. As one put it: *"Somehow she just knows what to do. She takes the upper hand. . . I'm just kinda going along, following along. If I'm needed to do something . . . I'll do it, but I won't decide. . . . I don't feel like I have that control."*

Mothers often engage in behaviors that exemplify actualizing their control in childbearing and parenting. Pregnancy and parenting are her turf. Fathers view these behaviors as impeding paternal involvement. A father stated: *"Part of the reason that men don't participate more in raising families is because of the negative reinforcement they get from their spouses. Either they aren't diapering right or they're not caring for the child right. . . . Men are hearing they're doing it wrong so they don't want to do it again; they pull back. . . . If a woman can understand that her husband is just doing it a different way and that it's okay, it would be a lot easier for men to continue to participate."*

There seem to be unspoken yet societally acknowledged role expectations as articulated by another father. *"I really do feel in the role of being an assistant parent, but I am an assistant parent . . . not totally absent from the program. [My wife] does a lot of the heavy duty serious parenting type stuff—thinking about what clothes to put on her . . . what to feed her. I guess part of being a mom, at least to her and maybe to me, too, is to kind of be the chief parent. I'm not prepared to say it's a bad thing at all that I'm in this assistant parent sort of role. . . . It relieves me of quite a few responsibilities. . . . [My wife] would like us to be called co-parents, but she also really likes to be chief among equals."*

In order to promote paternal involvement, the mother needs to develop an awareness of the perception of herself as chief parent and acknowledge to her mate the inaccuracy of this assumption, which not all women seemed willing or able to do. Once both parents are able to critically consider the idea of the mother's acknowledged expertise, the father is better able to perceive himself and his mate as being on equal footing. One such father stated: *"[My wife] grew up in a family with very traditional roles. It's been a struggle for her to give up more [of the parenting] than she had anticipated . . . to have me have him as much as I do. . . . Breastfeeding was something that she had exclusively with him and when I could begin to share the feeding, it was difficult for her."*

This mother had difficulty getting beyond the expectations developed from role enactment in her family of origin. Few of the mothers actively promoted paternal involvement, but those who did, particularly during pregnancy, seemed to have a powerful impact that carried well into later stages of parenting. As one father emphasized: *"Part of the mother's role is to nurture the involvement of the father."*

Fathers needed to have time alone with their children to develop competence and their own style. Most of these men came to parenthood with impoverished behavioral repertoires for parenting, having minimal or no previous experience with children. Rather than assuming innate superiority in parenting on the part of their mates, these fathers realized that confidence and competence came from time spent taking care of the child.

Sharing parenting also involved the father becoming more assertive as a parent, which conveyed the father's perception of parenting as an appropriate male endeavor. Some fathers realized they could not wait to be invited into parenting by their mates, but had to assert themselves in enactment of the paternal role. One said: *"I have told her on a couple of occasions, 'Look, I can handle it. Go find your own space. I love you and I care for you, and it doesn't change my lifelong ambition to stay with you the rest of my life, but I just want to be alone with my son now.'"*

Taken together, this investigator's studies illuminate the father's perception of the strategic role of the mother in promoting or impeding fathering behaviors. Participating fathers perceived themselves to be lacking in the essential resources to assume the position of chief parent. They lacked a uterus and breasts, the essential organs of gestation, parturition, and lactation. These men believed their mates possessed innate knowledge, skills, and instincts that gave them advantage as parents. Participant fathers conceded their mates dominated the planning for the child, including controlling conception, and the degree to which the father was allowed to be involved in the experiences of pregnancy and parenting.

MOTHERS' EXPECTATIONS OF THEIR MATES AND NEEDS OVER THE PERINATAL PERIOD

Women are recognized and supported as parents, even by their partners. Mothers tend to function as *gatekeepers,* controlling fathers' access to the child and enactment of the paternal role. The findings discussed above indicate that men empower women as parents based on their attributions of them as superior parents. If the mother has so much influence on paternal behavior, what is it she wants and expects of her mate as they become parents? This information is necessary to be able to effect changes in maternal behavior that influence paternal behavior. To address this question, eight first-time mothers were interviewed using grounded theory methodology.

Each participant mother was interviewed two to six times from early pregnancy through 6 months postbirth. The mothers were asked what they wanted and needed from their mates, both as their partners and as the other parent of their child. They were also asked what expectations they had of their mate as a father. As the study progressed, additional questions included: *"Whose child is this?"* and *"What are you doing to bring your mate into the pregnancy or parenting?"*

The mothers' expectations and needs of their mates fell into three primary categories that were related to their stage in the childbearing process: *understand and support me* (pregnancy); *be with me* (labor and birth); and, *help me* (parenting). Although each category is most closely associated with the specified period of the childbearing process, each carries over into the subsequent time periods. For example, understanding and support were needed most during pregnancy, but were also needed during labor and birth and into parenting.

Understand and Support Me

During pregnancy the mothers needed their mates to acknowledge that things were different due to the pregnancy. Mothers wanted their partners to understand they were often feeling tired and sick and were therefore unable to perform all of their normal functions. For these mothers, "support and understanding" had several referents, including: (1) taking up the slack with cooking, cleaning, and other household tasks; (2) understanding how they were feeling emotionally, including tolerating unpredictable mood swings; (3) showing interest in the growing baby; (4) preparing the nursery or other "nesting" behaviors, such as refinishing a crib, decorating a special room, or moving to a larger apartment; (5) dialoguing together about the baby, life after the baby, and parenting; (6) accompanying on visits to the obstetrical care provider, being present during labor and birth, and attending childbirth preparation classes together; (7) reassuring her about her competence as a mother; (8) being financially and emotionally more responsible; (9) expressing a love for her and acceptance of her changing body; and, (10) understanding her lack of desire for sexual relations, particularly early in the pregnancy (when she was feeling fatigued and sick) and again late in pregnancy (when she was feeling huge, uncomfortable, and unattractive).

Be with Me

During labor and birth the primary need of each mother was that her mate be physically and emotionally present. This need began to be expressed during late pregnancy when each woman needed to be assured her mate would be accessible for labor and birth. The mothers wanted their mates to be home more or available by phone, pager, or specified itinerary.

As pregnancy progressed, the mothers focused on their needs during labor and birth. These included using the techniques learned in childbirth education classes, reassurance that they could make it through labor and birth, and that if the mother panicked or lost control, they would rely on their mate to get them through. As one mother described it: *"Basically I expect him to get me through labor and birth. I'm gonna need him there to coach me. I expect him to read my moods and change with those and stay real close to me through the whole thing and help me."*

Only one mother anticipated that her mate might have his own needs during labor and birth and arranged to have an additional support person present. The presence of a supportive other better assured that the mother's needs would be met. When it came to the actual experience of labor and birth, these women wanted most for their partners to just *be* with them, not to *do* for them.

Help Me

The need for the father's understanding, support, and presence persisted throughout labor and birth and into parenting. Each mother needed reassurance that her mate would be home and available to help her care for the child. These needs were particularly great immediately after birth, during her physical recovery and adjustment. The mothers then needed time and space to develop competence and confidence with infant care. As the novelty of parenthood began to wear off, mothers wanted more help with the baby and household tasks. By 6 months postbirth, the mothers desperately wanted time alone, time off from parenting, and greater sharing of parental and household responsibilities. The mothers' need for help from their mates crescendoed over time.

Each of the mothers dealt with the ongoing challenge of the division of labor. Though they acknowledged and appreciated their mate's role as provider and the demands on him outside the home, they nonetheless wanted help with the baby and household responsibilities. One mother said: *"It's been a struggle for me to try and come to grips with the issue of how much am I willing to do and how much should I do and how much I should ask my husband to do because I feel really grateful that he's working and we don't have to have me go back to work."*

Each mother also struggled with the tenuous balance between her need for help and the need for things to be done *right.* One mother said: *I'm so used to having things done my way, and probably it shouldn't be like that, but I'm real picky. So there are certain things I just won't let him do. I like things done right and I like things done well. . . . He doesn't dress her very well. When she's tired or hungry she'll start to cry while you're getting her dressed 'cause she gets fed up with putting her arms in the little holes and stuff. He gets flustered and he can't do it so I usually take over."*

As time wore on the mothers wanted more help from their mates and began to resent having to tell them what to do and when to do it. In the words of another mother: *"I need him to take the initiative in the care of the baby. It used to be I was just so new at this and I just loved doing all these little things that I didn't really care if he took the initiative as long as he helped. Now I really need him to start taking some initiative and putting some thought into what needs to happen next."*

In addition, especially for stay-at-home mothers, there was a need for their mates to provide them with adult conversation and contact with the outside world. One mother termed this a need for *intellectual intimacy.* In the same vein, each mother needed her mate to validate that staying home with the baby was an important and valued activity. Mothers wanted their mates to understand the intense demands of taking care of an infant all day, that there were good reasons why nothing else got accomplished. Each mother longed for the father to have to take care of the baby for at least an entire day to get a dose of *reality,* believing only then would the father understand how much work parenting entailed.

Mothers also expressed a contrasting lack of desire for physical intimacy with their mates, however. The adult couple relationship took a back seat to parenting, and often to the mother's work outside the home. Although these women wanted and needed to know they were still loved by their partners and had not been replaced by the baby, they did not particularly want this expressed in a renewal of their sexual relationship. For example, one articulate mother said: *"I certainly don't need as much cuddling as I used to, which is funny because now I think my husband needs it more. After work he's all ready to cuddle and stuff and I'm like, 'I would love to have a nice conversation with you, but don't touch me. I've had somebody hanging on me all day and I'm all touched out.'"*

As the babies neared 6 months of age, each mother expressed an intense need for time alone, time away from the baby. They needed more help with the baby and more sharing of responsibility.

Ownership of the Child and Involving the Father

Throughout the childbearing process mothers grappled with whose baby this was: hers, his, or theirs. This struggle then impacted the degree to which she was able to share the experience or the baby through involvement of the father. Issues of ownership were represented by the mothers' choices of words. They spoke of the fathers *helping out* and *baby-sitting.* Rarely did they speak of sharing the responsibility or co-parenting. These mothers perceived themselves as the chief parent.

Two mothers exemplified extremes in their underlying feelings of power, control, and ownership of the baby. The oldest mother and her partner had taken years to conceive a child. Facing the challenges of infertility, they were forced to fully explore their desire to parent and the meaning and place of parenthood in their lives. This mother's beliefs express this reflection and her maturity: *"I have certain expectations of my husband, but superimposed on that are my own expectations of myself as a mother. . . . I don't want to make being a mother the only place in my life where I have power. I see a lot of women who use their mothering as the place in their life where they get control. They choose to exclude the child's father rather than bringing him into the process because it's the way they feel good about themselves. I feel okay enough about myself at this point in my life that I don't have to compete with my husband. . . I think I really want my husband to have the space to be the father he wants to be, and not have me dictate to him what that is going to be or how that is going to be . . . . A lot of my concern about my husband's role as a parent is that we have a much more balanced model. . . . and that I not get hung up on being the primary parent who is in control, and not end up with a child who only wants Mommy. . . . And I've told my husband that I think part of his job as a parent is to make sure that he puts a reality check on that. . . If he does just let me take over he's in part responsible for that."*

Toward the other end of the continuum was the following mother who exemplifies the internal struggle between ownership of the pregnancy and child and involvement of the father: *"The biggest thing I've wanted was just understanding. If I go into the bathroom to throw up don't run in there with a cold compress. I need privacy. . . . What's inside of me doesn't belong here yet. Everybody has to let me sit down for a minute and catch my breath. I needed that space I needed that privacy."*

This mother's ambivalence was persistent. She wasn't even certain she wanted her mate present during labor and birth, yet she decided not to breast feed because she wanted the father to be able to participate in what she perceived to be a very important parent–child interaction. She believed there was nothing that promoted bonding like holding and making eye contact with your baby as you provided essential nutrients and love.

Mothers' Expectations of Their Mates as Fathers

Each mother anticipated her mate would be a good father and was surprised when he surpassed all expectations. Mothers found their mates to be attentive, patient, enthusiastic, interested, and playful. Mothers noticed differences in their mates' style of interacting with the baby. The fathers did things to, and with the babies that the mothers would not have thought to do. One mother observed: *"It is such a joy to watch him with the baby. It makes me feel so good. If I had any apprehensions about his interest in parenting or his practical skills at parenting, they went out the door. He's right in there changing diapers and asking questions and really coming to understand everything that's going on."*

The results from this particular study support the conclusion that mothers perceive themselves as the primary parent and want and need support from their mates in parenting. These mothers struggled with whether or not they really wanted to share parenting with their mates. They both wanted and needed their mates to function in a supportive role rather than a situation of shared responsibilities and co-parenting. The direction of action was toward the mother, with minimal identification of paternal needs or the need and responsibility of the mother to bring the father into the pregnancy and parenting. These mothers did not want the baby to replace them in their mates lives, but the relationship between mother and child took priority over the adult couple relationship.

CONCLUSION

As we move into the twenty-first century, both men and women, individually and within their couple relationships, need to be able to dispel myths and free themselves of the expectations and limitations of traditional gender-role stereotypes. Although women often complain about the lack of paternal involvement while suffering the effects of superimposing work and family roles, they nonetheless seem reluctant to truly share family responsibilities with their mates, opting instead to remain *chief among equals.* In order to effect change in the degree of paternal involvement, attention must be paid to altering the mind sets of both mothers and fathers in order to change the dynamics and division of labor within the adult couple relationship.

With guidance and support both mothers and fathers may be able to negotiate enacting work and family roles in ways that are individually and mutually more satisfactory. Intervention strategies need to include confronting power dynamics within the family while focusing on enhancing couples communication, including role negotiation, decision making, and problem solving. Men and women as couples need to assess their individual and combined resources and actively negotiate how best to use those resources to meet and better share work and family demands. Satisfactory resolution of these issues has the potential to significantly impact the health, well-being, and life satisfaction of women, men, and their children.

In this chapter, Dr. Biller summarizes the various types of potential inadequacies in a child's experience with his/her father. Paternal deprivation is explored in emotional as well as physical ways. Correlates of paternal deprivation, such as child maltreatment and abuse are described with reference to methods for healing. A holistic, transactional perspective is proposed, which explores biological, familial, and social system factors and their interactions.

6

Preventing Paternal Deprivation

Henry B. Biller

An understanding of the impact of inadequate fathering on child development is important in arguing for the increased participation of men in the parenting process. In preparing for parenthood and in assuming the initial responsibilities for their infant, both the father and mother need to be aware of paternal factors in child and family development. A crucial strategy in preventing paternal deprivation and child maltreatment is to support the positive involvement of men during the pregnancy period and in their relationships with their newborns. The purpose of this chapter is to summarize and integrate some major issues concerning the interconnections between paternal deprivation and child maltreatment. A much more detailed account of the material presented in this chapter is available in *Child Maltreatment and Paternal Deprivation* (Biller & Solomon, 1986). For research underscoring the impact of positive paternal involvement, see also Biller (1993) and *The Father Factor* (Biller & Trotter, 1994).

BASIC PERSPECTIVES

Paternal deprivation is a term referring to various types of inadequacies in the child's experience with his or her father. Most typically, it refers to the actual physical absence of the father, but it can also relate to the father's uninterest in, neglect of, or rejection of the child (Biller, 1974). The child does not necessarily have to be separated from the father; paternal deprivation can occur when the father is available but there is the absence of a meaningful father–child relationship. The child of a verbally, physically, or sexually abusive father can also be viewed as paternally deprived because he or she is not being exposed to appropriate fathering behavior.

Interrelated problems of child maltreatment and paternal deprivation pose a great threat to the healthy development of our children and the future of our society. Directly or indirectly, paternal deprivation is a factor in the great majority of incidents of child maltreatment, both within and outside the family.

A biopsychosocial perspective is crucial for an understanding of the interrelationship between paternal deprivation and child maltreatment. Unfortunately, although our society has expected men to financially provide for their families, it has not held them accountable for the quality of parenting that children receive on a day-to-day basis. Many child and family development problems are associated with inadequate father participation and an overburdened mother (Biller, 1993a).

Compared to the fathering role, the mothering role is more consistent from society to society, as well as from family to family. Because men are more variable in their involvement with children, the overall quality of family relationships is especially apt to be linked to the level of father connectedness.

There is a strong association between variations in fathering and the resultant personality adaptations of males and females in a society. Cross-cultural research points to the benefits of the active participation of fathers in the parenting process. Societies with a clear expectation of paternal involvement with infants generally also have more positive attitudes relating to the rights of women and children. Low father availability tends to be associated with an emphasis on boys and girls being compliant, whereas children in societies with high paternal involvement are more likely to receive encouragement for assertive behavior (Biller, 1974).

In societies and subcultures where fathers are excluded from infant care, young children tend to be more restricted and overly dependent on their mothers. Men who are father deprived early in life are likely to engage later in rigidly over-compensatory masculine behaviors, however. The incidence of crimes against property and people, including child abuse and family violence, is relatively high in societies where the rearing of young children is considered to be an exclusively female endeavor (Levinson, 1988).

This is not to say that an individual's level of psychological well-being is just a function of the quality of paternal involvement experienced during childhood. Many different biological and social influences impact on personality development. Some individuals who have been the recipients of attentive fathering still have serious developmental difficulties, whereas others are extremely well functioning despite having had a history of paternal deprivation. Nevertheless, variations in the quality of fathering generally have a crucial impact on infant and child development. Children who experience positive father involvement are likely to be at promise to develop their personal resources and social competence, whereas those who are paternally deprived are at risk to suffer from psychological problems. Biological predispositions and social circumstances have much to do with the details of how variations in paternal involvement affect particular children. Inadequate fathering may increase the vulnerability of a child to developing a poor self-concept, insecurity in peer relationships, and other types of dysfunction depending on the specific intermix of individual predispositions and social circumstances.

In contrast, high-quality paternal involvement enhances a child's opportunity to live a satisfying and productive life. Effective fathering increases the child's chances of developing a positive body image, self-esteem, moral strength, and intellectual and social competence (Biller, 1993).

The father's involvement must be analyzed within the context of the many interacting biological, psychological, and social influences on child and family development. For example, consideration must be given to how the child's temperamental predispositions, as well as broader cultural expectations, affect paternal behavior and family relationships. Attention must also be paid to the impact of the child's evolving maturity on parents and their marital relationship. Ongoing emphasis must be on the dynamic interplay among paternal involvement, child development, and family relationships (Biller, 1974; Biller & Meredith, 1974).

EARLY RELATIONSHIPS

Insufficient attention has been given to the father's role in child development. Men are very variable in their family relationships, but a clear connection exists between the degree of positive paternal involvement and the quality of personality adaptations at both the individual and the social level. Children and families develop best when fathers and mothers are partners in parenting, giving individualized attention to sons and daughters. Both boys and girls greatly benefit from positive father–child relationships. Young children who receive inadequate fathering are unlikely to encounter other men who will be positively nurturant to them on a regular basis. The father's impact needs to be viewed from a biopsychosocial perspective with greater attention being given to life span developmental research considering the reciprocal impact that parents and children have on one another.

A major way to improve family effectiveness is to increase the amount of constructive father influence, especially during the pregnancy and infancy period. This includes educating and sensitizing both females and males to the importance of the father becoming a full-fledged partner in parenting. Both parents benefit when they cooperatively share childrearing responsibilities. A frequent roadblock to positive family functioning is that the father is not an actively involved parent.

The father should have confidence in his ability to contribute to his child's development. In order to prevent his children from being paternally deprived, he needs to feel secure that effective fatherhood is a basic part of being masculine and is important to his own continuing development (Biller, 1993; Biller & Meredith, 1974).

The degree to which the father as well as the mother is nurturant, caring, and accepting is highly related to the successful development of the child even during infancy. The father's constructive support of the child's individuality is especially crucial to early self-concept development. Children in two-parent families who are deprived of positive interaction with their fathers, either through some form of father-absence or in the context of neglect (or other form of maltreatment), are more at risk for later psychological and emotional difficulties.

Both men and women have something special to offer children. For various important cognitive, emotional, and social learning experiences, the presence of two parents is advantageous for the child. Boys and girls need to learn how to interact adequately with both men and women, and the two-parent family situation can provide the possibility of an effective model of male–female communication (Biller, 1993).

Children develop best when given the opportunity to form a basic relationship with both a positively involved father and a positively involved mother. Fathers are as important as mothers in the overall development of children. Nevertheless, with sufficient compensatory resources, children may develop relatively well in families with one competent parent, especially with respect to those from less-than-adequate two-parent families. Analyzing the impact of paternal deprivation requires consideration of the interaction of a myriad of factors (Biller, 1974).

If we focus on father absence, for example, we must examine the type and reason for the absence (divorce, death, employment); the child's age, developmental stage, and adequacy of functioning at the time of the absence; the preabsence father–child and mother–father relationships; the quality of the mother–child relationship and the mother's adjustment and attitude toward the father's absence; sibling relationships and the availability of surrogate models; sociocultural and socioeconomic factors, including the family's financial resources and social support system; and the amount of other family changes related to the absence (moving to another residence, changing schools, and the like).

CHILD MALTREATMENT

The concepts of paternal deprivation and child maltreatment should both be viewed in a multidimensional context. Child maltreatment includes more than severe neglect or physical and sexual abuse; various forms of inappropriate verbal and emotional insensitivity, rejection of individuality, and over-restrictiveness must also be considered. With respect to the behavior of fathers and mothers, child maltreatment pertains to those patterns of parental involvement (verbal abuse, physical abuse, sexual abuse, infantilization, over-restrictiveness, and so on) or uninvolvement (disinterest, nonresponsivity, neglect, abandonment) that may potentially undermine adequate affective, social, sexual, intellectual, and/or physical development (Biller & Solomon, 1986; Garbarino, Guttman, & Seeley, 1988).

If we are to gain a fuller understanding of child maltreatment, more attention needs to be given to gender differences in both effective and ineffective parenting. There are both similarities and differences in the ways in which fathers and mothers maltreat their children. In two-parent families, fathers are much more likely than are mothers to be chronically neglectful and also to have a higher rate of reported physical abuse, especially severe battering, and incestuous behavior.

Because of the large number of single-parent female-headed families, mothers do outnumber fathers in committing some types of maltreatment, including physical abuse. In two-parent families, mothers are more likely to overprotect, over-restrict, and infantilize their children, whereas fathers are more apt to reject or withdraw from their children (Biller, 1993).

In many families both parents are abusive and/or are involved in multiple forms of maltreatment. Again, it is crucial to examine the total family and social system as well as child-specific variables if we are to understand the short and long-term consequences of specific forms of maltreatment (Gelles & Strauss, 1988).

Father neglect is the most prevalent form of child maltreatment in our society. Paternal deprivation in its many forms (including emotional disinterest, aloofness, rejection, and verbal derogation, as well as physical unavailability) has a particularly negative impact on child and family development. There has been a double standard concerning parenting, with paternal disinterest being accepted or even expected, especially if the father is very achievement and work oriented.

Fathers as well as mothers must be held accountable for providing adequate parenting. Children need the opportunity to interact in a positive, stimulating manner with both of their parents. In terms of the number of children affected, paternal deprivation is much more of a problem for our society than is maternal deprivation. Inadequately fathered children, particularly if they are young, are relatively unlikely to receive a compensatory male influence, whereas most children, even if their mother is somewhat inadequate, are exposed to a variety of caring females, including other female relatives and teachers (Biller, 1974).

FAMILY-SYSTEM FACTORS

Mothers are more likely to maltreat their children when fathers are uninvolved in child rearing. Father neglect in both two-parent and one-parent families is often associated with a high incidence of maternal stress. The acting out of the overburdened mother's frustration can be expressed in a variety of inappropriate ways, including overdominance, overprotection, and sometimes direct physical abuse and neglect of her children. Many fathers in two-parent families are uninvolved or are involved in only a very narrow way in disciplining their children, often in an inappropriate or maltreating fashion.

The high level of maltreatment of children by single mothers can also be viewed, at least in part, as being related to a set of social values that tends to put too much pressure on the mother's accountability, and not enough on the father's participation in child rearing (Biller & Solomon, 1986).

Even during pregnancy, the cooperative involvement of the expectant father is important. The health and well-being of the fetus can be affected if the pregnant mother does not get adequate prenatal care (Shapiro, 1993b). Economic and subcultural factors certainly are involved in the availability of high-quality prenatal care, but expectant mothers with supportive husbands or committed boyfriends are more likely than those without a partner to be accepting of their pregnancy, to go for regularly scheduled obstetrical visits, and to be appropriately concerned about the effects of their own well-being and health on the fetus (Biller & Solomon, 1986).

Partner support can be crucial for the expectant mother's self-esteem and positive concern for her health. Inadequate concern for the fetus can be construed as a particularly serious form of child abuse, with potentially irreversible and devastating consequences for later development (Holmes, Reich; & Pasternak, 1983).

Given the chance to interact with them, fathers as a group have just as great a capacity to be sensitive to their infant's needs and to be responsive to them as mothers do. Although men do not appear as generally interested in children who are not their own as women do (which is also a factor in the widespread extra-familial paternal deprivation in our society), they are fully capable of being involved with their own children, even with their neonates, if they have the opportunity (Greenberg, 1985).

There are similarities and differences between the ways in which involved fathers and mothers interact with their infants. Although their styles of stimulating and caring may differ, however, fathers can parent even young infants adequately. The infant who has both an involved father and an involved mother receives some special stimulation from each. The degree to which the father and mother are supportive of each other's participation with the infant also influences the quality of parenting the child receives (Pedersen, 1980, 1981).

Fathers and infants are fully capable of forming reciprocal attachments with one another. Even in the first few months of life, the infant can have a very special relationship with the father. Attachment to the father and paternal social play and stimulation have been found to facilitate infants' sensory-motor and cognitive development, as well as their comfort and confidence in exploring the physical and interpersonal environment. More and more evidence is accumulating of the long-term developmental benefits for children who had positive relationships with their fathers during infancy and early childhood (Biller & Trotter, 1994).

The failure of a father to form an early bond or attachment with the child is one factor that may increase the likelihood not only of early paternal neglect, but also, given other family system factors, of probable emotional, physical, and/or sexual abuse later in the child's development (Biller & Solomon, 1986).

It is crucial for the father to develop a feeling of responsibility and protectiveness toward the child. Such a commitment-attachment can do much to facilitate the father's capacity for positive nurturance and stimulation, as well as helping him not to act out inappropriate impulses toward the child. The formation of an early and reciprocal attachment also increases the probability that the infant will be responsive in a way that the father perceives as positive (Biller & Solomon, 1986; Shapiro, 1993b).

Attachment is a two-way process, and there is a need to consider the characteristics of the child as well as the parent. Some parents have difficulty in bonding sufficiently with their infant because of the child's constitutional predispositions, behavior, and/or appearance. At one extreme are infants who remain so totally unresponsive or atypical in their response patterns to others that few, if any, parents would have the capacity to develop a strong attachment to them. Fathers are more likely than mothers to have a problem in developing an attachment to a handicapped child or a child whom they perceive as permanently defective (Lamb, 1983).

Many parents also have difficulty in bonding when they are separated from their child for a significant period of time while the child is an infant. The parent who is most likely to be separated from the infant is the father (Biller, 1974). When an infant has special problems, it is particularly important that a strong bond develops with both parents. On the other hand, some children either are less likely to be targets of maltreatment or are more resilient in the face of negative family experiences (Biller, 1993).

Family-system factors beyond the individual parent—child relationship must be examined. The quality of the father—mother relationship and the husband-wife relationship is extremely crucial. A severe imbalance in the family system, typically with the mother being over-involved and the father under-involved, can result in problems for the parents as well as the children. Parents who feel supported by their partners in their child-rearing efforts are more effective in dealing with their children and less likely to maltreat them. On the other hand, a parent who is frustrated in the marital relationship, or is spouseless, is more apt to deal with the child in an inappropriate manner, including possible physical or sexual abuse (Biller & Solomon, 1986).

Stress factors are more predictive with respect to whether a parent will maltreat the child in some way than in identifying the particular form of abuse. Taking into account the personal characteristics and background of the parents along with the stress factors and the individual behavior of the child can promote a clearer view of the probability of occurrence of a specific type of maltreatment. For example, a parent with poor impulse control and low frustration tolerance is likely to abuse the highly active child physically (Chess & Thomas, 1986).

Support from other family members in addition to the spouse can be crucial when a particular parent, typically the mother, feels totally responsible for child rearing. Factors such as economic pressures, the presence of several children close in age or of a handicapped child, and lack of neighborhood and peer resources can all add to parental stress and increase the likelihood of child maltreatment (Garbarino et al., 1988). It is important to emphasize, however, that two parents cooperating together have a much better chance in dealing with such challenges (Biller, 1993).

Constructive Approaches

Among children living with their mothers subsequent to a divorce or separation, there is tremendous variation in the amount and quality of contact they have with their fathers. In some families, children whose parents are divorced may never see their fathers again; in other families they may have contact with their fathers on a daily basis and may even spend more time with them than they did before the divorce.

There are clear advantages of a high level of positive father–child interaction, even when the parents are divorced or separated. In most cases, joint or shared custody arrangements are more beneficial to the development of the child, and of the parents, than are traditional custody arrangements, which tend to limit father–child contact and to overburden single mothers (Biller, 1993).

Many fathers in two-parent families could learn much from those divorced fathers who constructively share parenting responsibilities with their ex-wives; it is ironic that some fathers make more of a commitment to child rearing postdivorce (Rosenthal & Keshet, 1981). A major impetus in divorce prevention and in family therapy should be to strengthen the cooperation of fathers and mothers in parenting (Biller & Trotter, 1994).

Paternal deprivation and child maltreatment are strongly associated even when the father is not directly abusive. The most common type of maltreatment is father neglect, but the mother is also much more likely to be abusive, or to allow others to mistreat her child, when she does not have the support of an actively involved partner.

In both one-parent and two-parent families, the mother is more at risk to abuse or otherwise inappropriately socialize her child when the father does not adequately share parenting responsibilities. Preventative and treatment programs designed to help families and children must recognize the importance of men and women becoming partners in parenting, even before they, themselves, have children (Biller & Trotter, 1994).

Both men and women should be sensitized to the crucial role of the father prior to their becoming parents. Preparenting experiences can increase the likelihood of the new father and mother constructively sharing child-rearing responsibilities. A strong focus should be on the importance of husband–wife cooperation during the pregnancy period. Just as both partners should be fully involved in the decision to have a child, they should continue to share responsibilities while they are expectant parents. The pregnancy process is a very significant developmental phase for the expectant father as well as the expectant mother (Biller, 1972, 1993). Typically, there are some difficult periods in most pregnancies, but overall, expectant parenthood is likely to be a very happy time for couples who are able to accept and support one another.

Moreover, cooperation between the expectant parents can go a long way toward increasing the likelihood of a positive father–infant relationship and the prevention of later child maltreatment.

An exciting concomitant of our growing core of systematic data following child development into adulthood is the substantiation of the powerful intergenerational impact of "The Father Factor" (Biller, 1993). Active paternal involvement in childhood is associated with highly positive developmental outcomes for adults, whereas early paternal deprivation is often linked with serious psychological and social problems for both men and women. "The Father Factor" has much to do with parents passing constructive values to the next generation and increasing the chances that their sons and daughters, too, will be successful in their child-rearing efforts (Biller & Trotter, 1994).

Inadequate fathering in its many guises looms as the most serious threat to our country and future generations of children. We should surely be concerned about the national fiscal deficit, but even more we need to address the escalating cost of our rampant "paternal deficit." A child without an involved father should not suffer from generalized paternal deprivation (Biller, 1974). A sense of community and intergenerational commitment can strengthen the positive bonds between families and society by encouraging men and women to value the nurturing potential of fathers. Whether they are fathers or not, men must take responsibility for meeting more than just the financial needs of children and families. *The Father Factor* is all about men and women becoming full-fledged partners in parenting (Biller & Trotter, 1994).

In this chapter, Dr. Greif explores the beginnings of fathering from a less genetic perspective. Although most fathers begin fathering with a pregnancy and birth, some fathers have a quite different marker. They become active fathers through the breakup of marriage or being suddenly thrust into the role by the death of their spouse. He describes the unique difficulties these men suffer due to male socialization and the over-participation of women in the nurturing role. Looking at the concern from both a social acceptance perspective and from a psychological one, Dr. Greif explores the goal of single fathers and all fathers achieving equality in parenting.

7

On Becoming a Single Father with Custody

Geoffrey L. Greif

Whereas the bulk of the other chapters in this book focus on the experiences of men who become fathers for the first time, this chapter examines the experiences of fathers who become sole custodians following a marital separation or the death of the mother. Allow me to be provocative for a moment. Fatherhood in its broadest sense is, of course, a matter of definition that varies from one man to the next. What is the essence of fatherhood in all its glory for one man may be merely a break in a work routine for another. For many men, it is when they gain sole custody, rather than at the birth of the child, that they first experience becoming a father.

As is obvious from the nature of this book, men have not traditionally been the caregivers in the two-parent family and have often been unprepared for such a role. Even though this situation has changed for many, there are others who fervently believe that the nurturing and daily physical care of the children are the primary responsibility of the mother. For fathers who hold this view, becoming a biological father may mean simply assuming an additional financial responsibility (that is, another mouth to feed) and the possible necessity of working overtime to feed it. This would be in accord with the breadwinner role that many men see themselves fulfilling in the family.

What happens then to the father when he first gains sole custody, when he has to be the breadwinner and the nurturer? When faced with that responsibility, as is true currently of 1. 4 million fathers (U.S. Department of Commerce, 1990), he must attempt to balance, often for the first time, a number of conflicting roles for which he may have little or no experience. No longer can he turn the children over to the mother, as he might have done in the past when he went off to work or play. In assuming custody he has to deal with all of the tasks of parenthood. For many, this results in a psychological crisis. The father is forced to choose between the traditionally competing definitions of manhood and full-time parenthood.

COMPETING DEFINITIONS

When a father assumes custody, either by choice or necessity, he has to fulfill all of the roles. The father may never have had to consistently deal with his children's emotions other than as disciplinarian. He may never have been responsible for shopping for clothing for them, preparing daily meals, arranging household chores, and overseeing homework and sex education. The question I will address is: How do they cope with this new definition of themselves, with becoming a father/parent?

My research on single fathers began in 1982 with a national survey of over 1130 separated or divorced fathers with custody who were members of Parents Without Partners (Greif, 1985a). It continued with a second survey in 1987-1988, also of over 1130 single fathers as well as fathers who were widowed (Greif, 1990; Greif & DeMaris, 1990). Follow-up interviews have been conducted over the years on a variety of topics ranging from how they are coping with the demands of parenting (Greif, 1987) to an exploration of their feelings about their own fathers (Greif, in press). It is clear from the survey data and from in-depth interviews that when fathers first gain custody they are confronted with a public perception that they (and all men) are incapable of raising children alone. While being heaped with praise on the one hand for their desire to parent, they were frequently encouraged to turn to their mothers, sisters, and their children's female teachers for help.

The Message?

You're a nice guy but this is woman's work! Such "encouragement" is debilitating and often feeds the fathers' own sense of anxiety about their capabilities. Some men give up in the face of this and do not keep the children. Others do press on. I will talk first about separated and divorced father and then widowers.

THE SEPARATED OR DIVORCED CUSTODIAL FATHER

To understand the process of becoming a single father, we must first look at how they gained custody. The majority (61%) of the more than 1100 fathers surveyed in the late 1980s said they wanted custody very much. Roughly 20% had to fight to win it in court (Greif, 1990). The reasons the fathers give for gaining custody cover the spectrum. In descending order they are: the father was the more emotionally competent parent; he was in a better financial position; he was acquiescing to the wishes of the children; and he was deserted. Some fathers added that they wanted their children because, with their wives leaving, they did not want to lose the remainder of their family.

What are the first few months like for fathers when they begin raising their children alone after a marriage has ended? It should be noted that some fathers gain custody a few years after the divorce when the mother and/or the child have decided that a change in residence is necessary. Mendes (1976) refers to fathers who actively seek custody as seekers, differentiating them from assenters, who often reluctantly agree to do the solo parenting. Her research, as well as mine, shows that those who actively seek to raise their children adapt more easily to the demands. This obvious point needs to be asserted because desire as well as preparation for single parenting are keys to success, as is true for the first-time fathers described elsewhere in this book. In addition, the prepared father will have less emotional stress than the one caught by surprise. To illustrate, imagine on one extreme the father who has been participating in all aspects of childrearing during the marriage and has gained custody with the support of the children's mother. He not only has the history of involvement, he has the desire. On the other extreme would be the man who came home from work and found his wife had left him and the children.

As the father struggles emotionally with the circumstances surrounding his gaining custody, a number of tasks have to be immediately accomplished. These are presented below. Other tasks or rites of single-parent life that need attention later are also discussed.

Housework and Childcare.   The first day that Dustin Hoffman is alone with his son in *Kramer vs. Kramer* (the first Oscar-winning movie about a single father with custody), he burns the french toast. Over time, the household is shown to lose a little of its lustre but Hoffman is depicted as becoming a competent housekeeper. This is emblematic of what happens in real life.

Fathers who gain custody without going through a period of living alone report an initial period of chaos. It is not simply a matter of their frying the water and vacuuming the bird out of its cage; rather they report not knowing exactly how appliances work nor how to prepare the children's favorite meals. The age and gender of the children become a key variable. Fathers with older children and with daughters are more willing to share chores with their children (Greif, 1985b) and appear to have an easier time. In the latter situation, fathers seem to expect daughters to help out more than sons. At the same time, the daughters want to assist, perhaps either continuing a pattern that started when the mother was still in the home or filling a vacuum they perceive. With time, the fathers report that household chores get sorted out even though the home, like Ted Kramer's, does not shine as it did when the mother was living there.

Child care also becomes an immediate concern, particularly with younger children in the home. Although teenagers can clearly be left on their own, younger children need levels of supervision that vary with their age. In almost all of the families studied (many of whom were quite traditional in the division of family labor), the bulk of the child care had fallen to the mother during the marriage. With her out of the picture, the father often had to pick up the pieces.

Let me introduce you to John. He is in his early 40s, and has been raising an 8-year-old son for 7 years. In some ways he is typical of single custodial fathers, yet in other ways he is not. During the marriage he, unlike most fathers, did a great deal of the housework, in part because, as a mortgage banker, he had a flexible schedule. He gained custody after a long court battle because he was able to prove that he was the more stable parent. His wife apparently was more wrapped up in her work than in parenting. When he first gained custody of his 1 year old he arranged child care through a patchwork of his parents, hired babysitters, and occasional time off. His son entered full-time day care as soon as he was old enough.

Contrary to popular thinking, fathers rarely can afford housekeepers. Makeshift arrangements have to be made that involve placing children in day care, using relatives, finding a roommate, having sitters come into the home, or shifting of work hours. Sometimes those shifts in work hours have serious consequences.

Building a Relationship. A few fathers admitted to having little insight into their children when they first embarked on single parenthood. Whereas the bulk of the fathers did not report an initial inability to build and maintain a relationship with their children, those who did cited problems understanding the normal childhood reactions of anger, tears, sadness, and anxiety. The situations were especially difficult for fathers when the expression of these feelings coincided with the breakup of the marital relationship. One way that John was typical is exemplified by his reply when asked about initially gaining custody of his then 1-year-old son, *"I felt that I was capable (in fact he had argued this point extensively in court) but I was not too emotionally stable because of everything that was going on."*

With time, as the father's feelings about the breakup become more manageable, his ability to respond to his children improves. In a real, as well as metaphorical sense, the father's own individual growth can mirror the growth of the relationship with his children. Despite this, daughters are noted to cause the father more puzzlement than sons. It is not that the fathers do not have positive relationships with daughters [according to one study they have especially close relationships with preadolescent girls (DeMaris & Greif, 1992)]. Rather, they have difficulty understanding them and need reassurance from others that they are responding appropriately to their daughters' emotional needs. With time, the mystery of raising daughters does seem to abate.

Handling Work. When the demands of being at work and at their child's school, doctor's appointment, or in a car pool clash, the father must reorder his priorities. About work, John says, *"At first, when we divorced, it was in a very small town where everyone knew what had happened and people were not very supportive. Then the company that I was working for went under and I had to move. They had not been very good about my shifting schedules a lot. Where we moved the people were supportive. Where I went to work next I told them I was a father first and they were more accepting."* This is one of the areas where fathers have the most immediate problem.

For some men, de-emphasizing work in their lives is a blessing; but for many it can have negative psychological ramifications. No longer can they define themselves through their work as many have done. No longer can they hope to succeed at work at the same pace that they had before. As a result, their self-esteem may suffer at a time when it is perhaps already at a low ebb from the loss of the marital relationship. Some fathers have to quit their jobs and take ones that often pay less but allow more flexibility, whereas others are fired. John elected to assert his fatherhood role when looking for a new job. This was not detrimental to him because he found an accepting atmosphere.

Dealing with the Courts.   For many men, establishing legal control of their custody situation is an important component in building a sense of themselves as a father. As mentioned, about 20% of the fathers in the research had to battle their wives in court for custody; the remainder either did not go to court or used it to rubber stamp a prearranged agreement. Many fathers do not feel secure with their situation until they have at least obtained a custody decree. Even among those who do obtain a decree, there is the fear that custody will be removed from them if the ex-wife attempts to dispute it. Thus, until the children are legally "theirs," some fathers cannot begin the psychological process of accepting their full-time parenting status.

John's battle for custody continued. He returned to court a second time 3 years later when his son started kindergarten. *"She keeps dragging me back to court,"* he complained. *"I think she saw him as a source of income* (from child support) *and was not really interested in him."*

Like most fathers, John does not receive any child support. Research shows that only one-quarter of the fathers may be court-ordered to receive child support and that fewer than half actually receive what they are owed (Greif & DeMaris, 1991). Some fathers report that they are satisfied just to have custody and do not even attempt to win a child-support award. Regardless of the arrangement, fathers report that until they have legalized their situations, they only feel as if they are parenting on a part-time basis.

Socializing and the Ex-wife.   Although this final area has less to do with "becoming" a father, it is worth noting as it centers around the father's self-perception about intimacy and sexuality, which can affect his relationship with his ex-wife and his children. As his social life and his relationship with his ex-wife stabilize, the father is more likely to feel comfortable in his role as single father.

Simply put, the more burned the father feels from the marriage, the less likely he is to immediately begin dating. Fathers tend to wait 6 months before they start any serious socializing. They often feel their first loyalty is to solidify the situation with their children. They are not usually encouraged by their children to date as such activity dashes the children's hopes of their parents reconciling, and also takes away from time their father has available to spend with them. In addition, some fathers are hesitant to date because socializing may provide fuel for a custody battle. A trusting relationship with the ex-wife can free the father to date more comfortably. With a satisfactory and appropriate social life he is able to role model for his children the necessity of establishing new significant relationships and moving on with life.

John is dissatisfied with his social life and has been for years. He reports that he dates infrequently and rarely has sexual relationships. For him, time has not helped him grow into this aspect of his life. Yet he does express a certain degree of comfort overall when he is asked about his role as single parent. At the same time, and somewhat contradictorily to John's experience, it has been found that those who find success socially tend also to be fathers who are doing well in other areas and are thus happier overall (Greif, 1985a,b).

The first few months of parenting are a unique period of time for the divorced father. He often is thrown into uncharted waters and expresses surprise at the demands of parenting. The more emotionally upsetting the divorce, the more difficult the sailing is. During these first few months the father may realize, when faced with the burdens of the many tasks of parenting, just what becoming a father means.

THE WIDOWER

According to the U.S. Department of Commerce (1989), there are nearly 100,000 widowers in the U.S. raising children under 18 years of age. In many ways their experiences mirror that of the divorced and separated fathers. When a father is unprepared for the death of the spouse (or her desertion), he is likely to experience much more emotional upheaval than if there is preparation for the death as happens after a chronic or lingering illness. Avoidance of dealing with the death, including feelings of anger and depression about the death, are common in varying degree. Despite the emotional turmoil that a father is in, arrangements for housekeeping and child care still have to be made immediately.

One key difference between widowers and divorced fathers appears to be in the nature of building a relationship with the children. Usually, the widower does not feel he has failed in his primary love relationship. Thus he is dealing with a loss from a positive relationship rather than from a failed one, where he may shoulder some of the psychological responsibility. His capacity to cope with his children's emotions is thus affected in a different way.

For example, following a death, a family is more likely to pull together than following a marital separation. With a death the dividing force has usually been accident or disease-related, though suicide may have also been the cause. With separation, the same forces that pulled the family apart (lack of intimacy, emotional differences, infidelity, problems with physical or substance abuse, etc.) may still be operating and can work to separate family members from each other.

Widowers are confused by both their own feelings and reactions about death and by their children's. One father, when asked how his children coped, told me, *"It was weird. At the funeral, the six year old didn't cry at all. And then, later in bed with me patting her back she sobbed for a long time. I was dumbstruck. It made my skin crawl. But I guess when kids cry about that stuff adults feel better. The oldest two were also weird. They were (my deceased wife's) from a previous marriage. I had tried to adopt them during the marriage but their grandparents wouldn't allow it so my wife hadn't pushed it. They had no idea how to react but were initially very emotional."*

In this father's story one sees the beginnings of his realization that children have emotions that he does not understand. Yet, in fact, a child choosing to cry in private rather than public should not have surprised him. His reaction, of course, is filtered through his own feelings about the death, which he also may not understand.

Many fathers choose to deal with the death by discussing it immediately with their children and then dropping it as a topic of conversation. Often these men believe something need only be talked about once and only once. Such fathers tend to look at the world in black and white terms and are less comfortable with the gray hues that shadow emotions. The fathers who have an easier time are those who are more comfortable with their emotions and realize the complexity of their children's feelings. They understand that the death of their mother has to be brought up a number of times over the ensuing months and years and that each new developmental stage for the child is a renewed opportunity to discuss the death and its meaning.

The rituals of death (the funeral, mourning period, etc.) are different than are those for divorce, which are virtually nonexistent. These rituals in some cases may forestall the emotional impact of fatherhood. Fathers report blocking out the first 6 months as they focus on their children, the funeral, and other related arrangements. When the noise dies down and people stop coming over (they are less likely to make a fuss and visit after a divorce), the finality of the death seeps in and the impact of the demands of parenting starts. In other ways, with a death, the rituals serve to pave the way immediately for fatherhood to begin. Because there is a finiteness to it, the father can move into parenting sooner.

CONCLUSION

The beginning of fathering as well as the path to becoming a father can take many forms. For some fathers, birth is the marker. For others it does not begin until they are in it up to their elbows. Men's socialization and the over-participation of women in the nurturing role may slow men from becoming fathers and add to their discomfort when they first become sole custodians. The sooner society can accept fathers as full-time parents hand-in-hand with mothers, the sooner they will become fathers in the fullest sense from the moment of conception.

In this article, Dr. May, one of the premier researchers of expectant fatherhood, explores the expectant fathers' reactions to high-risk pregnancies. She underscores many of the findings reported by Shapiro (normal pregnancy fears) and Freud (fathers of premature babies) in this volume.

Her particular focus on paternal stress adds dimension to this aspect of the forgotten parent. She describes the exacerbation of a special bind experienced by men in high-risk pregnancies. At the time when he needs the most emotional and pragmatic support, an expectant father is likely to be particularly isolated, especially if his wife comprises his entire support network.

8

Men and High-Risk Child Bearing

Katharyn A. May

The scientific and clinical knowledge about expectant fatherhood has increased dramatically over the last 20 years. As is typical of the growth of knowledge, however, progress has been uneven. Although clinical and scientific attention has been increasingly focused on the experience of high-risk childbearing, and specifically on what impact high-risk childbearing may have on the transition to parenthood (Mercer,1990), precious little is known about expectant fatherhood in the context of high-risk childbearing.

Most of the literature addressing high-risk childbearing concentrates more or less exclusively on the experiences of women. When high-risk expectant fatherhood is discussed, it is often as an interesting footnote to the central issue of high- risk expectant motherhood. The clinical and scientific knowledge that is available on men and high-risk childbearing provides much raw material for reflection and investigation, but provides few firm conclusions. Thus, the arguments presented in this chapter are based as much on the writer's 15 years of research experience with expectant fathers in a variety of circumstances as on current scientific and clinical knowledge.

92

MEN AND HIGH-RISK CHILD BEARING

Pregnancy is generally regarded as the first phase of the larger process of the transition to parenthood. During pregnancy, expectant parents move through a complex set of psychological, social, and physical changes as they come to grips with the reality of themselves as future parents. These processes of psychological and social adaptation during pregnancy are probably as significant in men as they are in women, although they are not as well described to date. When a pregnancy is complicated by increased obstetrical risk, both partners face additional stress because this situational crisis is superimposed on a significant developmental transition. Although some elements of the high-risk childbearing experience are similar for both men and women, others are unique and rather gender-specific. In order to understand the effects of high-risk childbearing on expectant fathers, it is important to first consider the nature of the risks involved.

THE NATURE OF HIGH-RISK CHILD BEARING

The concept of "high-risk childbearing" has evolved as perinatal health care has become more sophisticated and has allowed women who are likely to require specialized care to be identified in advance. The "at-risk" identification is designed to ensure that appropriate care is given in a timely fashion to prevent complications to the mother, and more often, to the unborn. Health care for women thought to be at risk during childbearing includes more frequent screening for complications, a greater number of professionals involved in care, and often requires intrusive or demanding self-care regimens. Instead of the family's own obstetrician or nurse-midwife, care is often provided solely by specialists, sometimes at locations far from the family's place of residence.

In addition to the physiological risk to the woman and unborn child, both parents are thought to be at increased psychosocial risk during a high-risk pregnancy. The emotional and physical demands of high-risk pregnancy and additional stressors limit the emotional and physical energy available to expectant parents to deal with the normal stress associated with childbearing. They may grieve the loss of the expected normal, predictable, and happy pregnancy, while simultaneously trying to adapt to the demands of the high-risk condition.

Parents may lose any sense of control they might have had over events related to the pregnancy, and the sudden and unexpected human and financial costs associated with high-risk care may be overwhelming. They often feel that they are isolated and have no one in their social network who truly understands their concerns. Finally, they face the very real threat of physical risk, even death of the woman and more frequently, the unborn child (Mercer, 1990).

Risk in childbearing, as is in other realms of life, can be estimated in a general sense, but the implications of any particular high-risk pregnancy can not be truly known until after the pregnancy is completed and the infant is born. Thus, parents in a high-risk pregnancy must also come to grips psychologically with a series of unknowns unique to this experience: how serious is the high-risk condition likely to become? will treatment be effective in this particular case? will it seriously affect the health of the mother? if so, will the effect be temporary or permanent? will it seriously affect the health of the baby? if so, how difficult will this infant be to care for and raise? These questions plague both parents during a high-risk pregnancy. Some aspects of the expectant father's experience are probably unique and are only now beginning to be understood, however.

HIGH-RISK CHILD BEARING FROM THE FATHER'S PERSPECTIVE

A comprehensive search of the health science and social science literatures yielded only four studies and one literature review specifically addressing the experience of the expectant father in the context of a high-risk pregnancy (Conner & Denson, 1990; Ferketich & Mercer, 1989; May, 1993; May & Sollid, 1984; Mercer, & Ferketich, 1990; Mercer, Ferketich, DeJoseph, May, & Sollid, 1988a; 1988b; Ross, 1993). A synthesis of the findings from these studies suggests that the high-risk pregnancy has at least three distinct kinds of impact on the expectant father. First, the high-risk pregnancy forces the expectant father to come to terms with threats to individual and family well-being, a concept described by one father as "seeing dark clouds on the horizon" (May, 1993). These threats include the burden of high-risk care for the pregnant woman, and the potential loss of the unborn/newborn and of the partner. The second clear impact of a high-risk pregnancy is that it tends to isolate the expectant father from his major sources of emotional and social support as he assumes domestic responsibilities from his spouse and supports her in her high-risk care regimen. Finally, the high-risk pregnancy creates its own set of un-anticipated consequences for the expectant father; some are clearly negative, some are neutral, and some may be positive, but all are unexpected and require the father to adjust to a different personal future than the one he may envisioned at the beginning of pregnancy.

"I See Dark Clouds on the Horizon": Coming to Terms with Challenges to Individual and Family Well-Being

Expectant fathers who find themselves in a high-risk pregnancy ini-tially describe a feeling of foreboding about anticipated threats to their partners and their family. As the high-risk pregnancy unfolds, these threats usually become real and challenge their ability to cope and maintain some balance in their lives. The most significant of these challenges created by a high-risk pregnancy include: bearing the physical, emotional, and financial burdens of the high-risk regimen, and confronting the potential loss of the unborn/newborn and the partner.

Bearing the Burdens of High-Risk Care.   A high-risk preg-nancy imposes additional burdens on the expectant father, burdens that he may not have anticipated and may not be able to manage effectively without assistance. Usually, the father must compensate for any lost income from the woman's temporary disability, manage most of the household responsibilities (including coordinating or doing childcare of older children), as well as be a sensitive and responsive spouse and help his partner cope with her situation. The emotional and physical exhaustion and time pressures are often quite over-whelming, especially if the father is inexperienced or has difficulty in any of these areas (Mercer & Ferketich, 1988; Ferketich & Mercer, 1989; May, 1993).

Ross (1993) reported that expectant fathers in a high-risk pregnancy recognized that they had to fulfill two primary familial roles: giving emotional care to their partners and other children in the home, and sustaining the family by maintaining financial support, and taking on additional domestic responsibilities. Typically, men coped by main-taining a positive attitude, "taking one day at a time," holding on to their faith, and gathering knowledge about their situation. Their coping was not without some personal cost, however; these men reported that their physical health deteriorated as a result of this role overload.

The stakes associated with providing solid emotional support for the high-risk pregnant woman may be higher than might be apparent at first. Several early studies have suggested that strong emotional support from the expectant father to his mate appears to be important to her psychological as well as her physical health (Grossman, et al., 1980; Entwisle & Doering, 1981). In one recent study, there was a negative correlation between maternal blood levels of stress hormone and her satisfaction with her spousal support during a high-risk pregnancy (Kemp & Hatmaker, 1989).

By contrast, in at least one study (Mercer, Ferketich & DeJoseph, 1993), men in high-risk pregnancies reported significantly less satisfaction with their spousal relationships than did men in low-risk pregnancies. This finding could suggest an early negative effect on the spousal relationship as a function of stress from the high-risk pregnancy, or perhaps, that in some way, couples with less than optimal spousal relationships may be more vulnerable to complications of pregnancy. The first explanation is, on its face, more likely, but the latter has some interesting, if not distinctly troubling possibilities.

Confronting the Potential Loss of Unborn/Newborn.   The high-risk pregnancy reinforces the normal fears most fathers have about illness or loss of the unborn/newborn child. Most men recognize the fact that the unborn is vulnerable, even in a normal pregnancy. The diagnosis of a high-risk condition, even if it affects the unborn only indirectly, intensifies the expectant father's concerns. One of the ways in which the threat of loss of the unborn can be understood is by looking at the process of prenatal attachment, that is, the parent's emotional connection with the unborn. Relatively little is known about parent–fetal attachment during pregnancy in general, although several studies have attempted to measure this both in normal and high-risk pregnancies (Mercer et al; 1988b). Although research in this area is preliminary at best, it is generally thought that men demonstrate similar, but less marked attachment to the fetus during pregnancy when compared to women. This is understandable, given the constant physical reality of the unborn and the physiologic changes women experience as part of pregnancy. The woman has a direct experience of the unborn, whereas the man's experience is necessarily somewhat indirect, that is, through the woman's body. One father described this as a process of focusing on the unborn, saying his wife "just had a better microscope" (May, 1982a).

The quality of a man's attachment to the unborn during a high-risk pregnancy may be affected by the quality of the spousal relationship as well as timing of the pregnancy. A man's readiness for pregnancy is clearly and inextricably tied to the quality of his relationship with his mate. Early research suggested that men defined readiness for fatherhood in terms of a sense of security and satisfaction in their spousal relationships, a sense of being finished with the child-free period in their lives, and a sense of relative financial security (May, 1982b). The association between readiness for pregnancy and the quality of the spousal relationship was reaffirmed in later work (Mercer et al. 1993).

There is no evidence to date of differences in paternal–fetal attachment between men in low-risk and high-risk pregnancies (Mercer et al., 1988b). The nature of paternal–fetal attachment may be subtly different in a high-risk pregnancy, however. Results of this same study suggested that stress from negative life events, self-esteem, marital adjustment, father's anxiety and the father's birth position in his own family predicted only 7% of variance in paternal–fetal attachment in low-risk expectant fathers. In high-risk pregnancies, stress from negative life events, marital adjustment, as well as depending on help from his own parents, family functioning, and received social support were related to paternal–fetal attachment and predicted 31% of the variance. The relationship between family functioning and paternal–fetal attachment was the opposite of the expected direction, however, in that paternal–fetal attachment increased as quality of family functioning decreased. This suggests the possibility that the high-risk expectant father's connection to the fetus may be relatively unaffected by the personal and family disruption caused by a high-risk pregnancy, as long as the father feels ready for the pregnancy and that he has adequate available support from his mate and others.

Readiness for fatherhood may significantly enhance the emotional connection the expectant father develops with the unborn and this factor may be even more important in the context of a high-risk pregnancy (May, 1980). One father identified himself to a researcher as a "first-time expectant father" even though his partner had been pregnant and had miscarried six times before. This man had not wanted the earlier pregnancies, but had acquiesced to his partner's desire to start a family. Although he was supportive of her through these multiple pregnancy losses, they were not truly losses for him since he felt no connection with the unborn. In the last pregnancy, however, he described himself as ready to become a father; unfortunately, this pregnancy also was lost. Despite the fact that the pregnancy had not progressed beyond 14 weeks of gestation and he had not yet even heard the fetal heart or felt fetal movement, this father actively grieved the loss of that unborn child (May, 1978b).

This association between readiness for pregnancy and a developing bond with the unborn in the context of a high-risk pregnancy has also been seen in more recent research. Some men in particularly stressful pregnancies complicated by a risk of preterm labor described difficulties in "connecting" to the unborn when they regarded the pregnancy as coming "too soon". This sense of distance from the unborn intensified their own emotional distress as they attempted to support their partners and deal with the disruptions caused by the high-risk condition and its treatment. These fathers thought they "should not feel this way," and strived to hide their feelings from their partners as much as possible. In some cases, however, this sense of unreadiness and distance from the unborn was overcome, in part, by the very nature of the high-risk pregnancy; women often were advised to attend to fetal movements on a daily basis and to have multiple diagnostic tests during pregnancy (such as ultrasound), which in some cases served to stimulate and reinforce the father's sense of the unborn as a separate person (May, 1993).

It is clear that a high-risk pregnancy exerts a powerful effect on how men view their unborn children. Responses to an interview question late in pregnancy ("what are your thoughts and feelings about your baby now?") showed that men in low-risk pregnancies usually expressed curiosity about the unborn, whereas men in high-risk pregnancies usually expressed concern and anxiety about the well-being of the unborn (Mercer et al., 1988a). Men in pregnancies complicated by preterm labor (a condition that poses a direct threat to the well-being of the unborn) talked extensively about almost constant worries for the unborn. To cope with this worry, these men developed complex "communication links" with their partners so that they could stay informed about developments while they were at work. They often went to great lengths to be present at prenatal visits and diagnostic tests in an effort to be reassured about the unborn's condition, and reported that this made them feel "more in touch" with their partner and the unborn (May, in press).

Thus, it appears that the expectant father in a high-risk pregnancy may be more acutely aware of the unborn by virtue of his understandable concern about its well-being. Whether or not this intense awareness of the fetus contributes to a stronger emotional connection and attachment during pregnancy is not yet known, however. The power of a secure couple relationship in helping the father forge an emotional connection with the unborn is evident. Thus, it is not surprising that, while the potential loss of the unborn is a significant stressor for most expectant fathers, this potential loss is overshadowed by the fact that a high-risk pregnancy also presents the possibility of the loss of the partner.

Confronting the Potential Loss of their Partner. Perhaps the most powerful and unique aspect of high-risk expectant fatherhood is the need to confront the fear of losing the partner through severe maternal injury or death. The phrase "she died in childbirth" is layered with multiple meanings for men, and has been so throughout recorded history; it represents the loss of a treasured loved one in the prime of life, guilt and the dark consequences of sexual activity, the mystery of feminine power and vulnerability, and the conflicted states of being a new father and a new widower. Men generally acknowledge the threat of maternal injury and death inherent in childbearing, although they may be hesitant to discuss these fears, even with close friends. In two studies, one focusing on father's responses to unanticipated cesarean birth and the other on the impact of home-managed preterm labor on families, fathers acknowledged that they had considered the possibility that they would "leave the hospital alone." These fears were raised in interviews only after a strong rapport had been established between the father and the investigator, and after the investigator specifically alluded to the unpredictability of childbirth (May, 1993; May & Sollid, 1984).

It is probably this deep fear that drives the fiercely protective and sometimes aggressive behavior of some expectant fathers in high-risk situations. This behavior may be incomprehensible to others (especially health care providers) because, from their perspective, the objective threat to the woman's health and well-being is usually quite small, when compared to the risk of fetal/neonatal death. It is important to understand that, for most men in high-risk childbearing situations, however, the highest priority is the well-being of their partner. Thus, they focus on any hint of threat to her. When hospitalization is required during a high-risk pregnancy, the expectant father may attribute worried looks and a sudden crisis orientation on the part of health care providers to mean his partner is in danger, when instead the objective risk is to the unborn. Health care providers may be genuinely surprised when they discover (usually after the fact) that the father's acute distress (usually demonstrated by near-panic, aggressive, or obstructive behavior, or sudden withdrawal from the situation) was a result of fear for his partner's life (May, 1991).

"No One Ever Asked about Me. . .":
Paternal Isolation in High-Risk Pregnancy

Another compelling theme in the experience of high-risk expectant fatherhood is the extent to which the experience isolates men from the emotional support of their partner as well as from the social support of others around them. In the Mercer and associates studies (1988a, 1988b), expectant fathers whose partners had been hospitalized because of pregnancy complications repeatedly expressed surprise that the researchers wanted to talk to them. These fathers had clearly become used to being overlooked as part of the surroundings for the "real" story of the pregnant woman. In a more recent study of how families manage maternal bedrest during pregnancy for treatment of preterm labor (May, 1993), expectant fathers consistently reported that no one (other than their partners and their own family) asked how they were doing, despite the fairly obvious nature of the family strain and disruption. It is as if the expectant father was considered a "prop" for the pregnant woman rather than a person with his own emotional and physical needs (May, 1989).

The level of paternal strain during a high-risk pregnancy can be considerable. During one 45-minute interview with a father in the Mercer and associates project, the researcher noted that the father repeatedly drank from a bottle of antacid he had in his pocket. When the researcher eventually commented on this behavior, the father denied that he was under unusual strain. During the course of the interview, however, he reported that for the previous 3 weeks while his partner had been hospitalized, he had been working 16–18 hours a day to try to make up for the loss of his partner's income, was trying to keep up with household duties, as well as coordinating the child care of their preschool-age child at home. This same pattern of high levels of paternal strain with low levels of visible social support has been evident in May's (1993) more recent work.

The fact of high levels of paternal stress is, in itself, of some concern.

This stress is probably exacerbated because most men feel they can not go to their partners for emotional support for fear of intensifying their partner's own distress at the disruption caused by a high-risk pregnancy. As one father put it, "you would have to be a complete SOB to go home and tell your troubles to your wife, when she's the one taking the risks, getting the needles and the medicines, just to have your baby" (May, 1993). In fact, both partners in a high-risk pregnancy are likely to have significant levels of emotional distress. Levels of anxiety and depression have been found to be significantly higher in couples with high-risk pregnancies when compared to low-risk pregnant couples (Mercer & Ferketich, 1988). Thus, both partners are likely to need much additional emotional support, but may not be able to meet their own needs or their partners very effectively.

Men may be at particular risk in this regard. It is generally thought that men tend to have smaller social support networks and rely more on their partners for emotional support than do women (Antonucci, 1985). Indeed, Mercer and associates found that men were likely to report their own father-in-law, male friends, and the physician in their social networks during a high-risk pregnancy (Mercer & Ferketich, 1988). May (1993) found that men identified other men as a source of support, but were reluctant to take advantage, saying "it hasn't gotten that bad yet." Fathers looking back on a high-risk pregnancy reported that they wouldn't wait for a stressed-out high-risk expectant father to ask for help, because "he won't"; instead, they would just "jump in and mow his lawn, take him some food, whatever. . . ." Thus, it appears that expectant fathers in a high-risk pregnancy are likely to have high levels of emotional distress, yet have few opportunities to seek and receive emotional and practical support.

"If I Knew Then What I Know Now . . .":
Unanticipated Consequences of the High-Risk
Pregnancy

With relatively little scientific information about the immediate impact of a high-risk pregnancy on the expectant father, even less is known about the longer-term implications of this experience. The study by Mercer and associates included data collection from high- and low-risk pregnant women and their partners by mailed questionnaires until 8 months after childbirth. There was a 51% refusal rate among high-risk expectant fathers invited to participate in the study, however, and a subsequent 40% attrition among the high-risk fathers over the period of the study, resulting in a subsample of 41 high-risk fathers remaining at 8 months after birth. Thus, conclusions about the consequences of that experience were, by necessity, somewhat limited. Overall, in the first year after childbirth, men who had experienced a high-risk pregnancy reported improving emotional and physical well-being, and declining marital satisfaction (a pattern consistent in the transition-to-parenthood literature). Their appraisals of their family's level of functioning improved, but not as much as appraisals reported by men who had experienced normal pregnancies (Mercer & Ferketich, 1990).

One clear long-term effect of a high-risk pregnancy has to do with planning for future childbearing. Focus groups were recently conducted in which women and men were interviewed separately about their plans for future pregnancies after one high-risk pregnancy. Analysis shows that women were more positive about attempting a second, probably high-risk pregnancy. Men expressed many reservations about their ability to cope with the stresses a second time, and openly questioned among themselves whether "it was worth it." Generally men indicated that, if their partners wanted a second pregnancy, they would be willing to go along. As one man said: "At least this time, I'll know how terrible it is going to be, but I'll know we can get through it together, and get a good baby" (May, 1993).

This comment points to one unanticipated, but notably positive effect of living through a high-risk pregnancy as a couple and as future parents. Men repeatedly remarked on how satisfying it was to know that they could function with their partners as part of a team, to cope with, and overcome, the challenges the high-risk pregnancy put in their path. For many men, this was their first opportunity to learn that particular lesson, and it seemed to be an important one. Further, for some men, surviving a high-risk pregnancy was the price paid for having a truly cherished child. They described in eloquent terms how every sacrifice made their child more special and more a part of themselves (May, 1993).

SUMMARY

In summary, there is growing evidence that emotional distress and family disruption are an inherent part of high-risk pregnancy, and that these factors have a significant impact on the psychological and physical well-being of expectant fathers. High-risk pregnancy requires men to assume a significant burden as they attempt to maintain employment, household and child care, and to provide support to their partners during the period of treatment. This overload may result in high levels of worry, physical and emotional distress in men. Standard health care practices barely seem to acknowledge the existence of fathers in high-risk pregnancy, let alone provide support for them. To the extent that men are strong, resilient, and resourceful in themselves and secure in their relationship with their mates, they can cope with the challenges of a high-risk pregnancy, with enough energy left to provide love and security for their mates and their newborns. If they falter, if they need help and support and cannot find it, the experience of a high-risk pregnancy may be the first step away from a secure future as men and as fathers.

Beginning with an exploration of changes in fathering and differences between fathering and mothering, the authors explore differences in late-timed fathering over the past 3 decades. Noting that delayed fathers are reportedly more interested than younger first-time fathers in parenting, and more likely to engage in caretaking with their children and that their quality of play also differed, the authors call for study of fatherhood in a life-span perspective. Finally they underscore the need to consider timing of entry into the fatherhood role.

9

Late-Timed Fatherhood: Determinants and Consequences for Children and Families

Ross D. Parke
and Brian Neville

Changes both in the structure of American families, as well as in the roles and functions of individual family members are a continuing focus of theoretical and empirical investigation. Many of the most significant of these changes are reflected in the role of the father in the contemporary family. In this chapter, the qualitative and quantitative shifts reflecting changes in social conditions that have taken place in fathering activities since the 1950s are assessed. Our focus is on historical change in fathering, but to appreciate shifts in the paternal role, complementary changes in the behaviors of other members of the family are also noted. A second aim is to illustrate the value of examining historical change in families for increasing our understanding of family functioning. A final purpose is to cast the study of fathers and families in a life-span framework in order to explore the utility of this approach for future theory building and research in this area.

104

THEORETICAL ASSUMPTIONS

We begin by presenting assumptions concerning the study of families. First, to fully understand the changing nature of the father's role in the family, it is necessary to recognize the interdependence among the roles and functions of all family members (Parke, 1988; Parke & Tinsley, 1987). It is increasingly recognized that families are best viewed as social systems. Consequently, to understand the behavior of one member of a family, the complementary behaviors of other members also need to be recognized and assessed. For example, as men's roles in families shift, changes in women's roles in families must also be monitored.

Second, fathers indirectly influence other family members, in addition to their direct influence through interaction. Examples of fathers' indirect impact include various ways in which fathers modify and mediate mother–child relationships. In turn, women affect their children indirectly through their husbands by modifying both the quantity and quality of father–child interaction (Belsky, Levine, & Fish, 1989; Parke, 1990; Parke, et al., 1979; Parke & Tinsley, 1987). In addition, recognition is being given to the embeddedness of families within a variety of other social systems, including both formal and informal support systems as well as the cultures in which they exist (Bronfenbrenner, 1989; Cochran, Larner, Riley, Gunnarsson, & Henderson, 1990; Parke & Tinsley, 1987).

A further assumption that guides our chapter is the importance of distinguishing among individual time, family time, and historical time. *Individual time* is each family member's life course. *Family time* is defined as the timing of transitional life events for the family as a unit (e.g., residential relocation). *Historical time* provides the social conditions for individual and family transitions; an example is the 1960s Vietnam War era. These distinctions are important because individual, family, and historical time do not always harmonize (Elder, 1984; Elder & Hareven, 1993). For example, a family event, such as the birth of a child—the transition to parenthood—may have very profound effects on a man who has just begun a career, in contrast to one who has advanced to a stable occupational position. Moreover, individual and family time are both embedded within the social conditions and values of the historical time in which they exist (Elder & Hareven, 1993). The role of father, as is the case with any social role, is responsive to such fluctuations.

A PORTRAIT OF TRADITIONAL FAMILIES

In studies of relatively traditional families, it has been consistently found that from birth on, mothers feed and caretake more than fathers with both infants and older children (see Lamb, 1981a; Parke, 1981, 1990; Parke & Tinsley, 1981; 1987, for reviews). Even when adjustments are made for the amount of time available for caregiving activities of mothers and fathers, the same pattern of greater mother participation is evident. This pattern is present not only in U.S. samples (Kotelchuck, 1976; Rendina & Dickerscheid, 1976), but in other countries, such as Great Britain (Richards, Dunn, & Antonis, 1977), Australia (Russell, 1983), France and Belgium (Szalai, 1972). There are, however, both wide individual differences across families in the level of father participation. In a later section, some of the factors that modify the father's contribution to caregiving is considered.

Two qualifications merit brief mention. A distinction between *competence* and *performance* is useful in studies of father involvement in caregiving. According to Parke (1990; Parke & Sawin, 1976), fathers are capable of executing caregiving tasks (e.g., feeding) and exhibit as much sensitivity to infant cues during feeding as mothers. Moreover, using the amount of milk consumed as an index of competence, fathers and mothers were found to be equally skillful in this task. Fathers do have the capability to execute caregiving activities competently even though they generally contribute less time to this type of activity than mothers.

Second, although research on the father's influence in infancy has centered primarily on the direct impact of the father's behavior (e.g., as a feeding or stimulatory agent), his influence may be indirectly mediated through the mother or other members of the family as well (see Parke & Tinsley, 1987; Parke et al., 1979; for detailed discussion of this issue). For example, even when they are not directly participating in feeding, fathers can indirectly affect this activity by modifying the behavior of the feeding agent. The father's indirect role in feeding is well illustrated by Pedersen's (1975) investigation of the influence of the husband–wife relationship on mother–infant interaction in a feeding context. Feeding, however, is not the only important interactional context and next we turn to another significant context—play.

PLAY: THE DISTINCTIVE ROLES OF MOTHER AND FATHER

Although mothers contribute to caregiving more than fathers, fathers are not necessarily uninvolved with their infants. Both mothers and fathers are active playmates for their infants and children; however, fathers devote a higher proportion of their time with their children to play than do mothers. For example, in one early study of middle-socioeconomic-status (SES) families, Kotelchuck (1976) found that fathers devote nearly 40% of their time with their infants to play, whereas mothers spend about 25% of their time in play. Further evidence comes from Lamb (1977) who observed marked differences in the reasons that fathers and mothers pick up their infants: Fathers were more likely to hold the babies to play with them, whereas mothers were more likely to hold them for caretaking purposes.

Fathers and mothers differ not only in quantity of play, but in the style of play as well. Fathers' play is more likely to be physical and arousing, whereas mothers' play is more verbal, didactic, and toy-mediated (see Parke, 1990; Parke & Tinsley, 1987; Power & Parke, 1982). Mothers and fathers provide distinctly different types of stimulation and learning opportunities (Carson, Burks, & Parke, 1993; Power & Parke, 1982). Only by considering both mother and father as separate but interdependent members of the family system can we understand early infant development.

THE IMPACT OF TIMING OF PARENTING ON THE FATHER'S ROLE

Patterns of the timing of the onset of parenting are changing, although those changes are not evident from an examination of the median age of parents at the time of the birth of their first child. In the first half of the 1950s the median age of a woman at the birth of her first child was the early twenties, whereas in the 1980s it was approximately the same. This apparent pattern of stability, however, masks the impressive expansion of the range of the timing of first births during the 1970s and 1980s. During this period, women were having babies both earlier *and* later than in previous decades.

Two particular patterns can be identified. First, there was a dramatic increase in the number of adolescent pregnancies, and second, there was an increase in the number of women who were postponing childbearing until their 30s. Between 1970 and 1990, there was an increase in the rate of childbirths to adolescent mothers. Similarly, between 1970 and 1981, the number of first babies born to white women in their thirties doubled. Moreover, between 1976 and 1988 the rate of first births among women in their thirties has increased from

19% to 33% (U.S. Bureau of the Census, 1989) and recent estimates suggest that this trend toward "childbearing at the later ages will continue to be the norm throughout the decade" (O'Connell, 1991, p. 13). This trend is positively associated with the educational and occupational status of the women and the tendency to delay marriage (Baldwin & Nord, 1984; Bloom, 1984; Bloom & Trussell, 1984; Rindfuss & St. John, 1983; Teachman & Polonko, 1985; Wilkie, 1981). What are the consequences of this divergent pattern of childbearing?

A number of factors need to be considered in order to understand the impact on fathering of childbearing at different ages. First, the *life-course context,* which is broadly defined as the point at which the individual has arrived in his social, education, and occupational time-table, is an important determinant. Second, the *historical context,* namely the societal and economic conditions that prevail at the time of the onset of parenting, interacts with the first factor in determining the effects of variations in timing. Let us consider delayed childbirth in light of these issues.

The Contexts of Postponed Fathering

A variety of contrasts exist between becoming a parent in adolescence and initiating parenthood 15 to 20 years later. In contrast to adolescent childbearing, when childbearing is delayed, considerable progress in occupational and educational spheres has potentially already taken place. Education is generally completed and career development is well underway for both men and women. Men who have their children early have more energy for certain types of activities that are central to the father role, such as physical play (Parke & Tinsley, 1981). Similarly, the economic strain that occurs early is offset by avoiding financial problems in retirement due to the fact that children are grown up and independent earlier. In turn, early fathering generally means beginning grandfathering at a younger age, which in turn, permits the early-timed father to be a more active grandparent (for a discussion of these issues, see Tinsley & Parke, 1984).

In spite of these advantages, when men become fathers early, there are two main disadvantages: financial strain and time strain, due to the competing demands imposed by trying simultaneously to establish a career as well as a family. In contrast, the late-timed father avoids these problems. The late-timed father's career is more settled, permitting more flexibility and freedom in balancing the demands of work and family. Second, patterns of preparental collaboration between the parents may already be established and persist into the parenthood period. To fully appreciate the context in which late-timed fatherhood takes place, we will briefly examine each of these issues—the work, marital, and social networks of late-timed fathers.

Work Relationships of Late-Timed Fathers

Delayed fathers have described themselves to be in more stable work situations than early-timed fathers, to be more experienced workers, and have their jobs and careers more firmly established than early-timed peers (Daniels & Weingarten, 1982). Although they are expected to be more satisfied with their jobs, as job satisfaction has been found to be positively associated with age until mid-life (Kalleberg & Loscocco, 1983), and less likely to experience the "life cycle squeeze," during which one's ability to generate income has not yet progressed as fast as the need for income with the introduction of children (Rodman & Safilios-Rothschild, 1983), support for this view is limited. Recently Neville and Parke (1993) in a study of early- (under 25 years of age at first birth) and late- (over 30 years of age) timed fathers found that delayed fathers were more satisfied with their jobs, but the effect was due to SES and salary differences between the groups rather than timing of birth, per se.

The financial strains associated with early career status, therefore, may be more likely to create conflict between the work and family demands of early/normal-timing fathers than delayed-timing fathers. Again, in one of the few direct tests of this issue, Neville and Parke (1993) found some support for this proposition but was qualified by the sex of the child. Specifically they found that younger fathers of girls and older fathers of boys reported more interference by work in family life than older fathers of girls and younger fathers of boys.

The work of fathers has been found to both support and interfere with their family relationships. Studies have shown the amount of time fathers work to be associated with less instrumental and emotional involvement with his child (Crouter, Perry-Jenkins, Huston, & McHale, 1987; McHale & Huston, 1984; Reppetti, 1989), and observations of anxiety in children and irritability in fathers during father–child interaction (Cowan & Cowan, 1985). Alternately, support by co-workers of parental responsibilities, job satisfaction and involvement have been linked to more stimulating and responsive father–infant interaction (Volling & Belsky, 1991); positive parenting attitudes, such as authoritative style and demand for maturity (Greenberger & Goldberg, 1989); and father's support of their 5-year-old children's autonomy and affiliation attempts (Grossman, Pollack, & Golding, 1988); respectively.

Social Network Attributes of Late-Timed Fathers

Social networks of parents have been posited to influence child development and the transition to parenthood (Cowan & Cowan, 1992; Cochran & Brassard, 1979; Power & Parke, 1984). Among mothers, satisfaction with support from family and friends has been linked to more positive ratings of parent–child interaction (Brassard, 1982; Cotterall, 1986; Crnic, Greenberg, & Slough, 1983; Crockenberg, 1981) and to be positively associated with both cognitive and social development in children (see Zarling, Hirsch, & Landry, 1988).

Earlier studies have found that the association between fathers' involvement with their children and social network attributes is influenced by the employment status of mothers. Within single-earner families, men were found to play less with their children if a local female kin network existed and if their social ties were predominantly with men (Riley, 1985). In dual-earner families, men's involvement in routine child care was greater if they had access to multiply supportive bonds with friends, especially other parents from whom they could gain child-rearing advice, and if work did not conflict with home life. Moreover, fathers who reported low levels of advice from their own fathers, were more likely to get it from nuclear kin, whereas the high-advice group was more likely to use neighbors. Significant positive correlations were found between use of nonkin and salience of the parental role, educational status, and occupational status (Riley & Cochran, 1985).

Given that delayed fathers have been found to be more likely to be in dual-earner families and less attached to nuclear families, their social networks should reflect those fathers in Riley's studies. Indeed, among mothers, late timers have reported relying on emotional support of friends during the early years of parenting more frequently than early timers, and reported it to be more important to them than early timers (Walter, 1986). Early timers reported relying heavily on parents for child-rearing and emotional guidance, and on extended family for general emotional support. The late timers in this study tended to be geographically removed from their parents, leading them to develop a more heterogeneous social network to cope with parenting stressors.

Consistent with this earlier work, Neville and Parke (1993) recently found that the social networks of early and delayed fathers differed. Early fathers were found to have stronger ties than delayed fathers to kin and delayed parents had stronger ties to nonkin, at least regarding child care issues. Delayed fathers were found to talk about their children to more nonkin than early fathers, whereas early fathers sought physical child-care help from more kin, and were inclined to go to kin for child-care advice, at least when they had boys. That early fathers were more likely to go to their families for child-care advice when they had boys may be due to the increased likelihood of problematic behavior among boys (Achenbach, Howell, Quay, & Conners, 1991; Rutter & Garmezy; 1983), or to greater investment by early fathers in their relationships with boys over girls, which has previously been found in a general sample of fathers (Parke, Hymel, Power, & Tinsley, 1980). In either event, the data provide limited support for the hypothesis that stronger connections would be found between delayed fathers and nonkin, and early fathers and kin.

This tendency to rely on familial versus nonfamilial sources of support may be due to several factors. It my be simply a matter of geographical distance from kin, as found by Walter (1986) among mothers, which prompts delayed fathers to look elsewhere. Alternatively, it may be that early fathers are more reliant on their families-of-origin due to issues of emotional attachment and development, as well as financial limitations. The current data did not permit explorations of these alternatives. Further research on the development of social networks across the life span is clearly warranted.

An asset of greater access to a broad social network for delayed fathers may lie in the enhanced resources to cope with the stresses inherent to parental responsibilities. A broader array of people with whom to consult when problems arise should help delayed parents to cope with the daily hassles of parenting and any major traumata, as social support studies attest (Brassard, 1982; Crockenberg, 1981; Crnic et al., 1983; Cutrona & Troutman, 1986; Wolf, 1987). Further, both cognitive and social development in children has been found to be positively associated with the parental access to social support (Zarling et al., 1988). The children of delayed fathers should profit from these connections, providing a margin of protection against both social and cognitive difficulties.

Marital Relationships

Research has clearly supported the hypothesis that marital relationships influence parent–child relationships, but differently for mothers and fathers (e.g., Belsky, Rovine & Fish, 1989; Dickstein & Parke, 1988; Goldberg & Easterbrooks, 1984; Levy-Shiff & Israelashvili, 1988; Volling & Belsky, 1991). Specifically, paternal involvement has been found to be positively associated with marital satisfaction.

A positive linear association between age and marital stability and happiness through age 30 has been found by a number of studies (Booth & Edwards, 1985; Carlson & Stinson, 1982; Vanden Heuvel, 1988). Recently, Neville and Parke (1993) found that delayed fathers were not more satisfied but the early and late groups were distinguishable mainly by the age at which they married and the length of the marriage when the child was born. Thus, the marriages of the delayed fathers were more firmly established than those of early fathers, but not necessarily more satisfying. Children of delayed parents may, in the long run, profit from the stability of their parent's relationship. In their study, however, Neville and Parke (1993) found no relationship between marital stability and the father–child relationship.

THE IMPACT OF DELAYED FATHERHOOD

In this section, the effects of late-timed parenthood for both quantitative as well as qualitative aspects of the father–child relationship will be examined. First, are fathers who delay parenthood more or less involved with their offspring? Second, are their styles of interaction different from early or on-time fathers?

Father Involvement

What are the consequences of late-timed parenthood for father involvement? Retrospective accounts by adults who were the first-born children of older parents report that having older parents was an important influence in their lives. Many reported having felt especially appreciated by their parents (Yarrow, 1991) and described fathers who were between the ages 30 and 39 when the respondent was born as more accepting than fathers who were younger or older (Finley, Janovetz, & Rogers, 1990). Parents' retrospective accounts of parenting have also been found to vary with timing. Nydegger (1973) found that late fathers expressed greater self-confidence in the parental role, as well as greater ease and composure in discussing the role than early-timed fathers. Both mothers and fathers have reported that delayed fathers are more interested than younger first-time fathers in parenting, and they are more likely to engage in caretaking with their children (Bloom-Feshbach, 1979; Daniels & Weingarten, 1982). In their study, Daniels and Weingarten (1982) found early-timed fathers are less involved in the daily care of a preschool child. Three times as many late-timed fathers, in contrast to their early-timed counterparts, had regular responsibility for some part of the daily care of a preschool child. The increased paternal responsibility assumed by fathers in late-timed families may account for the more optimal mother–infant interaction patterns observed by Ragozin, Basham, Crnic, Greenberg, and Robinson (1982).

Other evidence is consistent with the finding of greater father involvement when childbearing is delayed. Bloom-Feshbach (1979) reported that the older a father is at the time of this first child's birth, the more he is practically involved with the caretaking of his infant. Age of father was not associated with expressive-nurturant aspects of the father–child relationship; however, possibly infant–father attachment, for example, may not be altered by age of the father. Other research suggests one possible mediator of greater father involvement among older fathers. In a short-term longitudinal study, Feldman, Nash, and Aschenbrenner (1983) found that one of the predictors of paternal involvement in infant caregiving was low job salience. Although it is possible that older fathers can afford to invest less in their career and therefore, low job salience may be tapping a similar dimension, it is possible that time in career and job salience are independent. Assessment of job salience and its relationship to paternal caregiving in early- and late-timed fathers would help clarify this issue.

Recently, Cooney, Pedersen, Indelicatto, and Palkowitz (1993) found in a nationally representative sample that compared to "on time" fathers, late-timed fathers were more likely to be classified as being highly involved and experiencing positive affect associated with the paternal role. Delayed mothers have also reported being more psychologically ready to take on the responsibility for raising a child and attaining more satisfaction with parenting (Daniels & Weingarten, 1982; Ragozin et al., 1982; Walter, 1986).

As these findings demonstrate, the timing of the onset of parenthood is a powerful organizer of both maternal and paternal roles. In the future, investigators need to examine not only both maternal and paternal interaction patterns with each other and their children, but within the context of careers as well. More detailed attention to cohort issues is warranted as indicated by the suggestive findings of Daniels and Weingarten (1982). Presumably the decision to delay the onset of parenthood was easier in the 1970s than in earlier decades, due to increased acceptance of maternal employment, less rigid role definitions for men and women, and the greater availability of support services such as day care, which would permit a simultaneous family-career option.

Interactional Characteristics of the Late-Timed Fathers

There are qualitative differences in styles of interaction for on-time versus late timed fathers. MacDonald and Parke (1986), in their survey study, found that age of parent is negatively related to the frequency of physical play, even after controlling for the child's age. This relationship appears stronger for some categories of play than for others, however. Some physical activities, such as bounce, tickle, chase, and piggyback, which show strong negative relationships with the age of parent, are also activities that tend to require more physical energy on the part of the play partner. This assumption of the energy expenditure required by different types of play activity is based on an independent survey of adults who rated the categories of play according to their energy requirements.

These findings underscore the importance of considering the age of the parent in studies of physical play. The negative correlation between age of parent and physical play may be due to either the unwillingness or inability of older parents to engage in high-energy affectively arousing activities, such as physical play. Alternatively, children may elicit less physical activity from older parents. Moreover, Neville and Parke (1987) found older parents to be likely to engage in more cognitively advanced activities with children and to report holding their children more than younger fathers. These and other studies (Zaslow, Pedersen, Suwalsky, Rabinovich, & Cain, 1985), suggest that older fathers may be less tied to stereotypic paternal behavior, adopting styles more similar to those that have been considered traditionally maternal.

One of the limitations of prior studies of the timing of fatherhood is their reliance on self-reports. Few studies have based their conclusions on direct observations of father–infant or father–child interaction.

One exception is a recent study by Volling and Belsky (1991) of fathers interacting with their infants at 3 and 9 months. These investigators found that older fathers were observed to be more responsive, stimulating, and affectionate at both 3 and 9 months. In another recent observational study, Neville and Parke (1993) examined the play patterns of early- and late-timed fathers interacting with their preschool age children. Not only does this work extend the prior infancy-based work, but confirms earlier interview studies of father–child play style as a timing of fatherhood. Results revealed that early and delayed fathers' play styles differed, the early fathers relied on physical arousal to engage their children, whereas the delayed fathers relied on more cognitive mechanisms to remain engaged.

Timing effects are important not just for fathers, but for grandfathers as well. Moreover, as we will see, not only is age per se important but the timing of entry into familial roles may be a determinant of interactional style as well. In their study of 30 grandfathers who were observed in interaction with their 7-month-old infants, Tinsley and Parke (1988) found that grandfather age was related to the level of stimulating play. Grandfathers were divided into three categories: younger (36–49), middle (50–56), and older (57–68). Grandfathers in the middle age group were rated significantly higher on competence (e.g., confident, smooth, accepting), affect (e.g, warm, interested, affectionate, attentive), and play style (e.g., playful, responsive, stimulatory). From a life span developmental perspective, the middle group of grandfathers could be viewed as being optimally ready for grandparenthood, both physically and psychologically. Unlike the oldest group of grandfathers, they were less likely to be chronically tired, or to have been ill with age-linked diseases. And, unlike the youngest grandfathers, they have completed the career-building position of their lives and were prepared to devote more of their time to family-related endeavors. Moreover, the age of the middle group of grandfathers fits the normative age at which grandparenthood is most often achieved; thus, for these men, the role of grandfather was more age-appropriate than it was for the youngest and oldest groups of grandfathers.

CONCLUSION AND FUTURE DIRECTIONS

A variety of issues remain to be explored in future studies of the determinants and consequences of late-timed fatherhood. First, as suggested by a life course perspective, the impact of the historical period in which the late-timed decision is made needs to be given more consideration. As Daniels and Weingarten (1982, 1988) found, the impact of late-timed motherhood clearly had different consequences for women in the 1980s, 1960s and 1970s. Similar work needs to be completed for late-timed fathers. The historical context clearly is an important modifier of how men's roles are managed.

Second, we know surprisingly little about the effects of late-timed fatherhood for children of different ages. More attention to the impact of the developmental studies of the child is clearly needed.

Third, the social, cognitive, and emotional consequences of being reared by a late-timed father needs to be considered more carefully. Although some research (Parke, 1990) suggests that the capacity for parent–child physical play is an important correlate of young children's peer relationships, no direct test of this proposition with older fathers has been undertaken. Although one would expect that late-timed fathers who engage in less physically playful interaction with their children may have a detrimental impact on their children's social-emotional development, this remains a hypothesis. Perhaps, the compensatory cognitive activities, such as book reading and pretend play may offset the hypothesized negative impact of reduced physical playful interaction.

Fourth, longitudinal studies of the long-term impact of late-timed fatherhood are needed as well.

Fifth, more attention to the impact on the fathers themselves is needed. Are late-timed fathers more satisfied then early-timed fathers? Or alternatively do they feel burdened by the energy demands of children?

In conclusion, this review underscores the need to place the study of fatherhood in a life-span perspective. Finally it underscores the fact that our assumptions about the determinants and consequences of fatherhood for both men, women, and children need to be qualified by the timing of entry into the fatherhood role. This essay is a further reminder that there is no single portrait of fatherhood, but rather multiple forms of fathering and fatherhood need to be both recognized and better understood. The challenge of understanding diversity of fatherhood is one of the important challenges for future research.

Late at night I listen for you.
Your music astounds me.
It is the music of a human being
coming to birth.
Taking birth and waking up
is our business,
and the business of your mother.
But the music while you are doing it
is the splendor no king can buy.
It exasperates me with the distance
and finesse of its sonorities.
Your mother's gentleness of breath after
our day of yoga preparing for you,
our day of buying pure foods and
managing the pains of her body,
is music to me, but not so great a music
as the rustling as we pass those curtains into flesh.
I can hardly dance like your body dances
as it awaits you. But I can love and
be astounded by these harmonizing tones.

—David Debus

In this chapter, Dr. Shapiro provides an inside look at the psychological experience of pregnancy for men. Considering social changes and pressures, he focuses on particular double binds for all fathers (i.e., be involved, but not consumed) and seven specific fears reported by the vast majority of expectant fathers. After exploring differences between male and female experiences, he provides specific advice for expectant fathers.

10

When Men Are Pregnant

Jerrold Lee Shapiro

'Twas so good to be young then
To be close to the earth
And to stand by your wife
At the moment of birth

The Green Leaves of Summer (Traditional)

The biological event that results in fatherhood takes an incredibly short time by comparison to the lifelong emotional commitment that it sets in motion.

In March 1992, actor Warren Beatty was interviewed for a PBS broadcast, *Warren Beatty talking with David Frost.* The conversation took place just prior to the "Oscar" awards in which Beatty was nominated in several categories for his film, *Bugsy.* He had also recently become a father for the first time, after a long career as a Hollywood bachelor.

Frost: *This must be the happiest time of your life.*
Beatty: *You're talking about the baby. It is. . .and yes. . . I wouldn't have guessed the level of happiness that brings you.*
Frost: *Years ago I was waxing eloquent about the joys of deferred fatherhood. . . but nothing prepares—it's more than you expected.*
Beatty: *It's much more and in an odd way it frees you to go about business in ways I wouldn't have anticipated. . . . No longer questions I'll do it well.*

118

> Frost: *I must say the most awe-inspiring moment of my life was the moment Miles, our firstborn was born.*
> Beatty: *Well I remember it in milli-seconds. The detail of it from 24 hours before and the labor and the birth and the 24 hours later. There is nothing that isn't indelibly imprinted on me. It's the biggest experience I ever had.*

Most fathers would agree that the birth of their children feels like the biggest experience one could have. It is how we become fathers.[1] The pregnancy and birth experience may also set the tone for the way the baby is incorporated into the existing family. A couple who closely shares the experience may well continue that bond into the child's early life. Conversely, when a pregnancy is alienating, the baby may be experienced as the cause for that distancing.

Particularly for fathers, early connection with children counteracts prior generations of absence and underinvolvement. Lacking the nurturing biological link to our infants, we attach socially and emotionally. We also have to establish our intimate connection with our children in the eyes of our partners and society.

Pregnancy

A woman's status will change dramatically with pregnancy. She will be afforded special considerations, respect, and attention in modern Western culture. Preceded and introduced by her growing belly, she is commonly pampered by those who know her, and is approached in friendly ways by strangers, who will often spontaneously describe their own pregnancies or children.

This is surely appropriate. A pregnant woman probably feels more vulnerable as well as more special at this time. Her body is changing; there is new life inside her; her chemistry is acting in novel ways;

---

[1]This chapter is primarily devoted to men who are the biological fathers of their children. Adoptive fathers usually do not have the opportunity to bond with their infants during a pregnancy. If you are an adoptive father, there is a lot of catching up to do, especially if your child arrives suddenly. Although the chapter may not be directly relevant, the psychological tasks described are probably just as necessary. It is certainly an additional complication to have to experience the initial mix of feelings that accompany your new child, after the child is already in your home. In addition, some adoptive fathers may have to go through these feelings before knowing whether they will definitely be able to keep their infant.

and she definitely deserves any extra support and care that may be offered.

Pregnancy for Fathers

Although men do not have any biological signs of pregnancy, they often begin to experience a host of emotions and thoughts. Psychologically, expectant fathers are just as pregnant as their wives. We too, will soon be responsible for the care of a helpless infant. In modern Western societies, men are expected to be increasingly involved during pregnancy, birth, and the early years of child raising.

An expectant father will soon become aware that the extra support, understanding, and caring that rightfully is offered to his pregnant partner is unlikely to be extended to him as well. In fact, he may well become the butt of apparently good-natured jokes about his potential loss of freedom or about the paternity itself. In a very significant way, expectant fathers commonly experience a double bind: the confluence of two opposing messages.

On the one hand he is invited, encouraged, perhaps cajoled, into full participation into the pregnancy and birth of his children. At the same time, he is clearly given to understand that he is to remain an outsider.

The Double Bind

This contradiction is particularly confusing and problematic for expectant fathers. The difference is between a verbal message, *"Please be involved,"* *"You must be involved,"* and the unspoken codicil, an amendment sent nonverbally and unconsciously, *"thou shalt not upset the pregnant woman with any negative feelings."* It is quite acceptable to be supportive. It is unacceptable to be express worry or anxiety.

An aware and involved expectant father has a serious dilemma. To be fully involved, he must recognize and experience his personal feelings about the pregnancy and impending fatherhood. When he does, he will soon realize that the feelings embrace a wide realm. As Paul described them during a counseling session, there were few reactions left out: *"First of all, I was shocked, then very excited, couldn't believe the joy that filled my heart. We had wanted this for so long. I just wanted to hug Elly and hold on and just be like one. Later, there was this feeling of love for the baby and the three of us that was unexpected; a pleasant surprise. . . . As I was alone during the middle of the pregnancy, I began to have other feelings . . . completely unexpected . . . fears, anxieties. I was even angry as incredible as that might seem. It wasn't that I had second doubts or anything . . . I just was blind-sided by my emotions. I just didn't know who to talk to. I tried talking to my mom, but she just said, 'don't trouble Elly with any of that nonsense.' That made me feel like I was weird or something. I was happy about being a father. You know you're the first person I ever told this to."*

Paul's mother suggested that he retreat to the traditional male role: strong, silent, and distant from his wife and the pregnancy. Such advice went against the current mores of sharing as fully as possible in the pregnancy. It also left him feeling lonely and disconnected from his wife and baby. To share all his feelings, he would have to risk upsetting his pregnant wife, and feeling guilty for making her feel as bad or confused as he was.

What is particularly interesting is that Paul's experience is almost universal for men who are invested in being involved fathers. That is what his counselor told him. He also advised Paul to share his feelings with his wife, suggesting that her feelings may be similar. Paul did so and later reported that it turned out to be excellent advice. He and Elly felt much closer with the knowledge that they were being more fully pregnant together.

Paul's feelings were quite typical. He was fortunate on three counts, however. He had a counselor. He and his wife had the kind of relationship that welcomed his feelings, and *he was aware of his feelings.*

For many of us, knowing and labelling our specific feelings is truly difficult. We are caught in a quandary. Pregnancy is a time when a couple desires togetherness and teamwork. If the expectant father remains unaware of the range of his feelings, stifles, or masks a significant portion of those feelings, he will feel further away from the pregnancy, his wife, and their baby. If he tries to describe those feelings, he may be at a loss for proper labels for them. His wife, already feeling vulnerable, may not initially be completely receptive to *his* concerns. Should he be set back by these challenges, he risks increasing the emotional distance. The dilemma is that if he attempts to express what is in his heart, he may find himself pushed away, and if he avoids those emotions, he pushes himself away. It is a time for men to struggle to discover and articulate all their feelings, and to persevere when and if they are rebuffed.

Different Pregnancy Experiences

Any sensitive person can understand the vulnerability that a young pregnant woman might feel. She is going through a host of physical, emotional, and psychological changes. We expect that she might be frightened and ambivalent about labor, childbirth, and the anticipated stresses of mothering. It is very important that the expectant father pamper, humor, and especially show love, affection, and caring for her. He cannot fully experience her "morning sickness," but he can take extra responsibilities around the house and give her extra support she may need. It is proper for a pregnant mother to be fearful, sad, angry, or confused.

Psychologically, an expectant father is just as pregnant. He does not have the biological basis, nor automatic social support for the novel thoughts and feelings he is experiencing. Yet expectant fathers do have a variety of pregnancy symptoms and need some extra attention if we truly expect them to be actively involved in the pregnancy, birth, or early parenting.

It is hard for men to express these needs directly. Should he express the need for extra support, nurturance, or attention, he may be seen as selfish, demanding, inconsiderate, or chauvinistic. An expectant father is discouraged from excessive preoccupation with developing his relationship with the fetus, or for feeling "out of sorts." Some men unconsciously express these needs indirectly. Many modern men actually experience some sympathetic pregnancy symptoms. These symptoms, called *couvade syndrome* are far more common than the literature would suggest. They include weight gain, lower back pain, nausea, achiness, etc. These symptoms, which are moderately displayed in most men, represent an unconscious attempt to be more connected to the pregnancy. By sharing the physical symptoms, even though they are psychologically generated, a father may be able to feel closer to his wife and baby than otherwise.

Generally speaking, these sympathetic pregnancy symptoms are treated humorously by family and friends, and generate little sympathy for the father. His path to fuller involvement is often more complicated.

The Wife as Gatekeeper

Men who want to be fully involved have to be invited into the pregnancy by their wives. Expectant fathers have no direct access to their baby while it is growing in their wife's womb. Access to kicks or other movement is generally by invitation. She places his hand on her abdomen when the baby is active. She describes what it feels like inside. The woman who wants her husband involved tries to give him connection to their baby by description and action. Without her permission, his bonding is purely intellectual. Arnie described his "secret midnight activity," "When she's asleep, I watch her belly. Sometimes I see ripples under the skin, and once in a while an elbow or knee moving under the skin looks like a locomotive traversing some secret underground passage. That's when I sing to the little guy and try to go on journeys with him. I can't wait until we can go on the ride together."

Arnie sensed that his wife guarded her relationship with their baby too closely. He felt rejected when she would tell her girlfriends by telephone about every move the baby made, yet was unresponsive when he asked her for details. His response to this "closed gate" was to peek surreptitiously through the bars at night.

What is particularly significant is that patterns established during the pregnancy may extend long after the birth. Many mothers continue to be gatekeepers between their children and husband long past any biological necessity for that role. Fathers who want to be more directly involved with their children, will be well served to request more direct, nonmediated interaction with their babies, as early as the pregnancy. By expressing these feelings early, an alternate pattern of father access will be established.

Many men do talk to their babies in the womb. Others sing to them. Besides the obvious psychological effect that may have on the father, there is some evidence that babies do hear sounds before birth. Subsequently, they orient toward those familiar sounds after they are born.

The Credibility Gap

In addition to the double-binding message that expectant fathers are to be involved, but not fully, there is another message that defines father participation. During pregnancy it is made clear for the first time to most men that their wives have more credibility about parenting purely on the basis of gender. As a female, his partner is considered more reliable, better informed, and correct regarding any questions of relationships or childrearing.

It is true that women may have had more experience caring for younger children when they were girls. They may also have thought much more about being parents. The assumption that a woman's opinion is inherently more credible in any particular relationship, however, is more a reflection of current gender politics than a statement of fact.

When their wives are pregnant, men are given to understand that she has suddenly become an expert on all manner of child-rearing skills. Some women truly do become experts. Their pregnancy propels them into reading, questioning, and personal reflection that will serve them very well as mothers. They learn the skills that match their feelings of mothering. However, as my colleague Kate Pizor, a family therapist, mother, and parent educator is wont to point out, "nobody is born with a gene for diapering." Research supports this contention. Several studies indicate that when their babies are born, men and women hold, diaper, and soothe their babies equally well. Over time, women, who spend more time with their babies, become much more adept at these routine parenting duties.

Good parenting requires preparation, motivation, ego strength, perseverance, and plenty of on-the-job training. It is not exclusively the purview of mothers. Expectant fathers who have lots of feelings, beliefs, or learning about pregnancy and parenting may well have an extra struggle to get their position heard. The input may well be just as valuable as that of their wife.

Michael was not the only expectant father who became more concerned with the baby's, and the mother's health than did his pregnant wife: "We had the biggest fight we ever had about the smoking and drinking. She was never a big smoker, but when she got pregnant it started to increase because she was afraid that otherwise she'd eat too much and get too fat. No matter how much I told her that she needed to just be careful, exercise, and if she put on extra weight, it'd probably be good for the baby, it had no effect. The beer too. She would always have a beer with dinner. I threw a fit one night when I came home early and she was sneaking a glass of beer, because she wouldn't drink it in front of me. She told me that I was a man and just couldn't tell her how to act when she was pregnant. Her doctor didn't know. So I called her up and told her that Jill was drinking and smoking. Even the doctor didn't believe me until she asked Jill herself in person. I was going crazy thinking about how my baby could be harmed and my wife could be hurt. Really that was a helpless feeling that I hated and don't ever want to revisit. One time I actually thought it would end the marriage, but I just knew I had to get through."

Michael had a battle on his hands during the pregnancy. He believed that he was right and he struggled to convince his wife. Not all men face such clear-cut issues. Sometimes there is just a different style of parenting that each person feels is better. A man must also be careful not to assume that he is correct and his wife wrong, and bully her into agreement. It is important to anticipate that as a father, he will have a responsibility for, and lots of feelings about, his children. These feelings are not automatically less important than those of a mother.

There is an ironic side to this credibility gap. Much of the increase in men's participation in childbirth and early parenting, resulted from the busting of strict gender role demands that accompanied the women's movement. Through the tireless efforts of feminists and their supporters, there has been an increasing equality for women and men, regardless of gender. During the crucial period when a couple becomes a family, sex-role stereotypes remain strong, however. On the one hand, women are considered experts who are automatically more credible. On the other, she is reinforced for being helpless during pregnancy, unable to handle her husband's true feelings. At the same time, her husband is being rewarded for keeping his feelings to himself, keeping distant from this women's realm. In short, the traditional stereotyped gender-roles that we have tried so hard to minimize are very much maintained.

THE EXPECTANT FATHER'S EXPERIENCE

A remarkable transformation occurs when a man becomes a father. Over the course of a pregnancy, fears, anxieties, and concerns generate new sensitivities to relationships, children, and the world as a whole.

Expectant fathers experience a number of changes in their internal lives. Two of these are a reassessment of the fathering that they received as a child, and a reliving of feelings they experienced as boys.

Many men respond to the surprising feelings that accompany a pregnancy by attempting to reconnect with their own fathers or other significant male role models in their lives. Being placed in the ultimate masculine role by the pregnancy, they attempt to find a deeper attachment to other fathers. They seek an instant apprenticeship to an established expert. When many expectant fathers attempt to make this connection, they have to bridge a gap of emotional distance from their own fathers. Often they feel rebuffed, misunderstood or in John's words: "exactly the way I felt as a little kid. Every time I asked him (his father) anything, he made me feel stupid for asking. There were the looks of distaste on his face, the perturbed tone of voice, the way he'd look at you. It was always like, any idiot would not have to ask such a question. When I was a teen, I figured out that it was his cover. If he didn't know the answer, he'd act like the question was dumb. But still I felt it."

As John describes, many an expectant father attempting to bridge the gap finds himself re-experiencing painful feelings of his own childhood. Whatever emotional deficiencies a man experienced as a boy are likely to be rekindled. If he grew up feeling rejection as a child, his wife's withdrawal during pregnancy may well reactivate those feelings. Conversely, if he felt trapped in his original family, he might well re-experience feelings of suffocation, when he considers, during a pregnancy, his impending responsibilities. Becoming a father often has the impact of exaggerating any unresolved problems from boyhood.

Many boys go through their early years feeling alone and helpless. Not belonging to the world of women, separated from the world of men, a young boy has to fill his emotional needs personally or from his peer group.

It is easy to see how a pregnancy restimulates some of these feelings. It is frustrating for a man to have increasing responsibility along with diminishing authority. During a pregnancy, his wife will be more needy and rely more on him. Her own attention is divided. She is beginning her relationship with the child growing inside her. During the first and third trimesters of the pregnancy, she is likely to be fatigued. Thus, while she is asking her husband for more attention, affection, and responsibility for household chores, she has less emotional energy to give back to him.

Security and Freedom: Basic Emotional Needs

We all have a lifelong need to feel secure and free. When these needs are inadequately resolved as children, we are prone to a continuing struggle to find freedom and security. If we experienced too much freedom as children, we will likely fear abandonment. If we had too much security, we may have a long fear of suffocation. The expectant father may have grown up with fears of being ignored, rejected, or discarded. The enforced separation, resulting from his wife's exhaustion, inward focus, personal emotional concerns and need to relate more to other women who have shared the female experience of motherhood, can make the time of pregnancy a true test. Interviews with several expectant fathers revealed the following scenario:

- He suddenly finds that his spouse is unavailable emotionally.
- She may also be unavailable physically and sexually.
- He needs to reflect on the impending changes in his life.
- He does not have friends who can fully relate to, or talk about, his current dilemma.
- He believes that he should be strong enough to handle these concerns without help.
- He is not aware of exactly what is creating the internal discomfort, often ascribing it to financial or job concerns.
- He feels disconnected from all sources of support.

Normally, such a man would turn for support to his partner. She knows him, he trusts her, and they are going through a similar experience. Unfortunately, she is precisely the person who is unavailable. When he attempts to recapture support from his past, the feelings of rejection are magnified.

This is particularly difficult for men who have fought feelings of rejection their whole lives and believed that marriage and family was the antidote. Here on the brink of the best in family life, he is faced with escalating fears of abandonment.

Fears of Suffocation and Entrapment

Although the majority of men carry unconscious fears of rejection and abandonment from their families of origin into their families of procreation, not all have such experiences. Of course, there are men who do not carry any particular unresolved emotional baggage into their marriages. In addition, there is another group of men who had a quite opposite experience. Having had parents who were overintrusive, they find aloneness a welcome relief. Such an expectant father may find his wife's sudden neediness a powerful threat. Tom, describing the change in his relationship with his wife said,

She was a real independent woman in the best sense. All of a sudden she was pregnant and crying a lot, always wanting to know where I am every minute of the day. . .I don't think I have read an entire section of the evening paper without her sitting on my lap. . .wants me to hug her all the time. . . . It makes my skin crawl. I just want to escape.

It is easy to imagine "the dance" that goes on at Tom and Joan's house. The more needy she feels, the more she approaches. The more she approaches, the more he is repelled and withdraws, which in turn makes her feel more needy, and so forth.

For a man who is prone to protect his privacy, pregnancy has a way of eliminating much of the safety zone he uses between himself and others. This dilemma can make the pregnancy feel like torture to both partners.

It is not unusual that men who fear abandonment are attracted to women who fear suffocation and vice versa. Throughout their relationships they have to adjust to, and deal with, the conflicts that arise when both are feeling anxiety, and react by either approaching for comfort or withdrawing for safety. Because a pregnancy reactivates a number of unresolved unconscious feelings from childhood, it prompts the couple to a more extreme struggle for distance or closeness.

Security and Freedom

Beginning in infancy, each of us has two significant psychological needs: security and freedom. These needs are not limited to childhood; they are lifelong. Often they seem to be in direct opposition. To be free means to push the limits of safety; to be safe means to eschew exploring the unknown. In a sense this is accurate. At different developmental stages, we need to advance one rather than the other.

When our child is growing in the womb, our needs for both security and freedom may be severely tested. As we feel too much freedom and distance, we begin to experience feelings of rejection and abandonment. When we feel too secure in our nest, we are likely to feel suffocated and entrapped. The balancing act to serve both needs will be a lifelong endeavor. Recognition of these apparently opposing desires will go a long way towards resolution.

THE SEVEN SPECIFIC FEARS OF
EXPECTANT FATHERS

In addition to these general psychological concerns and sociocultural binds experienced by expectant fathers, there are certain specific fears that are reported by a majority of expectant fathers. These feelings, born during the pregnancy, reoccur in increasing depth and intensity as men and their children age. Among these feelings, described by over 500 surveyed men, are four major categories of fears and concerns: performance fears, security fears, relationship fears, existential fears.

Performance Fears

Queasiness in the Delivery Room. Desire to be a part of the pregnancy and childbirth does not reduce a man's anticipation of discomfort regarding an abundance of blood and other bodily fluids. An expectant father anticipating his first birth participation, wonders about his ability to "keep it together" and truly help his wife, instead of fainting or "losing his cookies" during the delivery. The importance of this concern is revealed in recent fathers' accounts of birth of their children. Immediately after describing the birth as "wonderful," and commenting on the courage of their wives, they described with pride how well they personally came through the pregnancy with the contents of their digestive tract intact.

The reality that very few men actually have such trouble does not diminish the concern. What passes for humor by physicians contributes to men's fears of experiencing the birth of their children from a prone position, under the table on a delivery room floor. The popular media also regularly portray the pregnant woman, about to deliver her baby, wheeling her unconscious husband into the hospital.

Financial and Emotional Responsibility. "One day I was going along happy-go-lucky. The next day I was the sole support of three people."

More than 80% of the fathers I surveyed shared the feelings expressed by this 22-year-old father of 3 days. Nowhere is the socioeconomic programming so "hard-wired" as in the intense pressure fathers feel to provide financial support for their families.

The new child demands financial, physical, and emotional adjustments in the relationship. For many couples, the first pregnancy brings with it a change from two salaries for two people to one salary for three. Tradition and social expectations, as well as the inequity in male and female salaries, typically makes it inevitable that the father will bear the brunt of the enhanced financial burden. It is common during a pregnancy for men to "moonlight" or switch jobs to build a "nest egg"—a peculiarly appropriate term under the circumstances.

Becoming a father to one's own child also engenders feelings of responsibility and fatherhood to all children. Many men report a shift in awareness and involvement in world events. Individuals whom heretofore showed little interest in political stability, pollution, or nuclear arms, became involved in movements designed to make the world better for children.

Security Fears

Dealing with the OB/GYN Establishment.   Medicine that deals with female reproductive anatomy remains mysterious and alien to many men. Expectant fathers often experience feelings of dehumanization, infantilization, and embarrassment during their initial contacts with obstetrics and gynecology staff. Several men who accompanied their wives to prenatal pelvic exams reported nonacceptance from the same obstetrical staff that had previously praised their involvement. Their questions were frequently silenced with looks that implied, "only a fool would not know that." Many expectant fathers reported feelings of "being treated like a child" or "being dismissed" in their contact with these professionals.

Paternity.   "I was joking when I told my wife, if that kid has blond hair and blue eyes, I'm gone."

What is surprising about this "joke" is that more than 50% of the men surveyed acknowledged some fleeting doubts about not being the biological father of the child. This discomfort, which was often reinforced by unintentionally cruel jokes about the physical appearance of the mailman, was based less on any real concern that the wife had been unfaithful, than on a general feeling of inadequacy to be part of anything so monumental as the creation of life.

Such questions over paternity are not new. In the 4th century BC, Aristotle, wrote "the reason mothers are more devoted to their children is that they suffer more in birth, and are more certain that the child is their own."

The feeling of inadequacy to create life also manifests itself for men (and women) in psychological denial of the pregnancy—a phenomenon that may last for men until after the birth—and in a repetitive concern that the hospital staff has mixed up the babies in the nursery.

Health and Safety of Spouse and Infant. Usually during the second trimester a powerful fear that something might happen to his partner or baby begins to arise. Often based on dreams of such a loss, refreshed family memories or tragic stories, this fear may also be rooted in personal fears of abandonment or of being replaced. Because his pregnant spouse is normally turning inward toward the infant, and away from him, at a time when he is feeling particularly insecure, it is easy for his unconscious mind to transform her temporary emotional distance into a premonition of permanent loss.

A related fear that something will be wrong with the child often thrusts itself into the consciousness of both expectant parents. It is a rare parent who doesn't worry about birth defects or neglects to count fingers and toes on the newborn.

Relationship Fears

Being Replaced. It is common and important for pregnant women to turn inward and begin bonding with the life growing inside. At such times, husbands may feel neglected.

It is not surprising that we fear the loss of our most important relationship. Many of us have survived periods of great turmoil in our marriages. Expectant fathers of today may well have experienced first hand, the pain of their parents' divorce or the loss of their own prior relationships. As children, most of us have experienced a feeling of abandonment by a mother or other women. Such experiences can affect our expectations of how likely our marriage can survive the additional stress of a child.

If my own father, committed to the "earning a living," division-of-labor-standard, was somewhere in the background (at work or in the garage), the primary bond in the home was between mother and myself. Can I not then expect that as a father, I will also be pushed aside?

Existential Fears

Mortality. "I became aware, when Mary was pregnant that I no longer had any right to die . . . I stopped taking such huge risks. I found myself driving slower, avoiding rougher areas of town, actually listened to a life insurance salesman."

Of all the changes, fears, and novel experiences a wife's pregnancy brings to men, none is so subtle and yet so dramatic as a new consciousness of the biological life cycle. Reflecting on their intimate involvement with the beginnings of life, many men describe feeling closer to their own deaths. They also described an increased sense of connection to their own fathers.

Because death is so much avoided in our youth and action-centered culture, most men were surprised by their sudden feelings about the fragility of human existence, and particularly with their own mortality. Until a man is a father, he remains identified as a member of the younger generation. His living parents or grandparents act as a psychological buffer against death, because he expects to outlive them. When he becomes a father, there is now a new younger generation, one he cannot expect to outlive.

This concern over life and death epitomizes all fears portending loss, helplessness, inadequacy, or limitations. As the ultimate limitation, mortality colors the experience of expectant fathers.

Pregnancy and birth are only the origin of a major transformation. The last five fears expand and grow as our children do. Unaddressed and unchecked, they will plague dad with anxiety and push him from fuller participation in his family.

Sustaining these seven common fears is the powerful, nearly omnipresent double message that expectant and recent fathers receive throughout the pregnancy: the sense of being verbally invited into the pregnancy and birth, and simultaneously, and nonverbally, rejected. Men are expected to be part of the pregnancy, labor and birth, and they are expected to be supportive and happy about it. Their other feelings have not been welcome.

This double message and the concerns that arise in pregnancy provide a genesis for men's confusion about opposing demands normal in fatherhood today. One expression of which are the simultaneous demands for a man to be "the protector" and a "sensitive partner."

Similarly, when my partner tells me she wants me to be in charge of certain home or child care responsibilities, and then tells me how I'm to do them, she creates a scenario where I am in charge, and she retains supervisory power. It is imperative that I share with her my unwillingness to do the job unless it is my way, without an overseer. The very act of giving permission creates a power imbalance. These family negotiations may well be predicated on early discussions about the rights of a gatekeeper.

In my research over the past dozen years, a few basic "truths" have emerged from the experiences of hundreds of expectant and recent fathers. This pragmatic advice is replicated here both as a summary and as a set of guidelines for men experiencing this most momentous change in their lives.

ADVICE FOR EXPECTANT FATHERS

1. Expect, accept, and pay attention to the emotional changes you feel.
2. Expect to be confronted with double messages from others indicating a desire for your presence and a simultaneous discomfort with your true feelings.
3. Become aware of your feelings of fear and if possible the relationship of the specific fears to your personal history and life-style.
4. Once you are aware of your concerns about the pregnancy, share them with your pregnant partner. It is wise to choose quiet times when you are alone to do so.
5. Talk to her about her concerns and joys about the pregnancy.
6. Understand as well as you can, her shifting moods, fatigue, and physical symptoms.
7. Personalize the birth experience:

   - Investigate all available options available. Be careful to talk to recent parents and check out their experience.
   - Visit and walk through any special birthing rooms and facilities. Find out how many such rooms are available and whether you can reserve one for your labor and delivery. If a birthing room is unavailable, ask if the birth can occur in the labor room.
   - Meet any of the obstetricians who might deliver your child. Be sure to go over with each of them what you want for the birth.
   - Take childbirth education classes together, even if you do not

plan to be present for the birth. You need to know about your wife's experience even if you plan to be absent. If you change your mind at the last minute, you will be better prepared.

- Find out the hospital policy on caesarian sections. If you want to be present for an emergency surgical birth, be sure that you have taken any required classes, and made advance agreements for your presence.

- Plan ahead for financial arrangements, admission policies, etc. Give yourself plenty of time to deal with hospital policies. If the birth is only 2 weeks away, a 3-month delay in answering your questions will not be in your best interests.

- Be assertive about what you want, but don't become so argumentative that your wife and baby suffer. Remember, unless you live in a rural area, military base or are locked into a single location by an health maintenance organization (HMO) or preferred provider organization (PPO), you can shop around and take your business to someone who will give you what you want.

- Take charge of the check in. A woman in labor is in no position to deal with health care bureaucracies.

8. Try to be prepared to experience the exquisite joys and the miracle of your child's birth.

Although fathers are now a regular part of hospital births, there is little attention to any needs they might have in the process. In this chapter, Ms. Shecket describes an innovative ongoing program sponsored by one hospital in Columbus, Ohio. As one of the originators of the program and as the co-leader of the fathers' groups, she brings a unique expertise and insight into expectant and new fathers' needs. The Elizabeth Blackwell Center at Riverside Hospital is described and recommended steps provided for program planning at other sites.

11

Support for Fathers: A Model for Hospital-Based Parenting Programs

Peggy Shecket

Even though the delivery went like we hoped, I was very afraid. I thought my wife was dying. She was screaming and I didn't know if that was normal. In those movies we watched the women never screamed.

I'm so upset! They told us at the ultrasound that it was a boy and she just had a girl. How am I going to talk to her about this?

I'm going to be staying home with my kids when my wife goes back to work. Do you know how I could meet other fathers who are staying with their children?

The birth of a baby creates a crisis for parents. This life transition can be affected by many variables, including the parents' own early history, their coping skills and supports, and the degree to which this is a hoped-for baby. Many studies have focused on the needs of mothers and fathers during labor and delivery, offering suggestions for further research and alterations in nursing care. By contrast, little has been written about service models to deliver to make this life transition easier. Of the extant models, most focus on the pregnant couple, and on postpartum support services for mothers rather than for fathers.

Several researchers have identified the need for more attention to mens' needs during the transition to fatherhood. It is a time of change, stress, and crisis. In her research on first-time fathers, Hangsleben

135

(1993, p. 270) suggested that nursing staff should be alert to signs of depression in fathers so that referral can occur. She recommends that nurses should assess the learning needs of fathers and mothers, discuss with them their available support system at home, and make referrals to "counselors, public health nurses, support groups and parenting organizations." Her advice addresses a significant need. There is a scarcity of programs nationwide that address the unique needs of fathers from preconception through the early life of the infant.

Only recently has there been information available about fathers' feelings during pregnancy, labor, and delivery. Lemmer (1987, p. 273) analyzed 31 studies regarding expectant fathers. Her conclusions were that nurses working with families during their postpartum stay should be sensitive to fathers' "somatic and emotional needs." Yet most nurses already feel overwhelmed with the tasks associated with the care of the mother and baby.

Shannon-Babitz (1979) discovered in home visits with fathers during the first week postpartum that when given the opportunity, fathers wanted to openly discuss the thoughts and feelings they had about the birthing. She suggests that if staff can be available to listen to fathers' feelings, there will be more of an opportunity to resolve those feelings during the hospitalization. She also suggests that nursing staff closely observe the father's verbal and nonverbal communication, and that they pay attention to his physical and psychological needs—providing him with a comfortable chair, a pillow, and rests when he needs them. A follow-up visit was recommended by the labor room nurse during the first or second postpartum day to help fathers and mothers discuss and integrate their birthing experiences. Despite these observations, and the increasing presence of fathers in the delivery room, no such trend has been reported.

Fathers and Childbirth

In the 1960s, in order to provide justification for fathers' presence during their partners' deliveries, a role was created for them. They were called the "coach" (Wonnell, 1971). Classes were designed to prepare couples for birthing. These classes taught basic anatomy, stages of labor, and breathing techniques to manage pain. Increasing numbers of couples chose to enroll in these childbirth preparation classes. The goal was a successful labor and delivery for the mother with the father as an equally successful "coach."

One childbirth class provided a special hour of instruction just for fathers where there was an analogy used between a labor coach and a football coach. Part of the "script" for this particular hour read, "You can't play the game if you are the coach. All you can do is help your wife play a good game and help her prepare for the game" (Campbell & Worthington, 1982).

There has often been an expectation by health care professionals that fathers would play a specific role. May (1982a) confirmed this role expectation and wondered if these value judgments might have led to potentially inappropriate care. She concluded that it might be best for nurses to encourage fathers to find their own levels of involvement in labor and delivery rather than pressuring them to fulfill a role ascribed to them by the medical staff.

Throughout the research on fathers and coaching there is rarely a suggestion that a father might have any needs at all throughout this emotionally draining time. One textbook suggests, "The coach should be someone who is able to devote complete personal attention to the mother during the childbirth process" (Butler, Luther, & Frederick, 1988, p. 280).

At least one group looked at the role of the nurse in supporting the "coach" (El Sherif, McGrath, & Sonyrski, 1979). They listed suggestions for support of the coach in these areas: (1) physical, (2) learning and thought, (3) social, and, (4) inner. Under the category of "inner" there was the suggestion to "respond to him as an individual." Asking a father what he might need was not part of this plan.

Recently, Chapman (1992) explored alternative roles to the usual "coach." Behaviors observed during their partner's labor included comforting, encouraging, helping, directing, and observing. Three roles were then described: coach, teammate and witness.

Brazelton (1969, 1992) has taught through his research, his writing, and his beautiful videotapes the unique ways that babies interact with their fathers. This work affirmed the differences and importance of father–infant interaction. He has also identified "touchpoints"; connections can best happen with fathers, establishing a trustful relationship between father and physician.

Shapiro (1987) gave us important data about men expecting babies and becoming fathers, and added his own personal perspective. Men's feelings were validated by the research and by the very poignant narratives. Dr. Shapiro provided information for professionals working with new fathers to better understand their fears during pregnancy planning, pregnancy, labor, delivery, and early months of parenting.

In his recent book, *The Measure of a Man,* (1993a) Shapiro

discusses the revolution that has occurred in this country in the last 30 years as men have been permitted to be present at the births of their babies. "We begin fatherhood with sexual intercourse. During the pregnancy we have access to our baby only to the extent allowed by the mother. We are present at the birth of our children, wanting to help, yet feeling helpless. Soon we are home with our family and we feel the pressure of being sole support and protector of the people we most love. Where in the world can we learn how to do these well?"

The Program

There is little question that fathers have unique educational and psychological needs throughout this period of transition. Yet it is rare to find a hospital-based parenting program that specifically addresses the needs of fathers. One program, at the Elizabeth Blackwell Center at Riverside Methodist Hospitals in Columbus, Ohio, has paid special attention to fathers at several crucial times: prepregnancy, pregnancy, labor and delivery, postpartum, and postdischarge.

The parenting program was created with the assistance of Dr. T. Berry Brazelton, the late Virginia Satir and the late Dorothy Briggs, each of whom visited the Elizabeth Blackwell Center to share their wisdom and their vision. This unique program was created to address the needs of parents from preconception through the years of parenting adolescents.

The program begins with a forum called "Baby Maybe" to assist men and women with their decision to parent or to remain child-free. At the "Baby Maybe" classes men and women openly discuss their fears, their ambivalence, and their expectations about parenting. They leave with more information, and a more realistic sense of what it might be like for them to be a parent. *"Before I came here tonight, all I could imagine was a little boy who was into sports. I would watch all his games and cheer for him. Now I see that the kid might not be good at sports. Man, that would be hard for me."*

I'm really not sure that I want to be a father. I think my Dad hated being a father. He never did anything with us, so I guess he hated it. I don't even know what fathers are supposed to do."

When a couple is pregnant, there are childbirth education classes available: infant care for pregnant or adopting couples, breast-feeding classes and sibling preparation classes. During labor and delivery, staff nurses pay careful attention to the expressed and nonverbal needs of the fathers.

During the hospitalization following the birth, the parents receive a support visit at the bedside of the mother. Initially, the purpose of this support visit was (1) to inform the parents about classes and support groups available to them postdischarge and (2) to provide a listening ear when mothers needed to talk about their labor and delivery or about their babies, (3) to respond to mothers whose baby was in the neonatal intensive care unit or was being transferred to another hospital, (4) to provide special support for teen parents, (5) to answer questions about their older children and explain what might be normal reactions to the birth of a sibling at various ages.

As these bedside visits began, it soon became clear that fathers also needed support. For many fathers, the question, "How was this for *you?*" was the first time that they had an opportunity to talk about what they saw and what they were feeling after the delivery. *"I cut the cord! I didn't think I'd be able to do it! I thought I might get sick—but I didn't feel sick at all! I can't believe it! I cut the cord!"*

"I feel sad for my Dad. He wasn't allowed in there when I was born 30 years ago."

Once fathers' needs for support became clear, all were visited as the parenting consultant made rounds throughout the postpartum unit. Fathers were found in patient rooms, in the waiting room, and sometimes standing outside the nursery. One father stood at the window of the Neonatal Intensive care unit, where he could see his baby through a window. The parenting consultant introduced herself and looked through the window with the father.

"Is that your baby?"
"Yes. He was born last night."
"Oh. How did the delivery go?"
"Terrible. He's 2 months early."
"That must have been quite a shock."
"Sure was a shock."
"Has anyone talked to you about how he's doing?"
"The doctor said a few things but I can't really remember. I was pretty shook."
"Would you like to go in and see your baby? The nurses can tell you more about how he's doing."
"Oh, no thanks. I think I'll just stand out here."

"It's pretty scary to walk in there the first time. We could go in together. I'd be glad to show you how to wash your hands and put on a gown, and we can ask the nurses some questions."
"I'd appreciate that a lot."

Sometimes births happen at a time when friends can be present within the hospital, or family can be reached by phone, but often it is impossible for fathers to connect with a trusted person with whom they can begin to process all that they felt and saw. For many men, their need to cry as they experience the joy and excitement of the birth, or their need to talk about the fears they had throughout are not sentiments that they are able to share easily with others. For some there is hesitancy to tell their wives what they are feeling.

One father stood outside the door of his wife's room, 2 hours after their birth. As the parenting consultant put a hand on his shoulder he began to sob. *"I can't tell her what I saw. I don't want to upset her. I was there to be strong for her. I wasn't strong at all. I had to look away! It was awful in there. There was nothing I could do! They started to cut her. I couldn't stand it! They kept cutting and cutting and I could hear the sound! I will never forget that sound!"*

Occasionally fathers are referred to the consultant even when their wives are not on the postpartum floor. One father was referred the day after his wife was taken to the intensive care unit. She had become ill during her labor, and by the time of the delivery was gravely ill. Immediately after delivering the baby she had a grand mal seizure, which the father witnessed. *"I kept yelling, 'I'm here! I'm here!' but she couldn't hear me. Now I keep seeing that over and over again. The seizure seemed to go on so long!"*

This father went on to talk about the fear that not only would his wife die, but he feared his infant would die also. He worried that his baby would live—but wouldn't have a mother. He did not want to attach to the baby until he knew that his wife would live, and had chosen to not see the baby. The parenting consultant saw this father every day during his wife's hospitalization. He was able to see and hold his baby soon after the first meeting and went on to become a competent care provider of his son during the stay in the hospital. When he handed the baby to his wife several days later for the first time, he was able to demonstrate to her how the baby preferred to eat.

Before discharge each parent is given a bright yellow "Parenting Warm Line" card with a phone number printed on it which they can call when they have nonmedical questions. Each mother and father has a support link through this phone service before discharge, which eases the anxieties about going home. The phone is answered at the Elizabeth Blackwell Center and, depending on the question, is then transferred to one of the nurses or a parenting consultant. This is a free service. Parents who call with medical concerns are referred to their health care provider.

"I was wondering if you could tell me what I'm supposed to put on a one month old baby when it's 50 degrees outside."

"Our 2 year old wants to breast feed now that we are home with the baby. What should we do?"

The Birth of the Fathers Group

After fathers began to use the Parenting Warm Line service and come to parenting classes, they began to express an interest in forming a fathers' support group. In June 1990, a group of fathers agreed to gather in a focus group with two facilitators to create what would become a parenting program for fathers. Within the focus group were expectant fathers, fathers who were parenting children in a second marriage many years after their first children were born, single fathers and widowers. Their years of parenting experience ranged from 0–20 years. Despite the differences, what they shared was a common interest in planning a fathers' group. None had ever been asked previous to this gathering time, about what they might need to function effectively as a father. Of those who were fathers, none had been asked what would have made labor and delivery easier for them. Some felt that they had been helpful to their wives and others felt as though they had been "in the way." None of the fathers present in this focus group had ever had the opportunity to talk honestly with other men about what it was like for them to be fathers. Within their workplace it felt "inappropriate" to discuss these issues. In social situations they heard complaining about children, bragging about the children's accomplishments, and jokes about them, but not one father had an experience of talking in a social situation about his real concerns.

> Wouldn't it be great to be able to say to another guy at a party, "Our 2 year old is waking up every night. Do you have any ideas that we could try?"

Together, the group of fathers listed their needs. They were:

1. To have the opportunity to meet on a regular basis.
2. To have facilitators present to monitor the discussion.
3. Have the meeting be low cost.
4. Beer at every meeting (the facilitators could not meet this need.)
5. The understanding that a person could say whatever he needed to say without fear of ridicule.
6. An agreement of confidentiality within the group.

In August 1990 the Dads' Group began with 15 fathers and two facilitators, one of whom was a father of two sons and the author, who is the mother of two sons. There were no children present. At this first official gathering of the new group, one father after another expressed his joy at the opportunity to come together.

"This is the first time I have ever had the chance to talk honestly about what it has been like for me to be a father."

"My daughter was born on Tuesday and I haven't had a chance to talk to anyone about it. Would you guys mind if I told you what happened?"

"My Dad was never around when I was growing up. Sure he lived with us, but he was at work all the time. When he came home, he'd hide behind the newspaper. He never even talked to me!"

Consistent themes emerged that night and have re-occurred over time:

1. How can I be a father in a way that is different from the way my father parented me?
2. Where are the role models for me?
3. I miss the way our marriage used to be before the kids.
4. How can I be a good father and also a valued employee where I work?
5. What is the best way to find excellent child care providers?
6. How can I learn to feel competent about medical issues that come up with my child?
7. What is realistic to expect of a 2 year old?
8. At the end of the day when I go home, I feel very stressed. How can I make that transition easier?
9. My wife is so wrapped up in our child and I feel like I've lost my best friend, like my best friend died.

10. What is the best discipline technique? I don't want to hit my kids, but I want them to know that I mean what I say.

In addition to the Dads' Group, fathers used the Parenting Warm Line, When the questions were too involved for a quick phone call, the men were invited to come to the center for an individual parenting consultation. Some came with their wives and others visited alone.

From the start of this parenting program, men have been courageous and have said what they have needed. The men were heard and there is now a program in place that attempts to meet their special needs. This unique hospital-based parenting program has been a model for other hospitals. The key components are:

1. A preconception class that presents factual information about parenting but also allows time for sharing of concerns and questions.
2. A childbirth education program that educates men and women and also pays attention to individual differences and needs.
3. Labor and delivery staff who see the father as having needs for encouragement and support, and not just as a support person/coach for the mother.
4. Nurses on the postpartum unit who validate the importance of fathers and who are available to teach fathers and answer their questions.
5. A professional solely dedicated to new families, whose role it is to respond to the special needs for support of mothers and fathers during the hospitalization following delivery.
6. Immediate support systems in place after discharge for questions related to parenting.
7. Ongoing classes and support groups for parents as their infant grows.

SUMMARY

There must evolve in this society a new mind set about fathers and fathers' needs. The decision to begin a pregnancy, the time during the pregnancy, and the labor and delivery are stressful for all. In order to provide appropriate support and care for the whole family, health care professionals need to see fathers—not merely as support people for their wives—but as *men* in the midst of a powerful life transition, who have unique needs of their own.

In this approach to helping fathers through the pregnancy and birth, Dr. Levant begins by describing the difficulties for men transitioning to fatherhood, particularly vis-a-vis the necessary skills and roles in todays dual-earning world. Using clinical examples, he explores the beginning psychological skills required of involved fathers. He concludes by describing some means for expectant fathers to develop emotional awareness.

12

Fatherhood, Numbness, and Emotional Self-Awareness

Ronald F. Levant

Men are much maligned these days, portrayed in popular media such as the hit film *Thelma and Louise* as oafish, sleazy, or just plain dumb. Popular books such as Arlie Hochschild's *The Second Shift* and Deborah Tannen's *You Just Don't Understand* decry men's lack of involvement in family life and their inability to communicate with their wives and children.

I think the media have hit on important points, but I strongly object to the shrill blaming tone. The fact is men today are being asked to perform many roles for which they have received little or no preparation. Focusing on fatherhood, the expectation today in most dual-income households is that the father will do his fair share of the family work, perhaps taking either the morning shift—of getting the children up and ready for day care or school, dressing and feeding them and preparing their lunches—or the evening shift—of getting the children settled into their play or homework routines, and getting dinner ready.

Yet these fathers were prepared to be very different kinds of dads. Their fathers—their primary role models—were cut from traditional cloth, and enacted the good provider/chief disciplinarian paternal role. As boys, they were socialized to be like their fathers. They did not play with dolls, mind their younger siblings, offer baby-sitting services, nor go to home economics classes. While our sisters visited nursing homes with their girl scout troops, as boy scouts we rubbed sticks together to make them burn. At a more fundamental level, as boys the current generation of adult men did not learn those psychological skills basic to nurture and care for children: the ability to be attuned to the feelings of others (empathy), and the ability to access and to become aware of their own feelings (emotional self-awareness).

The focus of this chapter is the latter; emotional self-awareness. I will discuss this skill in the context of fathering. I will describe some of the traps fathers fall into, as a result of not having this skill, and then discuss ways that men can develop it. I will conclude with the discussion of a case of man who came into therapy because he felt "numb" on the occasion of his wife's pregnancy.

Socialized to be emotionally stoic, men are unlikely to have developed the skill of emotional self-awareness. Growing up we were taught, "big boys don't cry," or to "play with pain," in sports, exhortations in effect to be out of touch with our own feelings, particularly vulnerable feelings.

As a result of such socialization experiences, men are often genuinely unaware of their emotions, and suffer from at least a mild degree of alexithymia—the inability to identify and describe one's feelings in words (a-lexi-thymia . . . a = without, lexi = words, thymia = emotions). In my experience, this is more often a result of trained incompetence and skill deficits than of repression and denial, though those dynamics are certainly part of it. In the absence of emotional awareness, men tend to rely on their cognition, and try to logically deduce how they should feel. They cannot do what is so easy for most women: simply sense inward, feel the feeling, and let the verbal description come to mind.

I recall asking Tom, a divorced father, what he felt when his son, Max, stood him up for a father–son hockey game. Tom's answer: *"He shouldn't have agreed to go with his mother that weekend. We had planned this for weeks."* When I reminded Tom that I didn't ask him what should have happened, but rather what he was feeling, he was able to focus: "Oh. Well . . . I think I felt . . . hurt." But even then he had to think in order to identify his feelings. This is so different from what happens when you ask a woman an equivalent question, such as: *"Mary, what did you feel when your daughter stood you up for an afternoon of shopping at the mall?" Mary's answer: "Well, at first I was hurt, and then I was afraid, thinking that something might have happened to her, and then I was angry when I realized that she did this to me again. . . ."*

However, it is not accurate to say that men's lack of emotional awareness is complete; rather, it is selective. Men are allowed to feel and become aware of emotions in the anger and rage part of the spectrum, as prescribed in the "give 'em hell" injunction of the male code. Anger is in fact one of the few emotions males are encouraged to experience, and as a consequence, a lot of other feelings, such as hurt, shame, and even fear get funneled into it.

Thus, the male role socialization process makes it very difficult for men to decipher their own feelings, which are instead experienced as vague discomfort or general "antsyness." As a result, when they come to have any one of the myriad feelings that can get aroused in parents in the course of interacting with kids, their ability to carry out their parental role becomes handicapped. There are at least four ways that this can occur.

FOUR SYNDROMES OF PATERNAL UNAWARENESS[1]

Distraction

We saw this a lot in the Fatherhood Project at Boston University, because after fathers improved their listening skills, and actually spent time listening to their kids, they would sometimes hear things that they found difficult, disconcerting, or embarrassing. Not being able to read their own feelings, they were unaware that they were embarrassed or uncomfortable with what the child was saying. Instead, they experienced a buzzing sensation in their chest, and found their minds wandering to daydreams, or to tasks that needed doing. Dave Pulio for example (Levant & Kelly, 1989), is engaged in a fairly intimate conversation with his daughter Keri, of the type that he has only recently started to have, when the topic of a boy that she knows comes up. Dave is particularly uncomfortable with the fact that his daughter is becoming a young woman, and has not yet come to terms with the idea that she may develop romantic feelings for boys. He discovers that he has disengaged from the conversation, and fallen deep into a daydream about baseball, when his daughter slams the door, having left the room in tears.

---

[1] The material in this section is drawn from R. Levant and J. Kelly (1991) *Between father and child.* New York: Penguin. Copyright(©) 1989 by R. Levant and J Kelly. Used by Permission of Viking Penquin, a division of Penquin Books USA, Inc.

Dave subsequently learned the power of simply being able to identify the feelings that he was having. By putting a verbal label on the feeling—saying to himself, as Dave learned to do, "I am really uncomfortable with the idea that my little girl may be getting involved with guys"—he brings it into awareness, and that very often stops that vague buzzing discomfort. Further, once he has identified a feeling, he can then learn how to manage it.

The Rubber Band

In this case, instead of trying to cope with the buzz of unidentified emotions by distraction, the father lets the feelings build and build, until finally, like a rubber band stretched to its limit, they release, snapping in an explosion of anger. This syndrome obviously has the potential for very destructive effects on the father–child relationship. This occurs often enough that I am sure that the reader can think of many examples. Typically, in the Rubber Band syndrome, the father ignores feelings of mild irritation, which gradually build up to the point that they can no longer be ignored. The antidote once again is to identify the feeling. In this case it is particularly important to identify anger when it is mild and can be talked about, and before it has become unmanageable.

Tin Man

Instead of trying to divert himself from the buzz with distractions, or rolling it up into a hand grenade and tossing it at someone, the Tin Man takes it and the feelings producing it, puts them in a closet, locks the door, and throws away the key. Because Tin Men have a lot of self-control (having mastered the male code), they are usually able to keep those emotions in a closet. Unfortunately, when you lock up your feelings this way you also lock up your heart, and then you begin to lose the ability to feel at all. Once that capacity drains out of you, you become like those wind-up dolls sold in toy stores— rigid and mechanical.

The Tin Man syndrome is a very difficult one for children who thrive on parental emotions. Over the years, in many different ways, little Timmy Adams had told his dad this, and over the years Hal Adams had found hundreds of ways to rationalize the look of hurt and disappointment he always saw on his son's face when he failed to deliver. The night Timmy made a crucial error in an important playoff game, causing his little league team to lose the series, Hal finally ran out of rationalizations.

At dinner, Timmy, who understandably felt like he could never face his teammates ever again, violated a key tenet of the male code—never show feelings—by breaking into tears when he began talking about the game. This so annoyed Hal that he blurted out, "For God's sake, Timmy, stop crying like a baby. It was only a baseball game." To his credit, when Timmy shouted back, "You don't care about me, Dad, do you? You never have," Hal finally stopped ducking. This time he recognized his son's words for what they were, a sign of deep alienation, and 2 weeks later Hal joined the Fatherhood Project.

Mixed Messenger

Typically, the mixed messenger deals with the buzz of unidentified feelings by letting it ooze out in his body language, tone of voice, facial expressions, and movement. Meanwhile, he tries to keep his words calm, reasonable and even friendly, hoping to stonewall the buzz. Hence a discrepancy arises between his words—which represent what he thinks he's feeling—and his deeds—which represent what he's really feeling—sending a very mixed message to his child.

At first the discrepancy between the Mixed Messenger's words and deeds confuses a child. If the discrepancy continues for any length of time, the child's confusion will eventually disappear. After 1 or 2 years of hearing Dad's words say "I feel friendly," while seeing Dad's behavior say "I'm mad at you," the child concludes that it isn't his confusion but rather it's Dad's deviousness—he never tells you what he really feels, or never seems to mean what he says.

DEVELOPING THE SKILL OF EMOTIONAL SELF-AWARENESS[1]

The solution to all four syndromes is emotional self-awareness. For some fathers this can be learned relatively easily, by simply tuning-in and attending to feelings. Rather than pushing it away, this just requires a willingness to stop whenever an emotion tickles, and ask oneself "What am I feeling?"

Step One: Recognizing the Buzz

I should point out that, given his inexperience, even a dad who's trying to listen to his feelings will, at first, have difficulty putting specific names like sadness, anger, hurt, or warmth on what he experiences. What he'll usually notice is the physiological arousal, often experienced as a buzzing sensation inside the body, that accompanies the emotion. Because, in a general way, different emotions produce different buzzing sensations, taking note of these "buzzes" will give the father a handle on learning to identify his feelings.

General "antsyness"; difficulty concentrating; tightness in the face; clenching of the gut; jitters in the knees; overreaction to simple, inconsequential things; and a vague, global feeling of discomfort are all telltale signs of the buzz produced by upsetting emotions.

Warmth, tenderness, love, and other happier feelings also produce a characteristic buzz: ease of touch, unusual spontaneity, enjoyment, and tranquility being some of the more common signals. The dad who suddenly finds himself able to do what he and many men can't do comfortably—hold, hug, or otherwise physically touch his child— or the dad who finds himself talking with an unaccustomed freedom and ease, or liking a game he normally doesn't like, such as "Duck, Duck, Duck, Goose, " is a dad in the throes of a happy unidentified feeling.

Step Two: Developing An Emotional Lexicon

The next step involves developing a vocabulary for the expression of emotions, particularly the vulnerable and tender emotions. In the Fatherhood Project, I asked men to develop an emotional lexicon, by writing down as many words for feelings that they can come up with during the course of a week, which they would share at the next meeting. I would write their entries on the blackboard, and often got a list that looks something like this:

Anger	Burned-out
Irritation	Zapped
Frustration	Fried
Resentment	Stressed
Hostility	Aggression

Anger, hostility, stress—the list I compiled on the blackboard is a pretty good example of the emotions sanctioned by the male socialization process.

Contrary to this training, fully two-thirds of life involves emotions outlawed by the male socialization process—like sadness, hurt, love, joy, tenderness, pain, and disappointment. I tell the fathers that I'm afraid I don't have any magical solutions to these outlawed emotions, except to say, "Don't be afraid of them." There's nothing unmanly about being sad or hurt or tender or warm. These are the feelings that give life depth and richness. Once you acknowledge them, I think you'll be surprised at how many of these feelings you have, and how easily they flow out of you.

Step Three: Keeping An Emotional Response Log

The third step to developing emotional self-awareness is emotional record keeping, using a notebook to keep track of the feelings and buzzes that occur during father–child interaction, and the words or events that seem to produce them. These logs can then be discussed in a father's education group or used for self-study.

The basic procedure for emotional record keeping is as follows:

1. Record the buzzes (or feelings, if you notice them) that you become aware of, and when you first started to experience them.
2. Describe the social context within which the emotion was aroused: Who was doing what to whom? How did that affect you?
3. Go though the emotional vocabulary list, and pick out the words that seem to best describe the emotion that you were experiencing.

Emotional Record Keeping can be particularly helpful to fathers suffering from the Rubber Band syndrome, because it provides a means to get a handle on the stages that lead to an eruption. Through keeping such a written record, a father might discover, for example, that his anger proceeds through four distinct stages, each with its own markers, and this information gives him a kind of early warning system. He now knows that stage one of the buzz, inability to focus, signalled an incipient parental annoyance. Which meant that if he takes action at this stage he could prevent the buzz from progressing to stage two, antsyness; stage three, teeth-grinding; and stage four, eruption.

Step Four: Practice

The fourth and final step involves practice. Like any other skill, emotional self-awareness requires practice to become an automatic part of one's functioning. In the Fatherhood Project, we used role-plays, which were video-taped for immediate feedback, to practice the skill. Fathers were taught to tune in to their feelings through watching and discussing immediate play-backs of role plays in which feelings were engendered. By pointing out the nonverbal cues and asking such questions as "what were your feelings, Don, when you grimaced in that last segment?," fathers learned how to access the ongoing flow of emotions within.

Although working on these matters in a group context with video feedback is obviously advantageous, one can also practice this skill without such elaborate arrangements. By systematically keeping an Emotional Response Log, one can gradually build up the ability to recognize feelings as they occur.

When the Fatherhood Project was in its beginning stages, we conducted research on the skills approach to fatherhood education, and found that, as a result of the skills training program, fathers improved their communication skills, their wives reported that they functioned together as more of a team, and their school-aged children perceived positive changes in their relationships with them. This research is discussed more fully in Levant and Doyle, (1983), and Levant, (1988).

CASE EXAMPLE: A NUMB EXPECTANT FATHER

At the Fatherhood Project, expectant fathers would enroll in the Fatherhood Course. In the general discussion sessions they gave voice to their concerns. One expectant father reported "bursting into tears" on learning that his wife was pregnant, and he confided to the group that they were not tears of joy. Rather, he was anticipating the loss of the close and carefree relationship that they had enjoyed during their child-free years. Other expectant fathers expressed fears of adequacy; these fathers wanted to be good fathers but had doubts as to whether they would measure up. Still others reported concerns about medical issues, such as fetal abnormalities and congenital disorders, the risks of childbirth, and giving over control to the medical staff. Shapiro (1993b) discusses other fears and concerns of expectant fathers.

My most memorable case of an expectant father was a man whom I saw in my private practice. Raymond, a 40-year-old successful "work-out" specialist currently trying to turn around a failing New England computer company, called for an appointment because he "felt nothing" about the fact that he and his wife of 20 years were expecting their first child. Raymond was a hard-driving guy, who met or exceeded most of the requirements of the male code. As the first-born son of a rural midwest family, responsibility was his middle name. He took care of various members of his family of origin, and his extended family.

Apart from the fact that his wife was pregnant and he thought he "should" feel something about that, Raymond did not find it particularly odd that he "felt nothing." He usually felt nothing. The last time he cried was 10 years ago, when his dog was hit by a car.

I saw Raymond for ten sessions. Initially we worked on increasing his capacity to recognize his emotions, using the Emotional Response Log. Raymond was a quick study, and although he did not feel vulnerable emotions very intensely, and he certainly could not yet let his feelings pour out, he was able to discern quite subtle differences in his emotional states by the third session.

Raymond said at the outset that he thought that a lot of his problems had to do with his father. His father, 11 years older than his mother, was 38 when Raymond was born, and had died 13 years ago. Raymond believed that his father had a great life as an Army officer during World War II—a life that he had to leave behind when he married and started a family, and one that he seemed to miss greatly throughout Raymond's childhood. Because of the age difference and his father's detachment, Raymond never felt that he knew his father, yet he admired him greatly, and yearned to know him. For example, Raymond's lifelong hobby was participating in Scottish rites and learning about his (and his father's) Scottish ancestry, an activity in which he had earlier hoped he could involve his father. The first time I saw Raymond display emotions openly was when he spoke of how he had always wanted to see his Dad in a kilt, carrying a set of pipes.

Because Raymond had many questions he wanted to ask his father, we constructed a therapeutic ritual, in which he would spend 30 minutes in the evening, two evenings a week, writing down the questions that he had for his father on 3" x 5" cards. Using his newly developed emotional self-awareness, he also characterized the emotions that accompanied the questions with colors, using felt-tipped pens with different colors to represent different emotions.

The denouement to the therapy occurred during a trip to see his mother, during which he visited his fathers's grave. He described the experience as "raw emotion." His grief poured out of him, as he stood alone at his father's headstone, reading though his color-coded cards filled with unanswered questions.

Having broken through the walls that protected him from his grief, Raymond began to experience some strong feelings about his expectant fatherhood—fear, worry, and anxiety. He began to worry about whether the baby was going to be all right, given his wife's age (40 also). He also investigated some obscure genetic diseases that ran in Scottish families. I encouraged him to address his worries directly, by attending one of his wife's visits to he obstetrician. He did so, and was reassured about the baby's health, and also heard the baby's heart beat. His fear then turned to joy and excitement. We terminated after the tenth visit, 1 month before the baby was due. I got a postcard two months later that read:

> Ron, the baby was 2 weeks late. But he's a big guy, 8 lbs. 13 oz. And he definitely looks Scottish!
>
> —Raymond

Pregnant Father

So this must be my role:
As there's new life in her
It seems I'm bearing some new death
Here in my manly womb
We've made someone who will
And who will die
I swell with an embryo
Of endlessly ending night
It's a queer, dusty feeling
Giving birth to death
A smiling midwife awaits me
Her muscled hands tender with time
Urging me softly
Through this season of darkest labor

—Brad Sachs

Over the past 11 years, Charles Ballard has developed and run a unique and effective program for young African-American fathers at the National Institute For Responsible Fatherhood and Family Development in Cleveland. Focusing on helping these men become responsible as fathers and as members of society, the program employs a combination of psychological and social interventions. Recently, Martin Greenberg spent several hours speaking to Charles Ballard. The chapter represents an amalgam of these conversations and a brief summary of this most exciting program.

13

Teaching Responsible Fathering

Charles A. Ballard as told to Martin Greenberg

In October 1982, Charles Ballard developed The National Institute For Responsible Fatherhood and Family Development (NIRFED) in Cleveland. He has had remarkable success helping young African-American fathers to be more responsible, involved, loving, and concerned about their children. His program has become a model for other community programs nationwide and indicates the advances that can be made with caring and innovative leadership.

In describing some of the motivation that led him to try to reach out to young fathers, Ballard keeps coming back to his own personal experience. When he was $3^{1}/_{2}$ years old, his father entered a mental institution and subsequently died there 7 years later without ever returning home. Although his mother was described as "strong," he always felt a void related to the absence of his father in his life and he experienced a lack of significant male role models in his life.

Ballard became a teen father at the age of 17 and thereafter ran away to serve in the Army. While in the Army, he was wrongfully convicted of a crime and subsequently served a little less than 9 months in prison. While in prison he met an older African-American man who was kind and compassionate toward him. This was a new experience. Prior to that encounter, in his words, *"I grew up, I felt, in an angry, unsafe world and I was a very rough guy."*

Through his inspirational contact with this individual, Ballard him-

155

self got in touch with the importance of religion in his own life. He also began to feel that he wanted to be a part of his son's life. Thus, on leaving prison, he went back to talk to his son's mother and ended up adopting and raising his son.

Ballard indicates that he was and still is very close to his oldest son. His son, then in his late teens, pushed and encouraged Ballard in his work to reach out to fathers saying, *"Fathers need to get their act together. I think if any man can do it, you can. You have been a great father, you've been a loving father, you've been a responsible father and I believe you can teach men how to do it."*

THE EARLY BEGINNINGS

Ballard began his work as a social worker, with a position of community organizer of outreach workers at a hospital in Cleveland in 1976. In talking to expectant and new mothers, he would ask them if they would want the father of the baby to be involved in the pregnancy and/or the new baby. Most of the mothers indicated they wanted that and gave information so Ballard could contact the fathers.

Ballard then made a home visit and talked to the new fathers about their feelings about becoming fathers, if they felt they made a difference as a father and asked if they would be open to picking up their children on weekends. Primarily, Ballard encouraged the father to spend worthwhile valuable time with his child. About 80% of the time, the fathers were open to this. As the work progressed, Ballard noted:

> *I talked to men during the pregnancy and after the baby was born. I discovered if I got to a guy within the first trimester, invariably he would be there at the end of the pregnancy. So getting involved early on with the pregnancy situation is crucial to a lasting relationship between the couple.*
>
> *Early on I had groups of fathers in about five different areas in the city. We would meet in groups and have discussions around nutrition, choosing a doctor and so on. Then I noticed that some of the guys, no matter how much they learned in session, wouldn't talk. So I thought of the idea of doing one-to-one with them in their homes in addition to the meetings. Then I found out they did much better. Now, 90% of our time is spent in the home because we realize that is where the problem is.*
>
> *I was finding out that these young men had no idea as to how a child should be raised, taken care of, or how to change a diaper.*

They didn't have any understanding of that child's future. They didn't know about nutrition so there was no support for girls who were pregnant to eat better. The family was important but it was not a priority for these young men.

For most of these men I was the first positive African-American male in their lives. They had seen very few men who did not drink and smoke and have a self-destructive lifestyle. So I was the first that they had come across like that. And they commented that just having a man like themselves who they could talk with and ask questions and have discussions without having to play basketball or football or some other contact sport, this was very important to them and a new experience as well.

These young men found the groups to be very valuable and they wanted to talk about their own experiences. And that's why I started the program. I wanted it to be primarily for fathers because I discovered that these people have tremendous skills. If they don't have the skills, they can easily be taught. You can get out of the way and let them take over. When I was out of town or on vacation, they ran the groups and did an excellent job with it.

Ballard observes that in the past most programs for new parents were solely for the young mothers. " The message to the fathers was: get out of the way and don't interfere. You are the problem!" By contrast, Ballard emphasized how the young fathers could play a vital role in the lives of their children (Raspberry, 1993).

Ballard comments that the program (NIRFFD) has evolved from working with 100% teen fathers in 1983 to gradually serving different age groups, comprised as follows: 60% teen fathers; 25% aged twenty to thirty-five; 10% who were between 35 to about 45; and a group of older grandfather-type men.

DESCRIPTION OF PROGRAM

The basic program requires that a participant father:

1. Legitimize his children;
2. Goes back to school and does better in school;
3. Works at finding a job;
4. Changes a self-destructive lifestyle.

The lifestyle impacts on the mother, for example, if she is pregnant and the father is smoking cigarettes or marijuana, the secondhand smoke is going to affect her so what I did was to get him to be kind to her by taking care of himself. As he does that, he takes care of the girl and provides a better lifestyle for the child. As the child grow up, he sees his father's positive lifestyle. In this way, a father begins to teach his child how to live. . . It is not sufficient to help a man learn a trade if nothing is done to change a self-destructive lifestyle; that is, alcohol, drug abuse, or wife abuse. If a man beats his wife and he gets a good job, he won't stop beating his wife. If a man uses drugs or alcohol and he gets a pretty good job, he will continue to use alcohol or drugs, probably even at a greater level. So if a man learns a normal lifestyle then it creates not just the normal life for himself, but a positive relationship between him and other people.

The young men will work on those four major components, legitimization, going back to school, getting a job, changing a self-destructive lifestyle, at various personal speeds within a 6-months to 1-year period. The average father will go through the program in 6 months and will volunteer for the next 6 months.

As Ballard states,

One guy who is working and doing a good job is age 20 and has 3 children. He volunteered for 1 year. We are not saying that volunteering is as far as you are going to get, but in his case he was very young and part of his long-time volunteering was to complete his GED, which took him a little longer to do. The average father who goes through our program is ready to give back to the community in 1 year. I would say that within 2 years the average person can go anyplace and get a job. Some of the fathers who volunteer become counselors and some do outreach in other settings.

He tells his potential participants:

I am putting together a specialized 30-day training program that our workers go to. If you come to me as a potential outreach worker, then you come to get wisdom, you come to get knowledge, you come to get understanding. What you bring with you is desire, that's all we want from you is desire. What we do is put the meat on the bone. So when you come to us, we first of all work with your thinking about yourself, about your immediate family, about the other human beings in your life and institutions you have dealt with and then once you have resolved all your issues in those areas, you are now ready to be trained how to listen and how to communicate. In many cases, the counselors are young fathers (proteges) who have gone through our program.

Ballard learned, almost by accident, how valuable it was to require young fathers to work as volunteers with new fathers coming into the program. He observed, "The situation is more immediate for them. So many times they are better able than the professional staff to connect with their peers." He noted further, "First, we try to get them squared away, then they learn to work as volunteers with other young fathers and then they are candidates for full-time employment as counselors" (Raspberry, 1992).

Ballard observes that the individual counselors who work with the young father must have a risk-free lifestyle. He states, *"Kids know; they are looking at the kind of people who are working with them and they are very much affected by them. So we are looking for people who are not drinking or using drugs, not cursing or smoking cigarettes. We are looking for people who are happily married and respectful toward women. The reason for this is that young people need role models. They are looking for people that are different from them, that are role models for them. And yet who also can relate to them, can respond to them, can understand and empathize with their pain and where they have been and where they have come from."*

Ballard further emphasizes that when an individual goes through the NIRFFD Program that person is changed, that person becomes a role model. Thirty years ago doctors, lawyers, accountants, etc., lived and worked in the urban community and kids saw these role models at the cleaners, cafes, barber shops, shoe shops, and movie theatres and at the grocery stores and at church. "They saw these people who could be hopes and visions of their own lives." Over the years he noted the community gradually lost its role models as they moved away.

The program (NIRFFD) is creating role models within the urban community. He comments, *"You take a young man who's been in a gang. He gets his GED, he does better in school, he gets married, he has no other kids, he legitimizes his child. He stays in the community. He's taught to renovate his house and he buys his own house. He's taught to respect women. He walks around the community in a suit and tie and he stops fighting and has a good job. This person then becomes a protector and a role model for the community. He brings something back to the community. Furthermore, he becomes an image and a vision for other young men within the community."*

There is a an attempt to rapidly respond to new clients. Within 72 hours of a young man's presentation at the agency, a home visit is made. If he is staying with his parents, attempts are made to talk to his parents.

As much as possible, if the young father is going with his girlfriend, the team tries to get everybody together. The girl has to be involved as well, especially if the child has not yet been legitimized.

In the first 2-hour intake session ten areas are addressed. Those first 2-hours set the pattern for the next 3 to 6 months. The ten intake topics include

    1. the father's feelings about himself,
    2. his father,
    3. his mother,
    4. his siblings,
    5. his girlfriend,
    6. his baby,
    7. his peers,
    8. county welfare,
    9. the school system,
   10. the justice system.

Ballard notes that in this first 2-hour session, the worker maps out with the young father both of their outcome expectations. This conference regarding outcome expectations are repeated on a monthly basis. In this way there is a continuing reality check of the father's needs and aspirations.

An example of this interview according to Ballard:

Ballard: *"I would like for us to look at your infant. What is significant to you that needs to take place with your child."*
Father: *"Well, a friend of mine was in a gang and he got killed. He's got two kids, man. What if it happened to me."*
Ballard: *"So what do you see that you must do to insure that one year, 10 years, 15 years from now that that won't happen to you."*
Father: *"I gotta get out of the gang."*
Ballard: *"And what else are you doing?"*
Father: *"Well, I'm selling drugs; I have to stop selling drugs."*
Ballard: *"What else do you think your child needs as an example."*
Father: *"I need to finish school. I need to get a job."*

At this point, the young father is actually telling you the four things that we want from him: getting a job, establishing paternity, staying in school or going back to school, and changing his lifestyle. In most cases it comes from them. So we don't have to say it for them.

Once these are established, the team addresses the matters more specifically.

> Ballard: *"Now at what point on this annual planning sheet do you want to establish paternity?"*
> Father: *"As soon as I can."*
> Ballard: *"Well, it takes about 30 days so can we say about the end of August?"* So we put down as an expectation that we are to establish paternity by the end of August. *"I noticed that you mentioned your GED. How far are you on that?"*
> Father: *"Well, I haven't thought about it yet."*
> Ballard: *"Okay. Well, I know a program that takes 6 months. Are you up to going to that program?"*
> Father: *"Yes I am,"*
> Ballard: *"Now we are looking probably by the last of December you will be almost completed with that. How does that feel to you? The next thing you mentioned was getting a job. Tell me about your work habits. If you had a job will you be at work at 8:00. How much time would you think it would take to get from here to your house. Let's look at what point you would like to be on that job. What kind of job do you think you could do and do well.*
>
> *Now you mentioned a gang; now give me a date that you think we can have you out of this gang. How can we support you to get you out of the gang. Can I go and talk to the gang member?"*

At this point, the interviewer is already planning from the protege (new father) standpoint. Requirements are minimal because the program is predicated on the notion that these young men have what it takes for it to come from them. "When you ask people creative questions, people will tell you what's inside them."

Ballard emphasizes that he is teaching people (i.e., his staff and teen fathers) to communicate. He states, *"most people talk at people. The listening is even worse. We are listening about who the person is—whether he is an African-American and he doesn't count; or she is a female and she doesn't count or he is 'just, a kid or he is just an older person and they don't count."*

He likens true communication to a "kind of dance where the individuals are highly attuned to one another."

Ballard has observed that the young men he and his program work with often have tremendous rage. This has also been observed in groups with teen fathers in a juvenile detention setting. (Greenberg & Brown, 1994) Many of these youngsters do not fully understand the origin of this rage. He states:

> We've discovered that most of the anger, most of the rage that these young men experience happens preverbally, before the person begins to speak. So sometimes the young man cannot identify the real problem and so we have to use certain creative questions and methods to get to the source of the pain. For instance, he may say, "Well, I don't need a father because my father wasn't there for me and my child doesn't need a father anyway because he is going to make it on his own." So some questions are asked, "Okay, I appreciate you saying that you don't need a dad and I know a lot of guys are nodding their heads and are saying the same thing but what I want to ask you is this. If you could have had your father there and if he was a certain way toward you, then let's go around the room and tell me what kind of father would he have been." And these guys pick it up and they begin opening up. And what they say is that they wanted their dad to be loving; to show compassion, to be there, to be around for them, to take them places. All of this is coming out of all these years, an indication that they have displaced this anger and hate and this malice toward other people. The idea of dealing with the pain is probably one of our more dynamic approaches but it is also very much at the core of how we work with these young men.

Understanding the deeper reasons that the fathers come to the program helps in reaching these individuals. Ballard notes that the young men give a variety of reasons for coming into NIRFFD for help. There are the surface reasons and these include: (1) wanting to get help with getting a job; (2) wanting to learn how to get along better with their children and how to be better fathers; (3) because the mother of the baby or the mother's mother has requested (demanded) this; (4) and for a small percentage, attendance in the program is a condition of probation.

There are also deeper reasons that these young men have a hard time putting into words, however. Many of them feel insignificant and meaningless. The real reason that they come to the program is that they want to make a difference, to give some meaning, some direction to their lives. They want to know that their lives are important, that their existence on the face of the earth is important and meaningful in the lives of their children and their future grandchildren and great grandchildren and so on.

Ballard's gift is his unique ability to capture the young father's longing for meaning, put this into words, and to let the father know that he understands. He captures this longing in his use of visual imagery as he encourages young fathers to look into the future. For example, he says to a young father of a little girl, *"As you look into the future 10 years from now, when your daughter is going to be 12 or she is going to be 17. What kind of man do you want her to be married to. Because my experience has been that usually the girl marries the kind of man her father is. There is then a shift in him looking at himself to see what part of himself he is passing on to his daughter to be kind and productive.*

An aspect of this visualization Ballard calls *"future pacing"*—looking at the future and creating ones own future. To do this he asks the young father to look at his life with the absence of that thing (anything) and visualize how his life would be if that thing was there. For example, Ballard comments to a young father, *"If your father were there, would you have ended up in juvenile court, would you have ended up as a young father, would you have ended up as a school dropout or kicked out of school. I am not saying that you wouldn't or would have, but I am asking for you to take a good look at it. What would be the difference if your dad were there."*

Ballard indicates to the young father that he can recreate his past. For example, he states:

> *Let's say this young man's past is a past where his father wasn't present and there was a lot of anger and hurt and he has gotten into trouble with the juvenile authorities. What we tell the young fathers is to hold your past over here in your right hand. Now in your left hand go ahead and take the power that you are and create this new past that will have a far more profound impact than the old past. Now if you are going to throw one away and keep the other one, which one would it be. Almost always they throw away the old past—"the negative past." Then we say, from time to time this past is going to revisit you and that is all right, there is nothing wrong with that as long as you don't dwell on it.*

Similar to recreating the past, Ballard helps young fathers to get in touch with early hopes and desires (dreams) that they had as children and adolescents. Often, he notes, these *dreams for the future* may have been crushed by adults in their life, by the young father's parents or grandparents, by uncles and aunts, by neighbors or teachers who made fun of those dreams. Those dreams were far beyond what they could imagine was possible.

Ballard observes: *"So what happened is that those dreams put into effect a lot of hurt, a lot of put downs. They are put into a mental sack and they are closed up and they are put into the subconscious mind. What we do is massage the mind. We say to the young father, "talk about some of the dreams you had as far back as you can remember."*

For example, in response to this encouragement and support to share his dreams, one young father stated: *'Well, I was 7 and I said to my dad that I wanted to be a paratrooper, the one who just steps out of planes and opens his own parachute. My dad told me that I was stupid; he had been drinking and I can remember that. I can almost smell the alcohol; he was drinking and he slapped me!'*

In conclusion, Ballard further notes: *What we do is we keep working with those issues. We keep looking at those dreams—those dreams that the individual had at age 7 and he looks at where he is now and goes inside and talks to himself about what he needs to do to fill that gap.*

CONCLUSION

Two years ago, with a grant from the Cleveland Foundation, Dr. G. Regina Nixon, Principal Investigator and Dr. Anthony E.O. King, Co-Investigator were commissioned by the NIRFFD to conduct an extensive study of program participants.

Dr. Nixon stated:

> *the efficacy of the NIRFFD's non-traditional counselling appears evident, particularly for the outcomes of young fathers who participated in the survey. For example, the fathers took advantage of the legitimization (paternity) services and improved their educational and employment status. The program also had a positive influence on their attitudes toward self and parenting. Quite significantly, there was an overwhelming consensus that The National Institute improved their problem solving abilities and helped them to become better parents.*

Ballard has noted that "if comprehensive non-traditional services are provided to fathers, life opportunities will be enhanced for children and their mothers." Mr. Ballard also indicated that "young fathers, if approached in the right way, would be open to receiving human services and providing the best support for their children and the mothers of their children."

Teen fathers have been understudied, neglected, ignored, and misperceived. Beginning with the engrossment construct, Martin Greenberg and Henry Brown describe the needs and desires of teen fathers in a correctional institution. Far from the stereotypes, these teen fathers are viewed as very involved emotionally in their childrens' lives. A group-therapy program designed by the authors in the institution is explored. The reciprocal impact of teen fathers and their children is examined and a call is made for greater attention to these truly forgotten fathers and their therapy needs.

14

Teen Fathers: The Search for the Father

Martin Greenberg and Henry Brown

Over the past 20 years, the senior author has been researching and writing about fathers in general. In 1974, he coined the term *"engrossment"* to describe aspects of new fathers' involvement, sense of absorption, preoccupation and interest in their infants (Greenberg & Morris, 1974). Subsequently, he has elaborated on the subject, describing the "falling in love" experience common to new fathers (Greenberg, 1985). In 1987 Greenberg described specific interventions that can help fathers feel closer to their developing children.

TEEN FATHERS

The observations noted above had been completed with normative age fathers. The question arose regarding the generalizability of these results. What is the impact of impending birth and becoming a father on teen fathers?

Historically, programs for teen parents have focused on the mother and there has been an attitude of neglect toward the teen father. This attitude mirrored the past general neglect of the father's role as it relates to child development and the care of the child (Elster & Lamb, 1986; Greenberg, 1985; Lamb, 1981; Lynn, 1974; Nash, 1965;

Vinovskis, 1986). Fatherhood had been viewed as a social obligation rather than a state having biological roots and involving psychological satisfaction (Josselyn, 1956).

Nowhere has this attitude been so powerful as it has been with teen fathers. Even the importance of the teen father's, financial assistance is challenged by the array of other financial resources available from federal, state and local agencies. (Lamb & Sagi, 1983; Vinovskis, 1986). Vinovskis (1986) notes that:

> *When policy makers confronted the issue of adolescent child-bearing in the 1970's there was little thought or attention given to the responsibilities or needs of the father—especially if he was a teenager. Indeed, in the attempts to help the young mother and her child, little effort was made to involve the father and many even suggested that encouraging these adolescents to marry was counterproductive.*

Robinson (1988) noted that the teenage father was stereotyped as being uninterested, uninvolved, unconcerned, and unavailable with respect to his pregnant girlfriend and his new child. By contrast, numerous investigators have noted the teenage fathers' interest in participating in pregnancy, parenthood and childrearing (Redmond, 1985; Rivara, Sweeney, & Henderson, 1985; Robinson, 1988; Westney, Cole, & Mumford, 1986).

Moreover, there has been documentation of the powerful impact of impending fatherhood on teen fathers. For example, Elster and Panzarine (1983) noted that the prospective adolescent fathers experienced stressors related to vocational–educational concerns, concerns for the health of the mother and/or the baby, concerns about parenthood and problems with relationships. They concluded that the premature role transitions accentuates the stress for teen fathers.

It is the purpose of this chapter to attempt, in an exploratory fashion, to understand more about the experiences of the teen father, how becoming a father affects him and his feelings toward his baby and how these feelings were expressed in his reality relationship with his child. We were also interested in what thoughts and feelings he had about his own father, as well as other father figures (stepfather, grandfather, uncle, older sibling, adopting father, teacher, etc.) and how this was different than feelings about mother figures. We also wondered whether the event of fatherhood had the possibility, with support, to lead to positive behavioral changes among teen fathers. Finally, we hoped to use the data from this exploratory study to make some preliminary statements as to what type and intensity of services would be helpful for teen fathers in the future.

THE TEEN FATHER GROUP

An attempt was made to utilize themes associated with the concept of engrossment (Greenberg, 1974, 1985, 1987), which was introduced in a storytelling format with groups of teens. Finally, role modeling by the leaders of the group was an important aspect of the groups.

Description of Setting

Both authors consult within a juvenile detention setting; M.G. as a psychiatrist and H.B. as a teacher. During a lunchtime informal gathering, spontaneous discussion about being a father occurred in which large numbers of youngsters joined in spontaneously. It became apparent that there was a need and desire for many youngsters who were expectant or recent fathers to talk about their feelings and to learn more about being better fathers. In his clinical role in the institution, Greenberg had also observed heightened anxiety, depression, and increased expressions of concern about the welfare of the baby and their girlfriends when these young men found out they were fathers.

A pilot group of seven sessions was completed on the maximum security unit, which helped us to develop the format for later "father groups." After the first group meeting three youngsters were transferred to other settings (placements) and requested "father groups." All of the youngsters who participated were intensely interested in the father group meetings. Subsequent groups were held on nonsecurity units.

Method

The method consisted of group therapy meetings 1 hour and 20 minutes in length, held in the day room of one of the units. Expectant or recent fathers were invited to participate, but were not obligated to do so. Prior to participation in the group, youngsters were asked to complete *The Greenberg Teen Father Survey,* a 50-item questionnaire dealing with their feelings about fathering and about their girlfriend and baby. Initially the attempt was to try to have youngsters complete this survey before they entered the group but in a couple of cases some of the youngsters completed the questionnaire after they had already been in one group meeting. (We had hoped to be able to give the questionnaire again after their participation, but most youngsters moved on too rapidly to other settings.) The plan was for youngsters who attended the group to attend at least five times. However, the vagaries of a juvenile detention facility resulted in youngsters moving on to other settings or home after they had only met one or two times. A few youngsters were able to continue coming for three or more times. The basic rules for the group consisted of the following:

1. The need for confidentiality.
2. The need for respectful treatment of other members of the group.
3. People were not allowed to verbally abuse members of the group and needed to be respectful of different points of view.
4. Those in the group needed to remain seated and to not get up and/or threaten other members of the group.
5. School rules were in affect, meaning no swearing was allowed although this rule could be relaxed when a youngster used a four-letter word to express intense feelings and was not using it for verbal abuse.
6. The group was run in an open, nondirective fashion by two co-leaders.

There was a certain structure to the group. The group first opened with a review of the previous group and a summary of the major themes that the group touched upon. Frequently a member of the group was asked to talk about this. Then the first author opened the group with a story; usually a story depicting a powerful engrossment theme, or in other words depicting a close father–child bond that had been personally experienced (Greenberg, 1985). Both leaders shared stories from their own lives from time-to-time to demonstrate a particular point. Other creative modalities were used as well. A teddy bear, at times would be passed around the group. In addition, role play and psychodrama were intermittently employed to look at different fathering themes. Although the group was nondirective, at times different child development themes were brought up by the group leaders. These themes included infant-centered concerns such as coping with a crying baby, understanding the reasons for a baby's crying, learning proper methods of child discipline, dealing with anger toward the child, ways of showing caring and nurturing for an infant, and potential problems such as dealing with a child who has struck a parent.

Members of the groups could join and leave voluntarily. Referrals came from announcements by the probation staff, identification of expectant or recent fatherhood during mental health consultations and subsequent invitation for interested youngsters, and requests for admission from probation staff in other units.

Attempts were made to limit the population of the groups to a maximum of 10 to 12 youngsters. However, due to the vagaries of the criminal justice system, the population of the group was intermittently in flux. Drastic changes could occur as several members would be discharged and perhaps three or four or more new youngsters would come into the group. On several occasions, there were unexpectedly larger numbers; up to an unwieldy 16 and 18 members.

The groups consisted of 45% African-American, 45% Hispanic and 10% Caucasian teens. The majority of the youngsters were seventeen years of age (about 75%–80%). Usually each group had at least one 18 year old and at times there would be a 16-year-old member of the group. Our perception was that the African-American members of the group tended to be more vocal, enthusiastic, and eager to share and receive information about fathering related themes. This may also have been partially related to the fact that the co-author and co-facilitator, Brown, is African-American.

Group Interview Data

A number of prominent themes seemed to emerge in the groups. These major themes are elucidated in the words of the fathers themselves:

1. The Absent Father. Many of the youngsters frequently described a father who was often physically and/or emotionally unavailable. One expectant father stated: *My dad left when I was 2 and I always wondered where my dad went. I feel kind of bad because my sister used to get letters from him but I never did. Then he came back when I was 14 and I didn't have any kind of feelings about him; it was a strange feeling.*

Teen fathers who experienced early close contact with their fathers reported a heightened sense of loss at his departure. This 17-year-old teen father commented: *My dad and I were really close up until the time that I was 6 years old. It was like he was my best friend. We used to go to church together. We used to fix things with him. We did all kinds of things together. I kind of want to be a father like he was. At least a father like he was in the beginning. I mean, he would pick me up at school and he would take me to school. He would teach me things. . . . He would just spend a lot of time with me. Then he just sort of went away!!*

At times, the absence of the father is perceived to be created by the father's constant work demands. For example, this 18-year-old teen father observed: *Like my father was there but he was working all the time and I got tired of being at home and watching all this TV and then I started hanging around with the fellas (and getting in trouble).*

2. *Reversing the Cycle.* They want to be the kind of father they wish their father had been. They want desperately to change the pattern, to reverse the negative cycle. *It's not my fault my parents disagree. It's not my fault I was born. I think it was all messed up. That's why I plan to be the father I never had for my son. Because I know how it feels to grow up without a dad.*

3. *They Feel the Father Would Cure their Problems.* They feel the absence of the father has caused them to be in trouble, to engage in delinquent behavior. *If he had been there, things would have been different,* they surmise: *It would have been different if my father was there right from the time when I was little . . . when I was growing up. You know, like when your father is talking to you— you know what he says goes.*

Another 17-year-old father stated: *My pop cut out too. I never had seen him . . . slam bam thank-you-ma'am. If my dad had been there when I needed him; I probably wouldn't be here (Juvenile Hall).*

The way in which his father would have made a difference is graphically described by one teen father: *I don't have the kind of anger at my father you guys do. My father was shot when I was two and a half. Moms can only go so far. You know, like a mom's voice is not as loud as a dad's. A dad can say get your ass in the house .. I don't know what I can do except to be the best dad I can be to my kid.*

4. *Searching For the Father.* There is a desperate searching for the father and then a sense of pain and loss when the youngster realizes that he is not there and not coming back. This realization comes at

different ages and when it does come, for some there is a "hardening of the heart." An African-American teen father described his father this way: *He scat, he cut. I don't know who he is. I seen him and I still don't know why. I'm going to try to do the opposite. That's what I want to do. I don't want to leave when my baby is born and then come back 13 years later and have him say to me, 'You're still my son.' He's gone so long, he's no more. You get so mad and maybe you feel like crying and then your heart starts to hardening up.*

When asked if he could ever forgive his father, could ever let him earn his way back into his life, this young father stated: *He's gotta show up to apologize . . . You're always going to have love for your father, but he's not your father anymore . . . you know? When he leaves and comes back [many years later—sic] you're his son, but he's not your father. Part of being a father is loving your kid and taking time out for him and spending time with him—not coming back 10 or 12 years later and you haven't seen him in 10 or 12 years and then what(?) . . . you think you're a father . . . NO it goes beyond that! . . .*

Some teen fathers still very much want their fathers to be a part of their lives even later. The possibility of change, hope, and healing is seen in these two teen fathers' comments: *My father wasn't around the last three years. He was there with his side of the family, but if my father still was trying to make it work, I'd give him a chance . . .*

My father was locked up in the pen and then he woke up and he pulled his life together. He remarried to his fiance and he doesn't leave me and my little brother out and he wants to do things on weekends. Before it was like he popped up and he was locked up and then he was home for two or three months and then he was locked up again. But now he's remarried.

5. *Ambivalence.* Some of the youngsters describe missing their father and wishing he would come home. But when he comes home, they wish he would go away due to his abusive behavior. One teen father commented: *My father left when I was 6. The last time he was here he beat my mom and set the bed on fire. If I saw my dad, I'd try to tear his head off . . .I'd miss him and then I would also wish he would go away because I was afraid of him. . . It makes you mixed up. Like you want to see him and yet you don't want him around because he beats up on your mom.*

Some youngsters describe feeling angry and/or disconnected from their fathers despite their presence. They feel wounded by past hurts and struggles. This 17 year-old commented: *I had a father, but not a dad. He was never there. He was never there when I wanted to go fishing, when I wanted to go bowling, when the school had an open house . . . until I got all messed up, he wouldn't be there for me. . . . I love him for being my dad; he is totally opposite from my mom. I can't stand his ways . . . his alcoholism. . . saying everything is my fault . . . and he and my mom used to get into all kinds of stuff . . . get into stuff with me and my big sister.*

The importance of this relationship and the mother's mediating role in his continuing effort to talk to his father although he regards this as a failure, is noted in these words: *You know like with my father, I would keep trying with him. I'd try to talk to him and it didn't work. My mom would say, 'Go talk to your father, go talk to him again.' Then I would try and it just didn't work out.*

6. *Wanting To Share Feelings Related to Being a Father.* Invariably, these youngsters had no opportunity to talk about their feelings of being a father with their fathers, with other male role models or even with friends. As a result there is a great release of energy and enthusiasm as they talk about these experiences in a setting where they feel valued, respected and listened to. Some of this enthusiasm in communicating is captured in the comments below as they describe why they want to return to the father group. *You get different views and I can be a better husband and person. I want to be like my father (he emphasizes).*

In this group you get to let out all the feelings that you are holding in, so it feels good to share it and people can tell about their fathers and they can open up . . . instead of keeping all the angry feelings inside . . . you realize they might be able to bring you, your father and your whole family close together.

I want to be there when my child is born. By talking to the other people in the group you get to experience and learn how to take care of your child and how to be a good parent. The group is good because of the information.

You get to hear what other people have shared . . . it helps.

7. *Engrossment.* Many of these fathers, from their descriptions, appear to be "engrossed" in their newborns and children. They describe themselves in words that show them to be focused, involved and fascinated with their children. For example, a 17-year-old African-American teen father commented, *"My baby recognizes me right*

away; she knows it's me. I hold her on my lap and kiss her and look at her. It feels really good and it's just intense pleasure. I go see her almost every day."

The experience of a connection, of a bond with their child, is experienced as very pleasurable and further reinforces the father's desire to have contact with his child. He is *engrossed* in his child. The pleasure in this experience is noted in these words by this 17-year-old teen father. *I feel all happy when I see my daughter. You know I do things with my child. I let her play with coloring books and I sit on the ground and watch her. Then our eyes meet and we both start to laugh. She asks me, "What are you laughing at."* (His daughter is now 3.)

A few teen fathers, however, feel disconnected from their children. They don't feel engrossed or bonded to their children. In some cases, this may be related to a lack of contact with them and/or a poor relationship with the baby's mother and is associated with a sense of sadness. For example, a 17-year-old father stated with some sadness: *"I don't have any feelings when I see my kid. I don't feel much of anything now. By the time I get out, she'll be 1½. I can't stand the mother."*

8. *Fears of Losing Freedom.* Often, the experience of feeling close and connected with their babies exists side-by-side with fears that they will lose their freedom, that they will be "owned" by the mother of their child, that they are too young to assume all this responsibility. For example, a teen father commented about his delight and enjoyment in being with his daughter. He then commented further on what having a baby meant for his relationship with his girlfriend and his feelings about issues of responsibility. *She thought that if I had a baby she was going to keep me but it didn't work that way. I told her just because I've had a baby, that doesn't mean you can keep me. . . . I was growing up too fast. I wanted to be like my brothers, to jump around, to hang out, to get girls, to have money, to do it all. And school was one of the last things I wanted. School was the place I went to find more girls. I was doing "bad."*

DISCUSSION

The results from this preliminary study indicate that teenage fathers are very responsive to support and sharing of information through the model of "father groups." Although youngsters often had an opportunity to talk about their feelings about their own children and their expectant fatherhood, a major focus of many of the groups centered around these youngsters' feelings about their own fathers.

The "father groups" provided a role model for appropriate behavior and respectful treatment of one another. The specific structure of the group with concrete rules (no swearing, respectful treatment of one another, no threatening, respecting different points of view) enhanced this role modeling. As leaders we demonstrated this in our approach to one another as well as in our respectful treatment of the group members. The willingness of youngsters to follow this pattern was noted in that at times one individual would remind other members of the no swearing rule when there had been a lapse.

A major theme that permeated virtually all the groups was "the search for the father." Youngsters talked about wishing they had a father who was an active, involved part of their lives. They often shared the feeling that their lives would have been different if their fathers had been an active part of their lives.

At times it seemed that these youngsters were sharing an image, an ideal of an all-loving father. This image represented a father who was a nurturing and loving father who appropriately set limits and provided guidance. They wished that their own fathers were that father.

For many of these youngsters this ideal father is nowhere to be found. There were often expressions of anger, anguish, and sadness related to this absence, to this void. There is a gaping wound here with respect to their feelings about "father." Youngsters are often eager to have an opportunity to talk about this. The group provides an opportunity for them to share their experiences about their hurt and pain in an atmosphere that does not add to this pain and provides a sense of support and nurturing.

Often when these teen fathers are talking about what kind of a father they will be or about their own children (when they are already parents), they are talking about boys, and about reversing the cycle; becoming the kind of father that they wished their fathers had been (the ideal image of the father). It's as if they have become both that father and that child. Thus, they experience the healing in that loving image of father, giving both to themselves and to their child as well.

In many ways these youngsters are searching for some sense of meaning and a sense of direction—for a role model and a spiritual direction in terms of being fathers. For many of them, images of father have been associated with absence, loss, neglect, and abandonment and they desperately want to change the pattern, to reverse the cycle.

Unfortunately, they face a difficult task. For images of the father's roles and expectation of father are in disarray and confusion in our culture. Other cultures provide models or rituals both to help fathers get in touch with their feelings and to help him experience the importance of his role as father to the child. These rituals play an important part in helping the father to bond, to become *"engrossed"* in his child, to cope with jealousy and the transition of new fatherhood.

For example, among the Palikur Indians in Brazil, it is believed that the soul of the baby follows the father everywhere. If the baby's soul lost its way, then it is believed that the baby would die. So the father fashions a miniature bow and arrow and a baby sling, which can safely contain the soul of the baby. In this way the baby can safely be with her/his father wherever he goes and can accompany the father when he goes off to hunt. This powerful image also demonstrates that the father gives energy to the child and vitalizes him and the loss of this connection leads to the loss of a vital tie and subsequently to the loss of that child's spirit. (Fock, 1967) Furthermore, it demonstrates that the father's spiritual connection to his child exists even when the father is away and providing (hunting) for his family.

When we spoke with teen fathers we were often hard pressed to find positive images or feelings related to the theme of fathers and fathering in their own lives. Anger, rage, and disillusionment were common emotions that seemed to emerge. It was for this reason that we decided to use the model of storytelling using engrossment themes. (Greenberg, 1974, 1985, 1987; Greenberg & Brown, 1992) The basis for this was to provide positive and nurturing images of fathers and fathering with which youngsters could relate and that might trigger thoughts and images of their own.

We shared positive images of fathering and stories of experiences that focused on the positive father–child relationship, on fathers' feelings of *engrossment*, fascination, involvement, enthusiasm, concern, love, and care with their children.

Many of these youngsters have no positive role models, no positive images to base their strivings of wanting to be good fathers. They need to have something to work from; a starting point that gives them an inner feeling that it is possible, to be loving and nurturing fathers.

To this extent the story is like a catalyst. It gets the father system going. It gets the teen fathers thinking in positive terms about what's possible. In addition, because the story or images we choose are on an emotional level, it helps to get them out of their heads and more in touch with their feelings. These stories are always shared in an atmosphere of support and nonbelittlement.

Similar to storytelling, role play and psychodrama also provide new images and ideas, a substrata for a new structure to begin new possibilities. For example, in one of the groups a youngster shared that he had not seen his father in 3 years and felt unable to talk to his father. He described being cut off and disconnected. "I can't talk to my father," he kept repeating. Yet, at the end of the group in which he role played his father, he indicated that he was going to contact his father. In fact, he did contact his father who initially refused to accept his call. He tried again and subsequently made contact with him and his father came to visit him twice in the next week, subsequently arranging for his baby and his girlfriend to move in to his home.

Another expectant teen father shared that he felt fearful of his father. In a role play, he was able to assert himself to some degree and then felt more comfortable and stated he felt like he could now talk to his father.

We also used a teddy bear, which we would pass around the room asking youngsters to show how they might hug, cuddle, or comfort it. This was a way to understand and see how each individual related to the bear. Individuals would notice if one person was handling the bear in a rough way and then they might say, "Is that the way you handle your child? Is that the way you want your child to be handled?" Then we'd ask, "How are you feeling when you're holding your child like that?" In one group a youngster threw the teddy bear high up in the air. Other members of the group confronted him about this, particularly after he said "yes" he would do this with his child. In this way developmental issues could be taught through the medium of the camaraderie of the group.

In focusing on the teddy bear, it was almost as if we gave it life. We encouraged the youngsters to take care of that little teddy bear as they would want their own child to be taken care of. Youngsters began to learn how to show their emotions to their child in terms of hugging them and not to be threatened by these kind of emotions. They could see that men can display these kind of feelings and emotions in front of one another. At times, youngsters would ask the authors to show how we would hold the child (bear) and we would demonstrate this, although others would want to demonstrate a better way.

In describing their relationships with their children many of the youngsters frequently described feeling fascinated and talked about their enjoyment of having contact with them. Often they described being visually attracted to their child, enjoying holding their child, seeing their babies as perfect, feeling like they could distinguish their children from other children, experiencing intensive attraction to their children, experiencing a sense of elation at the birth (a "high") and describing an increased sense of self-esteem. In effect, many of these teen fathers often described themselves as experiencing *engrossment* in their children and this was particularly true for those teen fathers that had the opportunity to have regular contact with their babies (Greenberg, 1974, 1985).

The receptiveness of these teen fathers to the father-group experience suggests that there should be further opportunity within the community for father groups as well as individual counseling. The language that is used to describe the help that is available would effect the utilization of these resources. For example, an 18-year-old Hispanic youngster asked the psychiatrist leader how he could continue to receive help like he received in the father groups. I gave him the name and telephone number of a local community mental health center where I said he could receive counselling. He commented, "But I don't want counseling." At this I stated, "oh, excuse me; this is a place where you can talk about your feelings about being a father and your own father." "Yes," he replied, "That's what I want."

We also believe that it would be important to provide ways for these youngsters to be a success in their own lives. Therefore, we strongly recommend that there be access to vocational programs, vocational guidance as well as vocational apprenticeship programs. In addition, it would be extremely important for teen fathers to have the opportunity for educational guidance that would help youngsters in terms of their school, community college, and college goals. Furthermore, these youngsters need access to parenting classes as their knowledge of child development is often lacking.

As youngsters begin to think about what kind of fathers they are and could be, this is a unique time when they can look at their lives. They can ask themselves how can I make a positive impact on the life of my son or daughter? What can I do to change in a positive way?

The positive impact of counseling programs with teen fathers has also been dramatically illustrated by Charles Ballard's work in Cleveland at the National Institute For Responsible Fatherhood and Family Development. Youngsters that are part of that program receive counseling and are encouraged to legitimize their children, go back to school, and/or to seek gainful employment.

Mentoring programs would also be extremely helpful where the volunteers within the communities from which these youngsters have come would volunteer to provide contact with these youngsters demonstrating positive male and father role models.

The time around the birth of his child when a youngster becomes a father is a special time, a transcendent time when teenage fathers are more open to look at their lives, their hopes, and aspirations for the future. We believe that these youngsters are particularly amenable at this time to change and if programs were available to provide information, support, counseling, and mentoring, these youngsters would be particularly responsive.

In addition, a counseling program for teen fathers similar to the model of the National Institute For Responsible Fatherhood and Family Development is strongly recommended. If teens are able to receive support during the crucial time around the period of the birth, they may be able to redirect their lives in a positive way.

Other Teenage Boys—Nonfathers

Father groups may also have significant therapeutic benefit for delinquent teen boys in general. Opportunities to discuss the theme of fathering with teenage boys who were not fathers produced a similar fascination, interest, and involvement that we had observed with teen fathers. Further, it appears that "father theme groups" may provide an opening through which these youngsters may be reached and encouraged to discuss other aspects of their lives. Through this opportunity, change could occur.

It may be that the fascination and interest in father groups and fathering that we noted among teen fathers is a universal experience among teenage boys; this may be related to a general deprivation of information on parenting and birth, and a lack of positive role models in their lives. When the senior author has made presentations on fathering to mainstream populations of up-scale nondelinquent youths, he has found a universal receptivity, passionate interest, and concern. Teenage males are eager, almost starved for information in this area, and they are fascinated to hear about fathers falling in love with their babies, and loving them with passion, energy, and responsibility.

Part II

THE DEVELOPMENTAL PERSPECTIVE

Personal Experience

Psychological Issues

Blind Date

I prepared all morning
For this meeting
Scrubbed my body and hair
Though you wouldn't be seeing me.
At the hospital, I tightened my hand around my wife's
The wand sunk into her jellied stomach
We looked up
Saw you coaxed and coating the screen
The star of this joint production
At first, you were an algebra of shadows
A somber layer of thunderclouds
But with a few seconds' practice
We saw within the clouds
The beautiful, fish-like spine
The matchstick femur
Your heels pinned together
Like a frozen tap-dancer's.
Here a kidney, there a nose,
Then, the exquisite chambers
Of your lurching heart
That I quickened to keep up with
What silent words were uttered
By your hungry, gulping mouth?
The monitor shone with numbers
Measurements, averages, proportions
But I was suddenly blind
Blind to your delicate fingers
Blind to your skull
Blinded by an animal light
That poked the sight from my eyes
Sent me down to the darkness
Tapping my cane
Against this exile of terrifying love.

—Brad Sachs

Many men entering fatherhood become intensely aware of their lack of an older male mentor or guide. In this chapter, Dr. Lawrence Peltz provides the mentorship by describing in deeply personal ways his own development into fatherhood and his personal changes as a man.

Three Tries to Get it Right is an intimate account of the author's personal growth through the events of the births of his three children over a 13-year period. Deeply touching, this chapter illustrates a psychological maturing from performance to direct involvement.

15

Three Tries to Get it Right

Lawrence Peltz

After 22 years as "Dad," it seems important to put into perspective the father that I am and have been to our children. I have so much to say about our children; 22-year-old Jennifer, 16-year-old Aaron, and 10-year-old Cory. There is love and commitment; fear and uncertainty; all the thoughts and feelings related to this state of fatherhood.

I would like to "be" with you for awhile; to welcome you to the very private world that I inhabit. The internal world where I live fully or simply exist without being fully alive.

Many years ago in my work as a psychotherapist, I realized that it was vital to "be" with my clients in a way that went far beyond any technical competence. I had to risk truly caring in a way that let others know I was with them; that our connection was to be taken along in spirit when they left my office; somewhat like a good parent—present—seemingly a step or two behind, near their shoulder, offering support, genuine caring, perhaps love.

This connection reflects an even more important personal quest: to be fully with myself and my family in the place where duty, honor, loyalty, passion, and love reside in me. I've learned that we all share some thoughts and feelings as men. As we prepare for fatherhood, hearing, knowing, and feeling the experience of other parents, especially fathers, takes us farther down the road toward "becoming" father.

There is a vast difference between the role of father, and the immediate presence of a man who just "is" father. For me, "becoming"

182

involves a dynamic process called living that allows us to develop; to more fully experience ourselves and the people we love. In the process of becoming we don't always know what to do or who to be.

Becoming a father can be demonstrated by the experiences of three men. Each man is me, at progressive developmental stages: at the ages of 24, 30, and 36. I am now 46 years old and just entering what I believe is maturity as a father. All three children had very different experiences of me although they share the "same" biological parents.

JENNIFER

In January 1971 I was 24 years old. It seems incredible now that when I was merely two years older than she is today, I was married, supporting a pregnant wife, tasked with great responsibilities and almost no authority in my position as airman first class, United States Air Force. We were living in Honolulu, Hawaii, 6,000 miles from my suburban home outside New York City. Married less than a year, I was a former graduate doctoral student due to the necessity of fulfilling some military commitment during the Viet Nam Era. In addition, I was soon to become a new father. I don't remember even comprehending that impending change in status. My thoughts and feelings were organized in support of my wife and our newly formed marriage. My attention was almost entirely focused on the logistics of providing materially, and attending to the emotional needs of my partner.

This was a role I had learned very well from my own father. He has always been a valuable model of sensitivity to the emotions of others. He taught me to use gentle feelings in the service of those I cared about.

At 24, I had not yet learned to honor my experience as valuable in its own right, nor to honor myself as worthy of meeting my own needs. I had not granted myself the right to be attended to by those I loved. The words, "I want," "I need" etc., were absent from an acceptable vocabulary during my transition from adolescence to adulthood.

Cathy was due to deliver our first baby in January 1971. Because my mother had offered to travel to Hawaii to offer emotional support and logistical assistance, we thought it prudent to invite her to be with us a bit early, "just in case." As it turned out, the three of us shared a tiny cottage for 6 weeks waiting for Jennifer to make an appearance. During that time, it never once occurred to me that I had the right to attend to any of my emotional needs. In fact, it didn't occur to me that I *had* any emotional needs.

In retrospect, I believe that the predominant motivator available to me during my wife's first pregnancy was fear. Unfortunately, I was unable to acknowledge fear's existence. Thus, I automatically responded to every threatening situation with immediate problem solving, or when possible, circumventing the experience without acknowledging my avoidance.

The subject of my participation in Jennifer's birth lends itself especially well to my relationship with fear. I never admitted to anybody that I was relieved to not be allowed to participate in Jennifer's birth. In fact, I never acknowledged it to myself until writing about it now. It was especially easy to avoid the fear of not knowing what to do or how to be in a labor or delivery room by simply being excluded from participation. Tripler Army Medical Center was prepared to present me with a newborn daughter for the total price of $8.00. Tripler Army Medical Center was not prepared to allow fathers to do anything during the birth process except pace the waiting room floor.

As a young man, I was most comfortable when I had a job to do. The less structured the experience, the greater my fear. No guidebook existed to prepare me for fatherhood. If there had been one, I doubt that it would have been of much benefit, unless somewhere within those pages was permission to not know what to do or how to be. I now realize that unawareness may be preferable in many circumstances. When I trust that I am human and can only do my best at any moment, I find that I may avoid a tremendous sense of loss of self when a particular outcome is less than ideal.

When my wife was giving birth to our daughter, there was no guidance available to cope with my overwhelming feelings of helplessness and incompetence to aid and comfort the love of my life during an experience that was so alien to me. How could I comprehend what she was feeling, physiologically or emotionally? How could I possibly appear to be of any importance, let alone of any use, in a military hospital where everyone outranked me. In the confines of the safety and comfort of our rented cottage, I felt like a useful person. In the vast labyrinth of the hospital, I almost ceased to exist at all.

I could manage transporting Cathy to the hospital and I could manage waiting 12 hours for Jennifer to be born. I would have been terrified if anyone had offered to allow me to participate in the process of labor or delivery. I probably would have been equally terrified at the prospect of participating in Lamaze classes, had they been available to us at the time.

I accomplished transportation and waiting duties in expert fashion. Approximately 12 hours after arriving at the hospital, a nurse whooshed out of the labor ward obviously making a bee line for the nursery. Having flagged her down like a runaway cab (a throwback proficiency gained from years of living in New York City), I was afforded my first glimpse of our new daughter.

"Glimpse" is exactly what I mean. This "cab" was intent on leaving without me, and off to the nursery Jennifer was whisked. Looking at her through the glass wall, I saw a tiny infant, not unlike all the other tiny infants around her. I knew that I was supposed to feel love, joy, and experience a sensation of rapture; a "Kodak moment" in which a bond occurred, never to be broken.

What happened in reality, was an experience of some relief that my wife was safely through a painful and frightening ordeal, and amazement at my mother's intense emotions as evidenced by the tender tears in the corners of her eyes as she accompanied me through this unfamiliar terrain.

More than this, a state of great fatigue and shock predominated. To nobody did I admit this. After all, I was the proud new "Poppa" with cigars and flowers to buy and relatives to call. None of this did I resent, nor do I now. It was almost as if I wasn't inhabiting my body. I was out of touch with my own experience. I was relating to the arrival of our daughter, materializing out of *my wife's* body!

Looking back, I understand that my experience is common. I had so many expectations along with little familiarity or comfort in meeting them. It isn't a crime to be anxious and naive, but as a young airman with new responsibilities, I had to cope with my fear and inexperience in ways that denied their existence. I felt required to act "as if" I had it all together. Such acting rescinds permission to explore; to make mistakes in the service of growth.

As a family therapist, I know now how dangerous it is to maintain a split between internal and external experience. A discrepancy between how I appear to the world and how I feel inside represents a lack of permission to be enough as I am, and forces me to be false in some vital ways. The danger lies in institutionalizing the split so that I spend a substantial part of my life on this planet, hiding behind the image of the guy I send out into the world to represent me; the guy who "has it wired." He knows how to be, what to say, and he is always in complete control.

Of course, he is not real. He is an invention; my public-relations man selling a false image of me to the world. He is representing me as a performer, and a very good one at that. We know that the world of public relations can be treacherous. Selling an image to the public is one thing. To abandon the private self in the service of meeting expectations is quite another.

Of course, during times of crisis, it is sometimes necessary to wall off the inner self in the service of the "life and death" struggle at hand. To feel the terror or horror of the moment could be overwhelming, restricting the ability to survive. Fortunately, the times that require such a split are rare.

Psychologically, the danger occurs when the split becomes normal. The private self may become frozen in time, whereas the public self continues to adapt to the demands of the moment. Such a discrepancy retards the growth process. Instead, what is needed is a growing sense of competence that promotes greater self-acceptance, which in turn provides a path for the public and private self joining into a more unified, integrated being.

My next "try to get it right," illustrates this growing sense of integration of public and private, of competence and experience. It symbolizes my personal steps on the path to participating in this life in an increasingly rich, more present way.

AARON

June 14, 1976. Honolulu, Hawaii. So much had changed in 6½ years. Jennifer was now in first grade and Aaron was to be born. Military service was behind me. I had completed two separate master's degrees in related fields and was employed as a civilian psychologist, serving military personnel at the very hospital where Jennifer was born. I was now on the "other side" in my relationship with hospitals and felt very comfortable in my role as family provider and young professional.

By now, I knew that it was essential to build a sense of self before becoming comfortable with that self, accepting it, and ultimately striving to expand it.

Aaron was born in a private hospital. Prenatal care was provided by a private physician, and private classes were taken in order to guide us toward a rewarding, effective birthing experience. In essence, everything was done "right."

My wife's Ob/Gyn was wonderful. He was casually reassuring, able to use humor effectively to put us at ease, and provided a sense of confidence in his medical expertise. Cathy and I had met Dr.

Shimomura previously as a result of a PAP Smear that yielded abnormal precancerous cells and an operation to eliminate them.

I found myself fulfilling my idea of the role of the model husband by calmly listening to all information provided by medical personnel, accompanying my wife to appointments, driving her to the hospital for the operation, and in a concerned but reassuring way (Just like Dr. S.)[1] providing the support that I believed my wife needed.

It was only when I knew in some internal way that Cathy was safe, that I spontaneously began to cry as I held her tightly. I could no longer maintain the split between my role and my emotional experience. That experience would not be contained or denied any longer.

We were both very surprised by my behavior. I was surprised because I had not allowed myself to feel those overwhelming feelings of fear and anxiety. It was only when I felt relief that I allowed powerful feelings to emerge in one intensely tearful experience.

My wife was surprised because she still was not ready at that point, to come to terms emotionally with what could have been. She would be fine, because the screening had prevented the development of terminal cervical cancer. She was, however, greatly appreciative of my demonstration of deep loving, balanced by rational thought and emotional experience.

It is clear to me now, that this experience represented the beginning of an internal major life shift: from a survival orientation to one focused on growth and development.

My reaction to my wife's operation provided a model for the possibility of the integration of performance and feeling. In this instance, performance was related sequentially to emotional involvement. The task that lay ahead was to narrow the gap between cognitive and emotional experience until the two became entwined in a dynamic process, propelling me beyond my present limits of self-knowledge and self-acceptance.

It seems that there is no way to skip steps in the process toward emotional maturity. As a young child, my family readily accepted my feelings. My reaction to the shock of the outside world's nonacceptance of my most tender feelings was to learn to gain acceptance by performance. By attending to others' feelings I gained great apprecia-

---

[1]Dr. Shimomura's behavior and caring provided an excellent example of the physician's potential as a "father" role model and as a means to open the gateway for a father's emotional life.

tion and eventually learned that by doing good things for others I also gained acceptance.

The stage was set for an exemplary performance.

Cathy is timing her contractions. Good. She told me to return to bed and that she would let me know when it would be time to leave for the hospital. No problem. She has a bag packed and our friend JoAnn has been alerted to be ready to proceed to the hospital at a moment's notice, in order to render support from the wings.

Nothing much to do now but wait. Lamaze classes have been taken. We've practiced breathing exercises until we were doing them in our sleep. I've been trained for 6 weeks to be an effective birthing coach for my wife. I've learned that there are going to be times during the birth process when "the mother may become agitated and despairing." I've learned that she may become angry at me and hold me solely responsible for the unpleasant physical circumstance in which she may find herself. I've learned techniques and become familiar with the timing of the unfolding physiological process known as the birth experience. I've seen films in all their explicit detail to prepare me for the reality of birth. What's a little blood and mucus. I can take it. I'm a man.

In essence, I have been instructed to limit my emotional experience of this event and to devote my energies to serve my wife's needs. Paradoxically, I have been led to believe that this should be one of the most important, profound, deeply moving experiences of my life!

"Piece of cake." I could do all of the above as long as that feeling in the pit of my stomach remained under control; as long as that shaking in my voice didn't appear; as long as I could continue to be coherent; as long as I could con everybody into thinking that I really knew what I was doing; as long as nobody saw me glance at the clock whose hands never seemed to move, every 40 seconds; as long as I drew the line at losing control and fleeing!

That was where this downwardly spiraling self-realization could lead me: Out of the labor room, out of the hospital, out of my marriage, out of the self that I had constructed.

I never for a moment acknowledged any of the feelings from which I had divorced myself. I knew that some very disturbing physical symptoms commonly associated with anxiety could seize me without warning at any time. My means to cope with these physical sensations were denial and control. When denial broke down and physical sensation emerged, then cognitive control—mind over matter— kicked in. What couldn't be kept at bay could be vanquished. Of course, as always, the cost of this internal war was very high. In this case, the price for the illusion of emotional mastery was to relinquish the immediate, full experience of the present event. I was there, but I was distant; doing my best to conform to the message I had received in class.

In times of crisis, such extraordinary means to pull through, are sometimes necessary. To treat one's life as a crisis is to attempt to pull through without appreciating the experience as it unfolds. To not appreciate the moment-by-moment experience of life is to lunge toward life's ultimate conclusion, and in so doing, becoming immediately deadened.

"Time to get ready to head for the hospital dear . . . my contractions are 5 minutes apart." This was it! The wake up call to action! Cathy's mother bid us aloha and remained behind with Jennifer. Pulling on my (super)man costume we raced, *faster than a speeding bullet,* into Honolulu at the crack of dawn. We arrived at the hospital in time to check in and proceed through a 12-hour labor. Actually, my wife proceeded through labor. I proceeded to get very busy. Ice was forbidden. Cathy's lips were dry. Super coach would bring her ice regardless. It was our conspiracy. I had a job to do. I was the labor coach. I was the father to be. I was scared witless!

Not to worry. There were myriad things to do: time contractions; help Cathy focus on her breathing, check the clock; provide progress reports to the waiting room contingent; check the clock again; wait; step outside the labor room for a few minutes; consult with Dr. Shimomura (who fortunately came to the hospital several hours after Cathy checked in).

Although I was very happy to see him, I found myself uncomfortable in his presence and he must have sensed that. After advising Cathy that he and I would be taking a short break during a lull in the action, Dr. S. led me to the physician's lounge, where he produced two huge cigars. We smoked those cigars in silence as a sense of calm and the knowledge that in a very fundamental way I was cared for, settled into my being. I left the physician's lounge less anxious, and able to continue to help my wife through a long and difficult birth.

My contact with Dr. Shimomura was the most immediate genuine experience I encountered during those long hours until Aaron was born. Actually seeing our son, brought thoughts and feelings together. Although I don't remember any strong emotion at the time, I do remember a sense of absolute wonder that this inanimate little funny looking grey slimy figure, became a human being, gaining color and expressing his aliveness during his first few seconds on the planet.

Shakespeare defined courage as "grace under pressure." Cathy had been magnificent, showing tremendous courage. She knew this baby long before it was born. She had sung to it, spoken to it, stroked it, bonded with it before it's birth in a way that enabled her to meet Aaron in person as one would encounter a cherished friend that was very well known and loved. Her efforts during labor and delivery were focused on this mother/child connection. Her physical, spiritual, and emotional aspects were focused on bringing this child into the world.

My efforts were more focused on simply doing what was honorable. I wanted to do the best job I could for my wife and, as yet unreal, son to be. I believe that my participation earned high marks because I genuinely loved and honored my partner.

It was a rewarding time for me in the sense that we shared an act of love; not only through the conception of our son, but through the birth process as well. In *The Road Less Traveled,* M. Scott Peck defined love as "the will to extend one's self for the purpose of nurturing one's own or another's spiritual growth." He also noted that genuine acts of love take courage and work; courage to enter unknown territory in the service of an expanding self or other, and hard work to consistently persevere in the effort to nurture ourselves and those we love.

My capacity to love others was never in question. I had long been willing to nurture those I loved. My flaw was in my capacity to nurture myself. It was as if I had enough inside to sustain me, and sufficient resources to offer to those I valued. I could go no farther in my development, however, until I allowed sufficient attention to myself in the moment; to bring myself into each situation sufficiently, in order to grow, to develop; to become bigger; more than I had been before and therefore having even more to offer.

I had traveled far on my journey of self-development. I was no longer frozen with fear. A sense of worth enabled me to perform effectively in difficult circumstances. I could appreciate and deeply experience a range of emotional responses in reaction to meaningful events, yet there lingered a sense of incomplete fulfillment.

The ability to participate fully in the moment, regardless of the immediate circumstances became my goal. During the following 6 1/2 years, I made significant progress toward consistently being in my own life, rather than a custodian of it. That balance between being and doing developed so that I was less a manager and controller of my existence and so much more a spontaneous participant in my own life. My involvement in our youngest son's birth illustrated the growing richness and texture of life that emerged.

CORY

March 27, 1993

Dear Cory,

You are 10 years old now. A big boy who shows up on a daily basis. My son, you shout and laugh; you fight and hug and kiss; alive in every moment on this planet, in this family, and in your own life. You give so much to us who love you by your willingness to be with us so fully. You are so much already at 10. You are rich, Cory, in ways you simply take for granted.

I hear you in the kitchen as I type in the next room, sitting with your friend Nic; being silly as you joke your way through lunch. You are close to me right now; not a distraction or annoyance.

Although I don't know how much of this letter you will understand right now, you can save it for later and read it again perhaps when you too are a Dad.

I want to tell you about the day you were born, because it was a very special day. It was the very first day that you were here with us and one that I will always remember.

It would be better if I could show you the day you were born instead of just tell you about it. That's what I'm going to do—show you my day, November 29th, 1982.

But first there are some things I want you to know about that happened around that time. Jennifer was 12 then, and Aaron was 6 years old. We had moved to Santa Rosa the year you were born, into our very first and only house, the one in which we live today.

That year, I was 2 years from completion of my doctoral degree; a student, yet practicing my profession as a licensed Marriage and Family Counselor.

We didn't have much money then; not even enough for medical insurance, which would have helped pay the hospital bills when you arrived. But that was okay. Mom and I signed up at Community Hospital for help from the clinic that anyone could go to who was willing to be in the care of new doctors. These doctors were learning special skills to help with ladies about to have babies.

You see, the ladies were helped by not paying much money for medical care, and the doctors were helped by having patients to work with, in order to learn how to be most excellent.

Everybody that we met at the clinic was super nice and you and

Mom were really well cared for. The new doctors had supervisors who were very experienced. They made sure nobody made any mistakes while learning about this birth stuff.

You would not believe the equipment that they had at this hospital. There was a machine called a sonogram that let us see you on a screen while you were still inside mom's uterus. I got to meet you before you were even born!

You had a most interesting way of doing the darndest things in there Cory, because you decided to turn inside of Mom, to a position that would have made it impossible to be born without getting stuck coming out. You turned sideways instead of head down and although we would have liked to have waited for you to turn around so you could be born naturally, the doctors said that was not a good idea, because you might not want to ever turn the right way, and getting stuck would not be too much fun for you or for Mom. The doctors decided that an operation should happen in order to safely take you out of Mom's abdomen.

With Aunt Cindy holding down the fort, mom and I went to the hospital the day the operation was scheduled, and Mom was wheeled into the operating room. I couldn't go in because they told me that I had to wait outside. I didn't like that but I had no choice in the matter. I felt like you must in school sometimes when you must follow the rules, even though you know that the "Cory" way would probably work pretty well.

Something amazing happened next. A few minutes after Mom entered the operating room, she was wheeled out of the operating room because, just as the doctors were about to start the operation, they checked one last time to see where you were inside Mom. Well I guess you were not ready to be born that day because you had shifted at the last minute into the correct position to be born without having an operation.

Mom and I were pretty shocked at what happened. The doctors said that they could not do an operation that was no longer necessary, and that it would be best for you to be born when you were ready. The doctors also said that they had never, ever had this happen before in the history of Community Hospital!

Mom was taken upstairs to a room for awhile to relax and I came with her. After a while, a bottle of wine appeared, with two glasses and a note from the doctors. The note said that they knew it was hard for us to adjust to thinking we were going to have you come into the world that day, and then go home without you being born. The note and bottle of wine meant a lot to me because it kind of said that the doctors really, really cared. I think that it was another "first" in the sense that doctors gave wine to their patient, but in this case it was okay because we only had a very little bit so that you would not feel funny inside Mom.

After a while, we went home and a few weeks later you were born. I'm so glad that you arrived according to your schedule. Although the doctors thought you were late, you were actually right on time. Cory standard time.

What comes next is my showing you the day as I remember it. After I finish, we'll see if it's for reading now or for when you are older.

November 29, 1982

Here we are, Cath. We're leaving for the hospital in a few minutes, but there's no rush. You've been up for quite awhile; on your feet instead of lying or sitting down. You've told me that you know the course of labor and delivery will be much easier if you follow your own instincts. You've done it "their way"; made babies according to the recipe, and now it's time to take what you have learned, and apply it in ways that work for you, discarding what doesn't work at all. You have the luxury of using valuable knowledge in Cory's birth.

We're having a baby! We both know that it is you who must do the physical work, and it's you who occupies the special place of "mother" in our children's lives. We are not the same, but we are here today together in heart and mind and spirit.

There is help available, yet people drifting in and out of our experience seem slightly out of focus and cast in hues less colorful than we as we pass through check in and immediate admittance to a delivery room.

We've arrived at the hospital in the very last stages of labor. No busy work is required of me. Perhaps it never was.

I'm filled with anticipation and joy, and you are beautiful as you hold my hand tight, attending to competently bringing our son into the world.

Doctors and nurses play a supporting role in these intimate moments between us. They are so kind. So respectful of our shared miracle, that speech is reduced to hushed gentle murmurings.

Sunlight streams into the room, bringing nature's gift to meet another.

There is no world outside this room, at this particular time. There is only now, and that is all that matters. A clock on the wall tells us that there must be some need to measure experience. We needed it only to know the moment of our son's arrival.

Cory is ready to make his entrance and arrives in fine condition. He also arrives with his umbilical cord harmlessly wrapped around his neck (a fact only vaguely remembered 10 years later, on overhearing you say this in conversation). Some things are too frightening to recall, and I'm sure I have shut out the moment of terror when I realized the possibility of the horror of losing our son. I remember only the joy of his arrival.

I leave the labor room briefly as I'm sniffling, quickly blow my nose, and return. You mention from time to time, how touched you were by the feeling you saw me display. I can't convince you that my nose was running from purely physical causes. No matter, the tears of heartfelt emotion come as I write today.

I love you Cathy.

I love you, children.

For most men, becoming a father is far more emotional than theoretical. In this reprint of a classic column, Dr. Lawrence Kutner, spurred on by his "first Father's Day" reflects personally on the birth and first year of his son's life. He expresses some of the personal changes that are common to most fathers, such as his connection to all children, to his wife, to mortality, and to his father.

16

Essay for Father's Day

Lawrence Kutner

This is the first year in nearly three decades that I've given more than a passing thought to Father's Day. My own father died when I was 8 years old. Now I am a father. My son, who is less than a year old, is completely unaware of the holiday as he focuses his attention on keeping a spoonful of strained bananas inside his mouth and remembering where his feet are located.

I cannot honestly say that my first year of fatherhood has been blissful. More than anything it's been a humbling experience. Michael isn't the least bit impressed that his father's a psychologist and newspaper columnist. Whenever he sees my columns, he tries to eat them, which makes me wonder whether he'll be an editor when he grows up.

It's had its marvelous moments of course. I wouldn't trade anything for the first time I became convinced that my son actually recognized me and responded with a toothless grin of delight. I loved watching him as he became aware of his own hands and mastered the complexities of sitting up.

I especially remember his birth. Our family physician, who's also a good friend, knew that I had been present at about a dozen other deliveries as a labor coach or television producer. This was my first as a father. Toward the end of labor he looked at me and said, "Larry, go put on a pair of gloves." Under his artful guidance I delivered my son into the world. It was a wonderful way to begin the father–son relationship.

But there have been moments—mostly in the wee hours of the morning—when I felt like I would gladly trade Michael for his weight in potatoes. During our first few weeks together I, the alleged parent–child communication expert, had a great deal of difficulty distinguishing between his cries that confirmed a wet diaper and those that announced impending bladder activity. All too often I would undo his diaper and find him dry, only to have him immediately soak the clothes I was wearing. He appeared to take great glee in this. I was not amused.

There were times when Michael's crying was inconsolable and tested the limits of our patience. My wife and I would revert to tag-team parenting. "I've had it! I need a break! Maybe you can figure out something that will quiet him down." Tag, you're it.

Few fathers openly discuss these feelings of frustration. It's as if we feel ashamed of our imperfections and impatience. We believe, at some level, in the myth of the perfect father—an all-knowing and completely empathic man who can always solve any problem. Such fathers only exist on television.

A friend of mine, who's a nationally known psychologist and the director of a child development research center, once told me that when his children were very young he would sometimes find himself screaming at them, "Grow up! Grow up!" Another friend, who's a child psychoanalyst and was the director of psychiatry training at a major medical center on the east coast, told me during a moment of partic- ular candor how he used to fantasize about strangling his colicky newborn son when the screaming and crying went on for hours. There is a vast difference between occasionally thinking such thoughts and acting on them.

I've also found myself falling into many of the traps that I've written about over the years. All of my training and experience tells me that it doesn't mean anything if a child sits up or rolls over earlier than average. Yet I find myself getting especially excited when this happens. Minor events take on major proportions, "Hey look, Cheryl. He's drooling. And he's doing it so well!"

I also know that babies cry in definite cycles. They're more likely to fuss and scream during the evening than during the day. Many parents who don't understand this pattern become upset when their child's daytime caregiver says what a delight the child has been for 8 hours. The parents bring the child home and are suddenly faced with a screaming baby who refuses to quiet down.

What happened to the delightful child the caregiver described only an hour or 2 earlier? Is your child passing judgment on her parents or providing social commentary on their return to work? It's none of this, of course. It's simply a matter, according to some researchers, of the child getting rid of her accumulated tension from the day.

Even though I know this, and even though I see my child and his caregiver throughout the day since my wife and I work out of offices in our home, I still find it difficult not to take his evening crying personally. I wonder if he's upset because of some flaw in my skills as a parent.

More than anything, this first year of fatherhood has made me feel more like a father to all children. I've helped a few mothers on airplanes who were trying to comfort an upset child, instead of grumbling to myself about the annoyance. I can no longer keep the same level of clinical detachment when I hear about child abuse or crib death. I become furious when I see children standing on the front seat of a moving car instead of being strapped into a car seat.

And I wonder what Michael, who is named after my father, will be like over the years. As I look at him, sucking his thumb in his crib, I realize that he too might become a father. It seems so improbable an image for someone who gets excited at the sight of strained bananas. But that's probably what my father thought when he looked at me.

In this original contribution, Sam Osherson begins with a personal account of the isolation in men's lives. He relates the modern fathers' experiences to those of prior generations and emphasizes the need for intergenerational relating between men.

Dr. Osherson describes a new father's "search for a trustworthy sense of self through a thicket of competing impulses." As he explores the emotional issues for today's new fathers, Dr. Osherson points out the intense struggle of the new father to live up to an "idealized" image of fatherhood that feels impossible to meet. In it's place, he describes an image of fathers that would well serve expectant and long-time fathers. The image he proposes is of a father who is a real person, one who is warm, forgiving and reassuring; a man who understands his clumsiness and embraces it.

17

The "New" Father—and the Old: Understanding the Relational Struggle of Fathers

Sam Osherson

At the end of the film *The Wizard of Oz,* the unseen wizard has made a number of promises to Dorothy that he hasn't kept. All Dorothy knew of the wizard was his booming voice and the impressive spectacles that accompanied all his pronouncements. But then Dorothy becomes aware that the real wizard is hiding behind a curtain and operating the special effects. When she pulls aside the curtain, what does she find? Not a magnificent wizard but a small, balding man.

Infuriated that the wizard hasn't lived up to his promise, Dorothy scolds him: "You're a bad man!" Dorothy's words echo the refrain of so many sons and daughters whose hearts have been broken by their father's inability to keep promises.

The wizard, though, unlike many fathers, stands his ground: "No," he explains. "I'm a good man, just a bad wizard."

To really understand fathers, we have to forgive ourselves for being bad wizards and allow ourselves to be good men.

One sunday afternoon not too long ago, as part of my ongoing research on the changing nature of fatherhood, I spent several hours talking with a group of eight fathers about fatherhood. The men ranged in age from their mid-30s to close to 60. Their children ran the gamut from newborns to young adults, or as one veteran father said, "the stage when you realize you're still a father, and that no child ever completely grows up."

A friend of mine had set up the meeting from among his friends. I had hesitated to ask him, since I was asking for a lot of time from these busy fathers, but my resourceful friend didn't hesitate. "I asked guys from my basketball league," he explained. In the group were a fireman, film maker, several lawyers, a doctor, and a real estate developer.

I was surprised at the energy the men had to tell me about fatherhood, and each man had his own story of what it meant to him to be a father. Common themes united us: the unpreparedness of becoming a father, how much we all strived to protect our children from life, and how vulnerable we felt to their mistakes and experimenting, wanting to be a hero for our children and to be a real person at the same time, sex talks, the way marriage is changed by having children; sometimes for the better and sometimes for the worse. The newer fathers were hungry for information from the more "experienced" fathers, reminding me again how much the transition to fatherhood is a marker event in a man's life.

In my Adult Education courses on adult development I often ask parents to draw on a piece of paper a time line from the year of their birth to the present. Then I'll ask them to place an "A" at the point on the time line when they felt they truly became an adult. More men place an "A" for adult at the time of the birth of their first child than they do when they married or when they graduate college or choose a career.

When our first child is born we truly feel the mantle of responsibility on our shoulders, our choices are suddenly more real. It's a time when we may feel flooded by feelings, recalling the relationship with our own father, questioning what sort of father we will become, wondering what the future holds for our newborn and ourselves. The new father is often plunged back into memories of his own "son-hood" just at the time he is called on to make a developmental advance into his "fatherhood."

The men that I talked with were generous with their time, and there was much shared, good-natured laughter and howls of recognition as we each talked about our experiences. Two hours quickly turned into close to 3 hours.

As we wrapped up, the following exchange occurred: *"It feels good to talk about you and my children. I don't have a chance to do this very often."*

"How often do you talk to other men about fatherhood?" I asked the group.

Silence followed.

"Not really very much at all" was the common agreement.

Ned and Bill, though, were close friends, and Ned disagreed. Gesturing to his buddy Bill, he said, "actually, a lot. . .we call each other about once a month, and usually mention what's going on with our children."

Once a month.

As I drove away, Ned's comment made me think about the loneliness in fathers' lives. For many of us a glancing conversation once a month is a lot of contact about one of the deepest and most profound parts of our lives: being a father. Ned and Bill do better than me: I'm not sure I speak every month with a close friend about the normal, chronic emergencies or profound joys of fatherhood.

That's what made the "focus" group hard for me to leave: I too loved simply the chance to talk to other fathers about their problems, struggles, and confusion. We didn't arrive at many solutions, didn't really need to. There was instead pleasure in our common acknowledgement that it was okay to be a father and not have all the answers. The answers will come, I felt, once we can talk about not having all the answers. Women have known this simple truth for generations; men are just discovering it.

I relate this story because it feels to me that after all the social preoccupation with men over the last year, after several "men's books" on the bestseller list and scores of articles every week in newspapers and magazines on "the men's thing," we often miss the point about fatherhood today.

What I find most exciting about fatherhood these days is not that men are wrestling bare chested to find a "deep masculine" or drumming in men's groups, or that men will retreat to the woods to find their "inner warrior." What is most hopeful, I think, is that fathers often want to talk, and to put their most private and misunderstood experiences into words, their questions about love. Fathers today have a permission, tentative and unsure, but a permission nonetheless to be more emotionally present in their families, rather than having fatherhood defined primarily by the breadwinner/provider role. This is an opportunity denied many of our fathers, and their fathers before them.

In our time of changing sex roles, fatherhood is shaped perhaps most of all by our normal internal struggle with competing impulses and yearnings: to be present and not present in our families, to have our wives to ourselves and to share them with the children, to be similar to and different from our own fathers. Becoming a father can both enrich and transform us, and it can wound at the same time. Fatherhood gives us an opportunity to work out and heal old wounds carried over from our childhood. As a father the love I've felt for my children has been the most intense of my life, as has been the hate. I've heard this over and over from other men. And I know that in helping my children struggle with life I'm reworking my own stuff, over and over. I constantly struggle not to mix me up with them, but also not to distance myself so much from my feelings that I lose touch with their struggles.

One weekend visit not too long after my Sunday focus group, I asked my 78-year-old father how much he had talked about father-ing with his friends when we were all living in the suburbs in the 1950s. He seemed startled by the question: "Hardly at all," he recollected.

My father had friends, he's a sociable man quick with a joke, and he ticked off the names of several men as he thought, most of them now dead.

"We'd ask how the family was when we saw each other, but we didn't talk about those sort of intimate things," he mused. Then my father ventured to say: "Your generation is doing it differently, you have more opportunity to be with your families, to have the sort of intimacy that fathers didn't have when you were growing up. I think that's wonderful."

My heart warmed, at age 46, to hear my father pat me on the back: "You're doing a better job than I was able to."

He seemed warmed, too, by my reply: "You did a fine job, Dad."

The warmth between us, both fathers now, feels like a special gift, after years when my father and I had little to say to each other. Of course, the male dilemma follows us both when we are together—so much seems unsaid, unsayable.

Men these days are wrestling internally with intimacy: the wish to be seen and valued, to be loved and loving in their families. Often both men and women miss this internal battle. Culturally, we have a great deal of difficulty addressing men's relational needs and impulses. Preoccupations with whether or not there is a "men's movement," the focus on more comic aspects of men's groups, the attempts of men to "initiate" themselves in a variety of ways, obscures men's deeper needs today and the real opportunities of this time in our cultural history.

Among many of the men I know, the men's groups I've been a part of or observed, men want to talk about basic, simple relationship issues, the stuff that makes or breaks our individual lives. Often the opportunities and demands of being a father are foremost among the topics that men want to explore, often hesitantly, shyly perhaps, but explore nonetheless. The stereotypical image of a men's groups is a bunch of guys drumming, chanting, and wrestling as they strive to find mythic aspects of masculinity. Yet these activities don't represent what generally happens when men sit down to talk: at most groups men focus on basic, concrete life issues. Expectant fathers worry about what kind of fathers they're going to be after the birth of their first child. Dads of teenagers come in stumped as to how to defuse the tensions with their kids. *"I bark at my kids,"* one father said, *"it keeps me from biting them."* And he concludes: *"But how do I draw them closer if I only know how to bark?"* Men may worry that their fathers or mothers will die before things are worked out. For some men fathers have died before things have been worked out; a man may wonder how to put matters to rest, perhaps feeling he's been left holding the bag. Men will complain they don't feel like a real man in the family. *A successful architect father once said: "Women just don't understand the loneliness of men, our need to stake a claim in the world and prove ourselves."*

Some confess that they're scared their wives will leave them before they've worked things out.

These concerns reflect the changed world men live in today, different from the world of our fathers and mothers, different even from the world of 25 years ago. For example, family life has changed dramatically for men. The proportion of family work performed by men rose from 20% to 34% from 1965 to 1985, according to a careful review of a variety of academic research studies by sociologist Joseph Pleck.

More importantly, the very definition of what it means to be a good father has shifted from primarily the provider/ breadwinner role to more ambiguous expectations of emotional involvement and responsiveness. How do men today manage the costs of giving up the hero role and being the emotional provider, not just the financial one? What are the costs as well as the benefits to women of these changes? *One savvy woman executive said to me: "There's a price we pay when our husbands become more involved in the family—we lose that sense of being the Good Mommy for everyone."*

Women have identified the pain and loss that comes from not living up to impossible "SuperMom" expectations, whereas men have just begun to address the conflicting expectations involved in trying to be "SuperDad." Although we hear much criticism of men for not participating enough in their families, I find in my work that many men carry around oppressive performance expectations of what they have to do to be good enough as a father. Feeling like they're supposed to be able to earn the primary family income, support their wives emotionally, be encouraging of their children while still being traditional authorities in the family, all without any confusion, uncertainty or resentment, many men get more and more withdrawn and isolated from the very families they care very much about. Many men feel a loss about how things were with their fathers and try do better as fathers themselves but that's an open-ended task in the absence of realistic models. The result is that they feel that they're never really successful in their family. *One 30-year-old father who had lived through the painful divorce of his parents when he was a young teenager once lamented: "I didn't get all that much from my father, how am I supposed to give to my kids?"*

Relationships with aging parents are also a source of real, often unacknowledged pain for many men. According to a recent Gallup poll, 1 in 4 adult children feel emotionally distant from their fathers. Sizeable proportions describe their relationship with fathers as "tense" (21%), "cold and restrained" (20%), and "boring" (18%). Many of these men are grown children of divorce, who feel wounded and abandoned by fathers who have lost touch with their families after the breakup of their marriages.

Not all grown men are angry at their fathers—many men deeply love both their parents and wonder how to show their love in a time of changing gender roles. *One man, feeling pressured by his father to go into the family hardware business, remarked: "The only way to show my father how much I love him is to make the same choices he has made, but I don't want to live a life exactly like his—how do I be different and still his son?"*

In the old days, one imagines, men lived similar lives to their fathers, working hard and becoming the breadwinners and authority figures in families. In this way a son expressed his love for and loyalty to his father, and felt like a worthy son. These days fathers and grown sons often need to talk, to clear up the normal misunderstandings and disappointments that haunt the father–son relationship. At one weekend retreat a 38-year-old son and 65-year-old father confronted a painful moment of alienation 10 years earlier: the son had recently been divorced, the first divorce ever in the family, and—ashamed and disappointed in himself and his wife—went home to his mother and father for Thanksgiving hoping for a sign that he was still OK, still loved by his parents despite what he felt was his "failure." Alone with his father, he started to talk about the end of the marriage, only to watch his father turn on the TV set to watch the Packers–Lions football game, a family tradition. The son shut up and didn't mention his divorce again. Ten years went by until father and son, at the retreat, could talk about how the father had felt so bad for his son and didn't know what to say and so had turned on the familiar, comforting football game, while the son had felt rejected and worthless. Not knowing what to say either, he stopped talking to his father.

A search for reconciliation between men and their fathers often marks adult life as each age. This search can end prematurely for both men, leaving a son feeling that his father, in the words of poet Seamus Heaney (1988, p. 8), "keeps stumbling/Behind me, and will not go away."

Mothers, too, are often a source of unfinished business for grown men. There is so much writing about men and their fathers these days, much less about men and their mothers. Yet I must confess that after years of leading workshops on, and writing about, the father–son relationship, it strikes me that men's profound love for their mothers is one of the hidden secrets of our lives. Boys have to separate very precipitously from their mothers in order to feel as if they're "living up" as men. Often men are frightened of their tender feelings, perceiving them as too "feminine" and have difficulty knowing how to express their love for their mothers. We may fear becoming too "maternal" ourselves in our families, or with other men—and thus get angry at women for reminding us of our hidden attachment to our mothers. The protestations about the "deeper masculine" and men's pain with their fathers, and our need for men's groups away from women, may mask our fear of and resentment about how important our mothers are in our lives. *As one man once said in the midst of a weekend retreat on men's unfinished business with their fathers: "This is all great, but it feels as if my mother is sitting here on my shoulder, saying, 'what about me?'"*

Mothers will likely recognize themselves in some of these struggles: how to balance divided loyalties to work and family, to oneself and others, to parents and self, spouse and self, to the past and the future. In reality mothers and fathers share many common struggles today. It's not easy to feel beloved and loving today, that we're doing a good-enough job as a parent; neither gender is a Master of Intimacy, with oneself or others.

No one likes to feel that he or she is not "living up." For a man, to live up often means to have the answer, to be in control, to know what to do. The ideal image for a father may be of Ward Cleaver in "Leave It to Beaver," or brave Odysseus reclaiming his wife Penelope and his son Telemachus after returning from heroic deeds at war, (or the office), or of Lord Chesterfield who can give sage advice to a son who seems to want it, or of some other superhero who knows what to do and does it. Not to know for a man often brings embarrassment and shame, thrown back into unhappy feelings of being little and perhaps defective.

Recognizing how on the spot a man can feel in just saying that he doesn't know, doesn't understand, can be helpful and can cut through a lot of male avoidant behavior designed to mask moments when we feel inadequate. A man may feel quite on the spot right in the privacy of his family, whether it is being unable to comfort a crying baby enough to get him or her to stop, or in how to really say goodbye to a son or daughter going off to college, or how to manage the mix of abandonment, pride, and confusion that marks our experience when a wife goes off to work after 20 years of being a "Mom." *I always expected any wife of mine would work, I just never expected it to be like this." This was admitted by one savvy lawyer, who prides himself on supporting his working wife. Paul, for example, is a successful stockbroker whose wife, Mary, went to work after the kids were in high school. As she brought in her own income, the entire arrangement of the marriage began to change, including Mary's open and understandable yearning that Paul become more emotionally responsive and "talk about his feelings." Paul, who prided himself on being the competent man about the house now found himself in entirely new territory, one very different from the emotional terrain he had explored in 20 years of being the "strong, silent" provider and breadwinner. "I walk in the door and I know Mary wants something from me," he confesses. "I want to run and get a newspaper to hide behind. I feel so goofy when she looks at me."*

Women can understand how excruciating the feeling of not living up can be. For a mother, not to live up may mean feeling not nurturing or caretaking, not being the all-giving mother of our dreams. Often women are reluctant to show men their pain at choosing careers over family demands, at not being able to be perfectly successful at the "mommy track" as well as "the career track."

When men do feel in danger of being exposed as "inadequate," we try to puff up and defend ourselves by acting bigger, more threatening, or confident than we really feel. Bob, for example, is a father and business executive who confronted a changing family as his wife went back to graduate school after his children applied for college. "The house seemed lonelier than I can ever remember it," he observed to me one day. His adolescent children also tested him in a new way, particularly his 17-year-old son, Steve. Steve strained his father's emotional resilience by waffling for a long time about college applications, studying just hard enough to pass his courses but not to graduate with the honors his father hoped for, yet at the same time clearly wanting his father's attention. All this was very difficult for Bob, who had learned to think of himself as a high-powered executive who can get things done. Having so long thought of his contributions mainly in terms of protecting and providing, Bob wondered if he still had anything worthwhile to offer his family. As his own sense of "manliness" and self- worth became diminished, Bob retreated to his company's jet. He spent much of his week flying around the country in the jet, Nixon-like, attending important meetings and doing highly competitive "manly" work. At the very time he felt most vulnerable in his family he became the most hypermasculine at work, almost as if pleading with life that yes, I am indeed a powerful man who can get things done, who doesn't live at the whim of others.

Many male behaviors that imply distance and aggression are actually ways that men and boys learn to cope with that most basic of male dilemmas: how to connect with those we love without losing our self-esteem as men? A familiar sports scene: athletes competing with and beating up on each other, only to end with embraces, high fives, arms on shoulders and bodies intertwined.

In many families, aggression and closeness are bound together. For example, wrestling with dad or taunting or provoking him may be the best way for the little boy to get his attention. The 5 year old who jumps on a tired father who has just walked in the door; the 14 year old who berates his father about world events; the 25 year old who tries to beat his father on the tennis court! Each act is not just a competitive aggressive attack on a father but also an attempt to enliven or vitalize him, to get him out of his bubble of adult preoccupation. A wrestling match with dad—in whatever form it takes—is a way of wrapping oneself up in the father's arms and still feeling okay about oneself as a male.

Given men's tendency to act out and externalize their wishes to be caring and loving, as fathers we may wind up speaking a coded language about love that our families often don't understand and that we cannot translate for them. *One bemused father once said, reflecting on his children's accusation that he doesn't really love them: "How can they say I don't love them? If love is defined by what I do, of course I love them."* He meant that his hard work, his providing, were his way of showing his love for his family, the traditional way of protecting and providing by which men have expressed their love through the generations. Yet his family saw him only as silent and preoccupied, as unloving and disinterested in them.

Yet women are not the sole caretakers of relationships. Fathers are immensely important figures shaping the self-esteem and well-being of children. *The father of an adolescent daughter once explained to a group of parents why he calls home from business trips and talks to his wife but not his daughter: "She's into boys, dating, dressing up. Teenage girl stuff that her mother seems to know so much more about." Whereupon a mother who knew the pain of her father's withdrawal when she was young advised him: "When you're a teenage girl, others may have information but fathers provide the affirmation."* The affirmation of husbands is often crucial to the success of dual-career marriages: one of the primary correlates of a wife's marital satisfaction is her perception of her husband's empathy for and support of her choices about work and mothering. In the workplace, I have heard over and over how important supportive male mentors are for young women trying to make it in professional careers. Mentoring young men and women is a relatively unexplored way for older men to experience "fathering" the young, freed from some of the pressures and disappointments of the nuclear family.

BECOMING A FATHER

A struggle with intimate possibilities is often very intense for the new father. He may try to live up to an "idealized" image of fatherhood that feels impossible to meet. He draws on memories of his own father and mother, perhaps wondering how to combine close participation in his family with the demands of "providing" and career achievement. He may experience the painfully mixed sense of love and anger toward the newborn who has so much changed his life. The transition to fatherhood may be the first time a man struggles overtly with the painful sense of resenting the very being we also dearly love. Issues of shame, hope, and love are almost of crisis proportion for the new father.

We live in a time with many contradictory demands on men—that we be open with our feelings but also able to get the job done, that we be expressive but also stoic, be gentle but also strong and able to protect and defend. Gloria Emerson (1985, p. 2) has observed the mixed cultural expectations men live with today: *"At a time when women, with good reason, are asking men to make known their most guarded feelings, when we want them to love and raise babies and remember our birthdays, it is also required that they be the ones to rescue people in a burning building, and startle the dragons when they are heard in the dark."*

How's a father to make sense of these mixed expectations? We have images of wildmen with hair down to their feet, of fires in men's bellies, of mythic heros and of androgenous men. There's value in each of these, I suppose, but for me they all lack an image of men as merely human beings, an image warm, forgiving, and reassuring. For me the image of the involved father today would start with an image of clumsiness. *A father and son, one 60 and the other 40, once explained why they came 300 miles to a weekend workshop on "Men, Women, and Their Fathers: Unfinished Business," after years of alienation between them, "Because my son and I are trying to learn a new dance, how to dance together, he and I. The women in our family are graceful dancers, they know how to do this. My son and I need a place where we can be clumsy together."*

So do fathers and daughters, so do fathers and mothers.

As we all learn this new fathering dance perhaps we can allow ourselves to be clumsy as well as graceful.

A Coming-To-Birth Song

Oh baby, swinging in Heaven's cradle
Oh baby, swinging in the breeze
Oh baby, come down to Your momma and pappa
I thought I heard an angel sneeze

Oh baby, swinging in your starry cradle
Oh baby, living in Heaven's limelight
Oh baby, come down to your momma and pappa
Do we feed your tiny body right?

Oh baby, do you know the love that's waiting?
Oh baby, do you know the love that's here?
Oh baby, there's three of us in this together
It's your first birthday Party and you got nothing to wear

—David Debus

It is expected that in the process of becoming a father, a man will become increasingly in touch with the manner in which he was fathered as a child. During this inevitable psychological reconnection, many expectant and new fathers become increasingly aware of a suffering from a lack of adequate fathering or a deeper wound. In this poignant chapter, Joseph Pleck, relying on both his personal history and research explores this father wound and its implications for every man becoming a father. His conclusion that the child be allowed to heal the expectant father is perhaps the most powerful way for men to enter into the realm of fathering.

18

The Father Wound: Implications for Expectant Fathers

Joseph H. Pleck

Recently, I was stunned to learn that long before he died, my father had two heart attacks that he kept secret from his family, including my mother. They both occurred on business trips. He extended the trips, swore his business friends to secrecy. The secret came out to his family only 20 years after he died. He never faced up to how sick he was. To him, illness was a sign of weakness, something to be denied.

I lived my first 5 years during what was probably the time of the greatest security and happiness in my father's life. In his early 50's, he was increasingly successful in his work (the law) and his health was still good. In his office, he kept a framed set of photographs of his four children. I am about 3, sitting, holding a ball. My oldest brother (who just turned 60) is a teen. These photos seemed to capture a moment in his life that he wanted to keep; he never updated them.

But things did change. I was about 5 and he was about 55 when he had his first heart attack. Although he kept it a secret, I think I knew something had changed. He stopped picking me up to hug me when he came home from work. Perhaps he felt physically weak, or feared the exertion of picking me up would bring on another attack. He had a second heart attack at 60, again a secret he kept to himself. He developed painful calcifications in his shoulders, and in the last years, a golf-ball-sized cyst on his neck.

210

During his last several years, he looked so bad that after he died, my mother destroyed all the pictures taken of him then. About a year before he died, when I was a high-school freshman, I told a teacher that I knew my father would not live to see me graduate. It must have been terribly apparent, though never openly acknowledged, how sick he was.

In this period, he seemed to feel increasingly embittered by how his health, his family, and the world itself were changing around him. He spent his last years working full time on a case involving highly technical engineering matters that he never really understood, something terribly difficult and frustrating to him. He seemed to work all the time. He became chronically irritable and depressed, undergoing what textbooks call the "personality changes of later life." Perhaps he was having small strokes in his hardened arteries toward the end. Those years, when I was an adolescent, were hard for the family.

He also began drinking much more. I clearly remember his telling me when I was about 11 (which I now know to be sometime after the second heart attack) that his doctor had said if he stopped drinking he would live another 20 years, but if he continued drinking he would only live 5 years. I wanted to stop his drinking, but I couldn't. He in fact died suddenly just 4 years later, when he was 64 and I was 15.

Recently I've learned about some of the hurts and disappointments of his life. Growing up in a small town, German-Irish Catholic culture in the upper Midwest, he went to Chicago and became a partner in a major Chicago law firm in the 1920s. In any organization, before there is the first black, the first woman, and the first Jew, there is always the first Catholic. In most of the organizations and institutions he was involved with, he was it. Breaking out of the Catholic ghetto brought obvious rewards, but it also exacted some terrible costs.

My father worked in his own father's ice cream business until he was 18 and went to college. I remember him talking about his own father only once, describing him as "a good man, a good man, but he was a Prussian, he was strict. It wasn't that he refused to give me a vacation from making ice cream every day of my life, it just never occurred to him that a boy might not want to make ice cream every day, it just never occurred to him."

His voice expressed not so much resentment as an almost unbearable sadness. He left his family with a strong desire to succeed.

He and his family suffered some terrible losses. His older brother, Edward, the family's first child, died of a skull puncture in infancy, after several days of excruciating and grotesque head swelling. My grandfather, a tragically inexperienced new father, had playfully thrown him up in the air in a hallway without noticing the hanging lamp overhead. My father, born next thereafter, had a heavy burden as his replacement. Two younger siblings (Clifford and Alice) died of scarlet or rheumatic fever in infancy. (This was small-town Wisconsin in the early 1900s). In those days before telephones came to such communities, my father, as a teen, was the one sent to get the doctor, to get the priest, as they wasted away.

Another brother, Howard, with whom he was particularly close died at age 14 of influenza in the great flu pandemic of 1917, when my father was in college. Shortly before, my father had a premonitory dream, completely accurate in every detail, of the scene in his room when he received the telegram notifying him of Howard's death. This must have been a devastating loss. When I was a child (nearly five decades later), on more than one occasion at the kitchen table or in the living room, I remember Dad talking about Howard, and reading aloud to us, sobbing, the poem at the end of Thomas Merton's *The Seven-Storey Mountain* in which Merton says good-bye to his own brother who had died young ("Goodnight, dear brother, the stars weep for you as my tears . . .").

Such experiences of child death may seem almost incredible today, but they were not so uncommon then. Several years ago, after my own son was born, I came across the German lyrics to Brahms' "Wiegenlied" (or "Cradle Song"). Written only a decade or two before my father's time, it was no doubt the most popular lullaby in the German-American culture of my father's youth. It appears in every children's songbook today, but the words in current song books are not the original ones. In my father's time, its refrain was:

If God will, thou shalt wake
When morning doth break,
If God will, thou shalt wake
When morning doth break.

In my father's time, when you went to bed at night, you knew that before morning your children could be gone. It had happened before.

Dad was terribly concerned about child injury. I remember how he made himself a pest at school baseball games trying to get the players to drop the bat on the ground when they got a hit, rather than throw the bat wildly through the air as they usually did in their excitement, because it could hit someone in the head. Others seemed to regard him as a killjoy who was interrupting the fun. He would permit only a hand-powered lawn mower, because a gas mower could too easily cut off your toes. I am sure that every demand he made like this (and there were many others) was based on direct personal experience.

Once when I was about 10, I became very sick, vomiting uncontrollably all night and running a high fever. The next morning Dad told me that all night he had been certain that I would die (just like, I now know, his siblings). In therapy many years later, I re-experienced this incident, and recognized how deep his fear must have been. He was fatalistically convinced that I, his youngest child and the one he named after himself, would die just as his siblings had. The realization of how deeply he must have feared losing me broke me up. Perhaps his fear of losing me (and mine of losing him) was what the tension between us during my adolescence and his last years was really about.

He was greatly interested in literature and music, and when he was in college had aspired to be a college professor (of economics), but he felt a professor couldn't make enough to support a family. (Also, even as late as the 1920s, Catholics were discouraged from academic life; they were thought not to be intellectually free, totally enslaved as they were by the Pope.) Of his daily ride on the commuter train as a lawyer in the 1950s, he said: "If everyone else is reading the newspaper, you do not read a book." I remember him spending several years reading *War and Peace,* a few pages a day, at home, secretly.

He and I felt closest around music. He played the piano a bit, and I took after him. My involvement in music seemed to express a repressed part of himself. When I showed some talent, he wanted to take me to audition for professional study at a local conservatory. He especially liked to walk around in the back yard during the summer listening to the sounds of my piano practicing coming through the back windows.

As I was preparing a speech about 5 years ago, the lyrics of a song (to the melody of an Irish dirge I heard once on the radio) came to me. The experience of receiving them was extremely powerful, and something gave me the courage to sing them later that day, unaccompanied, at the end of a keynote address at a Men and Masculinity Conference:

Here's to our fathers, so deeply connected,
We know you in so many different ways.
Sometimes we think of the times we didn't have,
For we honor the future by mourning the past.

You never meant to hurt me, Dad,
But there were times you did so much.
After the last, worst time I cried myself to sleep,
When, the next day, you were gone forever.

Here's to you, my own dear father,
I know your life had such sorrow and grief.
Still, many times, I take strength from you,
And deep in my heart, I see you again.

It is important to be aware that there are *two* deep psychological shifts related to fatherhood taking place in many men today. First, as illustrated by other essays in this volume, men are discovering their own capacity to father, with the period of expectant fatherhood and new fatherhood as particularly critical periods in the discovery process. Second, many men are experiencing a *father wound:* profound distance, pain, and sadness about their relationship to their own fathers. These two "paternal shifts" are psychologically interconnected in complex ways. Here, to complement the understanding of expectant fatherhood offered in this volume, I offer a perspective on the father wound, and consider its implications for expectant fathers.

My file, clipped from magazines and books, of sons' poignant and bittersweet recollections of their relationships with their fathers grows steadily. Even in the *New York Times'* "About Men" column, usually devoted to either nostalgic longing for the good old days when sexism went unchallenged, or upbeat advice on upscale male grooming, such articles appear occasionally.

Psychotherapist Jack Sternbach, analyzing the father–son relationship in 71 male clients, found five subgroups: father physically absent (23%); father psychologically absent due to being too busy, not interested, passive (29%); father psychologically absent due to being austere, moralistic, unemotional (18%); father dangerous, frightening, crazy (15%). Sadly, in only 15% of Sternbach's cases was the father classified as appropriately involved, with some history of nurturance or positive connection. More sadly, the proportion of men reporting good relationships with their fathers was even lower in two other surveys (cf. Arcana, 1983; Hite, 1981).

The central argument of Ochberg's (1987) recent study is that father–son dynamics in childhood and adolescence often lead to a longing for affection, fear of humiliation, and fantasies of vengeance against the father, often expressed in repetitive, destructive behavior that continues even into the middle years. Many in this study describe poignantly their feelings of waiting in vain for a paternal blessing. Mike said. "I can tell him to his face that I love him for what he is—my Dad—and I can't get that through his fucking head. . . . He will never recognize me for what I am—his son." Ken remarked, "The thing that will always bother me as long as I live is never having had my Dad say that I have done a good job with the business. And he will never say that, to the day he croaks." (p. 143)

Perhaps these descriptions are one-sided; Harold Isaacs (1978) and Zick Rubin (1982) warn us that fathers' descriptions of these relationships are rarely heard, and may be quite different. Some men are truly fortunate to have a good relationship with their father. Nonetheless, it is clear that many men's experience (and women's, too, but I write here of men) is of an injuring and wounding father, a father who is often himself terribly wounded. So many describe fathers who are psychologically wounded, often literally physically disabled. At the cultural level, the wounded father is one of the great themes. Feminism, too, has made us aware, perhaps not always with sufficient compassion, of the sexism and homophobia that have crippled so many of our fathers. Confrontation with the "father wound" is a profound, increasingly common, yet still largely unspoken, experience in men's lives today. Men are asking themselves what their legacy from their fathers really is. Is it one only of tragic defects, or does it, can it include more?

The wounds of men are the wounds of fathers and sons. The grief of men is the grief of fathers and sons. Can the problems of the father–son relationship be the paradigm for the flaws in male culture itself? In listening to men talk about their fathers, I sometimes hear eerie echoes of conversations I have had with women who have given up on men, who have come to feel totally cut off from men, who utterly despair of the possibility of change in men. The words are so similar.

In the lives of fathers and sons, universal issues necessarily take unique shape in particular cultures. Every country has its own "father history." In the U.S., this history is only beginning to be explored, containing both positive motifs that are little known, and negative themes that are often stunning in their concreteness. Family historians have called attention, for example, to Alexis DeTocqueville's praise for the father–son relationship he witnessed in America in the 1830s:

In proportion as manners and laws become more democratic, the relationship of father and son becomes more intimate and more affectionate; rules and authority are less talked of, confidence and tenderness are often increased. (Degler, 1980, p. 75)

Consistent with DeTocqueville's observation, the diaries and correspondence of the Northern middle class in the late eighteenth and early nineteenth centuries frequently reveals a strong emotional connection between father and son, more so than between mother and son. Young or newly born sons were commonly described by their fathers as "my hope" or "my consolation." In 1794, Timothy Pickering wrote his son, John, of the "tenderness with which I love you." "Can any one love you better than I?" he asked the boy. Teenaged boys serving apprenticeships, and young men on their own, maintained contact with their family primarily through letters to and from their fathers (Rotundo, 1982, 1983). These relationships seem striking in light of today's pattern (which we too easily accept as a trans-historical universal) that the bond between males and their mothers is invariably stronger than their tie to their fathers.

But disturbing themes are evident in our "father history" as well. Consider this entry from the diary of Cotton Mather (Demos, 1982), the influential Massachusetts cleric most known for his active support of the Salem witch trials in the 1690s:

> *I took my little daughter Katy into my study and there I told my child that I am to die shortly, and she must, when I am dead, remember everything that I said unto her. I set before her the sinful and woeful condition of her nature, and I charged her to pray in secret places every day without ceasing that God for the sake of Jesus Christ would give her a new heart. . . .I gave her to understand that when I am taken from her she must look to meet with more humbling afflictions than she does now [when] she has a careful and tender father to provide for her. (p. 426)*

Mather was young and in excellent health at the time. The religious ideology of America's colonial beginnings established a long-persisting legacy in our culture that has wounded fathers and children alike.

In the nineteenth century, temperance and other social reform movements made the "bad father" a figure of popular discussion. Late nineteenth-century fiction gave considerable attention to the alcoholic, violent father who abused his wife and children, and to fathers who deserted their children, leaving them to founder in poorhouses. Historian John Demos also notes an "overflowing" prescriptive and fictional literature concerned with fathers who treat their sons in a "cold, indifferent, and authoritative manner," leading to resentment in the son, only causing greater rigidity and irritation in the father.

In some of these stories (Demos, 1982), the father accepts helpful advice to adopt a "softer" tone, but others end less happily. In one story discussed by Demos, a father imposes on his timid and sickly son a harsh regime of physical toughening—mostly outdoors, in wintertime, and late at night. Eventually the child dies, as much from "terror of his natural protector" as from overexposure and overexertion. In another, the father comes home "wearied and vexed" after his day's labor, and finds his son covered with dirt and grime. He "taxes and scolds" the boy severely, only to learn later that the dirt resulted from the performance of a good deed. The boy contracts pneumonia and dies before the father can make amends (p. 439).

Middletown, Robert and Helen Merrill Lynd's (1929) classic study of an American community in the mid-1920s, includes a snapshot of the father–child relationship the Midwestern small town of the early twenthieth century—what today's "pro-family" conservatives view as the ideal model for contemporary family life. "I'm a rotten dad," lamented one of Middletown's fathers. "If our children amount to anything it's their mother who'll get all the credit. I'm so busy I don't see much of them and I don't know how to chum up with them when I do."

Another Middletown father said: "You know, I don't know that I spend any time having a good time with my children, and it hit me all in a heap. . . . And the worst thing is, I don't know how to. I take my children to school in the car each morning; *there* is some time we could spend together, but I just spend it thinking about my own affairs and never make an effort to do anything with them." (p. 9)

The early part of this century gave us the normative conception of fatherhood that continues to be the dominant one today: father as psychologically absent and distant breadwinner.

Though I was born in the late 1940s, my own father was born in the 1890s—not one, but two generations before mine. I recently rediscovered the few surviving pages from a notebook of quotations he copied from the books he read. They gave me a profound insight into both my father and the culture of masculinity he grew up in. I found this passage from Romain Rolland's *Jean-Christophe,* a multivolume biographical novel about a composer, loosely based on the life of Beethoven, which won its author the Nobel Prize for Literature in 1915:

He saw that life was a battle without armistice, without mercy, in which he who wishes to be a man worthy of the name of a man must forever fight against whole armies of invisible enemies; against the

murderous forces of nature, uneasy desires, dark thoughts, treacher-
ously leading him to degradation and destruction. He saw that he
had been on the point of falling into the trap. He saw that happiness
and love were only the friends of a moment to lead the heart to
disarm and abdicate. And he heard the voice of God:

Go, go, and never rest!
But whither, Lord, shall I go?
Whatsoever I do, whithersoever I go, is not the end always the same?
Go on to Death, you who must die!
Go and suffer, you who must suffer.
You do not live to be happy. You live to fulfill my Law.
Suffer; die. But be what you must be—a Man. (p. 282)

When as an early adolescent I began to read real books, and asked
my father for suggestions, he told me *Jean-Christophe* was the book
that meant the most to him when he was young, and gave me his copy.
I think he re-read it several times as an adult, secretly, like the other
books.

In the same notebook, I found Robert Louis Stevenson's "A Prayer":

The day returns and brings us the petty round of irritating con-
cerns and duties. Help us to play the man, help us to perform them
with laughter and kind faces, let cheerfulness abound with industry.

Give us to go blithely on our business all this day, bring us to our
resting beds weary and content and undishonored, and grant us in
the end the gift of sleep. Amen.

On the same page is this from *King Lear:* "When we are born, we
cry that we are come to this stage of fools."

Many think that our culture has recognized the dark side of masculinity only in the last decade or two, and because of feminism. In reality,
in my father's time the darkness and risk of manhood was a profound
realization, indeed, the central meaning of being a man, to be overcome only with a world-weary, depressed stoicism. Manhood was not
a privilege, but a burden whose only releases were sleep and death,
and the latter usually with dishonor. Only the lucky and the few did
not succumb to masculinity's "uneasy desires and dark thoughts."

In a familiar mythic pattern, the father acts to bring his sons into
adulthood. This might seem the central father–son myth, but themes
of wounding and wounded fathers, who must be healed by their sons,
are equally if not more evident in ancient and contemporary cultural

images. Many of these have a positive resolution, showing the wish for healing. In the central mystery of the Grail myth, for example, the wounded King lies ill and the kingdom languishes until he is made whole by the virtuous acts of a knight-son who is spiritually pure.

Robert Redford's film *The Natural* (based on a story by Bernard Malamud) tells the oddly similar tale of a disgruntled, depressed, old manager of a losing baseball team, who is about to be cheated out of his ownership share by his unscrupulous partners. His nickname, not accidentally, is "Pops." But he and the team are saved by the son-figure's miraculous performances, deriving from his purity ("natural"-ness). As in the Grail myth, the son's purity is manifested by his avoidance of "bad" women and his attachment to "good" ones.

Watching a late-night movie recently, I was startled to see an only slightly disguised variation of the same theme in Frank Capra's Depression-era classic, *Mr. Smith Goes to Washington.* James Stewart portrays a naive young senator, elected largely because he is the son of an admired newspaper editor much mourned after his untimely death. Through his innocent integrity, he reforms the distinguished, respected, but secretly corrupt senator (Claude Rains) whom the evil political organization is using to manipulate him.

George Lucas' *Star Wars* trilogy, writes Joseph Campbell (1984), "contains a mythological theme, which is the same as that in Goethe's *Faust:* Are the machine and the machine maker going to dominate the human spirit, or is the human spirit going to be served by the machine? Luke Skywalker and his father, Darth Vader, represent the two positions. The father has capitulated to the machine and has become robotized; the son will not capitulate. He rescues his father." Campbell is right about the healing, but he gets the connection backwards. The father is not the symbol of the evil machine; the machine is the symbol of the wounding, unwhole father.

In other images, and in real life, the resolution is not so positive; the father–son confrontation ends with the father, and the relationship, left forever unhealed. In the pivotal moment in Arthur Miller's *Death of a Salesman,* for example, following scene after scene of father–son recriminations and self-inflicted wounds, Biff rejects his father (Willy Loman) after he learns his father visits prostitutes. Clearly the outstanding work of the American stage in the 1950s, its continued appeal today is attested by its recent successful revival on Broadway in a new production starring Dustin Hoffman.

Such personal accounts as Jim Covington's *Confessions of a Single Father* (1982) and Jed Diamond's *Inside Out: Becoming My Own*

Man (1983) poignantly portray both the opportunities and limits of reconciliation with the father, in their cases alcoholic or derelict. One man wrote me after a workshop I gave on "Healing the Wounded Father": "I was frustrated with myself that the depths of my own emotions seemed too deep to plumb there. I had already cried over how unbridgeable seems the chasm between myself and my own father. Indeed, I am advised that I should make no attempt, that attempt being too dangerous in view of a history of serious physical abuse until adolescence and psychological abuse since." But he goes on: "Nevertheless, for whatever reasons, I want at least to try to talk with my father."

So, too, do so many other men today.

A friend in his early 40's cried telling me about his visit to his elderly father following his father's stroke. Their relationship had always been difficult, but it had gotten better in recent years. My friend was worried about his father's health, and had looked forward to the visit. But his father had a nervous habit, made worse by the stroke, of constantly changing the TV station with the remote control device while the family tried to watch television together. When my friend asked him to stop, his father threw the control box hard at his face, inflicting a deep cut over his eye; hitting an inch lower, it would have blinded him. My friend left the family home immediately, vowing to never see his father again. Another friend, rebuffed by his father, said, weeping: "If my father saw a dog lying on the sidewalk bleeding, he would stop to do something. But his own son, he would step over."

Perhaps the most painful stories I have heard of men trying to connect to their fathers—and painfully failing—are the ones gay men friends have told me.

What can anyone say to these men? Of course, many men have always had good relationships with their fathers, or as adults have developed better relationships with them. When father–son relationships are difficult or distant, they of course do not always reach these depths. But when they do, there seem to be two paths that men follow. Some men come to view their fathers with compassion, to see them as more wounded than wounding (Pleck, 1987). It is too simple to say that their knowledge of the circumstances of their father's own life exonerates their father's acts, or leads them to forgive their fathers. Such terms may be inadequate and inaccurate, but somehow the son seems able to let go of his hurt, to unlock himself from acting only out of his pain about his father, to see something sustaining in his connection with him.

Other men, like my two friends, have finalized their relationship with their father at much greater distance, with considerably less positive feeling. I feel it presumptuous to evaluate them as any less "forgiving," or their stance as any less "resolved." Who can judge another man's feelings about his father? At least for now, they have simply stopped trying to find a more positive connection.

Attempting to heal a relationship with one's father is not without pitfalls. This attempt can be physically or emotionally dangerous, as my friends' experience testifies. Reconciliation with the father also risks being superficial, as Judith Arcana notes. After all, haven't men always been taught to pretend that the standard father/son arrangement is fine? No, you didn't mind not seeing Dad; you didn't miss him, he wasn't supposed to be there anyway; you didn't feel his discipline was too harsh, his demands too uncompromising; that's what a father is for.

Arcana (1983) writes of the further risk that the son's reconciliation with the father can serve to rationalize the son's own adult sexism, the ways he has now come to realize he is similar to his father. "Grown sons think they need to excuse their fathers, so that they can love them, and want to excuse them so that they, as men themselves, may be excused" (p. 177, 181). Although these and the other risks can be genuine ones for some men, they do not make sons' search for healing in their paternal bonds inherently illegitimate.

The title of Robert Bly's well-known *New Age* interview asks: "What do men really want?" At least one answer is clear: the unwounded, healed, whole father. Men—and women—want this not only for what it would mean for their fathers' lives, but also for themselves. To Bly, you must grieve for your father before you can grieve for yourself.

What to do? We have to help heal our real fathers' actual wounds when we can, and to realize honestly when we cannot. We need to heal the so-often destructive and alienated images of masculinity that surround us, the wounded father-images of our culture. Most important, we have to heal the wounded father so many of us carry in our hearts.

When you become an expectant father, your father wound inevitably becomes sensitized. I wrote many sections of this chapter before becoming a father myself. Then, I rewrote and added material simultaneously as our son Daniel was born and blossomed in our lives. In many ways, writing about the father wound was part of the preparation I needed to do to be a dad. Sam Osherson (1987, 1992) and others have written of the reparative or restitutive process in men's parenthood. I would add these points from my own experience.

Expectant fathers often say they feel that they don't really have any positive model from their own father about how to be a father. Perhaps every expectant father who has this sense experiences it a little differently. I encountered it in the following way.

Being an expectant father and being involved with a birth made me feel, at a deep emotional level, the "miracle of life." The triteness of the phrase has perhaps desensitized us to the reality that birth, indeed, is a miracle. One day I realized that perhaps even more miraculous than physical birth is the mystery of psychological attachment. Birth stimulates a process in which the infant "attaches" to a parent or parents, and parents "attach" to their newborn. This mutual attachment signifies psychological birth. A fear I had as an expectant father was that I would somehow fail to attach. I found myself wondering whether my father had ever really attached to me, and if he hadn't, how would I be able to? Of course, when Daniel was born, my engrossment in him was astonishingly immediate and permanent. Viewing my response, I realized that I was not acting like someone whose father did not love him. Experiencing this issue as an expectant father gave me a place to see something different about my father.

Fear of loss is central to both the father wound and expectant fatherhood. For many men, adolescence was when the primal split with their father occurred. Earlier, I recounted how I realized in therapy how much my father must have feared my dying, and that this fear must have contributed in some way to our tension when I was an adolescent. Throughout our pregnancy and Daniel's early months, fear of loss was very strong for me. Many clinicians say this fear is near-universal, but because of the history of child death and injury in my parents' families, for me it was perhaps especially powerful. Coming to terms with how scared I was that Daniel would die, helped me to understand better how my father's fear of my dying made my adolescence harder for him. My adolescent independence was, to him, in a way like my dying.

Children's literature contains some teachings about father–son relationships that can stimulate healing of the father wound. One I must share comes from a children's book telling the Chanukah story (Scrocco, 1987). Before Daniel, I knew the story only in broad outline. A few years ago, I found myself reading aloud to Daniel this description of the death of Mattathias, who first resisted the imposition of Greek religion on the Jews, and was the father of Judah Maccabee, who then led the armed resistance.

And the days of Mattathias drew near that he should die and he said to his sons:

"Be ye zealous for the law and give your lives for the covenant of your fathers. Remember what our fathers did in their generations. . . . Therefore be strong, my sons, and show yourselves men in behalf of the law; for therein shall ye obtain glory." And he blessed them and was gathered to his fathers.

Within this language lies a world in which men experience the death of their fathers not as the final splitting and ripping apart, as so many men do now, but as a time of mutual blessing and orderly completion. Daniel and I found this imagery inspiring.

If you are an expectant father, one of the things you should "expect" is that both before and after pregnancy, all your old memories about your father will be re-stimulated, and you will have many new ones. Some memories will be positive and some will not. In some ways, being a father yourself will make you experience your father wound less, but in some ways more. When new memories arise or old ones are seen in a different light, learn what you are ready to learn from them. You may see that you cannot heal your father, but you can let your child help you to heal yourself.

In 1974 and 1985, Greenberg coined and fleshed out the phenomenon of "engrossment": the sum of a fathers' emotional reactions to his newborn child. In the current chapter, Dr. Bader follows up this work with an empirical study of the engrossment phenomenon. Using a scale that is based directly on the earlier work by Greenberg, Bader concludes that the phenomenon of engrossment is measurable, has two factors (global infatuation and elated attunement), and provides some support for use of The Engrossment Scale (Bader & Greenberg, 1991).

19

Engrossment Revisited: Fathers Are Still Falling in Love with Their Newborn Babies.

Alan P. Bader[1]

Until recently, the study of parenting was essentially the consideration of the mother–child bond. Nowhere was the scarcity of literature as great as in the father–newborn arena (cf. Howells, 1969; Nash, 1965). In 1974, Martin Greenberg and Norman Morris broke ground with their clinical interview research of the emotional experiences of 31 new fathers in Great Britain. In this study, they coined the term *engrossment*, referring to the affective link-up of the father to the newborn from the point of reference of the father. The original study compared first-time fathers who were present at the birth to a matched group of fathers whose first contact occurred when the baby was shown to them by nursing personnel. Both groups were described as *engrossed* with their newborns. For many of these fathers the intensity of their emotions was surprising.

The "engrossed" father was seen as having a profound emotional reaction to the birth of his child: He has an enhanced visual and tactile

---

[1]This study was completed while the author was a doctoral candidate in counseling psychology at Lehigh University.

awareness of his baby; an awareness of the distinct characteristics of his infant; often seeing the child as the epitome of perfection; he feels strongly attracted to the infant; and experiences enhanced self-esteem and elation. These emotions were enhanced by the baby's reflex activity and behavior. This reaction was consistent with corollary studies in the extant animal behavior, transcultural, and obstetrics literature.

Greenberg and Morris (1974) and Greenberg (1985) speculated that the phenomenon may represent a universal potential for absorption, preoccupation, and interest in the infant that is released by contact with the infant.

Although there were no significant differences in observations of engrossment among fathers who saw their newborn's birth as opposed to those who did not, those fathers who were present at their infant's birth thought that they could distinguish their baby from other babies better than fathers who were not at the birth. There was also a trend suggesting that fathers who were present at the birth were more comfortable in holding the baby than were fathers who were not present. Furthermore, fathers who saw their child's birth, repeatedly and spontaneously commented that "when you see your child born, you know it's yours." This "paternity certainty" concept was not spontaneously mentioned by fathers who did not see their infant's birth. It is likely that the feeling is related to a father's sense of being connected with his newborn. These observations suggest that there may be a qualitative difference in the degree of engrossment in the two groups of fathers based on the degree of contact with the newborn.

The authors speculated that the greater the early physical contact with the infant, the more likely it is that engrossment will occur. They especially felt that the first hour after birth may be a significant period and it would be an important time for the father (as well as the mother) to have contact with the newborn. The father's development of engrossment in his newborn infant may have important ramifications in the subsequent development and mental health of the child. Numerous investigators have noted increased anxiety, juvenile delinquency, and emotional disturbance among father-deprived children (Barnett, Leiderman, Grobstein, & Klaus, 1970; Holman, 1959; Ostrovsky, 1959; Stolz, et al., 1968). A father who is early engrossed in his newborn is likely to continue to be involved and maintain his contact with his developing child.

Greenberg and Morris noted that often fathers who were *engrossed* may be reluctant to express theses feelings due to social demands (concern over his wife's feelings of competition; looking "unmanly" etc.). A father's engrossment might also be delayed or hindered by hospital procedures, if they are insensitive to the father's participation or limited his opportunity to visit his wife or child. Engrossment can also be hindered by feelings of rejection or anger at the treatment he and his wife receive from health care providers.

CHARACTERISTICS OF ENGROSSMENT

1. *Visual Awareness of the Newborn (VA):* Engrossed fathers enjoy looking at their own newborn as opposed to other newborns. They perceive that their infant is attractive, pretty, or beautiful. They perceive that in comparison to others, their own newborn child is especially beautiful. Engrossed fathers experience a powerful impact from looking at their newborn's face such that they perceive their newborn as a unique individual.

2. *Tactile Awareness of the Newborn (TA):* Engrossed fathers desire tactile contact with their newborn and they derive pleasure from this contact. They desire and achieve great pleasure from touching, picking up, moving, holding, and playing with their newborn. Engrossed fathers experience a strong positive impression from the feel of their newborn's skin.

3. *Awareness of Distinct Characteristics of the Newborn (DC):* Engrossed fathers have an awareness of the unique features and characteristics of their newborn to the extent that they believe that they can distinguish their own newborn from others. They can describe the specific physical characteristics of their newborn such as their eyes, noses, ears, or mouths and believe they can identify their resemblance to specific features of themselves foremost, their wives secondarily, and to other relatives more remotely. For fathers who have witnessed the birth, there is an emphatic knowledge that the newborn is "theirs."

4. *The Newborn is Perceived as Perfect (PR):* In spite of the so-called unsightly aspects and awkwardness of the newborn, engrossed fathers perceive their newborn as the epitome of perfection. To engrossed fathers, their own newborn is perceived to be functioning exactly as it is supposed to function.

5. *Strong Feelings of Attraction to the Newborn that Lead to Focusing of Attention on the Newborn (FA):* Engrossed fathers feel

drawn toward the newborn to the extent that they feel compelled to repeatedly contact and re-contact their newborn. They have a strong desire to hold onto their infant and to not want to yield their hold to others. They have a strong preference for interacting with their newborn. They perceive their newborn as larger than its actual size. Engrossed fathers tend to stare at their newborn with awe or amazement.

Normal reflex activity and behavior enhances the feelings of engrossment. Engrossed fathers have a sense of wonder and amazement at the liveliness and movements of their newborn. They are positively impressed that their newborn appears alive. When their newborn moves, they are drawn closer. Engrossed fathers have the perception that when their newborn opens its eyes in their presence, their newborn is communicating directly to them. They perceive that their newborn is responsive to their movements and voice. Engrossed fathers are positively impressed by their newborn's grasp reflex.

6. *Extreme Elation (EL):* Engrossed fathers experience sensations of extreme elation. They describe feeling high, stunned, stoned, drunk, dazed, off-the-ground, full of energy, ten feet tall, different, abnormal, taken away, or taken out of themselves. Often commencing at the birth, these feelings of elation are still present 2 to 3 days after. They experience feelings of relief that their newborn is healthy. Engrossed fathers feel that their newborn turned out better than they had hoped. These reactions are particularly triggered by looking at their newborn's face.

7. *Increased Sense of Self-Esteem (SE):* Engrossed fathers are proud, have a sense of feeling bigger, more mature and older after viewing their newborn for the first time. The first realization of actually being a father occurs to fathers after they view their newborn for the first time. They report a great sense of accomplishment at having produced new life. Satisfaction increases when others see their newborn.

Following Greenberg and Morris' (1974) landmark interview study of British fathers of newborns, a number of authors have described *engrossment-like* phenomena in subsequent studies. Leonard (1976) reported that fathers described their feelings as "great," "proud," and "fantastic." Similarly, Bills (1980) found that fathers scored high on a self-reported measure of affection toward their newborn.

This chapter reports on a recent study that was specifically designed to explore the degree of fathers' engrossment with their newborn babies, and to report on the development of Bader and Greenberg's (1991) "Engrossment Scale"; a self-report instrument designed to measure engrossment as defined above.

Since the mid-1970s a growing interest in the role of the father as an active nurturer has led an increased attention by researchers of the father–newborn connection. Several studies have found that fathers demonstrate sensitivity and attraction to their newborn (e. g., Frodi, Lamb, Leavitt, & Donovan, 1978; Jones & Lenz, 1986; Jones & Thomas, 1989; Parke & O'Leary, 1976). With the current attention that has been given to fathers' capacity for involvement with their children, and nurturance of their newborn in particular, it has become important to re-examine systematically the characteristics of engrossment defined by Greenberg and Morris (1974).

Are there discernible characteristics of engrossed fathers as Greenberg and Morris (1974) suggested? Is engrossment a universal potential for any father when he has contact with his newborn? Finally, is there some valid empirical measure of a father's engrossment?

DESCRIPTION OF THE STUDY

Subjects

This study was conducted with 72 fathers whose newborn babies were still in the postpartum ward of one of three suburban hospitals. As in the Greenberg and Morris study, only fathers of healthy "normal" infants were included.[2] Each father completed and returned the questionnaire; a return rate of 77%. Fifty-one percent of the subjects were first-time fathers. Two-thirds of the fathers attended childbirth preparation classes prior to the birth of their newly born child, and 93% were present for the delivery. The subjects ranged in age from 19 to 43. Sixty-seven of the fathers were married from between 1 and 18 years with a mean of 4 years of marriage. The fathers' level of education ranged from 10th grade to 4 years of graduate school with a mean of 13.9 years of education. Annual incomes ranged from $12,000 to $95,000 with a mean of $37,810.

THE ENGROSSMENT SCALE

The Engrossment Scale (Bader & Greenberg, 1991) contains 51 multiple-choice questions. Twenty-nine questions were designed to

---

[2] For an examination of fathers of preemies and at risk infants see chapters by Katharyn May and Ernest Freud, this volume.

measure fathers' degree of engrossment with their newborn. An additional 22 items asked for information about pregnancy, delivery, and child care. The items were derived from the results of Greenberg and Morris' (1974) study of engrossment, and based on their model.

Seven characteristics of engrossment, Visual Awareness, Tactile Awareness, Awareness of Distinct Characteristics, Perception of Perfection, Focusing of Attention, Elation, and Increased Self-esteem, were treated as subscales of the overall Engrossment Scale (Bader & Greenberg, 1991). For example, an item reflecting strong engrossment in the area of Visual Awareness was *"When I look at my baby's face: I am amazed by her beautiful features and that she already has unique character in her face."*

The strongest responses were written with very positive language to capture the infatuation or in-love quality of the engrossment experience. No items reflected strong negative reactions to the newborn because of the social undesirability of choosing such a response and because such negative reactions were quite rare in fathers' reports. Four items from the Greenberg First Father Engrossment Survey (Greenberg, 1976), the questionnaire that Greenberg and Morris (1974) used in their original engrossment study were included.

Each scale item has four response positions that range in intensity from strongly engrossed, which is scored a 4, to not-engrossed which is scored a 1. The precise language of Greenberg and Morris' (1974) subjects was the basis for writing the most strongly engrossed responses on The Engrossment Scale (Bader & Greenberg, 1991). For example, one of Greenberg and Morris' (1974) subjects described his newborn's skin as "incredibly soft, like velvet." A Tactile Awareness item on The Engrossment Scale is a question about how the baby feels to touch, and the most engrossed response is: "like velvet, incredibly soft and smooth." That response scored a 4. The items were written so that a score of 3 or above was considered an engrossed response, but stronger emotions were necessary for a score of 4, the Likert position of strongly engrossed. For example, in response to the following Self-Esteem item: "When other people look at my baby, I feel:

1. Thrilled and proud when others see her."
2. Pleased with the reactions of others."

Response (a) was scored as 4 and response (b) was scored as 3. Thus, engrossment was defined in operational and empirical terms that directly reflected the narrative descriptions of engrossed fathers.

Procedure

Data was collected on the postpartum units at the hospitals. A rotating schedule was used so that each hospital was visited approximately every third day. At times when a hospital's census was low, a longer period of time elapsed between visits.

To begin each visit, the examiner knocked on the doors of all those mothers who had uncomplicated deliveries and whose babies were not in intensive care. Permission was obtained from both parents for the father to participate. After the fathers signed consent forms, the fathers were given the instrument and instructed to complete it privately before they departed the hospital for the day. Completed instruments were placed in a sealed return envelope, which was left in a bin at the nursing station for subsequent collection by the examiner.

Results

On a scale of 1 to 4, the average full scale engrossment score was 3.17 and the mean subscale scores ranged from 3.57 for Perception of Newborn as Perfect (PR) to 2.74 for Awareness of Distinct Characteristics (DC). Cronbach's alpha for the full scale was 0.77 and alphas ranged from 0.68 for Elation (EL) to 0.17 for Awareness of Distinct Characteristics (DC).

Factor Analysis revealed two interpretable factors. Factor 1, labelled "global infatuation," appeared to represent an aggregate of Elation and all of the proposed subscales except Distinct characteristics. Factor 2, labelled "elated attunement," appeared to represent elation related to the awareness of distinct characteristics of the newborn.

Multiple regression analyses performed with the demographic variables (fathers' age, years married, etc.,) as predictor variables showed no relationship between the predictors and engrossment. That is, engrossment was not a function of the fathers' age, education, income, the mothers' income, or the newborn's age or weight. An analysis of variance comparing scores of first-time fathers and those with previous children on fullscale engrossment also showed no differences.

Discussion

The results of this study suggest that most fathers experience strong positive emotional responses to their newborn babies. The experience of elation appears to be the hallmark of the engrossed response. A review of the factor analysis suggests that fathers reactions may be characterized by two types of experience. One type of experience appears to represent a global feeling of elation represented by great happiness and relief, great pleasure when looking at or holding the newborn, great attraction toward the newborn, the perception of the newborn as perfect, and a feeling of pride and elevated self-esteem. This experience may be analogous to the earliest phase of romantic falling in love and has been labelled *"global infatuation."* The infatuation experience is one in which there is a strong attraction to the love object who is perceived as beautiful and perfect, regardless of its specific attributes. The infatuated father may be unaware of the distinct characteristics of the newborn, but still very much in love with and drawn toward the new baby.

The second type of experience consists of feelings of elation and the belief that one can distinguish the unique characteristics of the newborn such as its cry, its appearance, and physical features. This factor has been labelled *"elated attunement."* Here, the father feels attuned to the uniqueness of his baby and responds with joyful emotion. This attunement experience may be viewed as the beginning of a connecting process between the father and the newborn, whereby the father responds to the specific unique characteristics of his newborn. Though all engrossed fathers experienced elation, some believed that they could recognize the specific characteristics of their newborn. Therefore, engrossment may be experienced differently by different fathers.

The results of this study support the notion that engrossment may be a "basic innate potential among all fathers" as Greenberg and Morris, (1974) suggested, though some fathers may experience engrossment differently than others. This potential for engrossment may be triggered just by fathers having contact with their newborn. The fact that fathers who had previous children were no less engrossed than their first-time father counterparts lends support to the universality theory in that father–infant contact, not just the act of becoming a father, appears to trigger the engrossment response. Additional support for the universality theory is found in the fact that engrossment was not related to fathers' or mothers' incomes, the length of the parents' marriage, or the age or weight of the newborn. Of course, the study does not reflect a cross-cultural sample.

Another test of the universal nature of engrossment would be to study fathers who were unable to have contact with their babies immediately following birth. These include adoptive fathers, stepfathers, fathers of ill babies, and ill or absent fathers. Greenberg (1987) believes that engrossment can occur at various stages of infant development such as when the baby smiles, coos, giggles, laughs, sits, crawls, etc., as long as fathers have direct contact with their babies and are open to fully experiencing their babies. He has also suggested (Greenberg, 1993) that fathers need not be present at birth or be the biological parent, in order for engrossment to be triggered. Thus, by measuring fathers who have not had immediate newborn contact, Greenberg's hypothesis about engrossment being a universal experience that is triggered by contact at various times during early childhood could be examined further.

The Engrossment Scale (Bader & Greenberg, 1991) when used as an overall scale (i.e., 29 items) may be a moderately reliable measure of the responses that fathers have toward their newborn babies. The Engrossment Scale (Bader and Greenberg, 1991) achieved a modest level of full-scale reliability that could possibly be increased by increasing the number of items on the total scale. The relatively low reliability coefficients for the seven subscales may also be attributed to the small number of items per subscale and may be increased by adding more items per subscale.

RECOMMENDATIONS FOR FURTHER RESEARCH

Further study is needed to test the hypothesis that engrossment consists of two types of experiences, global infatuation and elated attunement. Possibly, engrossment parallels romantic love so that there is a point in time when infatuation with the image of the love object recedes and loving of the known individual becomes dominant. If so, it would be important to identify the components that constitute a successful transition from initial engrossment to future father–infant involvement.

Because for some fathers engrossment is related to their awareness of the distinct characteristics of their newborn, it would also be of interest to determine if those engrossed fathers who believe that they can recognize the distinct characteristics of their newborn can actually do so. This author recently conducted a study in which fathers were tested on their abilities to discriminate their newborn from others on the basis of touch, smell, and sight (Bader, 1993). The fathers in that study showed a remarkable ability to recognize their newborn by touch and by sight (Bader, 1993). In other newborn recognition studies, fathers have demonstrated attunement with their newborn to the extent that they were able to recognize their newborn solely by identifying their odors (Porter, Balogh, Cernoch, & Franchi, 1986) and by discriminating photographs of their newborn from other newborn photographs (Kaitz, Good, Rokem, & Eidelman, 1988; Porter, Boyle, Hardister, & Balogh, 1989).) No measures of the fathers' engrossment were taken in those studies. A future newborn recognition study that pretests fathers on engrossment, including their perception of their ability to recognize their newborn, could shed light on the relationship between engrossment and fathers' ability to recognize their newborn.

Finally, the Engrossment Scale (Bader & Greenberg, 1991) could be used to measure the effects of psychoeducational interventions with fathers during the early postpartum period. For example, fathers at risk for not bonding with their newborns would be exposed to a class in baby care that would address the practical (changing diapers) and psychological (nurturing) role of the father. Engrossment would be measured pre- and post-class to determine if the class was successful at increasing engrossment responses in those fathers.

In this chapter, Dr. Ernest Freud richly conveys the isolation common to most men becoming fathers, particularly those with premature and at-risk infants. The article begins with an interesting application of his famous grandfather's analytic method. Using a combination of personal experience, research and clinical acumen, Dr. Freud examines the sense of the father of a premature infant as a lone wolf. In the process, Dr. Freud explores the trauma and blow to a father's sense of manliness, and the social issues that accompany modern medicine's technologically centered Neonatal Intensive Care Units (NICU). He calls for increasing attention to the needs of these men and recommends both the need to turn men's enforced passivity into self-esteem enhancing creative activity and the use of a doula.

20

Premature Fathers: Lone Wolves?

W. Ernest Freud

Let me share with you a personal concern of mine pertaining to the subject matter of this chapter: bearing in mind how neatly Kaplan and Mason (1960) had shelled out a sequence of reactions to prematurity in "Premature mothers" (the four tasks of "anticipatory grief, acknowledgement of failure, resumption of active relating to the baby; seeing its special needs as a premature and prematurity as a temporary state yielding to normality"), I felt that something equally neat should be put together as characteristic for "premature fathers." I was searching for common denominators that would unmistakably describe them as a group, but found myself at a loss. Maybe, some or all of these tasks also applied to these fathers. I was not satisfied and then searched for a motto that would sum it up and could be put at the top of this chapter, but I still remained at a loss because I could not think of a suitable one.

I then told myself what I say to my patients when they don't know how to start a session: I encouraged myself to get hold of the first thing that comes to mind (because in the last resort everything one thinks is relevantly connected). But would I then project something of myself into it? Sure I would. So what came to mind was "lone wolf." I realized that this was me all right: one of my first names is Wolfgang, and I was

234

the little boy who had become a lone wolf ever since my mother had died when I was 5³/₄ years old. The other part was still missing, however, I had always reassured myself that I could think about prematurity sufficiently uninvolved because I myself was not a premature father. My son had been a full-term healthy baby and I had plumbed the deepest depth of my memory for the "true determinants of this special field of interest, prematurity" (W.E. Freud, 1992). That had been some 2 years ago, but as time goes on, usually more things tend to come to mind. So it was with me too: I suddenly recalled that some weeks before my son was born his mother's waters broke. From what we know, this might easily have precipitated a premature birth.

In this event, the mother was ordered prolonged bed rest to be able to carry the child to term. I had visited her in hospital until very late one evening when labor started in earnest (in those days fathers were not yet routinely encouraged to be present at the birth of their children). I had to walk home because the buses had stopped running by then, and I remember feeling very lonely, being once again the lone wolf. What had up till then not been so clear to me, that I am a "near miss" premature father became clear. So I can with a good conscience head the beginning of this chapter with the motto I had in mind.

Lone Wolves

Let us go back to what I think premature fathers have in common. They all experience a number of psychological traumas, usually multiple and cumulative ones. The first one is that of prematurity.[1] The second one is the traumatization through what is best termed, "NICU culture-shock." Third, they all have the responsibility of shouldering the burden of accompanying or carrying their at-risk child, usually for the rest of the child's or their own life. Apart from this, premature fathers seem as different from each other as they come, especially when, as a psychoanalyst, one has occasion to get to know them more thoroughly, as it were, from the inside. What can be clearly distinguished, however, is the father who has been alerted in advance to the likelihood of an at-risk birth from fathers who are confronted with the event around the time of delivery, as, for example, in the course of an emergency admission to hospital? As can be expected, the forewarned fathers have time to come to terms with the prospect of fatherhood

---

[1]I propose using the terms, "premature" and "at-risk" interchangeably, as they have much in common.

that is different from the idealized image, whereas unprepared fathers will experience, at least in the beginning, considerably more anxiety and stress.

Ideas are divided on the lengths to which preparing of fathers and (mothers) should go. Some parents and medical staff think it may be inadvisable to guide them through the NICU when they are first shown the hospital during pregnancy. Others, by contrast, console themselves with the thought that, as patients who have to undergo an operation benefit from being prepared before-hand, so families may be in a better position to cope with prematurity if they have been acquainted in good time with what may possibly be in store for them.

Traditionally, fatherhood is associated with taking on responsibility for the new life, what Greenberg (1985) has fittingly termed the "perils of responsibility." There it revolved around the father's ability to provide financially, which may in American culture have an even greater place value than in Western Europe. Psychoanalytically, earning capacity can be understood in terms of anal potency, that is, in terms of manliness, something that in the minds of men seems forever threatened and therefore often elicits overcompensation. When the spouse becomes pregnant, birth envy and lactation envy rear their heads. The father suffers from exclusion anxiety and may, as Liebenberg (1973) described, resort to pregnancy symptoms or to couvade-like behavior (Trethowan & Conlon, 1965). The mother's condition may become a challenge to his creativity or generally lead to increased activity to counteract fears of passivity. He has fantasies of showing off with his strong heroic sons and his stunningly beautiful Miss World-like daughters who will in turn attract strong masculine men to marry. It is clear, therefore, that a full-term baby stands as proof of male prowess, perhaps seasoned with a shot of "machoism."

Though the "macho" concept is still implicitly plugged by the media it is now increasingly falling into disrepute at least on the surface. The appeal of strong men of action, the impetuous, daredevil and at times cruel male rarely loses its attraction, even for the meekest and weakest (or perhaps especially for these), however.

When an at-risk baby is on the way all this comes to a halt. It puts an end to the hope for a perfect and healthy family. The father's self-esteem is severely shaken: suddenly it feels as if he will never be accepted in the society of "real" men—he will merely remain a second-rate father—looked down on, despised, and ousted. He will lose face and lead a pitiful existence, hardly worth living (thoughts of putting an end to his life may cross his mind) or he might want to desert his spouse who, he imagines, now no longer wants him. It feels like he is being taken from his masculine pedestal. The longed-for ultimate father authority has slipped through his hands as he is increasingly surrounded by the authority of medical men. Possibilities of fatherhood engrossment (Greenberg & Morris, 1974) slip away; instead of the expected "highs" there will only be "lows."

It looks like the end of his castles in the air. He feels perfused with weakness and when alone may for brief moments break into tears. Such states of despair and resignation can be fueled by the differences of readiness for sexual activity in premature fathers as compared to premature mothers.

Odent (1992) recently alluded to this still somewhat taboo problem area in a chapter on breastfeeding and monogamy. In the premature father's mind there is a close connection between his sexuality and it's outcome in the form of an at-risk child. It puts his masculinity into question. Therefore his need to reassure himself of his virility is stronger than in fathers of full-term healthy infants. He consequently reacts more strongly to any signs of sexual rejection by his spouse. The sensitive and informative Toronto film *Journey to Attachment: the Psychosocial issues of Prematurity* (Foresight Audio Visual Limited, 1983)[2] does not shrink from broaching the topic of the premature father's frustrated sexuality when in one of the vignettes the spouse points out that just when she wants to convey to him that in spite of the preemie still being in an incubator she is fulfilling her motherly duties fairly well, he begins desiring her as a woman. To safeguard the partnership it is essential that discrepancies in the partners' sexual orientation be openly discussed under the guidance of a psycho-therapist.

I think we tend on the whole still to overestimate the emotional resilience of fathers on account of their "halo" of manliness, whereas it can safely be assumed that the prospect of an at-risk pregnancy elicits consternation and bewilderment. Odent (1992) rightly points out that the label "high risk" is itself dangerous "in terms of the anxiety it triggers and maintains over a period of several months" (p. 93).

Stauber (1979) studied anxieties in pregnant women in Berlin and

---

[2]The film was produced by Nancy Shosenberg and Lesley Walker under the guidance of Klaus Minde of the Psychiatric Research Dept. of the Hospital for Sick Children Foundation, Foresight Audio-Visual Ltd., Toronto, Ontario. Because of its impact the film should be shown by a specialist used to handling relevant discussions (German introduction to the film, W. E. Freud; 1987).

found that their most frequent concerns (right at the top of his inverted pyramid diagram) were about malformations in the child. One could well imagine that their concerns are very similar to those of pregnant women. A recent analysis of perinatal statistics here (Rheinische Perinatalerhebung, 1993) found that 66% of all pregnancies (more than three ultrasound controls) are classified as high-risk pregnancies. But this is small consolation to the premature fathers, who feel isolated and bowled over. Sometimes these fathers can't help wondering to what extent high-risk babies' lives are saved at almost any price when they feel they have to pay for it.

Another aspect, recently described in the English newspaper, *Independent,* concerned the stresses for high-risk families that live on the bread line and raised the question of what the community is doing to support such babies. The article was entitled "we saved the baby; unfortunately the family is cracking up" (Williams, 1993). There is certainly no dearth of worries on these father's minds.

Once the baby has been delivered he[3] will no longer be the family's (cf. "The Whose Baby? Syndrome," W. E. Freud, 1991) but will belong to a host of "Gods or (Goddesses) in White," each claiming their share of him, and who are in a position to make far-reaching decisions about the baby's future. The fathers know that one had better not be openly critical of them lest they take it out on the baby (a common ever-present fear). It is understood, that medical procedures have priorities over psychosocial considerations (W.E. Freud, 1981).

In these realms of unholistic medicine (also with the connotation of "unholy") the premature father is a somewhat confused and disorientated but not necessarily wholly welcome guest and is sometimes asking himself whether the physicians should not really be the guests. The situation reflects just one aspect of role confusion (better: role paradox) in this new holding environment, called NICU. It is a weird place, literally buzzing with activity of one kind or another. Nurses are dashing in and out or cluster, sometimes with a physician, around an incubator and the fathers may feel uncomfortable in their presence and threatened by their knowledge and expertise (Consolvo, 1984). There may also be the occasional mother and father of other preemies around, when they are not conspicuous by their absence (which has remained my impression in spite of all that has been said and written about visiting). The premature father feels

---

[3]Rather than using "it" for the baby, "he" and "she" will be used interchangeably.

isolated (like his preemie in the isolette) and very much alone (a-lone: The lone wolf).

In my worst moments, in NICUs for extended periods of time, while empathizing and identifying with the premature fathers, I experienced the NICU as a kind of antiseptic prison. Day in, day out, one would be seeing mostly the same people but would be too preoccupied and weighed down to take much notice or talk with them. I was reminded of Van Gogh's painting of the circle of subdued prisoners trudging, seemingly forever, in the confined space of the prison yard. There is a high incidence of deaths in NICUs and the thought of death was never far from our minds while we were there. (There were echoes of lines from Oscar Wilde's *Ballad of Reading Goal* in my ears).

Initially, the preemie is still too weak and "untogether" physiologically (Gorski, 1979). The father may feel deprived of handling him and in the absence of the mother is aware of being expected to fulfil some kind of mothering role, for which he is ill prepared. The baby seems too frail and delicate to be touched and yet the nurse may encourage him to touch the baby, to call him by name and to talk to him. If he is lucky he may be in an NICU where the kangaroo method is accepted, and before he knows what has happened he and his preemie are bonding to each other during this sensitive period (Klaus & Kennell, 1982). Somehow the father is growing into his new role and the new role is growing on him.

The other unbargained-for role that is put on him again, usually without adequate preparation, is that of a go-between. He is made the "missing link" between his spouse on the ward and the preemie in the NICU, the live "umbilical," which is a good deal more than the customary Polaroid photo that is routinely given to the mother. It is also more than showing her a film of a far-away perinatal center while the preemie is stabilized for transport by helicopter (showing a film is used, e.g., by the Kaiser Hospital in Grand Rapids, Michigan). It is even better than closed-circuit television, as used in the Mayo Clinic. The father commutes, sometimes more than once a day while the mother may still be too immobile after a C-section.

Being able to share his feelings and his impressions of the NICU is of tremendous help to the couple. Through being given the opportunity of doing something useful, the father can surface from the sea of passivity and can begin to come to grips with his status of inmate and of "splendid isolation" in the NICU, with its many overwhelming stressors (Miles, 1992). What is more, once the swing away from passive dependency gets under way, it tends to potentiate, which is very reassuring. The father is now becoming aware of being able to cope, even though it may only be a beginning.

There are many ways of coping, and I recall one visiting father who visited regularly and always carried a large video camera with which he filmed the daily progress of his preemie for the mother, to whom this was a boon. It kept both of them going, until she became fit enough to come over into the NICU, where they could spend time together as a family, which helped all three of them to make a better and faster recovery.

The other side of the role paradox, which has not yet been sufficiently resolved, is that of active participation of the parents in caregiving. Of necessity, in the beginning this will have to be done by the nursing staff. It makes the father feel completely superfluous and in my opinion largely accounts for the widespread unsatisfactory visiting patterns (irregular visiting or too short visiting spells). It is an impediment to early bonding with the child. The father's readiness for participation in caregiving can be gauged by the impact of even brief and seemingly peripheral opportunities for sharing in caregiving can have.

I recall observing in a hospital in Southern California where a distance of some 30 meters separated the delivery rooms from the NICU. The hospital served a large population of less affluent Mexican-Americans, who usually gathered in front of the delivery rooms to catch a glimpse of their baby as it was wheeled on a trolley along the wide corridor to the NICU. The parents appeared to be particularly excited as they tried to identify the babies that the nurses wheeled out of the delivery room. Whenever a nurse appeared with a trolley they tried to get a glimpse of the baby. Suddenly one of the men, rushed forward and eagerly asked the nurse whether that was his baby on her trolley. She nodded and he put his hands on one side of the trolley, both pushing it together toward the NICU. A wide smile of fatherly pride and satisfaction remained on his face and one could not fail to see that in those few moments he had become a changed man through having been able to participate. I later learned that the Karolinska Hospital in Stockholm had made it a custom to let fathers wheel the incubator trolley from delivery room to the NICU. Another time I was told about a British NICU that also cared for U.S. Air Force personnel stationed in the vicinity: a monitor suddenly failed to function but no hospital technician was immediately available. Fortunately one of the visiting fathers who was an electronics engineer, happened to be on the spot and could do the repair within minutes. He was delighted to have been of some help and was described as a changed man. In all these episodes the effect of early bonding was striking and convincing.

In times when everything seems to fail, the predicament of the premature father is accentuated when he can no longer count on accustomed support systems. Friends and relatives have surprisingly little understanding for the situation and tend to withdraw because the idea of an at-risk baby is frightening to them. On top of everything else the parents find themselves deserted. Often, only people who have undergone a similar experience can really understand the emotional repercussions of prematurity. The "veterans" in the parents self-help groups are doing a great job, but investigators are needed to find out why enthusiasm for them frequently peters out after a while, particularly in Europe. My hunch is that this might not happen if they were integrated in ongoing research.

The worst hit families are usually those of ethnic minorities among whom the incidence of prematurity is often higher. They are especially handicapped through language barriers, discrimination, and a narrower choice of support systems. Communication has remained a problem with them as there are rarely enough competent interpreters available. At a recent conference about parents of premature babies one of the recommendations put forward was that independent interpreters should be provided to help family members("Frankfurter-Thesen," 1993).

Early on I mentioned that fathers are basically traumatized by the impact of two overall stressors, the at-risk condition and the effect of their acquaintance with modern medical technology-dominated neonatal intensive care. Ever since I came into contact with prematurity I have wondered how these hazards could best be avoided or eliminated, and it seems to me that there are good prospects for success in both areas: a coherent overall strategy of continuous accompaniment along an extended perinatal continuum (EPC), as outlined in my paper on the Prophylaxis of Prematurity (W.E. Freud, 1992b) could take care of the first, although we are already in the thick of a silent revolution of neonatal intensive care. The kangaroo method" (Anderson et al., 1986, Stening & Roth, 1993), to which even fathers of healthy full-term infants—besides premature fathers (De Leeuw et al., 1991)—have taken like ducks to water, is currently humanizing neonatal intensive care, as we know it, beyond expectation.

Application of the Doula concept (Sosa et al., 1980; Klaus, Kennell, & Klaus, 1993) both before and after labor, may in conjunction with other psychosocial innovations, tilt the balance in the foreseeable future. I am referring here, above all, to Kennell and Klaus's (1988) clarion call for changes, and in particular to their description of Dr. Jorge Cesar Martinez' setup in The Ramon Sarda Mother and Infant Hospital in Buenos Aires (Kennel & Klaus, 1988, pp. 807–811), where premature parents are accepted on the caregiving team. Much will depend on the extent to which these parents can and will be integrated in the team and on the composition of such teams. My own experience with small teams in a somewhat similar setup at the Cassel Hospital (a psychoanalytically oriented hospital for functional nervous disorders near London, with Tom Main (1968) as Medical Director at the time, has made me hopeful that patient participation can be implemented to a high degree. Last, but not least, the promising statistics of Dr. Marina Marcovich's NICU at the Mautner-Markhof-Kinderspital in Vienna, which have recently been presented by her in Germany and been described by a Swiss parents magazine (June 1993) seem to reflect solutions to the crucial issues of physician–nursing staff bonding as well as to the thorny problems of staff–premature parent relationships.

Above all, there is hope for the premature fathers themselves from the time onward when they can accept the challenge of prematurity and begin to turn their enforced passivity into the mobilization of activity. Their understandable feelings of anger and aggression about being victims of circumstance can fuel creativity. Devising strategies and tactics in dealing with the infant's later development remains a challenge to ingenuity, and moreover, the experience they have gathered along the way is invaluable and can be passed on through the parents' groups. Once the wolf-side of the "lone wolf" can gather momentum, their feelings of manliness will be reinstated and there should no longer be any need for feeling lonely.

One of the primary psychological duties of new fathers is to provide a timely and nurturing holding environment for the mother and their fetus, infant, and small child during the period when the mother–child relationship, characterized by primary attunement, is essential for the development of what Bowlby (1988) termed a "secure base."

In this chapter, Dr. Diamond discusses the emergence of the father as the primordial "protective agent" who enables the emotional relationship between the mother and her new baby to begin and, subsequently to develop naturally. The value of this "husbandry" function on the child, the mother, the father, and the marital relationship is examined. The psychodynamic developmental basis for this fatherly "holding" is outlined while both internal and external sources of interference with its attainment are considered. The chapter concludes with some reflections on the unique nature of male nurturance evident in this less conspicuous facet of fathering.

21

The Emergence of the Father as the Watchful Protector of the Mother–Infant Dyad

Michael J. Diamond

The archaic and universal wish to be tended to, protected, and provided for is experienced in both imaginary and actual relationships with others throughout the life span. These watchful, protective "others" include mothers and fathers, grandparents, caretakers, older siblings, and relatives, friends, teachers, and guides, wives and husbands, clergy, mentors, as well as societal, political, and symbolic leaders, and eventually even one's grown children. The Christian paternal imagery of "Our Father, which art in Heaven" is the foremost Western depiction of this fundamental longing. As this imagery implies, the preeminent representation of such a protector and provider role is that of *the father.*

This fatherly representation rests firmly on ubiquitous concepts of masculinity that are accompanied by traditional injunctions to achieve "real manhood" (cf. Gilmore, 1990). The protective, providing father imago reflects duties emblematic of such constantly sought manhood,

243

both among contemporary westernized men as well as among career-oriented women (Betcher & Pollack, 1993). The protective, providing, paternal representation arguably occurs even when the traditional gender divisions in parenting, in which the mother is the primary nurturing figure, is modified (cf. Ehrensaft, 1987; Pruett, 1987). Although we cannot know the biological or archetypal basis of this paternal depiction with certitude, it seems evident that this idealization of the father as a delegate of the outside world operates powerfully as a cultural representation even when the real parents do not reinforce it (Benjamin, 1988).

I have discussed elsewhere (Diamond, 1995a) how this initial paternal presence of protective watchfulness, when accompanied by subsequent "good enough" fatherly involvement and provision, proceeds to evolve and develop alongside other fatherly representations over the life cycle.[1] Thus, the involved father who is able to "watch over," "hold", and protect the mother and "her" fetus, infant, and small child is likely in due course to become the father who protects and encourages "his" young toddler's separation and individuation from the mother. Similarly, and years later, he must again "hold," bear, and support with interested restraint his adolescent child's identity experimentation and subsequent distancing from family dependencies. A father's *quiet* strength and *subtle* courage is required, in addition to the more *active mentoring* long associated with good fathering (see for example Bly, 1990; Shapiro, 1993a). The progressive, developmental accomplishments that depend on this fatherly contribution increase the chances that, even in a grown child's mid-late adulthood, a healthy, internal sense of being watched over will remain vibrantly alive.

In this chapter I will discuss the emergence of the father as the primordial "protective agent" who enables the emotional relationship between the mother and her new baby to begin and, subsequently, to

---

[1]Abundant evidence now exists demonstrating specific contributions that involved fathers make to their children's development (e.g., Lamb, 1986; Snarey, 1993). I discuss elsewhere these contributions and the accompanying internalized, paternal representation for sons who are sufficiently fortunate to have had such "good enough" fathering at varying points throughout their lifespan (Diamond, 1995a). Both Benjamin (1988, 1991) and Ross (1990) consider the important role played by such fathers with their daughters, particularly during the prelatency phases. Pruett (1987, 1993) emphasizes the unique importance of involved, actively nurturing fathers during their child's earliest years, whereas numerous other writers point out the relationship between the absence of such active, involved fathering and the many social and familial ills besetting the contemporary family (Comer, 1989; Herzog, 1982a; Lansky, 1992; Mitscherlich, 1969; Parker & Parker, 1986).

develop naturally. The value of this "husbandry" function will be examined as it impacts on the child, the mother, the father, and the marital relationship. Finally, I consider what is required for fathers to assume this function while reflecting on personal, systemic, and external disruptions to this fatherly "holding." I will begin by sketching out the nature of this protective, watchful function as a man first becomes a father.[2]

FATHER'S PROTECTIVE AGENCY: THE "HUSBANDRY" FUNCTION

Fathers provide a timely and nurturing holding environment for the mother and their fetus, infant, and small child during the period when the mother–child relationship, characterized by primary attunement, is essential for the development of what Bowlby (1988) termed a "secure base." In serving as the dyad's original "protective agent," the father shields the mother from impingement and interference from without, while she carries, bears, and suckles their infant. Thus, especially before the infant can make use of him in other ways, the "watchful" father frees the mother to devote herself to her baby. In "holding" the mother–infant dyad near the end of pregnancy and for several weeks after the baby's birth, the father is able to promote the mother's necessary "primary maternal preoccupation," which becomes the basis for the infant's ego establishment (Winnicott, 1956).

A father's respect for, and protection of, this "mothering dyad" is crucial in his child's relationship with mother as the "first other." This fathering position is aptly conveyed by the term *husbandry,* which Webster's dictionary defines as "the management of domestic affairs, resources, etc." Indeed both the *material* aspects of providing and the *emotional-physical* facets of availability and defending are called into play during the father's early, watchful protectiveness. Together, the *material-providing* and *emotional-responsiveness* dimensions reflect the "psychobiological, instinctual" basis of fathering (Benedek, 1970a; Pleck, 1995).

---

[2]My focus in this chapter is on the father as the *biological* parent able to accompany his spouse through her pregnancy. Nonetheless, the significance of and main issues bearing on fatherly "protective watchfulness," apply likewise for fathers of *adopted* and *step-children,* particularly during the child's infancy when the dyadic relationship with the mother is paramount.

In his *providing function,* the new father often "feathers the nest" by working diligently to gain greater income or career status in order to look after his wife and "young fledgling" (Betcher & Pollack, 1993; Pollack, 1995). Additionally, in his *empathic responsiveness* to his child's dyadic needs, the new father guards and gives sanctuary to the particulars of maternal biological contact and feeding. Thus, as a delegate of "the outside world" in his "husbandry" function, the father provides for and serves as an external beacon to his wife and child, protecting their intense, primary mutuality with one another (Benjamin, 1988; Stern, 1985).

The attuned father providing this watchful protection is especially able to "parent his wife" at the very time she most needs such care (Herzog, 1982b). Such fathers, moreover, seem better able to connect with their inner lives while maintaining a valuation of the outside world beyond the mother–child primary mutuality (Diamond, 1986). The "alliance of pregnancy" (Deutscher, 1971), characterized by the husband's empathy with his spouse (and vice-versa), subsequently evolves at delivery into a sense of the "whole becoming greater than the sum of its parts," while a "feeling of awe" tends to accompany this emerging sense of family and parenting alliance (Herzog, 1982b).

Fathers capable of such engagement, furthermore, are more likely to experience an increased sense of familial worth and personal self-esteem as they become "engrossed" in their newborn (Greenberg & Morris, 1974; Pruett, 1993). The selfless generosity, sacrifice, and servitude required by such early forms of fathering strengthens a man's sense of "real manhood," primarily because such fatherly protection and provision fulfill "the ubiquitous code of masculinity" (Gilmore, 1990). Furthermore, in accepting his familial caretaking role, fathers are provided an important opportunity for overcoming developmental obstacles, working through intrapsychic conflicts, and creating new family legacies of male nurturance (Benedek, 1959; Betcher & Pollack, 1993; Diamond, 1986, 1995a). Such fatherly provision additionally increases marital satisfaction, although the long-term effects remain unknown (Greenberg, 1985; Ehrensaft, 1987; Pruett, 1993; Shapiro, 1993a).

An infant is fortunate indeed to have the mother's ordinary "primary maternal preoccupation" and the father's sufficient "protective agency,[3] in combination with adequate physical endowment and

---

[3]"This "protective agency" can be understood as part of the father's *"paternal preoccupation"* namely, as an equally meaningful counterpart to the mother's *"initial devotion,"* as distinguished by maternal biological contact, feeding, and attunement.

freedom from unforeseen external trauma. Such an infant essentially is shielded from those primitive annihilation threats to personal self-existence, stemming from experiencing an overwhelming sense of helplessness involving terrors of falling apart and dissolving, which severely compromise subsequent cognitive, affective, and intrapsychic development. The fetus and then infant provided with "good enough" initial mothering and fathering is thus likely to "go on being" largely unriddled by the more primitive anxieties interfering with each subsequent developmental task (Winnicott, 1956, 1960).[4]

Children of fathers who are unable to provide sufficient protective agency during the earliest phases of their lives are unlikely to receive important fatherly provisions at the latter stages, even though there are subsequent opportunities for reparative paternal contributions (Diamond, 1995a). There is evidence, for example, that children of fathers less involved in these initial phases of fathering are more likely during later childhood (and adult) development to incur paternal sexual abuse (Parker & Parker, 1986), father abandonment (Comer, 1989), and the detrimental effects of uninvolved or ineffective fathering, including "father hunger" (Greenberg, 1985; Herzog, 1982a; Shapiro, 1993a).

A father's "protective agency" function remains important throughout his child's development, though its forms will alter and its significance recede as other fatherly provisions become more salient throughout the life cycle. Its early emergence is illustrated in the Homeric tale of Telemachus, which embodies a watchful father's loving, protective, and altruistic qualities toward his child. In the myth, Telemachus pretended insanity in order to avoid conscription into a life-threatening war. To ascertain whether he was malingering, however, shrewd military examiners placed his infant son in the path of the plow that Telemachus was guiding. Determined to protect his son rather than himself, Telemachus created a wide arc with his plow around the boy's helpless, infantile body. Thus, he constructed a "semi-circle of protection" to save his son's life, though relinquishing his own cover of insanity.

---

[4]Although either parent can serve *both* mothering and fathering functions (see also Ehrensaft, 1995; Pruett, 1987), it is nevertheless important for a child to experience the presence of *two* parents (or their surrogates) at certain key developmental junctions (see Diamond, 1995a). Each of these parents should ideally represent the culturally determined mother and father functions, respectively, within a triangular dynamic, in order to provide the child with sufficient opportunity for adaptive splitting and developmentally determined conflict resolution as well as culturally based group adaptation.

This capacity for the self-sacrificing role of fatherhood is the back-bone for paternal protective watchfulness. I shall consider next how this capacity grows to fruition and how it may become disrupted.

THE CAPACITY FOR PATERNAL PROTECTIVENESS

Attempts have been made over the last quarter century to examine the more instinctual basis of fathering despite the prevailing belief that fathers are further removed from the instinctual roots of parenting than are mothers (Benedek, 1970a; Ehrensaft, 1987; Greenberg, 1985; Greenberg & Morris, 1974; Pruett, 1987; Shapiro, 1987, 1993a). This psychogenetic approach to fathering has emphasized both the father's function as a *provider* and his capacity for *fatherliness ties,* which render his relationship to his children a mutual, developmental experience (Diamond, 1986).

Benedek (1970) posited an instinctually rooted character trait termed "genuine fatherliness," which enables a father to act toward his children with immediate empathic responsiveness. Redican (1976) discovered latent predispositions for such paternal caretaking, even among primates. Greenberg and Morris (1974) and Pruett (1987) observed such character trends in the form of fatherly "en-grossment" with their newborn and the achievement of father–infant "biorythmic synchrony," respectively. Ross (1975) examined the genetic precursors to such fatherliness in terms of *generativity* and *nurturance.* Nonetheless, the developmental forerunners of the father's capacity for *protectiveness,* particularly in its original *watchful* functions, have not been examined.[5]

The process of *becoming a father* begins long before conception and birth. Just as the roots of a woman's motherhood are traceable to the distant past of the little girl's wishes to be like her mommy and experience maternal yearning to (re-) create through nurturance, so too can the foundations for a father's attachment and relationship to his infant be observed in *the little boy's* generative and defensive

---

[5] I stress *watchfulness* as the preeminent characteristic of the father's protective function throughout this chapter in contrast to the otherwise significant aspects of fatherly protectiveness which involve holding, containing, defending, and providing. The salience of watchfulness is warranted ontogenetically, as evident in its serving as the foundation for these latter protective qualities. Watchfulness develops moreover throughout the mammalian species from an earlier precursor in the form of a built-in protective mechanism.

instincts, wishes and behaviors linked to both his own mommy and daddy. Consequently, a father's actual *attachment and relationship* to his infant commences long before labor and delivery (Gurwitt, 1976; Herzog, 1982b; Ross, 1975, 1982a).

An examination of studies of *adult men's* experiences during the sequence of prospective fatherhood indicate that the emerging father must deal with and adequately master a number of *emotional* and *psychological* issues that become manifest during the course of this sequence in order to achieve the caretaking role of "genuine fatherliness" (Diamond, 1986; Gurwitt, 1976; Herzog, 1982b; Shapiro, 1987). There are moreover many external sources of interference with a father's holding function. Both *social-economic factors* and *unforeseen trauma* may create *unfavorable birthing conditions.* These external sources include naturally occurring disasters, physical illness or death, severe psychological illness (particularly to the mother), as well as unavoidable financial, work-related, and/or social-political conflicts, such as war or under career circumstances requiring that the father be unavailable or removed from the family.

Extraordinary demands are placed on fathers, particularly during adverse birthing situations involving "high-risk" pregnancies with premature infants or with "high-risk" infants per se (W.E. Freud, 1995; May, 1995). Almost any father's capacity for "protective watchfulness" is severely compromised during these latter circumstances, which inevitably involve increased financial burdens and overwhelming needs to provide solid emotional support for his "high-risk" pregnant wife in addition to his "at-risk" fetus or infant. These fathers must also confront emotionally demanding blows to their self-esteem, painful issues arising from feelings of helplessness, and grief pertaining to potential loss, while at the same time, being forced to abdicate their paternal holding functions to the physicians and nurses of the neonatal-infant care units (W.E. Freud, 1995).

In considering the *psychodynamic, developmentally based* issues affecting this capacity for paternal protectiveness, it is evident that many unconscious wishes along with "neurotic" conflicts are triggered for men during pregnancy. These include: *envy toward the prospective mother;* concerns regarding *responsibility for impregnation;* anxieties pertaining to *adulthood and aging;* issues involving *competition* and wishes to re-establish *connections with one's own father;* wishes to *revitalize one's own parents; jealousy and guilt toward the fetus* who is the object of the partner's rapt attention; and unresolved *conflicts and mutuality wishes in the partnership* (Diamond, 1986; 1995b). Given sufficient spousal and social-environmental support, however, most men are able to weather these difficulties sufficiently so that their fatherly instincts are not undercut (Jordan, 1995; Shapiro, 1987).

The fundamental psychological task for most men during this period involves the ubiquitous need for *creative expression* and *sublimatory activity* in addition to the overcoming and/or "working through" neurotic and other forms of psychopathology (Diamond, 1992). Pleck (1995) describes this process in terms of the naturally progressive healing of the "father wound." The man who can find constructive ways to express his fatherly ties during the time of "wait," while simultaneously protecting this partner's (and child's) health and privacy by serving as a source of strength and support, emerges more fully with a healthy paternal identity. Such a man is well prepared for the "long and winding road" of fathering.

A father will naturally experience both jealousy and envy of the intense, mother–infant mutuality. His capacity to serve as a protective agent consequently depends on how he deals with his envy. The "holding" father must successfully integrate both the creative and destructive aspects of his envy of the primary maternal–infant bond (Hyman, 1995). This synthesis results both through his *creative expression,* which further establishes his tie to the infant (Diamond, 1992), and through his identification with the "blissful union" experienced by mother and her baby (Hyman, 1995). The mother's sensitivity to the father's needs and her attunement to her husband's feelings of loss help ameliorate his sense of exclusion, envy and rivalry (Jordan, 1995; Hyman, 1995; Shapiro, 1987). Additionally, through the new father's protective agency, involved nurturance, and increasing comfort with his "genuine fatherliness," such a "good enough" father fulfills his culture's code of manhood. This provides the new father with another opportunity to rework his masculine gender identity and enhance his self-esteem.

The *holding father,* in addition, must be able to perceive his child as representing an opportunity for self-enhancement (i.e., increased self-love) and as being a means for attaining immortality. Wolson (1995b) has clarified the crucial importance of paternal, "adaptive grandiosity", which entails both the father's *projection of his special, ideal self* onto his child (e.g., in ways he feels or wanted to be extraordinarily special himself), as well as his *capacity to differentiate himself* from his baby. Lacking these adaptive and reality-oriented abilities, more omnipotent, maladaptive grandiose expressions render such fathers unable to maintain empathic sensitivity with their wife and baby as separate individuals. Fathers who are deficient in adaptive grandiosity are unable to provide the necessary holding functions because they are both threatened by exclusion from, and overly needy of inclusion into, the mothering dyad. Such fathers cannot "defeat (their) childhood narcissism" and frequently require therapeutic treatment to foster a mature, adaptive grandiosity (see Diamond, 1995b for a clinical illustration).

CONCLUDING THOUGHTS

A father's "watchful protectiveness" helps provide a "good beginning" for his infant child while strengthening his own emerging paternal identity and the evolving parenting alliance with his spouse. The nature of his protective agency, his serving as the "someone watching over" from the *outside,* is multi-determined and based largely on the unique needs of his child, his wife, himself and the operative marital, familial, and cultural system.

Though I have given prominence to the significance of this less conspicuous, hitherto rather neglected facet of fathering, it is none-theless true that this fatherly characteristic has largely been relegated to those ill-fated realms of discourse where fathers are treated as "the forgotten parent" (Ross, 1982b). Certain parental phenomena, such as providing an ego-supportive "holding environment" (Winnicott, 1956), serving as a steady and responsive "container" for a baby's unpleasant feelings (Bion, 1959), and supplying "empathic mirroring" (Kohut, 1971), have historically been conceived of as *"maternal"* in function. It is not surprising, therefore, that the less "noisy" and visible, more receptive and serene *paternal* functions involving "holding," "containing," and empathy, as represented by fatherly "protective watchfulness," have long been ignored, presupposed as "mothering," maternal or feminine traits (see for example, Ehrensaft, 1995; Schwartz, 1993), or simply treated as insignificant, peripheral facets of "hus-bandry."

I have attempted in this chapter to emphasize the importance of a father's protective watchfulness, particularly as it emerges during his wife's pregnancy and at the early stages of his infant child's life. This protective agency will moreover be manifest in various ways through-out the course of his children's lives and will be shared with his wife within their parenting alliance. The inherent limitations in his ability to protect his loved ones from the pains and tragedies of fate nonetheless force an involved father oftentimes to endure, with some equanimity, the agonizing sense of helplessness in the wake of life's "necessary losses." All the while, yet another form of quiet strength and courage is required of this man, who must frequently bear with restraint a position lying *outside* the primacy of his child's (and frequently, child-mother) dyadic mutualities.[6]

The essential nature of this complex fatherly provision is powerfully revealed, initially in the delivery room when the father watches his child emerge from within his wife, "while touching anew the unspeakable awe of the miraculous world beyond his control" (Diamond, 1986, p. 466). The rich vicissitudes of this "holding" function are manifest subsequently by a father with his children throughout his life as he increasingly accepts the borders inherently restricting his protective agency. For the child who has grown up, this universal longing for fatherly watchful protection is boldly revealed in Ira Gershwin's haunting lyrics from the American jazz era:.

> There's a somebody I'm longing to see
> I hope that he
> Turns out to be
> Someone who'll watch over me.
> . . . . . .
> Won't you tell him please to put on some speed
> Follow my lead
> Oh! How I need
> Someone to watch over me.
>
> "Someone To Watch Over Me"
> (from *Oh, Kay*)
> —George & Ira Gershwin (1926)

---

[6]This should in no way imply that fathers do *not* experience their own unique *dyadic bonding* with their children. The mutual bonds experienced by fathers with their sons and daughters are powerfully rewarding and extremely important in each one's interactive development (see Diamond, 1995a). My point, however, is rather that this function of "protective agency" operates largely *outside of* these dyadic bonds, and consequently requires that fathers obtain their gratification from their "watchfulness" less directly and less interactively.

Part III
THE CLINICAL PERSPECTIVE

Psychodynamic Dimensions

Treatment Issues

Little by little as your body forms and buoys
larger in her pendant ocean,
your presence forms and buoys
in my oceanic heart
and in my daily mind.

Consider this office I am going to rent:
you get my old room for healing talk,
poem, painting and music, and it is
as Simone Weil says, "Emptiness
attracts grace." I am emptying out
my room to attract the grace of you.
The dapple through oleander will freckle you,
while I go dark oak and respectable in this town.
I would gladly strut the streets in coat & tie
to put bread and the bread of my heart on your table.
I feel and know you, making emptiness for you.
I almost hear your laughter coming out
from the pile of music paper I shall move.

—David Debus

In this chapter, Dr. Hyman brings an extended dimension to this volume by exploring the fathers reactions during the first 9 months of their childrens' lives. She sounds a clarion call, warning new fathers of potential intrapsychic conflicts that are likely to emerge or become reactivated during the pregnancy, birth and particularly the earliest parenting periods. New fathers who experience particular jealousies, anxieties, feelings of abandonment, isolation, or anger around their participation or lack of same in feeding their infants may have to focus more intently inwardly to resolve previously hidden early conflicts.

Among the needs she identifies are the developing capacity to restructure intrapsychic barriers and imbalances, and the need for new fathers to tolerate the uncertainties of shifts in gender-related expectations of fatherhood.

22

Shifting Patterns of Fathering in the First Year of Life: On Intimacy Between Fathers and Their Babies

Judith Partnow Hyman

I don't think of myself as a spiritual person, but having a child has made me such. It has put me in touch with my mortality, with aging and dying, and with my immortality—it has made me feel more of a whole person. My relationship with my son is a way of giving my child a way of redeeming my own earlier relationships; to give him the family I never had. I feel like a good father. I never thought I could love another person so much—it's almost painful.

39-year-old father of an 8-month-old son.

The birth of a mother and a father is initiated by the Promethean event of the birth of the first child. The evolving redefinition of parenting

256

roles presents an important challenge to the traditional bio-evolution-ary argument that the mother is more responsive to the infant due to her mammalian physiology and that parenting involves primarily the mother. This challenge is stated in Benedek's (1970a) psychobiologi-cal argument that the male's procreative role has instinctual roots that go beyond the drive organization of mating behavior. Benedek be-lieves that the father's function encompasses both provider and nur-turer, and that a trait coined *"genuine fatherliness"* can enable the father to act with immediate and empathic responsiveness toward his children. Benedek's "genuine fatherliness" foreshadows Pruett's (1983) empathic nurturing, which he termed *"bio-rhythmic synchro-ny."* Given the psychosociocultural atmosphere over the last few decades, the seeds for the flourishing of "genuine fatherliness" have been rapidly spreading.

The purpose of this chapter is to familiarize the reader with the changing nature of the involvement of the father (from autocrat to nurturer), and to describe the intensified desire among many men to become more intimately involved with their infants. Highlighted are emphases on the father's experience surrounding the issues of the feeding of his baby along with the reactivation and revisions of his gender identities. Special attention is given to the conflicts of envy and narcissistic vulnerability surrounding the father's relationship to his bottlefed and/or breastfed infant. Insights are used from psychoana-lytic literature and empirical research conducted by the author.

SHIFTING PARADIGMS

> The women's movement in essence stated that they were deprived, that they wanted it all. That reawakened the men that they've been shut out too. Now we are witnessing the flip side—that men want both too.
>
> —A 39-year-old father

The reverberations of the women's movement have had a funda-mental impact on the redistribution of roles, responsibilities, and power in contemporary American marriages. The fact that most contemporary women are concerned simultaneously with mothering and career implies that they no longer have to use their territorial rights to the child as their sole domain of power. The modern mother's dual interests in both briefcases and babies also has a significant influence on the way in which men make the transition to fatherhood;

among other things, there is generally an increased vacuum in the care of the child, and decreased pressure for him to be the sole provider. In this intermediate area a potential space is emerging that provides an opportunity for men to be engaged in the procreation and early care of children.

In this new constellation, fathers are expected to become intimately involved with children even before they are born. Intergenerationally, however, most men have limited previous role models for this responsibility; their own father for example, most likely related to them as a talking/walking/playing (oedipal) child rather than as a burping/nursing/pooping (preoedipal) infant. Many modern fathers may be committed to the ideal of relative equality in marriages and to themselves as actively involved parents. They may lack the relational and nurturing aspects of internal maternal/paternal identities and the abundance of psychological resources they need to fulfill expectations of intimate involvement with their babies from birth onward, however.

More likely, these men have had early experiences of maternal caretaking that appear to be unintegrated with later paternal caretaking creating a "disjunctive transition" (Gerson, 1989) in their development toward a paternal identification. The imbalance of their co-gender identifications can create an underlying tension, anxiety, or conflict intrapsychically and interpersonally.

SHIFTING PATTERNS OF FATHERS IN THE BIRTHING EXPERIENCE

> As a new father, I feel enhanced as a person, with increased patience and tolerance and a sense of purpose. I have something to come home to at night. They say you can tell a women is pregnant because she glows, but I think you can tell a father because of his glow. It feels really special to be needed. I think there is really something changing in our society for fathers. We are really allowed to be a part of it, beginning with the birth and all the prenatal visits. It's a comfort to express this to my other male friends as well.
>
> —Danny, a 27-year-old father of a 6-month-old daughter.

The starting point for this discussion are the findings of the author's study of the emotional experiences of 75 first-time fathers from intact families with babies 3 months (hatching) to 12 months of age

(Hyman, 1992). The fathers were recruited from pediatricians and obstetricians, newspaper ads, and the Warm Line at Thalians Community Mental Health Center of Cedars/Sinai Hospital. They were primarily college-educated, Caucasian, and married about 3 to 5 years. Sixty-five of these fathers had taken childbirth classes. All were present during their child's birth, the majority (59) remaining minimally 2 hours or longer. Between 3 to 12 months later nearly all the fathers reported being highly interested in their babies and very able to give them love.

In mainstream culture, these findings reflect the dramatic shifts in the delivery room from the total absence of the expectant father, traditionally pacing back and forth in the alienated bareness of the maternity waiting room, to his ubiquitous presence and emotional involvement in the birthing experience. Research has shown that the father's experience of birth and his behavior toward his spouse and baby during delivery is more emotionally profound and significant in shaping the father's involvement than prenatal attitudes (Peterson, Mehl, & Leiderman; 1969). In other words, even if anticipatory negative feelings toward fathering exist prior to birth, a favorable birth experience will ultimately transform the father's attitude to ultimately a positive one, and vice versa.

The dual experiences of prenatal education and the powerful intimate involvement in the birth environment reinforce the father's attachment to the newborn infant. His presence in the birthing room has dramatically expanded his ability to be an involved, active, and a nurturing caretaker in the preoedipal period. For many fathers birthing initiates an epic of self-identity revision drawn from a wellspring of early psychological bonding and relating; for some it is felt as a spiritual transformation.

> I realized in the birthing process how much I fell in love all over again with my wife—how heroic she was. She was so focused, she wanted to deliver vaginally and worked on it. I have never been a very spiritual person, but the birth and the creation of the baby is miraculous. The baby is part of me. My soul has becomes externalized in my child.
>
> —Randall, a 39-year-old father of an 8-month-old son.

These fathers' responses, their engrossed interest and engagement with their babies, supported by the literature, underscore one of the more striking themes in the author's data: early involvement in parenting activities stirs psychic shifts and thereby is a learning process during which fathers' attitudes and internal identities can undergo profound change.

Involved fathers in the author's research consistently referred to their expanded emotional repertoire, and to their enhanced sense of self-esteem and familial worth, which they attributed to their presence in the birth experience as well as their involvement in pre- and postnatal care. The increased "patience and tolerance" described by Danny (above), reflects a consistent pattern voiced among involved fathers reflecting the amelioration of aggression in men concomitant with an increased capacity for containment. An anxiety scale (Cattell & Scheier, 1976) used in the research indicated that the experiences surrounding the new baby tended to lower anxiety and not to elevate it. These findings are reminiscent of former studies (Scott-Heyes, 1982; Teichman & Lahav, 1987) wherein contrary to predictions, expectant fathers reported lower levels of anxiety and hostility. It may be that the presence of a new baby operates as an organized focus for working through various issues, tempering anxiety and stress.

The cultural shifts supporting the father's involvement in the preparation, birth, and postnatal care of the baby are reflective of many dramatic changes in America. Some of the more formidable themes are the Zeitgeist of the women's movement, which has stimulated the rethinking of gender roles precipitating in changes in the roles of mothers and fathers. In addition, the disenchantment with traditional values of the "nuclear family" and the economic shifts requiring dual careers encourages more fathers to be involved with their family. The confluence of all of these forces activate the father's nurturing qualities, his primitive maternal identifications, and his intensified desires to achieve intimacy with the new baby.

SHIFTING PATTERNS OF FATHERS IN THE FEEDING EXPERIENCE

It is important to emphasize and recognize that the increased stimulation of such forces can culminate in the heightened emotionally laden nature of men's psychological orientation toward fatherhood. Given that the involved father seeks to continue and deepen a personal connection with the new baby, his interest and narcissistic investment turns toward an arena of profound personal contact—that of feeding, the earliest means of intimate social contact (Fairbairn, 1952; Klein, 1948). For some involved fathers, this highly charged arena of increased narcissistic investment is accompanied by the likelihood of narcissistic vulnerability. This phenomenon was borne out in the father's reactions to whether his baby is being breastfed or bottlefed.

The benefits nutritionally and developmentally of breastfeeding are well documented in the literature but little attention has been given to its impact on husbands. The author's research compared matched groups of fathers of breastfed babies to fathers of bottlefed babies. The infants in the bottlefed group had for the most part been breastfed for 8 to 12 weeks (the current preferred mode of feeding); most mothers either terminated breast-feeding at about this time or commenced a mixed breast/bottle-feeding program. Weaning was attributed to a return to work, or loss of satisfaction, or in some cases, pressure from excluded fathers. Significant findings revealed that fathers of bottlefed or mixed breast/bottlefed babies (3 to 12 months) self-reported being less anxious, calmer, and more competent in interacting with their babies. In contrast, the fathers of breastfed babies reported greater levels of anxiety, excitation, and less competence. A significant number of the fathers of bottlefed or mixed breast/bottlefed babies wanted to be involved in feeding. In fact, the great majority (80%) of fathers of bottlefed babies (most formerly breastfed) reported giving their babies a bottle minimally once a day, with 40% providing two or more bottles a day.

One unexpected finding was a remarkable difference in response to the researcher's request for a clinical interview. Fewer than 20% of the breastfed group were willing to come in for an interview; in contrast, 80% of the fathers of bottlefed or mixed bottle/breastfed babies responded positively.

One father, whose 8-month-old son has been on a mixed bottle/breast plan since 6 weeks, explained his version of this discrepancy: *"I think the breastfed fathers are not here because they are not involved. I see the feeding very essential in being involved, else you feel very disconnected. You are not part of the loop. The caring and nurturing of the baby is then very disproportionate in the beginning. I want my son to know too that men are very nurturing. (Men too) can feel deeply and intimately."*

What other kinds of explanations can illuminate the phenomena of the involved fathers' absorbed engagement in feeding or, conversely, the unavailability for clinical interviews of fathers of breastfed babies?

A brief summary of the developmental tasks of fatherhood may be useful.

THE DEVELOPMENTAL TASKS OF FATHERHOOD

Fatherhood is a developmental phase requiring a man to undergo certain transitional passages activating earlier developmental struggles and conflicts and can bring about a developmental crisis comparable in many respects to the upheavals of early adolescence (Benedek, 1959; Deutscher, 1981; Gurwitt, 1976; Kestenberg, 1975; Osofsky, 1982; Osofsky & Culp, 1989; Parens, 1975). The re-emergence of these developmental tasks are reworked in the unfolding of fatherhood (Diamond, 1986; Gurwitt, 1989). A cursory synopsis of these tasks include: (a) early gender and gender-discrepant self-identifications; (b) infantile dependency needs; (c) early reproductive ambitions and envy of the woman's capacity to bear and deliver children (womb and pregnancy envy) and to sustain life (breast/lactation envy); (d) mastery over preoedipal/oedipal issues; and (e) separation/ individuation issues. Particularly central to this chapter is the developmental task of reworking early gender identifications which coincide with the current re-conceptualization of gender development amongst a group of psychoanalytic thinkers (Benjamin 1988, 1991; Chodorow, 1978; Dimen, 1991; Fast 1984, Goldner, 1991; Kaftal, 1991). The new debate about gender development bring to the fore men's relational and affective development rather than Freud's conception of manhood ensconced in the image of the heroic and the brave individualism, aggressive competition, and the suppression of emotion. As many new fathers move away from their stereotypic masculine modes of relating and toward affective involvement in the tenderings of their babies (cuddling, rocking, and feeding) they confront the opportunity to reintegrate the lost aspects of their gendered self-identities and to expand their capacities to relate.

To achieve this task fathers must rework their gendered self-representation, which means internally restructuring the older "orthodox" system of gender development referred to by Benjamin (1991) as "gender heterodoxy." Operating on a bifurcation model of heterosexuality (biological and developmental inevitability) this paradigm orders a fixed two-gender system of the masculine or the feminine, which forces men into a heroic, bravado model and assigns tenderness to women. The fathers of today, influenced by this two-gender model, were raised as young boys to turn toward their fathers to identify while negotiating a negative identification away from their mothers ("I am not like mommy," "I am not female"). In other words, to secure masculinity they have had to renounce, repress, and/or disidentify their primary maternal identification (Greenson, 1968; Ross, 1986; Van der Leeuw, 1958) rather than integrate it with paternal identification. Their own fathers have typically been absent from the nurturing matrix so that the experience of an affective, preverbal relationship is trapped in the world of women. What remains is a brittle false-self system of gender identity (Goldner 1991; Ross, 1986) and an unconscious fear and terror of women resulting from denouncing maternal procreative desires and assigning it solely to the feminine. The ensuing frustration (from the disconnection of these gendered identities), overdetermined in the developmental phase of fatherhood, brings about an intense envy of women's creative powers, which is frequently denied, reversed, and expressed through devaluation and degradation of maternal life-giving powers (Boehm, 1930; Chasseguet-Smirgel, 1970; Jacobson, 1950; Lerner, 1974, 1979; Van Leeuwen, 1965; Waletzky, 1979).

The new father who seeks an intimate relationship with his baby is faced with a developmental crisis dealing with intrapsychic conflict. He must find a way to restructure his "bravado" model of masculinity to be affectively involved in the preverbal relationship of his baby. He must also work through shifts in his dependency needs, feelings of envy, and competitiveness strivings. As with any developmental crisis, this involves testing and re-evaluating old patterns, improvising new ones, and, optimally, gradually evolving toward a more integrative personal self. When this fails, the new father is at risk (Gurwitt, 1989; Osofsky & Culp, 1989). He may experience dislocation, denial, or hostility, distancing himself from the mother/infant dyad psychologically or physically. Simultaneously he may devalue and degrade the women's life-giving capacities while intensifying a traditional masculine gender role, referred to as hypermasculinity.

The fathers interest in nursing supports some of the more recent challenges debated in the new line of development about gender— that is, that there are more natural gender consistencies and commonalities in masculine and feminine dispositions (Goldner, 1991; May, 1986) rather than an obligatory status of heterosexuality. This would support Fast's (1984) argument against an innate bisexuality disposition but rather a differentiation out of a common matrix. She states for the boy a broad range of identifications with the mother, including her functions in nurturing and care giving that may be included in his sense of himself as masculine. It may in fact be that "dis-identification" or "repudiation" signals failure in optimum development of masculinity, an organization too exclusively phallic, denying the actual procreative capacity and nurturing possibilities of a man.

ADDITIONAL INTERPERSONAL AND INTRAPSYCHIC CONFLICTS

In addition to the reactivation and conflicts of gender identities, other factors contribute to the interpersonal and intrapsychic conflict faced by new fathers of breastfed babies (Lerner, 1979; Waletsky, 1979). For example, a husband, although often proud and supportive of his nursing wife, may also begin to sense her increased competence in the biological and life-giving function contained in the new mother/baby dyad as her dependency needs on him decrease. The nursing mother's independence and intimate bonding may intensify his feelings of inadequacy, helplessness, superfluousness, exclusion, and isolation.

Conversely, the reawakened nurturance of the actively involved father whose infant is being breastfed is faced with a quandary: How does he cope with the fact that his partner is able to achieve a degree of intimacy with the infant of which he is totally denied? He has to deal with the paradox of being more involved, as he is expected to be, while simultaneously being excluded from the most intimate contact with his new baby (Shapiro, 1993b). Heightening this quandary is the frustration of men's reawakened procreative capacities and nurturing longings.

For the father of the breastfed baby, the constant awareness of the close bonding between the new baby and mother may make his unfulfilled dependency needs and newly aroused nurturings even more precarious. This threatening situation can transform his reawakened longings, awe and envy into shame and/or devaluation and subjugation of the maternal lifegiving powers with possibly serious implications for his capacity to nurture, such as flight from fatherhood (Gerson, 1989). In contrast, the father of a bottlefed baby fulfills his nurturing needs through his increased participation and involvement in directly feeding the baby. This experience can facilitate re-encountering his own wished for or experienced oral supplies, as well as reintegrating his gendered self-identities, thereby promoting the growth of his own internal nourishing paternal and maternal imago.

Optimally, the father of either breast or bottlefed babies works through these issues via identification with his own nurturing parental models or his nurtured baby. For example, the father, viewing his child feeding at his wife's breast may identify with the baby or the mother, and in the process reactivate his own met or unmet oral dependency needs, evoking memories of his own mother's goodnesses or inadequacies. In this way men's formerly lost gendered self-identities can be reclaimed and newly discovered intimacies can be facilitated. Depending on his internal/external circumstances, the identification with the nursing dyad can repair earlier deprivations. He may also be vulnerable to unresolved oedipal and preoedipal conflicts as he observes the baby/sibling/rival commandeering his territorial entitlements and symbolically competing for his wife's (mother's) affection, however, or viewing his wife's involvement in nursing as an envious reminder of his own narcissistic losses of the common gender matrix that he once experienced.

This issue may make the father vulnerable to experiencing and re-experiencing a narcissistic loss stemming from his wish heralding back to his preoedipal beginnings to possess everything, babies and breast, believing he owned the attributes of both sexes. The narcissistic injury from this early loss has the potential of reactivating a more intensive upsurge of unresolved developmental issues. Coping with this conflict effectively, and successfully amalgamating the creative and destructive experiences of his envy, and reworking his varied gendered self-identities is a major developmental challenge for the father. The task is too great to bear for some fathers whose desires to be involved have been reawakened and stimulated. Moreover, there are painful feelings of shame and rage of having these envious desires, which can be expressed as an attack or subjugation of women.

The danger of the breakthrough of raw envy is illustrated by the following interviewed father, an uneducated construction worker, who blatantly reveals his wish to usurp the mother's life-giving function. This father demonstrates the intense feelings of narcissistic rage that accompany the breakdown of the defensive structure of his formerly renounced maternal identifications. *"I was mad because I couldn't feed him. She insisted on 4 weeks because of her belief of bonding. She read somewhere that the baby should feel her heart beat and breath rate. At 4 weeks I brought home the breast pump. It was my turn! She cried. But I wanted to get involved! All I could do up to then was change the poopey. . . . I felt Corrie was pushing me out—that's why I got the pump. I feel a father should get the*

*chance to breastfeed and not that glucose stuff. That's not food—
that just makes them pee."*

On the other hand, some of the fathers interviewed by the author
conveyed a capacity to develop a nurturing paternal/maternal identity,
transforming their envy into an identification with the blissful union
of mother/baby, joining with the mother in a kind of corollary of
Winnicott's (1958) "maternal preoccupation" in what can be termed
a "paternal preoccupation." Such fathers felt a deep and sincere desire
to be close to the nursing dyad, perhaps identifying with the baby and
reliving their own earlier and fulfilling feeding experience or refueling
and repairing insufficient ones. These fathers experienced the baby,
the mother, and themselves as an integrated triad, living together as a
psychologically healthy unit.

The length of time of nursing and the attitude of the mother
appeared to play key roles in this fulfilling adaptation. Most men were
very excited and supportive of the nursing dyad for the first 3–4
months, but after that period of time their wishes for more direct
personal involvement began to emerge, breaking down their capacity
for containment. At that point in time for these fathers, providing a
bottle minimally once a day (either formula or breast milk) amelio-
rated their difficulties and maintained a supportive equilibrium in the
family.

The father's capacity to resolve his conflicts depends on the degree
to which the mother encourages her husband's involvement during
pregnancy and later child care. By being sensitive to her husband's
needs, the new mother can, to some degree, ameliorate his sense of
exclusion, envy, or rivalry particularly noted in breastfeeding. For
example, she can aid in helping the baby to discover more of daddy
(Atkins, 1982) and daddy discovering more of the baby. In this sense
the mother is very much the facilitator of the husband's connection
to the newborn, "if she welcomes him into the arena of symbiotic,
nurturing care, he will be better able to bridge the psychological space
between himself and his child" (Gerson, 1989, p. 141).

CONCLUSIONS

The emerging trends discussed in this chapter are highly dynamic, and
many questions remain to be addressed. Are the shifting roles of fathers
superficial responses to transient societal expectations? Is the nurturing father merely the current fad adopted to conform to current

pressures? Or is it possible that there is a fundamental shift of a reintegrated core gender identification of fathers and thereby their future paternal progeny?

The fathers interviewed in the author's research represent an emergent group of involved fathers who demonstrated their longings, struggles, and vulnerabilities toward a more intimate involvement in the birthing, caring, and feeding of their infants. This group of involved fathers reflect the contemporary shifting and decentering of gender paradigms and the restructuring of formerly disclaimed relational and nurturing capacities. For many fathers of newborns, this has released them from formerly stereotypic hypermasculine roles, transformed their longings and/or envy into an enduring nurturance and a unique capacity for intimacy, and enabled them to reclaim their renounced childbearing and childrearing desires.

The capacity to restructure intrapsychic barriers and imbalances to disproportionate self-gender identities and to tolerate the uncertainties of these shifts are a vital intrapsychic and developmental tasks in the unfolding of fatherhood. The contemporary generation of actively involved fathers, then, may be seen as transitional fathers who are somehow creating bridges from the imprints of their own internalized parents to possibly an unknown future prototype.

This chapter, which first appeared in expanded form in The Psychoanalytic Review examines the process of becoming a father from a psychoanalytic developmental perspective. It begins with a discussion of the neglect of the father during pregnancy and birth. It next considers the unique contributions made by fathers of the newborn. The less conscious wishes to become a father that emerge throughout male development are then explored. Finally, Dr. Diamond examines the specific phases of expectant fatherhood, from getting ready through parturition.

23

Becoming a Father:
A Psychoanalytic Perspective
on the Forgotten Parent

Michael J. Diamond

The man who does not believe in miracles surely makes it certain
that he will never take part in one.

—William Blake

THE FORGOTTEN PARENT

Several writers have recently called attention to the neglect of the father during the early stages of parenting. Burlingham (1973) argued for the end of comparative disregard of the preoedipal father in psychoanalytic writings, whereas Ross (1982b) has elaborated on the father as the "forgotten parent" in psychoanalytic literature. Burlingham's (1973) seminal paper invited her colleagues to investigate the psychodynamics of fatherhood, particularly the father's fantasies between impregnation and birth and during the first weeks of his infant's life; his hopes and expectations concerning the child's growth and development; his jealousies of the mother's preoccupation with the infant; the arousal of his own feminine attitudes; and the impact of these attitudes on his latent memories concerning the relationship to his own father. Nonetheless, as Ross (1982a) said,

268

the parental ambitions of the boy and man, their urges to create life, have generally remained linked to maternal, womanly ambitions and prerogatives. . . . It is almost, one senses, as if to be a parent one must be a woman. (p. 20)

Psychoanalysts have by no means been the sole perpetrators of this neglect. Lamb (1976) referred to the "unwitting contribution" made by social scientists toward the devaluation of the father's role; he subsequently advocated additional empirical study on the effects of increased paternal involvement (Lamb, 1984). He discussed the tendency to infer that mothers are more important than fathers and therefore solely deserving of investigation because they are the primary caretakers. Societal factors obviously play an important role in sustaining the belief that fathers are rather inconsequential, particularly when childrearing and socialization are widely considered the "duty" of the mothers.[1]

Jessner, Weigert, and Foy (1970) presented the prevailing cultural stereotype of becoming a father according to the phallic achievement of the boastful, beaming father making the maturational transition from a youth to an adult with first fatherhood. Such stereotypes, although inadequate, do set the stage for contrasting motherhood with fatherhood and eventually discerning the unique contribution made by fathers. Unlike expectant motherhood, expectant fatherhood cannot be described in terms of its biological immediacy with its more continuous, visceral knowing. As with adoptive parents, descriptions of the father's experience must rely on its experiential components, such as hope, appropriation, and responsibility (Jessner et al., 1970). The father must experience the impelling psychophysiological events of gestation, quickening, fetal growth, parturition, and lactation in a second-hand, yet typically highly affective manner.

Benedek (1970a) posited a "psychobiology" to fatherhood based on survival instincts, the derivatives of which produce the characterologic quality of fatherliness. Not surprisingly, the father is considered further removed from instinctual roots than is the mother. Benedek also

---

[1]Dinnerstein (1976) and Chodorow (1978), integrating feminist and psychoanalytic thinking, have dared to consider the social and psychological importance of fathers providing primary caretaking of their infants. This radically altered arrangement of mothering is then considered as it would affect those unconscious attitudes between men and women that ultimately determine prevailing societal standards. As Pruett's (1983a) clinical research suggests, the personal and social implications of viewing childrearing either as the "duty" of fathers or, perhaps, as more equally shared, are quite far-reaching.

attempted to show that fatherhood (i.e., the male's role in procreation) has instinctual roots beyond the drive organization of mating behavior. She believed these roots included both his function as a *provider* and a capacity to develop *fatherliness* ties that render his relationship to his children a mutual, developmental experience. She hypothesized a trait termed "genuine fatherliness"—an instinctually rooted character-trend enabling the father to act toward his children with immediate empathic responsiveness. Greenberg and Morris's (1974) observation of the "engrossment" fathers show toward their newborn offers partial support for Benedek's provocative idea. They found that engrossment went beyond involvement to include a sense of absorption, preoccupation, and interest in the infant that enabled the father to feel enlarged (i.e., with an increased sense of self-esteem and familial worth). This bond is viewed as an innate potential of fathers, released by early contact with the infant.

Others, both from a psychoanalytic and a developmental perspective, have presented evidence supporting the view that fathers make unique and important contributions to the development of their infants' personalities, while revealing characteristics often considered to lie only within the purview of mothers. For example, Pruett (1983a) studied infants *primarily* raised by their fathers. These "primary nurturing fathers were found to achieve a "biorhythmic synchrony" with their infants, a kind of empathic resonance similar to that displayed by mothers in the primary role. Abelin (1975) investigated the earliest role of the more supplementary father as he facilitated his child's exploratory and early phallic attitudes, his child's disentanglement from the regressive symbiotic tie with the mother, and his child's experience of early triangulation. Yogman (1984) demonstrated that competent fathers, in contrast to mothers, are more likely to develop a heightened, arousing, and playful relationship with their infants while providing a more novel and complex environment. Finally, Lamb (1976) summarized the literature demonstrating the importance of the father–infant relationship on the child's development and, not surprisingly, concluded that the *quality* of this relationship is far more important and influential than is the mere physical presence of the father.

MALE MOTIVATION FOR FATHERHOOD: A DEVELOPMENTAL FRAMEWORK

In view of the appreciable neglect of fatherhood, it comes as little surprise that there have been few psychoanalytic studies of the male wish for a child. Jacobson (1950) discussed this neglect of boys' pregnancy fantasies and wishes for a baby, which she posited was due to reaction formations against unconscious feminine wishes to grow children, and, at a deeper level, repressed envy of woman's reproductive functions.

Psychoanalytic understanding has been gradually influenced, nonetheless by numerous *societal changes, feminism,* the increasing influence of a number of *prominent female psychoanalysts,* as well as several important *theoretical advances* (e.g., the emphasis on object relational development in contrast to drive psychology). Using this increased understanding, I shall discuss the wishes for children among boys and men as they emerge throughout the developmental process. These overdetermined wishes are separated for expository purposes and tend to overlap within the psychic reality of the would-be father. Most of these wishes tend to remain unconscious and accessible to consciousness indirectly and/or through the psychoanalytic process.

Infantile Wishes to Bear a Child to Master Preoedipal Conflicts

Freud (1909) first discussed the reproductive wishes of little boys in the case of little Hans and his pregnancy fantasies where, "In phantasy, he was a mother and wanted children with whom he could repeat the endearments that he had experienced himself" (p. 93). Jacobson (1950) discussed the evolution of the pregenital boy's wish to have a baby, reflecting his *desire for active self-assertion and independence from the mother,* along with *mastery of his preoedipal conflicts.* The earliest wish develops during the oral and anal phase and fantasies tend to be of pregnancy and delivery by the oral incorporation and anal rebirth of the mother. For example, a child might fantasize eating up the breasts or whole body of the mother, only to restore her by reproducing her through the anus, mouth, or navel. These fantasies reflect the child's cloacal theories of birth wherein genital and excretory organs and functions are equated. The baby is equated with the breast, womb, intestines, or feces and such a primitive "theory" may remain alive in the unconscious, particularly of pregenitally fixed individuals.

The next set of pregenital wishes involve *fantasies about the parental relationship and concepts of the primal scene.* With early triangulation, these fantasies may involve the father impregnating the mother by defecating or urinating into her, or possibly that mother grows children by drinking father's urine, eating his feces, or part of his penis. Little Hans's "lumpf theories evidence these wishes (Freud, 1909).

The final set of preoedipal wishes involve a *shift toward the father* of desires previously directed toward the mother. These then become a part of the boy's homosexual fantasies and feminine identifications (with mother) as his early passive pregnancy wishes shift from mother to father, and concomitantly, from her breast to his penis. Thus, the child may wish to incorporate the father's penis or feces and to reproduce him as a baby boy with whom the father–son relationship can be reversed. The "breast baby" now becomes a "penis baby."

Jacobson (1950) widened our understanding of these desires to have babies as something purposeful, age-specific, and adaptive and not simply as expressions of instinctual urges. The process of identification by incorporating and internalizing love objects in the form of images of one's caretakers thus sets the stage for the subsequent development of this wish. Jessner et al.'s (1970) description of the pregenital parental attitudes displayed by little boys toward younger siblings and playmates suggests further this identification and accompanying wishes for a baby. These authors referred to the sublimation of such early infantile wishes as reflected in the creative endeavors of the artist; thus underscoring the parallel between procreation and creation.

Oedipal Wishes to Impregnate One's Mother

With the onset of the oedipal period, the baby fantasies of girls and boys take on different meanings and directions. This is ushered in by the discovery of the differences of the sexes and the ensuing castration conflict. As Jacobson (1950) describes it, the realization of their femininity intensifies wishes in girls for growing a baby in order to substitute for the supposedly lost penis. In boys, the discovery of the female genital mobilizes castration fears and affirms the boy's phallic identification with the father; consequently, active masculine drives to impregnate mother by sexual intercourse win out over homosexual feminine wishes. Thus, the boy has to sacrifice his wish to grow babies just as the girl must renounce her desire for a penis (Brunswick, 1940).

The little boy must renounce his feminine pregnancy-and-child wishes and advance to the "wish to have a child from mother" (Jacobson, 1950). Such an advance is regarded as a prerequisite for the normal subsequent development of a man's desire for children and his future attitude toward his children. This successful advance is largely influenced by the threat of castration and the birth of a younger child during this period. Unresolved castration anxieties may surface in adulthood to inhibit fatherhood, create guilt and anxieties around dependency needs arising during parenthood, or create difficulties during pregnancy as the pregnant wife is experienced as dangerous, castrating, and frequently nonerotic. Similarly, the little boy's more defensive maternal identifications in response to the traumatic birth of a younger sibling must be renounced by adaptive reaction formations that strengthen the young boy's phallic masculine position. It seems, however, that maternal fantasies need to survive in the healthy male father as they are alloyed with oedipal-level paternal wishes.

The successful resolution of the oedipal situation occurs as the boy identifies with his father, and in turn wishes to become like his father. Behind this more mature trend are typically deeper, more primitive strivings. Thus, postoedipal wishes to become a father enable the boy to achieve his goal of competition with his father—he can become a father. The man who does father a child then becomes a link in the chain of generations between fathers and their children. Although all men struggle with succeeding their fathers, some men are particularly fearful and thus inhibit or prevent their own fatherhood in order to keep from being exposed to their repressed aggression toward their fathers. Others may adopt a negative oedipal position to protect themselves from this outcome.

Sublimated Wishes Stemming from Envy or Awe of Female Childbearing Capacity

Envy can be a creative or a destructive experience. It so often serves as the bedrock for the healthy internalization (via identification) of the beloved maternal object. Ross (1982a) discussed male childbearing wishes as a kind of "identification with the aggressor" as the boy identifies with his active, producing mother. Thus, feminine maternal identification can no longer be considered as passive but rather, as achievement, power, and competition with the mother. Kubie (1974) stated that by fathering his wife's child and identifying himself with the child and mother at once, the father can assuage his archaic desire to possess his mother's breast (and the magical powers exclusive to women), thus "completing himself." The boy's envy and awe of his mother (i.e., "womb envy") are never completely renounced and when successfully sublimated, foster healthy fatherliness.

An intense envy of a woman's ability to grow and produce children may render it particularly difficult for the boy/man to renounce or sublimate his wish to bear children. Reaction formation defenses against such envy are developed during latency years and become manifest in the male's absence of a longing for children until the approach of marriage. At the point of marriage, the wish for a child resurfaces among those men who have largely mastered this envy; those who haven't done so frequently turn out to be impotent or, if potent, narcissistically invested in their children and frequently competitive with their wives in terms of maternal care. As previously mentioned, creative work is normally the main channel for the sublimation of such feminine reproductive wishes in men.[2] Ross (1982a) further suggested that the man's wish for a son may further serve to "drain off homosexual libido."

Sublimated Wishes for Dependency

Dependency needs are usually in conflict with the ego aspirations of young men, and self-esteem consequently is lost when dependent tendencies are recognized. Exaggerated phallic masculine behavior serves to repress such tendencies, which are associated with threatening feminine identifications. Benedek (1970a) discussed the exacerbation of young men's dependency conflicts on the threat of impending separations, such as during wartime. She noted that male nar- cissistic defenses increase in the attempt to conquer regressive dependent tendencies and, frequently, lead to a conscious desire for procreation which reassures the male of his masculinity through "virility." Thus, consonant with his ego-ideal, the (young) man finds an acceptable way of mastering his (regressive) dependency needs and the birth rate goes up!

Wishes for dependency and conflicts engendered by such unacceptable wishes persist for many men throughout the life cycle. Wishes for children and actual procreation serve to reassure the male of his masculinity through an identification with his own father's fatherliness" (i.e., nurturance), while elevating him above his fears by enabling him to reverse the dependent role by caring for the more needy infant-child. Many of a man's urges to bear and nurture babies reflect his desire to draw the strengths and virtues from his own history of

---

[2] In addition to creative work per se, specific activities may more fully discharge such sublimated wishes. Male psychotherapists, psychoanalysts, and related workers in the "people-helping" professions appear somewhat unique in their ability to express and gratify these tendencies more directly in their work activities (see also Diamond, 1992).

dependent relationships (Ross, 1982a). The importance of a man's relationship to the caretaking qualities of his own father cannot be underestimated.

Generative Wishes to Continue the Self

Erikson (1963) used the term "generativity" to refer to the concern arising in adulthood for establishing and guiding the next generation. He viewed this as an essential stage on the psychosexual as well as psychosocial schedule. Of course the mere fact of wanting or even having children does not "achieve" generativity nor is this drive necessarily applied to one's own offspring. Benedek (1970a), however, regarded the wish to survive or continue one's self through one's children as biologically founded in the instinctual drive for survival. Increased birth rates during World War II support the idea that departing fathers-to-be often left their pregnant wives reassured that their own lives would continue through their offspring. Various rites, religions, customs, and socioeconomic organizations suggest a universal desire to survive through children, particularly the child of one's own sex.

The male's wishes to continue the self through becoming a father may also reflect a more narcissistic component activated by the ending of a more carefree, relatively less responsible period of life as marked by marriage and/or aging. These developmental markers may stir up fears of death and, in turn, reactivate wishes for omnipotence. These wishes can be gratified by having children in whom the father will survive. The almost universal preference for a male child may indicate this more narcissistic or omnipotent dimension.

Wishes for "Primary Illusion"

Shor and Sanville (1978) coined the term "primary illusion" to refer to the powerful and oscillating images present in all human beings regarding the ultimate dream of simultaneous mutuality and autonomy. This "unquenchable wish to regain paradise" (p. 28) inspires numerous drives for fulfillment and repair of imperfections. Such wishes play a significant role in the male's desire for children, although the longing to be unambivalently loved and admired is rendered less conscious for adult males who tend to be conflicted around dependency issues. Jessner et al. (1970) suggest that on the verge of parenthood both spouses feel more intensely than at any previous phase of adulthood "that they can no longer find the way back" (p. 212), a feeling that creates a nostalgic yearning for a return to the mother's womb, or, in Shor and Sanville's lexicon, a longing for "the primary illusion."

The prospects of parenthood promise the possibility of recapturing fusional love without sacrificing autonomy, an illusion doubly important for the prospective father. The anticipation of an infant's or young child's unambivalent admiration and love seems to offer unlimited possibilities for repair among adult males so needy of gratifying their healthy symbiotic wishes. This hypothesis is supported both by Greenberg and Morris' (1974) observations on fatherly engrossment in their newborn and Pruett's (1983a) reports on father–infant biorhythmic synchrony with its truly empathic nurturing.

Wishes to Expand the Self

Parenthood represents an opportunity to develop one's personality and human potentialities, both along the self- and object-relational lines of development. Sublimated wishes to bear children are frequently seen in the creative endeavors of the artist while adult longings to have children embody the desire to create (Jessner et al., 1970). Procreation itself epitomizes creation and, as such, furthers self-expansion. The expectant father coming to accept his burdens and responsibilities, his sacrifices and curtailments of freedom, courageously "transcends the juvenile ideals of manliness" (Jessner et al., 1970, p. 216) and consequently advances both as an autonomous self and in relation to his beloved others. The adaptations of prospective and actual fathering, the evolving capacities for nurturing and caretaking visible during pregnancy, and the well-established reciprocal attachments of fathers to infants (Lamb, 1976; Pruett, 1983a) evidence the importance of self-actualizing tendencies in fatherhood.

Wishes to Expand the Partnership by Increased Mutuality

Wishes for children arise in both healthy and troubled marriages (or significant partnerships), frequently based on wishes to repair, improve, or expand and develop the relationship. Jessner et al. (1970) discussed these wishes among men attempting to make up for the lack of a meaningful partnership with their wives. They noted cases of "addictions to pregnancy" among dissatisfied partners. It is axiomatic that "dyads become triads during times of crisis" and male fatherhood wishes indeed frequently surface during troubled times. Such wishes occur also in healthy relationships, however, where the male may seek to increase the mutuality with his partner by expanding an already meaningful relationship.

Reparative and Identification Wishes to Revitalize One's Own Parents

Conflicts around separation and individuation are never completely mastered and, in fact, tend to resurface during significant phases of adulthood. Marriage and commitment to a partner mark a significant rite of passage for the adult male as he further separates and individuates from his family of origin. Simultaneously, both his mother and father are aging, and unresolved separation-individuation issues are often poignantly reexperienced. Guilt is a not infrequent companion for the individuating boy and, as such, it is often recapitulated during this period of adulthood. Like envy, guilt can inspire creative, healing, and prosocial as well as destructive, harmful, and antisocial tendencies. Reparative drives can take many forms and frequently serve to heal the pains of separation-individuation. The male's desire for a child may serve as a reparative wish, a desire to give to one's own father and/or mother the child that the individuating adult male can no longer be. Moreover, grandchildren revitalize their grandparents by providing numerous narcissistic gratifications and compensations for the failing powers of later life (Cath, 1982; Colarusso & Nemiroff, 1982). It is likely that wished-for parental revitalization combines with reparative desires to lessen the prospective fathers recognition of separation-individuation pains of later life. Finally, the father's wishes for children may signify his own wishes for such revitalization by virtue of his identification with his hopefully revitalized parents.

STAGES OF PROSPECTIVE FATHERHOOD

The importance of fathers begins quite early (e.g., Abelin, 1975; Lamb, 1976; Yogman, 1984) and fathers' attachment and relationship to the infant commences long before conception and birth (e.g., Gurwitt, 1976; Herzog, 1982b; Jarvis, 1962). Moreover, parenthood as a stage in the life cycle represents an important developmental step (Erikson, 1963; Jessner et al., 1970). Latent dispositions for parenthood become more manifest with pregnancy while the relationship between the prospective father and wife undergoes wide swings in terms of: (1) a new level of relatedness reflecting reactions to specific physiological and emotional changes in the wife; and (2) a reaction to the general fact and symbolism of pregnancy (Gurwitt, 1976). First-time expectant parenthood also involves dealing with the transformation of a dyadic group into a triadic group as the entrance of a third person causes considerable realignment and, with it, many risks. These are realized to some extent during pregnancy, particularly as the prospective father re-installs himself into the oedipal constellation.

The male experience of pregnancy is quite different than that of the female with its stronger psychobiological cast. Herzog (1982b) observed that men can, at least partially, *choose* how much they will be involved in the process and thus determine to what degree they will respond psychologically to physiological changes in their wives.

The male indeed undergoes evolution as the experience of fatherhood changes. Studies concerning the continuous evolution of fatherhood are even rarer than is literature pertaining to becoming a father (Colarusso & Nemiroff, 1982). Nonetheless, there is data available on the stages of prospective fatherhood obtained mostly from fathers choosing to be present at their child's birth.

McCorkel (1964) demonstrated that pregnancy was differentially experienced according to the expectant father's orientation toward marriage and fatherhood. He delineated three groups of prospective fathers: (1) those with a *romantic orientation* who evidenced a casual approach to parenthood marked by feelings of concern about new responsibilities that rendered fatherhood a maturational experience; (2) those with a *family orientation,* who accepted new responsibilities easily and considered pregnancy a gift—thus becoming closer with their wives; and (3) those with a *career orientation* who regarded fatherhood as a burden and, consequently, tended to deny transformations of their identity.

Gurwitt (1976; see chapter in this volume) presented a case report on a young male analysand's reaction to the psychological currents before and throughout pregnancy. His descriptions of the primarily psychological phenomena in his male patient were discussed in terms of four periods (getting ready; conception, bridging, and the early months; mid-pregnancy; coming-to-terms).

Herzog (1982b) studied expectant fathers whose wives gave birth to premature infants. He found that the men could be divided into two groups: (1) the most attuned group who were most in touch with their feelings and fantasies pertaining to the pregnancy;[3] and (2) those less well attuned who seemed to act out and were less integrated during pregnancy. The quality (and quantity) of the conjugal relationship tended to predict which of the two groups the men would fall into; those more empathic with and invested in their wives tended to be more cognizant of their own feelings and the impending arrival of their first child. A sequence of characteristic stages of expectant fatherhood unfolded with greatest clarity among those more attuned fathers who participated in an "expanding mutual intimacy" with their wives. Interestingly, this ability seemed to be inversely related to the man's own state of "father hunger" (i.e., longing for his own psychological father).

Shapiro (1985, 1993b) interviewed a number of fathers as to their experience of pregnancy and confirmed Jacobson's (1950) postulates concerning the reexperiencing of childhood memories along with unresolved childhood problems. He also reported seven major fears surfacing among expectant fathers participating in the birth experience: (1) queasiness in the delivery room; (2) paternity concerns; (3) anxieties involving the ob-gyn establishment and hospital procedures; (4) losing one's spouse or child by death or ill-health; (5) being replaced by the infant; (6) increased responsibilities; and (7) existential issues pertaining to life and death.

I shall next propose a seven-stage sequence of prospective fatherhood that integrates these four major studies of fathers' experiences of pregnancy with my own observations. These specific stages are discussed in terms of their chronological, behavioral, and psychodynamic vicissitudes.

Stage One: Getting Ready

There seems to be a distinct period in which both husband and wife know that they will try to make a baby soon (Gurwitt, 1976; Herzog, 1982b; Shapiro, 1985).[4] The conscious components of this joint

---

[3]This group seemed most like the men described by McCorkel (1964) who held a family orientation toward marriage and fatherhood. Similarly, fathers described by Shapiro (1985) seemed to lean in this direction.

[4]Of course many couples are not in agreement vis-a-vis the decision to have a baby. A discussion of those situations wherein one member of the couple actively or passively opposes the other's decision, as well as "accidental" and noncoupled pregnancies are unfortunately beyond the purview of this chapter.

decision pertain to: (1) timing (particularly regarding ages of the prospective parents and spacing of children); (2) readiness (i.e., coordinated versus differential readiness of the two prospective parents); (3) finances; (4) career issues; (5) division of labor; and (6) childrearing ideologies (Shapiro, 1993). This period is in fact often recalled as a more "rational and controlled" phase than are those that follow (Herzog, 1982b).

Men often display an intensification of external and internal activities as part of the process of getting ready (Gurwitt, 1976). Similarly, there tends to be a strikingly different feeling when "having sex to make a baby" in comparison with "just having sex" (Herzog, 1982). Marked ambivalence is frequently apparent along with such male concerns as: embarking on something new and foreign; transient worries of being sterile or not having sufficient "stuff" to do it; a feeling of urgency to "get on with it" before it is too late; and numerous reality anxieties pertaining to financial and career matters. Gurwitt (1976) considered unresolved developmental issues that may surface during this period including: (1) fears of revenge due to the wished-for impregnation symbolizing a surpassing of one's own father; (2) possible regression to a passive position and denial of one's own prominent masculine role; (3) fears of abandonment, female seductiveness, entrapment and becoming overwhelmed by the power of women; and (4) raising of (covert) envy of the female's unique creative capacity, which is often manifest in anger toward women.

Stage Two: Conception

The stage in which conception occurs and is medically confirmed is typically experienced as a time of fullness and ecstasy; a period during which the expectant father's characteristic affect is joy. Gurwitt (1976) examined the severe challenges to previously attained male equilibrium in describing the period of impregnation and conception as one that ". . . constitutes an important developmental challenge for the prospective father, which, . . . brings about internal upheaval and change" (p. 262). Some men become conflicted, although most report an expansion of the wish to love and to be loved. Many men report substantial improvements in their sex lives (Herzog, 1982b). Feelings of unabashed pride, an expanded sense of self, and images of "primary illusion" (Shor & Sanville, 1978) are apparent among many an expectant father during this brief phase. The cultural stereotype of the "phallic, boastful, and beaming" father (cf, Jessner et al., 1970) fails to do justice to such rich and far-reaching internal experiences.

Stage Three: The First Trimester

The early months of pregnancy are frequently characterized by the beginnings of the prospective father's developmental challenge or crisis—signified by the initiation of a major reworking of past and/or current relationships with his wife, parents, and siblings, along with a shift in his sense of self (Gurwitt, 1976). Inner splits, particularly in relation to the expectant father's own parents and their role as parental models, begin to surface during the time of bridging. Herzog (1982b) described perceptible changes in the fantasy lives of the well-attuned prospective fathers. Moreover, the initial mood of fullness and ecstasy had markedly changed by the end of the first trimester. For some, the internal changes were pleasing and enriching; for others they were more irritating and distracting with a compulsive quality. Oftentimes, signs of anger and ominous destructive forces appear, but remain unclear. Gurwitt (1976) examined several typical concerns at this time involving: the male and female within; fears of injury and death; starting life; being a son and being a father; and issues bearing on past-present as well as real-fantasy. He reported on the defensive pattern emerging in response to the progenitor role along with the male's attempts to cope with his sense of loss and change in relation to his wife. Many men respond with a particular enthusiasm for work while others develop neurotic behavior or symptoms as they identify with their pregnant wives (Jacobson, 1950). More attuned men do tend to become increasingly preoccupied with their own insides (Herzog, 1982).

The male's fantasies and feelings during this time tend to cluster about the theme of the "nurturing woman (or mother) and fetus" along with an attendant worry about the "adequacy of one's own supplies" (Herzog, 1982). There seems to be a blurring of differentiations both between the parent/child and mother/father at this time, a process that Herzog (1982b) speculates as reflecting a re-experiencing of the earliest stage in the boy's caretaking line of development. Thus, the boy's identification with the nursing mother as the furnisher of oral supplies is recapitulated for the expectant father. This is illustrated in a male analysand's dream occurring toward the end of the first trimester. In the dream, he was informed that his baby was healthy, after which he was taken to meet the infant for the first time. Upon greeting each other, the baby licked him, and as they played together, the father called out, "My boy!"

Stage Four: Midpregnancy

Pregnancy becomes more real during the second trimester as the wife begins to show and the baby begins to kick. Amniocentesis and the use of sonograms further establish the "reality of pregnancy" for many men. The fetus is experienced more as an alive being. Many husbands at this stage feel more excluded from their wives and the "creature within her," who may come to be viewed as a rival (Gurwitt, 1976). An increase in the male's envy of the woman's procreative and nurturing capacities may become manifest and exacerbate the appearance of the expectant father's nurturing wishes. Many men exhibit an upsurge in creative sublimation in the form of new projects and career activities; others may tend toward workaholism. Jessner et al. (1970) reported changes in the male's psychosexual responses when confronted by the more dramatic changes in his wife's physical appearance. These range from increased sexual desires for her to a complete deterrence in sexual feeling. Castration anxiety may be heightened during this period as a result of these aforementioned changes along with an increase in the male's exploration of his bisexual origins and nature (Gurwitt, 1976).

Many fathers become concerned with gastrointestinal and other somatic symptoms, including couvade (Gurwitt, 1976; Herzog, 1982b; Jessner et al., 1970; Shapiro, 1985). Herzog (1982b) speculated that this had to do with a developmental reworking of a stage wherein the boy's identification with his mother blended with his maternal or inner-genital phase (Kestenberg, 1975) when he became aware of early prostatic and seminal vesicle contractions. Issues from this latter phase are followed by hermaphroditic fantasies wherein the boy sees himself as able to both fertilize and bear children—able to carry a baby like mother while sustaining himself within the male role (Kestenberg, 1975). This is manifest in the expectant father by the wish to "have it both ways" These wishes, accompanying symptoms, and reactions to the beginnings of (prenatal) triangulation often render the father most aware of his ambivalence toward the child and its mother, creating a dialectic described by Herzog (1982) as shifting between the "nurturing" and "punishing" penis. This occurs in conjunction with a sorting out phase of midpregnancy, described next.

Stage Five: The Turn Toward One's Father and Fathering

During midpregnancy, roughly between 15 and 25 weeks, most men experience an increased pressure to sort things out within their families of origin (Herzog, 1982b). There is an attempt to re-establish connections with one's own father, particularly the "good father of old" as represented by the preoedipal father or an oedipal or latency years' mentor. A common preoccupation among the most attuned men was that their fathering would be blighted by unresolved difficulties in their relationship to their own fathers (Herzog, 1982b; Shapiro, 1985).

Herzog (1982b) viewed this turn as a "refueling" or "straightening out," as if to signal "a more masculine or less maternal quality associated with the second half of pregnancy" (p. 308). This appears analogous to Abelin's (1975) notion of a boy turning away from mother toward father at 18 months in order to help dissolve his "primary femininity" and embark on his "anatomically determined masculine course." Herzog (1982b) found that men who failed to go through this phase seemed to become progressively less able to participate in the "alliance of pregnancy" (Deutscher, 1971). Men who were in a "state of father hunger" and thus unable to revive contact with the "good father of old," struggled with this phase and concomitantly were unlikely to participate in the second half of pregnancy. These expectant fathers were most intolerant of their own feminine identifications. On the other hand, gentle and tender feelings that were formerly suppressed for the sake of "masculine toughness" often emerged among those men able to master the sorting out issues of this phase.

Stage Six: Toward the End of the Second Trimester

Changes in the fantasies and preoccupations of the expectant father occur sometime after quickening. Herzog (1982b) notes that men begin to think of the fetus as a child, *separate from* both themselves and their wives. The child's sex is routinely conceptualized at this time. Interestingly, Herzog (1982b) found that 100% of the less well-attuned men "expected" boys, whereas only two-thirds of the most attuned group expected boys.

Expectant fathers began to report blatantly aggressive fantasies in the form of intrusive imagery as they experienced the fetus as a separate, third entity (Herzog, 1982b). Jessner et al. (1970) reported increased jealousy frequently accompanied by increased needs for sexual intercourse or alternatively, deterrence to sexual feeling. This appears as an early-precursor to the "Laius complex" involving the father's rivalry and hostility toward the child. These fantasies took the form of wishes to hurt the baby, sadistic feelings toward one's wife, and strong concerns with child abuse. Herzog speculated that material recapitulated the little boys' oedipal issue of being forced to acknowledge the presence of three people and the necessity of bringing together wishes to be loved and nurtured with wishes to hurt and be punished. Regression may occur to preoedipal levels; in fact, Herzog (1982b) found pronounced urethral and urinary imagery among many fathers.

Stage Seven: The Last Trimester

The last trimester brings about the end of pregnancy and a new kind of experience for the expectant father. This final phase was humorously referred to as "coming-to-term(s)" by Gurwitt (1976) and is characterized by both an intensification of the reality-orientation, and a more uncanny kind of feeling with a sense of powerful magical forces being at work. The fathers empathy with his spouse further increases as he tends to actively observe other parents and his own interactions with children (Gurwitt, 1976). He may also experience apprehensions about his own role as a progenitor and future father while confronting anew such existential issues as birth and death, ending and beginning, and creating and destroying.

The sense of powerful magical forces was described by Herzog (1982b) as "the sensation that something powerful, magical, and big was going on" (p. 310). This "something" is beyond the expectant father's ability to control and while magical and mysterious for all, may be experienced as sublime for some and sinister for others. A "feeling of awe" tends to accompany the ending of pregnancy and the actual delivery. Herzog (1982b) discussed this in terms of the "whole becoming greater than the sum of its parts" wherein what has been willingly initiated becomes larger than past conflicts and resolutions and large enough to become a life of its own. Empirical support was reported by Brudal (1984) who found that very few fathers present at delivery escaped the experience of a new level of feeling, whether more intense or more distant. Intense affect, cognitive distortion, time alterations, depersonalization, and psychosomatic reactions were quite common.

Concurrent with this sense of awe, the expectant father's preoccupations of the previous months with his inner processes are replaced by a perceptible shift toward readying things in the real world for the child's arrival. Herzog (1982b), like Gurwitt (1976), found that most fathers increased their observations of children, concerns with child-rearing patterns, and preparental activities related to the actual arrival of the child. The most attuned fathers were also most able to "parent their wife" at this very time when she most needed care (Herzog, 1982b). These latter fathers were also able to get back in touch with their inner lives while maintaining a valuation of the outside world beyond the mother–child symbiosis. Such fathers were grooming themselves for their future role as the representative of this outside world but as a provider respectful of the mother–child symbiosis. In this respect, such men were able to serve as an external beacon to their wives who may feel submerged in their own inner processes and concerns at the time of parturition (Herzog, 1982b). Thus, the new father comes to hold a special and unique position—grasping as he does the principle of reality augmented so long ago by his earlier attempts to solve the "mystery of the sphinx," while touching anew the unspeakable awe of the miraculous world beyond his control.

From an analytic perspective, Dr. Wolson explores adaptive and maladaptive grandiosity of fathers with newborns. He distinguishes between fathers identifying with their children's accomplishments in appropriate and boundary violating ways. Of greatest import, Dr. Wolson elucidates the ways in which paternal grandiosity is normal and healthy and how such adaptive grandiosity can aid development of children and of the father–child relationship.

24

Some Reflections on Adaptive Grandiosity in Fatherhood

Peter Wolson

From the moment that a man becomes a father, he must struggle with his feelings of grandiosity. This is evident from the very start, when the father hands out cigars while waiting for his newborn to be delivered. It is a celebration of the birth of his child, with the emphasis on "his child." As his creation, the child represents a reflection of and an extension of him, particularly his ideal qualities and characteristics, "His Majesty the Baby," as Freud (1914, p.91) described it.

The child often serves as an enhancement of the father's self-love, particularly the ways in which he feels or has wanted to be extraordinarily special. His handing out cigars, in a sense, is a celebration of his own rebirth, through the birth of his child. The projection of the father's special, ideal self onto his child is part of fatherly love and glue that preserves family love and solidarity. This form of loving contact ultimately helps the child to separate from mother during the early years of life. For this to happen, the father must recognize that his child is a unique individual, not merely an extension of self. If he attempts to impose his ideal, grandiose self on his child, he can damage the child's self-structure and actually impair his or her independent development.

Thus fathers often struggle, consciously or unconsciously, with preserving the adaptive aspects of their grandiosity while avoiding maladaptive consequences in raising their children. I would like to reflect briefly on some aspects of adaptive and maladaptive grandiosity in fatherhood.

Originally I defined the concept of adaptive grandiosity in relation to artistic creativity as "the individual's exhilarating conviction of his potential for greatness, the extremely high value he places on the uniqueness of his feelings, perceptions, sensations, memories, thoughts and experiences" (Wolson, 1995a).

Furthermore, I said that "It is an ego-state which can be conscious or unconscious. This clearly differs from normal healthy self-confidence in which an individual believes in the value of his perceptions and in his capacity for successful achievement, but lacks the pervasive grandiose qualities described above" (Wolson, 1995a).

What makes this grandiosity adaptive is that it is inextricably intertwined with reality testing, with secondary process functioning and with the full acknowledgement of the separation of the self from others. Consequently behavior emanating from this ego-state is adaptive and reality oriented. For example, with respect to artistic creativity, adaptive grandiosity was deemed necessary to help the artist overcome his separation anxiety when confronting the empty canvas, and provided the motivational fuel for using his talents and skills. It enhanced rather than impeded his ego functioning during the creative process. As applied to fatherhood, adaptive grandiosity refers to the extent to which the father's grandiose perception and way of relating to his child is adaptive for the child's psychological development. The adaptiveness of the grandiosity depends on the father's ability to maintain empathic sensitivity with his child as a separate individual.

For example, when the father first sees his newborn, an adaptively grandiose response would be to perceive his child as beautiful, regardless of the way the child actually looks physically. It is, of course, quite common for people to respond to babies as beautiful, even when they may objectively be ugly. This is clearly an ideal, grandiose projection of beauty, and has the adaptive function of providing the infant with an emotional atmosphere of loving attention, which it vitally needs. This response implicitly acknowledges the child's separateness by lovingly accepting it, warts and all.

In contrast, a maladaptively grandiose response would be for the father to require the baby to exhibit an idealized conception of beauty. If the baby's appearance fell short of this ideal, the father might become enraged and withdraw his affection.

Maladaptive grandiosity is based on omnipotence, a belief in magical control of both external and internal objects, an inclination toward fusion states and an inability to distinguish between self and other. With maladaptive grandiosity (omnipotence), the father cannot see his child as a separate individual but merely as a self-extension under his omnipotent control. The child remains an idealized fantasy, not a real person in his or her own right. The maladaptively grandiose father would try to force his child to embody his own grandiose ideals rather than respect his child's individual integrity. The less capable the father is of differentiating himself from his child, the more likely his grandiosity would be maladaptive.

In an extreme case of maladaptive grandiosity, a father who hated his own mother for dominating and infantilizing him, refused to let his newborn son suckle at his wife's breast, accusing her of weakening him and trying to turn the son into a homosexual. The father had forced his omnipotent "masculine" self-image onto his child, and undermined his vital suckling relationship with the mother. In the final analysis, the adaptive and maladaptive aspects of paternal grandiosity are determined, respectively, by their positive and negative parental influence.

Extrapolating from the developmental considerations in my paper on artistic creativity, it would seem that fathers primarily demonstrating adaptive grandiosity were able to sufficiently separate from the symbiosis with their own mothers in childhood through a positive identification with their fathers. This permitted them to integrate good enough secondary process (reality oriented) functioning with their grandiose inclinations and to empathically perceive their children as separate individuals.

In contrast, fathers displaying maladaptive grandiosity remained fixated or regressed at a preoedipal level of development. They had not sufficiently identified with their fathers and continued to be pathologically merged with the maternal introject (the internal representation of the mother). Their archaic grandiose self remained largely unmodulated, and they grew up to feel entitled to exert omnipotent control over others, such as their wives and children.

With the regressive pull of fatherhood, most fathers struggle with the conflict between adaptive and maladaptive grandiosity to some degree. From the first moment of birth, they tend to project their ideal, grandiose self-images onto their child, and yet at the same time, with only a modicum of reality testing, they are aware of how different the child is from themselves, how it manifests its own distinctive personality.

When adaptive grandiosity is operating, fathers not only recognize and validate those characteristics that are part of their own ego-ideal, but also those traits that are different from that ego-ideal. The child's distinctiveness provides the father with an opportunity for self-enhancement. In other words, he may view the child's unique characteristics as an extension of his own personality. If the father tends to be shy and unassuming, for example, and he has a loud, attention-seeking baby, he can adaptively enhance his own personality repertoire by taking pride in and identifying with the baby's exhibitionism. The father's capacity to embrace and appreciate the baby's differences is what makes this form of grandiose identification adaptive. He may, however, have to internally struggle against the omnipotent, maladaptive side of himself that wants to reject the baby for its outgoing personality, and make it feel fearful or inhibited, more like himself.

As part of his adaptive grandiosity, the father typically communicates a sense of specialness to his child. He may eagerly notice every characteristic and behavior that the child manifests and attribute special meaning to these traits. For instance, he may single out the child's attentiveness and alertness, his affability, the power of his voice, his ability to persevere, his curiosity. The father's adaptively grandiose identification and absorption with the child allows him to validate and reinforce many aspects of his child's existence, providing his infant with a flow of loving attention.

As mentioned earlier, this special attention from the father serves the vital function of helping the child to separate and differentiate from its mother. The father has this influence because he is the parent from the "outside" and consequently comes to represent the child's relationship to external reality. This is in contrast to the mother with whom the child is symbiotically merged in fantasy at the beginning of life, and from whom the child must separate in order to enter the real world and become his or her own person.

The sense of specialness that fathers communicate to their children often implies that the child, through heredity, has innate access to the father's gifts, talents, predilections, tastes, etc. This provides the child with a special sense of being made out of "good stuff," as well as with a sense of belonging, relatedness, and of having strong genetic roots and ties to the father—a basic sense of grounding. One can speculate that without participating in this form of adaptive paternal grandiosity, children grow up missing an essential feeling of specialness and rootedness. They may feel just ordinary or unworthy of love or special attention and they may be alienated and cut off, without having a sense of "home" within themselves.

This sense of specialness can become maladaptive if the father attempts to force his own ideal personality characteristics onto his children without acknowledging, respecting, and appreciating their differences. In other words, if the father's grandiose identification with his child fuels his attentiveness and recognition of the child's unique characteristics, it adaptively reinforces the child's self-esteem. But if the father responds to his child merely as a special extension of himself, and rejects those characteristics that are different from his ideals while reinforcing those that are the same, he is laying the groundwork for a narcissistic personality disorder. Such fathers are often narcissistic personalities themselves (Kernberg, 1975).

For example, one father was totally identified with being a " jock" and constantly disparaged his son as a "sissy" for his involvement in art instead of sports. In another case, a father viciously attacked his daughter's preoccupation with studying to become a lawyer instead of learning how to cook for him. Such omnipotent invasions of childrens' self-structures can squelch their sense of autonomy and individuality and result in a confused, poorly articulated personal identity and a pathological grandiose self (Kernberg, 1975).

I recall one family in which the father encouraged all his children to become musicians and entertainers and insisted that they were superior to all the families around them. The children grew up with an inordinate sense of superiority, which masked an underlying feeling of alienation and inferiority. In another case, a father who lived a shady, transient nomadic existence living in seedy motels with his family, insisted that his family was superior to other families who led a more stable life. But the children, while manifesting an air of superiority about their so-called "adventurous, romantic" lifestyle, gradually realized that they did this to cover up their embarrassment and mortifying sense of inferiority.

At its most extreme, a father may come to perceive the birth of a child and the child's special needs for attention as an affront to his grandiosity, as a dreaded competitor. In one case, immediately after a son was born, the father became moody, pouted, and withdrew from his wife. He began to work long hours, had affairs and constantly picked fights for the negative attention until his wife felt totally depleted. Through reconstruction in therapy, it became apparent that he was reenacting his narcissistic wounding and rage from the birth of a younger brother when he was two years old. The rage was transferred from his mother and younger sibling to his wife and infant son.

A father may resent his child as long as the child diverts attention away from himself and value his child only when the latter enhances the father's self image. Instead of seeing the child as representing an enhancement of self-love and a means of attaining immortality, the omnipotent father may see the child as a threat and as auguring his own demise, as attempting to usurp the father's special place in life.

John Munder Ross (1985) wrote about the Laius complex, based on the Oedipus complex, in which the father (Laius) perceives the son (Oedipus) as a competitive threat and attempts to castrate him. Instead of seeing his children's growing strength and effectiveness as an adaptively narcissistic reflection of his own grandiosity, the omnipotent father feels undermined, as if there is only room for one successful person in the family, and may, in turn, reject and undermine the child's achievement efforts.

Through the expression of adaptive grandiosity, however, the father can provide the child with a sense of his inherent value as well as of the valuable characteristics and traits that will eventually allow the child to consolidate his own ego-ideal and life direction and goals. Kohut (1971) wrote about the importance of the father's comfort with being his child's ideal and with his ability to embody and contain that ideal. The father needs to convey his belief in the child's capacity to eventually attain that ideal, to become like the idealized father. Little girls, for example, often express, "You're the greatest Daddy in the world," and wear their fathers' shirts and jackets. Or, they may believe that their fathers understand everything and are the most handsome men they know.

Fathers who are uncomfortable with their grandiosity, with being their children's ideals, may discourage their children from idealizing them. Moreover, they may become upset when their children express pride in their achievements or some other aspect of their lives, accuse them of bragging and shame them into stifling their healthy need for attention. Kohut (1971) showed how this will undermine a child's self-confidence and his or her ability to develop healthy life goals.

Finally I would like to say a few words about fathers identifying with their children's accomplishments. It is certainly natural to take pride in the achievements of one's children as an adaptively grandiose reflection of both the child's and the parent's self-worth. Fathers may applaud their toddler son's aggressiveness, climbing precocity and physical strength and be in awe of their little girls curiosity, verbal agility and sweetness. But some fathers who have given up on fulfilling their own dreams attempt to preserve their grandiosity by overly identifying with their children's achievements, such as with a son's sports or business career or with a daughter's profession or marriage.

This grandiose identification is maladaptive to the extent that the father's self-esteem depends on the specific outcome of his children's efforts. The father is no longer relating to his offspring with the right to make their own independent choices but merely as objects for his own narcissistic enhancement. His love for the child as a separate individual becomes lost in the process.

In conclusion, it is important for fathers to be cognizant of their internal struggle between adaptive and maladaptive grandiosity (omnipotence) in relating to their children. The grandiose identification with a child is a normal part of parenting, and when it remains on an adaptive basis, it becomes an essential ingredient of family love and contributes to a child's sense of well-being, rootedness, self-confidence, life direction, and emerging individuality. But when it is maladaptive, it can undermine the child's self-cohesiveness and produce a sense of alienation, poor self-esteem and, at its worst, contribute to a narcissistic personality disorder.

The male seahorse gets to be
an eggbearer. His belly
has a pocket for loose change,
wallet, keys and the eggs
of his children. At labor he writhes
and wiggles mightily till
his young are out.
How proudly I would be a seahorse!

I do not get to be an eggbearer. I get to
get fat eating as if I ate for you.

—David Debus

Intrapsychic descriptions of the process of becoming a father are all too uncommon in the parenting literature. Many men experience a plethora of changes around the conception and throughout the pregnancy. In this chapter, Dr. Gurwitt provides us with a very intimate look at this process reviews aspects of his analysis with an expectant father. He explores the major upheaval that occurs around conception, and the unfolding stages of the pregnancy.

The author's skilled clinical acumen is evident as the young father uses his analysis and transference to his analyst to rework his relationship to his own parents and his wife. This analysis, slightly abridged here, which was first reported in 1976, is a classic article in the fatherhood literature

25

Aspects of Prospective Fatherhood[1]

Alan R. Gurwitt

The version republished here is an abbreviated form of an article first published in 1976, This brief commentary is being written some 20 years after the work on the original article was initiated. At that time a literature search on fatherhood was a frustrating task as there was relatively little available on anything to do with fathers and fathering, Fortunately, since then, there has been a growing interest in fatherhood so that now there is an increasing body of work covering a wide range of topics including even a history of fatherhood in this country that partially explains the social forces that for so long had diminished the importance of fathers and fathering (Griswold, 1993). We are now much more aware of the multiplicity of roles and influences, both positive and negative, of fathers on their children and reciprocal impacts of children on their fathers. We know much more about the importance of the mother–father relationship and the factors influencing that relationship, factors that in part have their origin during pregnancy.

---

[1]This is an abbreviated version of an essay published in Ruth S. Eissler et al. (Eds.), *The Psychoanalytic Study of the Child*, Vol. 31. New York: International Universities Press, 1976.

The good news is that active fathering is "in", but the bad news is that there are so many single-parent families where good fathering is absent. We are still learning more about the repercussions of father absence and the sad intergenerational cycles that play a part.

The very fact of this book, with its "classic" articles along with new research, demonstrates the recognition of the importance of the psychological roots and repercussions of becoming and being a father. It is a needed and proper focus because the issues involved can no longer be seen as being of relatively minor importance to children, families, and society. What transpires during the pregnancy and the early years of parenting, while not the sole formative factor, does indeed color the evolution of the family.

We now recognize that there may be typical patterns of responses of fathers-to-be and young fathers, some more positive than others, We know more about the development of boys and men (the growing mens' studies literature has helped here) including aspects that are pertinent to their becoming parents and the manner of their parenting. We are learning more about the external processes at work—within the family, extended families, peer, and workplace as well as somewhat more about internal phenomena involved.

It is with regard to the study of internal phenomena, however, that we still have a way to go. Although over the years many psychoanalysts and therapists have told me about their own or their male patients' reactions to pregnancy, there have been relatively few contributions to the literature. Although issues of confidentiality could well be a factor, I wonder if age-old repressive forces, seen in this republished case report, are at work. Fortunately, other chapters in this volume add to our understanding.

Becoming a father is an important episode in the life cycle of a man and his family. The character of that episode draws on all that preceded and influences all that follows. The very limited attention paid to prospective (or expectant) fatherhood (e.g., Arnstein, 1972; Blos, 1972; Colman & Colman, 1971; Jarvis, 1962) is thus remarkable, since it has long been recognized that the period of becoming a father is a time of important psychological transition (Benedeck, 1970a; Boehm, 1930; Jacobson, 1950; Jessner et al., 1970). That there is significant stress in this transition is evidenced by the clinical literature on the pathological reactions to the achievement of fatherhood (Freeman, 1951; Lacoursiere, 1972a,b; Towne & Afterman, 1955; Zilboorg, 1931). Moreover, the phenomenon of the couvade that appears in various forms in different societies probably serves to regulate apparently powerful forces within men in response to birthing (Howells, 1971; Jones, 1961; Reik, 1919). Although some reports have focused on specific phenomena in male analysands (e.g., Eisler, 1921a,b; Evans, 1951; Jaffe, 1968; Jarvis, 1962; Rose, 1961), there has not been a case report on a male's reaction to psychological currents before and throughout pregnancy. It is the purpose of this chapter to describe such currents in a young man whose wife became pregnant and delivered a baby girl while he was in analysis.

A CASE OF A PROSPECTIVE FATHER

Background

The patient was 23 years old when he started analysis. He had been married for 6 months, and was in his third year of graduate studies in a scientific field at the time. His wife became pregnant during the last year of the 4-year analysis. Their daughter was born about 4 months before termination of the analysis.

His concerns at the start of treatment were difficulty in coping with daily demands, a sense of poor control over his emotional life, insecurity in sexual relationships, problems in pursuing his graduate work, and problems in social relationships.

The patient had two sisters, one 2 years older, the other $2\frac{1}{2}$ years younger. His father was a mechanic who never gained much satisfaction from his work. During the patient's first 2 to 3 years of life his father was rarely home because of the war-related nature of his work. He was home more often shortly after the birth of the patient's younger sister, and the patient became strongly bonded to his father. The strength of those ties was influenced, we learned, by his mother's pregnancy, the birth of his sister, and what probably was a period of depression experienced by his mother—factors which, conversely, cast a pall over his relationship with her. The closeness to his father was short-lived, influenced not only by the rise of oedipal conflicts within himself but by the father's increasing moodiness and alcoholic tendencies. Although he tried, the patient rarely gained his father's approval (at least after the age of 4 or 5 years), and often felt rebuffed by him. It was only later that we began to understand how the strongly sadomasochistic relationship between the patient's father and paternal grandfather, a martinet of a man, left the father rebellious but cowed, covered with a thin veneer of manliness. These cross-generational influences played a major role in the patient's attempts to achieve fatherhood with a different model of fatherliness.

The patient's mother grew up in a strict setting. Her own mother died when she was young. She was very attached to her stern father, but in college, where she excelled academically, she began to rebel. During that "gay and wild" phase of her life, she met and married the patient's carefree father, a step that she later, resignedly, considered an appropriate punishment for her earlier wild ways. Her husband's later alcoholism, depression, and illness were part of the cross she had to bear, she once told the patient. Analytic work enabled us to see that the parents' marriage seemed to have changed after the birth of the patient's younger sister. As it soured, his mother devoted herself to being a 'model" mother and housekeeper. A prominent theme during the early part of the analysis was his mother's strong prohibitions against most sensual pleasures. It was she, not his father, who overtly condemned his early masturbation. It was she who put the brakes on his early (and later) active voyeuristic researches into the great mysteries of life: anatomical sexual differences and reproduction as it pertained to humans. She actively encouraged and at times participated in his investigations into the nature of plants and animals, however. (Both parents were active gardeners.) Of equal importance in channeling the patient's endeavors and later career choice was his father's unvarying reply to his frequent questions about the nature of things: "That's the nature of the beast, son." This unsatisfactory answer spurred the patient on to a lifelong desire to find out just what was the nature of the beast.

The patient early became a devoted naturalist, roaming through nearby forests and exploring ponds. Fishing with his father and walks with his mother were key influences. He also furtively roamed through his home, where he had many opportunities to observe his parents and younger sister in the bathroom in varying stages of undress. These observations left him in awe and confusion, more frightened than pleased. Most of these experiences had been "forgotten," except for a relatively late one: his older sister exhibiting herself when he was 8 years old and the family was staying at a beachside cottage. He not only remained "disgusted" by her, but this and other earlier experiences raised more questions than they answered. Female anatomy, no matter how sophisticated his later education, remained an area of bewilderment and fear and also gave impetus to his choice of career. Equally important in his quest to comprehend the nature of beasts was how they arrived on this earth. We learned that he knew and did not know.

The patient's wife was a nurse whom he had met in undergraduate school. She was a warm and giving person, less threatening intellectually and sexually than the young woman with whom he had previously been involved. Although they experienced considerable conflict, external and internal, later in the marriage, their attachment to each other was basically solid and positive.

Early Phases of Analysis

The early phases of the analysis were concerned primarily with reconstructing the patient's above-outlined developmental history. Much was learned about why he clung to infantile ways and why he felt small and flawed. He realized that his relationship with his wife was intertwined with remnants of the past and afflicted by ambivalence. He gained some insight into why he retreated from closeness to her and turned to men, only to flee from the threats of homosexual love and submission.

Issues around becoming a parent had come up from time to time. Indeed, one of the stated objectives at the beginning of the analysis had been the wish to be a good father. He often commented on how he and his wife would never become so all-involved as friends did with their children. He particularly berated his older sister's manner of parenting. Two years before the birth of his own daughter, however, he pushed away the thought of ever becoming a parent in spite of his wife's increasing insistence on becoming pregnant. He sourly anticipated being excluded during a pregnancy and the complications that would arise if they had a son. Following the chance observation of one of my daughters and myself going into a store, the negative tone seemed to alter. There was something remarkable about actually being able to help create a child, he commented.

During the summer before he began his third year of analysis, he spent much time with his nephew and was delighted at how well they got along and how well he understood him, in contrast with his "neurotic" and "self-centered" older sister. At first he did not see the connection between these activities and his announcement, early in September, that he and his wife were planning to have their first child the following autumn. That intention was played down as he reassessed his graduate work and career plans in a most positive way.

Perhaps the self-reassurances were necessary that autumn as he anticipated a new level and phase in the analysis in which he would "plumb the depths." Indeed, striking changes took place in the character of the sessions. Frequent dreams with deepening and more archaic associations led to earlier and earlier memories, fantasies, and theories of birth and body concepts. Body boundaries shifted, sexual and body secretions and parts were symbolically yet concretely equated. In retrospect, we were back to the time of his mother's summer pregnancy with his younger sister.

The Pregnancy

In descriptions of both psychological and physical events of pregnancy, a division into trimesters is commonly used. This division is clearly related to differential physical and psychological events in women. In approaching the primarily psychological phenomena in my male patient, I believe it is of value to rely on a similar division; in addition, I focus on the 2 months preceding the pregnancy, because in this preparatory period changes in the character of the analytic sessions took place.

In the four periods I describe (getting ready; conception, bridging, and the early months; midpregnancy; and coming-to-term[s]), two kinds of interrelated phenomena emerged: those clearly reactive to his wife's physical and psychological status and thereby influenced by the unfolding stages of her pregnancy; and those not so directly related to her immediate status but more broadly reflective of the very existence of the pregnancy and its implications for himself.

Getting Ready.   Following a Christmas holiday break of 1 week, the patient returned after the New Year, declaring that a new phase of work was to begin. Although ostensibly he meant finishing his thesis and embarking on new research, what unfolded were multiple aspects of concerns with impregnation and conception.

Shortly after his return he mentioned that his wife was now definitely planning to have a baby. Though the emphasis on his wife as the primary moving spirit partially reflected the overt nature of events, it was also indicative of his own ambivalence and defensive, innocent-bystander role against which he later protested.

In actuality he began to take an active role. The patient and his wife decided to move to a larger, more comfortable apartment. They chose a house situated near a pond. This quiet area, with the all-important water nearby and land for a garden, formed a setting that seemed to serve as a fertile environment for coming events. Although both the patient and his wife worked hard at remodeling the apartment, the patient in particular seemed to do so with a compulsive drivenness. It was the first time that he had taken so much interest in their living quarters. He was especially proud of his skill with tools, paying reluctant homage to his father whose mechanical and carpentry abilities were considerable. The move, the setting, and the settling activities had the quality of preparing a nest. Indeed, references to birds, nesting, and egg hatching, observations keenly made throughout his life, came up frequently during these hours.

A dream in which he had intercourse with the analyst's wife with his big, penetrating penis sent him running for psychological cover. Associations to this dream in later sessions further referred to his enfeebled and declining father, open criticism of whom (for being such a "lousy" father) would, he fantasied, lead to his father's suicide. Elements of a theme he repeated later were first seen in the transference: Namely, that to become an impregnator was not only the ultimate incestuous act but also a symbolic "doing in" of his father. The possible consequences of this dangerous action were reflected in concerns about accidentally injuring himself with the construction tools he used in his new home.

The sense of preparing for an ultimate act exhibiting his strength and ability was in the air, but it was fraught with danger from two sides: revenge from his father (or the analyst in the transference) and entrapment by his wife-mother (also the analyst in the transference).

Toward the middle of January, the patient's wife stopped taking birth control pills, but he did not mention this until the end of the month. It was introduced by several dreams. One dealt with two beautiful blonde women in revealing bikinis at whom he stared; the other starred his wife as a 10-year-old girl in a home movie. These two dreams, and others that occurred later during his wife's pregnancy, we gradually learned most prominently represented his mother, older sister, and wife as a mother-to-be; his sense of exclusion during the mother's pregnancy with his younger sister; fear of new exclusion during his wife's pregnancy; early voyeurism; and retaliation for his sexual activities. His associations to the first dream introduced other key themes as well. Although on the surface he was in agreement with the aim of their having a child, he bitterly resented both his wife's drivenness to become pregnant during the preceding weeks and his being used as a stud. He began to anticipate the future loss of exclusive control over his wife's body and attention. He expressed concern about the dangers of the pregnancy, labor, and delivery; and in his fantasies he saw himself as the perpetrator of a chain of events that was potentially mutilating.

The second dream, of the home movies, led to memories of "dirty" scenes in the past, including the episode of his older sister's exhibition. These memories stirred up oral, anal, and phallic fantasies that were tinged with sadistic overtones and contained primitive childhood concepts of reproduction. These archaic concepts, which coexisted with his sophisticated scientific knowledge, gradually were reworked.

He experienced renewed fears of the power women exerted by their sexual seductiveness. His wife's driven sexuality led to several biological analogies, such as black widow spiders in which the female kills and eats the male after fertilization. The male, however, could also do the mutilating, and he berated me for not making both him and his wife less dangerous and less vulnerable. As if in reaction to a sense of powerlessness, he began to retrace his own sexual curiosity as a child, recalling the warm and sensual summer evenings when his mother had allowed him to stay up late to investigate the wonders of fireflies. He remembered the combination of excitement and curiosity as he collected and squashed the fireflies to find out the source of their lights. He saw more clearly the merging of his curiosity, especially sexual, with the sadism of the scientific investigations as he attempted to understand and to master the mysteries of birth, life, and death, at least in these small creatures.

This theme could be seen repeatedly in his scientific research. Life, its beginnings, and the factors affecting it were key elements. Furthermore, the particular animals chosen for the research, types of amphibia, were linked in multiple ways to his childhood and both parents. The cloacal anatomy also seemed more compatible with his childhood concepts of anal reproduction, and its early embryological stages somehow were safer because of the sexual undifferentiation.

As a result of his current feelings of anticipated loss, he remembered and further worked through experiences of childhood deprivations. His mother was responsible for the loss of Pinky, the cherished soft, round, pink teddy bear that for years (probably up to the age of 5) had been his inseparable companion and comforter. He later recalled that he left Pinky at a neighbor's house and therefore might himself have played a role in its loss, but at this point he felt it had been his mother's insidious doing. When she told him Pinky ran away, he cried for hours. Indeed, in the sessions he seemed bereft. He later learned that she had asked the neighbor to throw Pinky into a burning trash heap. Bitterly, to emphasize the sense of maternal deprivation, he recalled being told that his mother breast-fed him for only 13 days. He was overcome by a sense of her cruelty, a feeling that spilled over and was related to the new depriver of his own needs. In this period he turned to the analyst (father?) in a dream:

> I was in a strange country or place and in great danger. People are after me. A psychiatrist lived there. I went to his home, an elaborate home with office, beautiful internally. I felt pleased to be there, safe and happy because of the threats. Someone had tried to strangle me. The psychiatrist was not you. It was someone who seemed openly benevolent and was older. Then the scene shifts, yet is related. I discover, while in the Middle East, old artifacts of Babylonian civilization and am going to tell someone in a museum so that they could be put there. It's a detailed plot and I can't recall it all.

His associations again emphasized the dangers of new and impending events. The psychiatrist's office was a refuge and a womb. Babylonian civilization seemed a time and place of evil kings and weird events where one needed protection. He recalled other dreams about shores, lakes, being a fugitive. Most prominently he thought of the word Babylon, splitting it into *baby* and *lon* or *lone*. He felt like a baby not only in terms of the infantile aspects he recognized in himself, but in relation to the eventual termination. The latter was like a rebirth out of the womb of the analysis (and analyst), when he would be alone and scared.

The intermingling of themes related both to the coming pregnancy and to the nature of his relationship with me and the analysis (particularly its termination) came up repeatedly during the remainder of the analysis.

During this preparatory time, he was faced with his thesis deadline and thesis defense. He insisted on typing the thesis himself, although he knew that it was very time-consuming. As he wondered why he did so and in such a compulsive manner, we recognized his need to deliver that final product of his own creative endeavors by his own hands. At the time of the actual and successful thesis defense, although he had been lovingly and encouragingly sent off by his wife, he almost totally excluded her from the subsequent celebrations. He preferred to include only fellow graduate students, mostly male and faculty. But there was an important exception. He saw the thesis not only as his baby but as a creation of both his mother and himself. He briefly allowed himself to see his mother as an important source of his own creativity, though earlier in the analysis he had had to play down her significance.

Thus it gradually became clear that before embarking on the voyage of impregnation, he felt it was essential to complete his own creation, which derived from his own efforts and those of a symbolic union with his mother as well as identification with her as a creative being.

In summary, there was a period of a few months before impregnation-conception when intensification of external and internal activities seemed to be part of a process of getting ready. The marked ambivalence was apparent in the active preparation of a new home in a setting linked with growing things; yet the symbolic nature of the progenitor role raised problems. It was as if to impregnate was a surpassing and doing in of his father, a wished-for event, yet one that also precipitated fears of revenge and regression to a passive position and a denial of his own prominent role. It also raised fears of abandonment, of entrapment, of being overwhelmed by the power of women, of female seductiveness, past and present; as well as covert envy of the unique female creative capacity. His anger was great and was linked with potential destructiveness in his progenitor role. The completion of his own endeavors (research and thesis) before the pregnancy served as a declaration of his own creative abilities, which in a very special oedipal way were linked with his mother. Furthermore, as if he had turned passive into active, the increased tempo of scientific work was connected with a lifelong attempt to control and master the forces of reproduction, life, and death, forces so long out of his grasp. At this point, it was already clear that there would be a merging of currents related both to the coming pregnancy and the analysis, especially change and termination.

Impregnation-Conception, Bridging, and the Early Months of Pregnancy. Shortly after the weekend during which impregnation probably took place (based on average length of normal pregnancies), the patient presented a copy of his completed and bound thesis to me. He looked on its completion as symbolic of the end of childhood and adolescence, the beginning of a new phase of life. He touched only briefly on the probability of his becoming a parent in the near future, and dwelt primarily on his career plans.

With the future and his independence very much in mind over the next several days, he began to think seriously about an appropriate time for termination. He wondered what work remained to be done in the analysis. He was particularly disturbed by a sense of being split, portions of himself being like his mother, others like his father. It seemed important to him to gain a better understanding of his past and present relationships with his parents. This aim led to a period of intense, though sporadic, working through of these relationships, a reworking that often occurred via the transference and was particularly colored by and perhaps intrinsically related to his wife's pregnancy. We saw that the split in himself pertained to each parent, who had both good and bad attributes. Early in this period he visited his mother at a time when his father "happened" to be away. They had long and pleasant conversations. Most important, they talked a great deal about parents and children and ways of childrearing. On his return, he began to soften his condemnation of both parents, but particularly of his mother.

Many more such visits and conversations followed. They were in marked contrast to previous times, when little visiting had occurred and the conversations had been limited and unsatisfactory. In the course of the next 9 months (and until termination), his view of his parents (and me) changed many times, but it remained important to revisit psychologically, now with a new purpose. Birth, children, mothers, fathers, were to have a new reality. In this context he reported the following dream:

I was anxious all week. It was weird, especially the sexual fantasies I experienced. A dream last night had the same tenor. In the dream I was in a town on Cape Cod, not far out, somewhere on the western part. I was going someplace close by, taking a shortcut. As I was walking across a bridge, I saw a girl not like anyone I knew before. She wore a bathing suit, possibly flesh-colored. Then I saw she had no suit top. She had incredibly beautiful breasts. Was she entirely naked? No, just her breasts were showing. I asked her how to get where I was going. I walked with her and was lost. Everything was confusing as if going away from my destination. Just a little bit off the track and yet so tremendously lost.

The locale reminded him of a place where he had done some research during his college years and where he met the girl who first stimulated his interest in intercourse. It also reminded him of the area where his family had spent the summers and where his sister had exposed herself. Bourne Bridge was exciting. It was a lift bridge. He wondered if he was anxious because he planned to visit his older sister the next day. It would be different from the recent visit to his mother. His father would be around. He then told of a recent party where he had experienced active sexual fantasies about both women and men, but had acted only on the former. All week long he had been preoccupied with "fantasy sex," with breasts, with masturbation. Did it have something to do with the visits to his mother? The associations then increasingly seemed "off the track." I said so, and brought him back to the dream. The sense of being lost was related to his confused sense of sexual identity and moving away, earlier in the week, from the closeness to his mother. I asked about Bourne. He thought of "to be born."

"Oh, by the way, my wife may be pregnant."

He said it in a monotone. He had tried to do a pregnancy test the day before by injecting urine into frogs. His wife's frog evidenced a vascularized cloaca; his did not. He then went on to elaborate thoughts about the girl known in college, reminders of his mother, then came back briefly to having been reading a book on obstetrics. It was unpleasant, frightening, especially pictures of female genitalia. It would only take a shortcut to be a girl. "Women scare the hell out of me. They, like my older sister, are so consuming."

Thus the pregnancy was announced by way of Bourne Bridge. Indeed, there was much to be bridged. Somehow he must bridge the male/female within, the real and the fantasized, the past and the present, starting life and the fear of injury and death, being a child-son-daughter and a parent-father-mother.

Over the next several weeks the pregnancy was most remarkable by its absence in the analysis, but by the fourth week there was no doubt that his wife was pregnant and that the pregnancy was having a major impact on them both. She had become very moody, nagging, demanding, preoccupied, unavailable—and just at a time, he complained, when he wanted to focus his sexual attention on her. After all, he had decided to give up masturbation to do so. Her breasts were sore; he could not play with them. As he had anticipated a couple of months earlier (indeed, 2 years earlier), she now was so much "more biological," and he at times felt enraged. The anticipated 3-month abstinence near and after term already loomed large.

He had a sense of familiarity, of similar things having happened before. His wife's ordering him about reminded him of his mother's behavior and his own volatile anger of his father's outbursts. His wife's expression of concern about his loyalty made him aware that for the first time there was severe strain on their marriage. This enabled him to recall his father's threats of leaving the family. More than anything, however, he felt apprehensive about his wife: She was so mysteriously different.

In spite of the turmoil, the realization of the fact of the pregnancy dawned slowly. As it did, he began to take small, conscious steps. He stopped smoking. Together, he and his wife spent much time that spring planting a garden. The analytic hours were filled with lectures on giving up being an indulgent, nasty little boy, on the joys of motherhood with condemnation of anyone who did not like children, on the responsibilities of fathers, and new. sympathy for his father. He said the lectures were like those of a reformed drunk and wondered not only why he was suddenly such a straight-shooter, but also why he seemed so preoccupied with concerns about death, his own, his father's, and—well, he didn't know yet.

During the next several weeks he barely mentioned his wife, except to say that she seemed uncomfortable and more distant than ever. (The distancing was two-sided, but temporary.) The major focus was a recapitulation of his relationship with his father in the transference. Many elements of that complex relationship were reviewed, but with new understanding. The wish to be close to me, to be like me, to be a father as he fantasied me to be, further stirred up passive homosexual concerns. The agricultural mode evolved into his feeling like a plowed field, like Mother Earth. The more he wanted my strength and received "seeds of insight" from me, the more he was compelled to react with fight (attack and themes of violence and being violated) or flight (missed hours, or hours that seemed to go nowhere). For some time he fought off the inevitable conclusion of the negative oedipal relationship, the wish to have a (penis) baby by his father, by me.

Interwoven were multiple aspects of competition. Deep down he wanted to be superman, but was afraid of the repercussions. What kind of an analyst was I if I was not perfect (a superman) and able to make him so? Would analysis enable him only to be a human being, "though a better parent"? His (preoedipal) father, once admired by him as a little boy as being perfection personified, was far from such. Indeed, as a rival for his mother's attentions, the patient had won an easy victory; or was he victorious? Why was he so disturbed now by his father's weakness and his mother's babying of him, just at a time when he felt such a need for her, or his wife, or someone? Well, in any case, he had surpassed his father by his wit, and now, with his wife pregnant, he had shown that he and his penis could also beget a child. That was evident for the world to see as she was beginning to show."

Gradually, he renewed his ability to see and tolerate feminine aspects in himself. Boundary strings, like those in his parents' garden that had stood for gender separation (trees and certain vegetables were male, flowers female), were falling away. The "all boy" image encouraged by his parents was a family denial of warm, nurturing aspects in men. His father seemed unable to tolerate these components, aspects both "feminine" (in the common but questioned use of the term) and passive-dependent in relation to other men. He began to wonder whether these were not only universal factors in men but also somehow important in his soon-to-be role as a father.

It was not surprising, then, when the theme of admiration for his mother and all mothers developed somewhat later. He once again became eloquent on the power and importance of mothers, not only in their ability to conceive and give birth but also to rear and mold children. The really important and powerful role in society was that of rearing children.

In June, toward the end of the first trimester, the patient's family visited on the occasion of his graduation. The "celebrations" were colored by the patient's anger and remorse about his father's too-eager anticipation of another grandchild and by his own fear of "contamination" of the child-to-be by his father. He also felt close to his mother.

A few days later he had a dream about a Cambodian child starving, while orgiastic partying adults ignored the child. The patient, however, tried to feed the child. His associations focused on his sense of starvation while both his mother and father cavorted. His parents' gluttonous ways required that children be protected from the evil doings of adults. Yet, whatever had been the case with his parents, it was he who was now gluttonous and wanted to cavort, because his wife was otherwise occupied and he lusted for other women to nourish him. His mother and his wife had not fully given of themselves to him and thus were prostitutes and deprivers. Nor did I do right by him, for I was about to leave on a brief vacation (to cavort), while he needed support and sustenance.

In summary, as the time of impregnation-conception approached the tempo of preparation for career decisions, in part related to a future supportive role, picked up. He was aware, however, of inner splits on many levels, particularly in relation to his parents and their role as models of parenting. The need to bridge so much within himself also served to bring about the actual impregnation-conception. His feelings about the pregnancy were muted by a defensive pattern related to his progenitor role, but also by his attempt to cope with his sense of loss and anticipated change in relation to his wife. His wife's determination to become pregnant engendered anger. He felt used and deprived, especially as the normal physiological events of pregnancy took their course. She seemed different and mysterious, yet he felt it was like an old story, feelings that facilitated further reconstruction of the events around his sister's birth.

He reached out toward the analyst for support and, in the process, further worked through his relationship with his father, recognizing his positive admiration for the preoedipal father and the negative oedipal aspects that included the wish to be a girl, to be impregnated, and to procreate. Previous masculine-feminine differences were reappraised, the old boundaries no longer holding up. He struggled to be a good husband and father, viewing the analyst both as an idealized image of the good father and an example of the procreator gone awry. Signs of ominous, destructive forces began to appear, but for the time being remained unclear.

Midpregnancy

This period covers only about 6 weeks of the 3-month second trimester because it was interrupted by the summer vacation, after which the character of the analytic work changed.

Soon after he had again raised the question of a possible termination date, a visit by his wife to her obstetrician established a due date. As it happened, this date was a month too early, an error not discovered until very late in the pregnancy.

In late June, he chatted cheerfully about accomplishing so much in his research, as well as doing "father-like" things such as seeing that the car was repaired and saving money. He had gone fishing and found a tiny lost kitten along the road. His cheerful mood gone, he told of almost crying at its plight. He picked it up, took it home, bathed and fed it. He felt at one with that motherless and homeless creature. "Mothering" it had been important.

Around that time he reported this dream,

There is a big auditorium where people are making speeches. I want to go in and listen, but there is a guard at the door who won't let me enter because the auditorium is full. I knew I couldn't go against the rules, but I really wanted to go in. His wife's uterus, we speculated, was the already filled auditorium. Not only was he left out in the cold, but he was prevented from looking inside. The guard at the door was me, the obstetrician, his father and himself.

This was followed by a period of increasing lability, and rapidly shifting themes grew. One day, while looking back at the tempest of the previous weeks, he recalled two events. The day before had been his birthday; and 2 weeks ago not only was his wife showing more but the baby had begun to kick!

The pregnancy now was more real, but so was the fact that it involved a baby. As he had previously concealed the pregnancy state, he now avoided the existence of the fetus.

At this time much of the material in the sessions dealt with fat, ugly women: his wife and probably his mother seen from the vantage point of a 2½ year old. Nevertheless, his repugnancy went to the point of his saying that not only did his wife seem ugly, but something about her appearance made him hate her.

Analysis of this disdain led to thoughts about the state of pregnancy and perhaps his mother's pregnancy as a kind of illness. He linked a recurrent childhood dream about crawling around in a sod-filled space, breathless and dying, with anal birth fantasies originating after his sister's birth at a time when he had been ill. Further associations to frogs clearing the cloaca and eating eggs added aspects of oral impregnation. Other dreams confirmed his envy of his mother's, sister's, and wife's ability to breast-feed.

Just before the vacation, another kind of interruption occurred that played on his worst fears and wishes. His father had what at first appeared to be a heart attack. Although, after a short while, no organic pathology was found and psychiatric consultation was recommended, the patient received the news with a mixed reaction. He condemned his weak, self-destructive father, who just wanted to get attention; he was like a baby. Yet the patient felt jealous, immobilized, and afraid.

In the last session before the vacation, he spoke of the tasks that he would have to deal with in the coming months. He already felt a sense of loss in relation to termination. He was to become a father in his own right, while at the same time having to struggle to deal with his father's need for help. He would have to make major career decisions as well.

To summarize this period, as his wife began to show and the baby began to kick during midpregnancy, the very reality of the pregnancy and an alive being could no longer be avoided. He felt excluded from his wife and from the creature within her, who now was increasingly seen as a rival. Re-experiencing the old sense of wonder and mystery, he revisited archaic, oral, and anal birth theories. The other source of his procreative and nurturing urge was now seen more clearly in his envy of women's procreative and nurturing capacities, the latter so marvelous when provided, so awful when withheld. His own nurturing wishes appeared most clearly in the incident with the stray cat. The further exploration of his bisexual origins and nature transiently heightened his castration anxiety, then mellowed even his concern about anatomical differences. He now felt sufficiently secure to bring about a rapprochement with his mother, identifying with her good parenting qualities.

Coming-to-Term(s): The Final Phase

The summer had been a bad time. There had been much to cope with, and he did not feel up to it. He blamed me for not enabling him to be "unflappable." Sadness and feelings of abandonment predominated. Termination and the last stages of pregnancy were interlocked, although the former experience was presently overriding.

His father was clearly depressed and, encouraged by the patient, had started therapy. His father's physical state was poor; he had partially lost vision in one eye. His mother rebuked the patient for not being more active in helping his father, as he now rebuked me. His wife and he felt apart and he was down on women. "I am not yet through being a son, let alone ready to become a father. Everything," he complained, "is awful."

Gradually, it became clear that this was not the case. Many significant steps had been taken; some openly revealed, others barely detectable, all played down. He and his father had begun to talk with one another. His father had, in one particularly emotional conversation, agreed that they had never been close as father and son, a fact that he regretted. During August there had also been an increase in the quiet observations of, and interactions with, married friends and their children. It was as if an active learning, practicing, preparing for parenthood was in process. And though he still had many complaints about his wife, their relationship was undergoing a transition; they felt closer to each other and intimately shared their experiences.

A week or two after he resumed analysis, his spirits picked up. That was embarrassing and sufficient reason to damn me, for it revealed the extent of his dependence on me. He was thus driven to throw his weight around, to engage in flirtations with young women, but his underlying self-doubts were clear in the sessions. In the vernacular of a current dream, could he "join the big boys of the hockey team of life" or was he "forever doomed to be subservient and have a short stick?"

For some time before a much-delayed trip to his family's home area to pick up hand-me-down items, he railed against his mother and other family members. Noting that he protested too much, he gradually became aware of his jealousy of his parents' new closeness and his reexperienced irritation about losing a favored position. These feelings were related not only to the events in his family, but to the baby coming and eventual termination. He could now understand how even before his own birth, but especially after it, when his mother put so much of herself into him, his father could have seen him as a threat.

At the time of the visit other conversations occurred with his father. He was delighted and yet uneasy about his father's new self-awareness. They talked about raising children. The patient was suspicious of his father's sudden enlightenment. He feared "contamination" from him. At one point during the conversation he said to his father that he loved him, only to have his father reply. "That's queer" (in the sense of homosexual). The patient, as if instructing his father, explained that men, fathers and sons, can indeed love each other.

With the purchase of a cradle by his sisters, the occasion of a baby shower for his wife, and the increased kicking presence of the baby, he felt very left out from time to time: All those soft things and music boxes; it must be great to be an infant!

For a while toward the end of the second trimester (late September), his wife and he both felt more positive about everything. She seemed particularly tranquil and pleased, his work was going well, and they were looking forward to the baby. Quite striking was a gradual change in his perception of his wife. Far from being ugly, she now seemed very beautiful to him; she had a special kind of beauty that he thought was intrinsic to the pregnancy.

As the (incorrect) time for the expected birth came closer, the tempo of preparation picked up. His wife stopped working, they built more furniture in their apartment to set up a nursery, friends and in-laws visited, and they both felt more apprehensive. His wife again seemed different, as if the need to mother were biological. The patient felt his life was not his own. After all, since providing a sperm many months ago, he supposedly had nothing to do with the course of events. His pleasure, goals, and work were being trampled on by women and "that baby," who now was viewed as a "pain in the ass."

No longer able to ignore indications of destructive wishes, he began to see signs of his anger and jealousy in many areas. Thus he recognized that his homogenizing frog embryos in the laboratory was not just in the service of science. He half-jokingly spoke of competing with his wife, stating he could grow better embryos than his wife any day. His sense of sardonic bitterness led to some further reconstruction of probable reactions to the birth of his sister. Was not the gamut of his present feelings similar to his childhood destruction of his mother's flowers and his father's trees following her birth? Was the pattern of wanting to create and destroy born of that period? Bringing to life and putting to death seemed so intertwined.

In late October, his father made a serious suicide attempt and was placed in a psychiatric hospital. These events set in motion a period of mourning for his father and concerns about dangerous thoughts and dreams causing harm to others.

In early November the patient began to take a new view of becoming a father. It was more than biological paternity, but the dilemma was, how much more? Gradually he was able to separate out his own sense of omnipotent influence, whether life-taking or life-giving, and to see that as his star and powers rose, his father's were declining. He had a sense of remorse and sadness, as well as new insights about future tasks of a parent. To be able to give, in spite of envy, to be able to shift and adapt one's needs and goals as one grew older and one's children came into their own were tasks of later parenthood. He cried for his father (it was perhaps too late for a reconciliation) and was able to go on to a better definition of his own goals. New ideals were being born, whereas old ones died.

The focus shifted back to his wife, the pregnancy, his work. One day he reported that he and his wife had gone to see a film on sexual practices in Denmark. In the movie was a scene of a delivery. He was overwhelmed with the skill and powers of the obstetrician. Could his father be reborn in the hands of a similarly skillful and powerful analyst? Was I so skilled that his analysis would result in a rebirth of a more perfect self? No, he later decided, I was merely human, and he would not become a superman. In any case, the latter event had supersadistic overtones, resembling a pact with the Devil of tyrannic aggression and submission, and would sustain the same pathology that had been passed on from his father's father and his father. Was that the cycle, the root of concerns about "contamination" from his father? In a telephone conversation his mother had predicted he would be a good father and not have his own father's hang-ups. Could it really be that the cycle would end with him?

Many of the sessions in November, toward the end of the pregnancy, were permeated by references to magic, mysticism, devils, and witchcraft. During this period, it seemed that early childhood fantasies were at work, but not only destructive ones. The more important of these became evident in mid-November, close to the time of the initial and incorrect due date. One day he was mildly ill with chills, fever, abdominal cramps, and diarrhea. He remembered similar episodes when he was a child. He thought there was something suspicious about these physical symptoms and connected them with the imminence of the baby's birth. Later that month, after they learned that the real due date was a month later, he experienced constipation for several days, frequently said, "I don't give a shit," and had a dream with elements of producing a big shit. His intestines, we finally concluded, were producing birth phenomena. "Now that is the biggest trick of all, speaking of magic; intestinal and natal alchemy," he said.

In early December, 9 days before the birth of a daughter, he reported the following dream:

> I was in some factory. It was a big, smelly one, which homogenized cats and dogs and dried them up for fertilizer. I was quite distressed, perhaps actually crying in the dream. There was a room for chopping up animals. A butcher came out, fat, with no hair, spattered with soup left over from homogenized cat. It was all over him, he was a mess. He handed me two kittens to hold before grinding them up. I went into another room, a classroom with youngsters of all ages and a male teacher who looked like a former history instructor. "Teacher," I said, "I'm sorry to interrupt, but I have a terrible problem." Then I told him about the butcher in the other room, starting to sob inconsolably as I spoke.

The dream was related to the baby coming and the birth process. Both he and his wife were now impatient, wanting to get it over with; his wife had cried earlier in the week out of fatigue and apprehension. While waiting, he thought it best to finish some papers, and was surprised that he could be so productive in spite of feeling resentful of "this whole baby business." They had two cats, one of which had kittens. He ground up animals in the lab, and the butcher-monster in the dream was his father and himself. Would he be an intimidating father and, if not, what kind of father would he be? He would want to protect the baby from his father and himself. The history teacher might be me, helping in that protection.

The following week he concentrated on whether the baby and future children would impair his career, while at the same time coming to more definite conclusions about seeking a position where he would be in command of his own ship (family, living circumstances, research) and pursuing issues around termination,

A week later, after the birth, he indicated his new understanding of how children develop a sense of omnipotence. "Eight pounds of baby," he said, "are completely dominating 300 pounds of adults."

In summary, during the summer break that occurred toward the end of the middle trimester, the patient carried on more actively than ever his observations of other parents and his interaction with children. This continued on resumption of analysis in spite of some inner and outer turmoil, the latter related to the illness, depression, and suicide attempt of his father. His father's travails increased the patient's apprehensions about his own roles of progenitor and future father, as he again became concerned about his competitive strivings and successful deeds, especially his successful marriage and the fathering of a child. He mourned for his father and in the process began to clarify and separate out his own developmental tasks from the particular nature of his father's development (with a view of the vicissitudes of later stages of being a parent).

Aspects of ending and beginning, of birth and death (Schafer, 1968), of creating and destroying were confronted anew, not only in terms of the pregnancy and the father's illness, but also via the transference, in relation to termination. He developed somatic, particularly gastrointestinal symptoms, which were couvade-like sympathy pains (Trethowan, 1965; Trethowan & Conlon, 1965). Termination was seen as a rebirth. All of these events, intrapsychic and external, with the enlarging fetus making its presence felt, seemed to invoke archaic mechanisms of splitting (Lichtenberg & Slap, 1973), introjection, and projection. In the latter part of the last trimester he had a sense of good and evil forces at work, endangering all, especially the baby. Against such powerful and seemingly magical forces, equally powerful counterforces were needed. The analyst was called on for all his wizardry, but was found to be only human, alas, a fact that would pertain to his own "rebirth" at the end of analysis. Although these regressive phenomena transpired, progressive efforts were at work; for they, like the baby girl that was born, did not wait.

DISCUSSION

The period of impregnation and pregnancy constitutes an important developmental stage for the prospective father, which, like other developmental crises, brings about internal upheaval and change. The outcome is of critical importance to the whole family (Ross, 1979).

These psychological events occur in the context of the special tasks of young adulthood. As was the case with the patient described, by that time important decisions about sexual identity, career, and marital partner have already been made. But when a man prepares himself to produce an offspring, it is likely that the equilibrium attained is challenged severely, although perhaps less noticeably than in the mother-to-be.

Ritvo (1971) describes how in early adolescence retreat from the object under the pressures of the upsurge of libidinal impulses leads to some degree of resurgent narcissism and ego disorganization. In late adolescence, there is a shift to new objects. The new object, the sexual partner, is an essential nutriment as well as an organizing influence.

As a new task arose for my patient, that of becoming a father, the ensuing upheaval resembled that of early adolescence as well as other developmental crises. Thus my patient's preparation for the pregnancy and the pregnancy itself initiated a major reworking of the past and current relationships with his mother, father, siblings, and wife, as well as a shift and resynthesis of his sense of self. All of these coalesced to color the psychological atmosphere into which his daughter was born.

Loewald (1951), Abelin (1975), and Lamb (1975), among others, in pointing to the early importance of the father in the child's development, indicate his modulating influence in the gradual separation-individuation process. With the resurgence of aspects of maternal envy, engulfment, and deprivation as a result of the pregnancy, my patient's admired preoedipal father stood as a protector, a refuge, someone who in fantasy actively sacrificed himself to rescue the patient from the primordial waters of the pregnancy. In addition, by taking over some of his father's specific and useful skills and attributes, forms of the ego ideal, the patient was able to begin gearing himself to become a supporter and protector of his own family, despite recognizing the flaws of his father of old and, especially, the old and sick state of his father of the present. His father was a model of fathering to whom he could turn to sort out what was useful as well as to discard what would contaminate and impede.

For my patient, the joint creation of a child introduced a new level of relatedness. Into this dyadic world peopled as it was by imagos in a state of transition, the child-to-be stepped gradually. At first it was more symbol than fact, yet at an early fetal age it already exerted powerful influences. As it got bigger and then finally made its kicking presence known, it gave warning to its parents-to-be to get ready. On the positive side, as a wondrous achievement, a marvelous experiment in the ways of nature, its existence was welcomed. Though often ignored as a new entity, it was what would make them a family, something they both desired. But in my patient these positive vibrations were buffeted by negative forces. For even before and certainly early in the pregnancy, the child-to-be stood more for the loss of a hard-won position, a rival at the breast, a depriver of sustained support and attachment, an agent and accomplice of his father, an envious and envied sibling, an instigator of change ambivalently anticipated, evidence of dirty work, a potential mutilator or mutilatee, and thereby, all in all, an invitation for trouble. To add insult to injury, no matter how great an innovator and scientist he was, he could not do what his mother, his wife, his sisters could do. At times he seemed driven back to the infuriating role of a passive observer. This passive role was also welcomed, however, for he could take refuge and disclaim having had much to do with the baby.

It was remarkable that by the time of the birth and clearly in the months that followed, he came to terms with his child. Their relationship following the birth actually began on a most positive footing, the turmoil that had preceded being quietly and gradually covered by an amnesic blanket.

The analysis and the analyst via the transference probably influenced the nature of the experience of prospective fatherhood, as the latter influenced the former. I was at different times seen as each of the important persons of the past, with all their negative and positive characteristics. But I was also seen as an ally in the work of understanding, and as neutral in the war of conflicts, desires, and fears. The pregnancy and becoming a parent became an integral part of the analysis, a synergic interplay useful to both (Hurn, 1969).

Finally, I want to draw attention to an important phenomenon. In the second, but mostly in the third, trimester, my patient had the intense experience of powerful magical forces being at work. This has been observed by others in describing women's experiences of pregnancy. Bibring (1959), and subsequently Jessner and others (1970), have commented on the number of women who are haunted by the fear of producing a monster or a dead infant. Jessner and co-workers say, "These concerns . . . reflect the experience of the uncanny and of magic powers" (p. 222). In the third trimester, "most women experience the fetus now as an enemy, who is injuring the kidneys or the womb" (p. 223), and later, "experiences of anxiety in many forms and morbid preoccupations in women during the last weeks of pregnancy were observed in all pregnant subjects studied. . . Delivery initiates in the mother fantasies of death and rebirth" (p. 224). My patient had similar fears, an expression of concern for his wife and of his own aggressive rage at his wife and child-to-be. The degree to which his fears were reactive to her fears is not clear. It seems to be particularly in relation to the commonly heightened apprehensions in the later stages of pregnancy that many societies exert the strongest ritual controls of which the "couvade" is a prime example.

Furthermore, there was a remarkable sharing of psychological and physical events during the pregnancy similar to earlier descriptions of women's experiences (cf, Bibring, 1959; Colman & Colman, 1971; Jessner et al., 1970).

Whatever the reasons for the past silence on fathers may have been, it appears that we are at last beginning to recognize the significance of the early role of the father. As a way to gain a better understanding of that role, we must turn our attention to the early developmental processes involved in becoming a father. Prospective fatherhood is a critical stage in that development. Further case reports can bring more understanding of the phenomena intrinsic to prospective fatherhood, at least from the vantage point of the analytic situation, unique though that may be.

It has been well documented that the advent of fatherhood brings on a host of new anxieties for men. In this chapter, Dr. Pollack points out that it is also a unique opportunity for men to resolve long-dormant unconscious issues. He claims that for many men, fatherhood presents a second chance to rework issues of gender identity, self-balance, and intimacy conflicts in a manner that may result in both a renewed sense of personal meaning and psychological safety. Specifically, an expectant father gets the opportunity to balance needs for autonomy and affiliation in gender specific and appropriate ways. Through the use of theory, research, and case studies of fathers "coming of age" well after his children were born, Dr. Pollack expands the notion of becoming a father to a psychological transformation involving new understanding of autonomy and affiliation.

26

A Delicate Balance: Fatherhood and Psychological Transformation—A Psychoanalytic Perspective

William S. Pollack

Traversing the path that leads to parenthood is, for many men, an arduous journey. For becoming and being a father presents men with a challenge much akin to the duality represented by the Chinese ideograph for change: CRISIS/OPPORTUNITY. A crisis—for many of the long-buried struggles and "unfinished business" from childhood threatens to become dramatically unearthed; and an opportunity because, as men, we are given life's greatest *second chance*: to father in a new way that both transforms ourselves and leaves a legacy of paternal nurturance for the next generation.

This chapter will focus on the psychological, emotional underpinnings in men's transition and accommodation to fatherhood as illustrated by clinical vignette and research interview. Throughout, there will be an emphasis on how the unconscious processes mobilized by becoming and being a father run deeper and tie us more closely to our past than we usually like to imagine. Yet, they also offer us the

316

opportunity for genuine transformation in a way rarely encountered in everyday life. Fatherhood for many men really is life's second chance to rework issues of gender identity, self-balance and intimacy conflict in a manner that may result in both a renewed sense of personal meaning and psychological safety.

MEN'S SURPRISE AND SHOCK

Almost 20 years ago, a pioneer researcher on the impact of fathers on their children's lives decried the academic wasteland in which men's contributions to family life had gone unheralded and unstudied while calling fathers, "the forgotten contributors to child development" (Lamb, 1975). Yet, it was many more years before we came to realize how having children, that is, how becoming a father, was a forgotten contribution to men's development. Perhaps, that was because our developmental models so narrowly focused on the very early years, and were so woefully inadequate when it came to late adolescent and adult stages. Yet, it was also because we had so championed the ideal of autonomy and separation, especially in "normal" men's development, that we neglected to understand the significance of affiliative attachments in male psychological health. As a result, we overlooked the powerfully transforming role of becoming a father. Men's nurturant urge, often suppressed in boyhood and adult socialization tasks, can be stimulated dramatically by becoming a father. Greenberg and Morris (1974) call it one of the most joyous recognitions surrounding men's experience of paternity.

Alan, a man whose progress to fatherhood we observed in the Boston University Pregnancy and Parenthood project[1] expressed this joyous shock and the subsequent psychological changes wrought by becoming a father in a poignant and articulate response to our interview:

> It has been a lot of fun to watch her grow but at the same time it is a lot of responsibility . . . I just had never been around babies, and I didn't know. I just didn't have any idea of what being a father was all

---

[1]The Boston University Pregnancy and Parenthood project was a longitudinal study under the direction of Francis K. Grossman. The work on father autonomy and affiliation was done by Dr. Pollack in collaboration with Dr. Grossman and his colleagues, Drs. Ellen Golding and Nikki Fedele. See Pollack, 1982, 1983; Grossman, Pollack, Golding, Fedele, 1987; Grossman, Eichler, Winnickoff et al., 1980, and Pollack and Grossman, 1985.

about . . . And I am really attached. I find myself thinking about her at work.

My personality has changed a lot. I take things a little slower. All of a sudden, you've got to be somebody's *father* It is different, but it's fun.

Yet, John, another man struggling with his new fathering role made manifest the ambivalence inherent in taking on such a nurturant responsibility versus one's own self (sometimes called narcissistic) needs:

Well, it's difficult for me to live with anyone . . . I could spend a great deal of my time alone. Without having a wife . . . without having children. But, at the same time, all those things are very important to me. So it becomes—obviously if I could be a 100% selfish and just have my wife when I wanted her and just have my kids when I wanted to—that would suit me. But I can see that marriage wouldn't last. So it becomes a . . . *balancing act, a constant balancing act.* Between her needs, my needs and the child's needs.

THE BALANCING ACT: THE BOSTON STUDY

The findings of the Boston University Parenthood and Pregnancy project (BUPP) provide empirical support for a model of healthy emotional development for adult men that requires a gender-specific *balance* between the capacity for *autonomy* and *affiliation,* between separateness and relatedness—I-ness and We-ness. The BUPP was a longitudinal developmental study of 90 couples first seen during the expectancy period of the birth of the indexed child. Women were seen, in individual interviews, close to the beginning of their pregnancy (half of the sample with a first child); and with their husbands later during the gestational period. The entire families (mother, father, and indexed child) were studied at birth, and at 1, 2 and 5 years later. Data were collected from home visits, naturalistic and structured observations, semi-structured interviews, paper and pencil scales, and child assessments. Standardized clinical ratings derived from interaction observations and video/audiotaped segments of play, interview, etc., also were utilized in complex time-linked statistical analyses. (Details of the larger study may be found in: Fedele, Golding, Grossman & Pollack, 1988; Grossman, Eichler, Winnickoff, Anzalone, Gofseyeff & Sargent, 1980; Pollack & Grossman, 1985). Among the issues explored were the nonparent-to-parent transition, marital couples needs/satisfaction, men's and women's changing sense of self, children's affective and cognitive functioning/development, the quality of parenting, and general adaption (Fedele et al., 1988; Grossman, Pollack, Golding & Fedele, 1987; Grossman, 1987; Grossman, Pollack & Golding, 1988; Pollack & Grossman, 1985).

One of the most robust findings from the BUPP was the predictive power of *autonomy* scores and *affiliation* scores during the cross-section of the life cycle that was studied; and the necessary dialectical and developmental *balance* between the capacity to remain related and connected to significant others, and the capacity to maintain a sense of self-focused interest and achievement. For both men and women it was the achieving of this healthy balance between autonomous functioning and affiliative relatedness that was predictive of marital satisfaction, "good-enough" fathering, general parental capacity, children's positive mood and family adaptation (Grossman, Pollack et al., 1987, 1988; Pollack & Grossman, 1985; Pollack, 1982, 1983).

An example of a man in the research who could be scored high on both autonomy and affiliation was Greg. In speaking about his wife and children he said: *"My wife is really warm, she can handle herself well, which I really like. The marriage is important to me. I also love being with my daughter. Saturday morning is our special time. But it's also important to me to have my own time—to read, to think by myself. Being alone makes me feel refreshed and more complete."*

These findings stand in contrast to traditional views of *autonomy* as an alternative to or opposite of *affiliation* and relatedness (Erikson, 1963). The perspective offered here is one of a dialectic (Grossman et al., 1988, Pollack, 1990)—autonomy is related to but not defined solely by participation in separate activities, and affiliation is not just a matter of engaging in relationships. Stechler and Kaplan (1980), two child psychoanalysts who built on the work of George Klein (1976), defined the beginning sense of self in children and its later integrated form in adults as a combination of two apparently disparate aspects that must be integrated into one identity. They hypothesized these two poles of the self being felt as an autonomous center of activity, versus the self as part of a transcendent unit. They called the autonomous pole the "I" component and the more affiliative pole the "We" component. I agree with Stechler and Kaplan that the self can simultaneously be separate and part of an entity greater than itself. In our research, when we talk about autonomy we are referring to the sense of the "I" within the self and when we talk about affiliation we are referring to the sense of the "We" embedded within an independent self. (Grossman et al., 1988; Pollack, 1982).

Although the autonomy-affiliation balance was important for women as well as men, men's definition of what was affiliative and what was autonomous differed radically from women's. Any attempt to measure these two concepts required awareness of these basic differences. For example, the men in the study would often show a strong proclivity to be close to their children but would express this by attention, physical play, or teaching. Women appeared to be more comfortable in holding and hugging their children. We felt, however, that both of these types of interactions were evidence of affiliative capacities. Indeed, the children's responsiveness to these very different parenting styles corroborated this. (Pollack & Grossman, 1985).

So for affiliation/autonomy scoring it was necessary to use distinct measurement scales, for men. Not merely an artifact of one empirical study, this finding has been replicated by other major research groups on empathy (Hoffman, 1977; Lennon & Eisenberg, 1987) substantiating the gender-specific nature of such concepts as self-sufficiency, warmth, empathy, relatedness, etc. (See also Pollack, 1982, 1983 for a full discussion). Rather than creating a rigid gender-linked dichotomy between capacities for relatedness and self-sufficiency—I-ness or we-ness—(i.e., the "independent man" versus the "interdependent woman"), the empirical data suggest a basis for recasting of these functions along the lines of a balance; and the recognition that there may indeed be, at times, a his relatedness and a hers relatedness; a hers autonomy and a his autonomy. *Mental health, then and psychological well being is not reflected solely in the achieving of autonomy for men, but rather is a balance of both relatedness as well as independence.* Fatherhood both upsets that balance as well as offering opportunities for its re-alignment.

FATHERHOOD: A SECOND CHANCE

In reviewing our research, we found several major trends in healthy couples' negotiations about parenting: For example in a traditional family structure when women take on the primary role of child care, men shy away from competing with this role of primacy with the children. I am not talking here about a dysfunctional setting in which women feel "stuck" with their children and men are off doing something else. Rather, these were couples who decided on such an emotional "division of labor" for their mutual benefit, and needs. And when something goes wrong in this set up, (e.g., the mother becomes ill or incapacitated), the father was more than ready to step in, give support and take on an alternative nurturant function. We described this balance as one of *complementarity*. Perhaps, at times, such complementarities need to be renegotiated, and the possibilities of excluding the man from emotional connection, or abandoning the woman to too much, need to be addressed. Yet, with this said, such an arrangement can continue to allow the father a significant role in parenting—meaningful for child and mother as well—even though it may not always be the *"leading"* role.

Yet, sometimes unconscious expectations based on deeply in-grained gender roles may impede fathers from taking up their new task of parenting. In our study we found that the mother could become an inadvertent *gatekeeper*, keeping her newborn babies from her hus-band. This was usually subtle, such as handing the baby to the father at an inopportune moment and then saying, "Oh, dear, don't hold her like that," or "That isn't the way to change a diaper." Often the father, who already felt inadequate, would unconsciously collude by hastily giving the baby to his wife and then backing off. With men and women increasingly invading each other's traditional "turf," it is understand-able that women may feel inclined to maintain some control over the household, especially over parenting. This may entail significant strain and sacrifice, particularly for career-oriented women, who are already juggling the burdens of work and home.

On the father's side, we noticed a parallel unconscious process, occurring around the birth of the newborn and into the child's first year, which I've called *nest-feathering*. The new father often felt that the best way to provide for his wife and child was to work assiduously in order to gain greater income or career status—to "feather the nest" which the young fledgling and his/her caring maternal parent were placed in. What we found, however, was that women in the study were most distressed by the emotional absence of their husbands during this expectancy period. So, much like the O'Henry story "The Gift of the Magi," the husband was sacrificing for the wife, and the wife for the husband, in ways that were terribly out of sync.

Our advice to these new fathers was that they spend some of their time supporting their wife and newborn by being physically and emotionally present. We suggested to their wives that they try to facilitate their husbands' learning how to take care of the newborn. We believe that men need to accept that their wives can "mentor" them in some nurturing skills. At the same time, they also need their wives to recognize that "male" ways of parenting can be a valuable complement to mothering.

In contradistinction to such *complimentarity of balance*, we found an important result concerning the effect of the *quality of the father's time* on their interaction with their children. All parenting research has shown, without exception, that fathers spend an extremely small period of their day with their children, even if they are "highly" involved (Grossman et al., 1988). What our findings showed, however, was that the *quantity* and *quality* of the time need not be the same. In other words, fathers in our study who were highly involved with their work, and were satisfied with that work—spending a fair amount of time at it, could not spend equal amounts of time with their children. The quality of the time that these 'job-satisfied fathers' spent with their children directly and positively affected their child's mental health, however. Work-invested fathers who care about their children and spend significant time with them—albeit not the same level of quantity as mothers—can still have an important effect on the emotional well being of their sons and daughters—due to the quality of the interaction. *Fathers, even actively at work fathers, do count and indeed do make a big difference!* Even if men are not the primary caretakers, they may have an important effect on the mental health of their families and children; and, by extension, on their own selves. Often this is a "second chance" for a reparative relationship and via this repair to an enhanced sense of intimacy for themselves, their mates and their families.

In the interviews of men who were found to be healthy supporters of both autonomy and affiliation in their children, a particular trend was revealed. These men stated that they were invested in learning how to parent correctly, and learned to do so from a combination of not only their own memories of parental nurturance, but the direct observation of their wives. These men often observed their wives parent as experts so that they could learn to be good parents themselves. We called this trend, for the men, *identification*. This process, I think, offers another chance for repair, and especially in the couples' situation. A man's ability to value and identify with the tasks that women do traditionally, particularly in mothering and child care, helps to undo at the deepest unconscious layers the fear and dread that many men feel about being dependent on a woman.

Becoming a man should not entail one single rigid pathway, but rather a multitude of possible journeys toward fulfillment. Both men and women become trapped when the personality characteristics necessary for mature involvement in our complex industrialized world become divided along gender lines. It is no more useful for men to be protectors and providers without the capacity for deep empathic feeling or the sharing of sadness with their mates, than it is for women to be the nurturing care givers to a child but he denied the capacity for achievement at work.

One way that such balance between the I and the We, and mutual respect between the genders can be realigned is in the *self-reparative role* of parenting in men's lives. Fathering is one of men's greatest opportunities for personal change. The research findings of our longitudinal study, corroborated now by a number of other innovative interventions (Barnett, Marshall & Pleck, 1992; Levant, 1990) suggest that "good-enough fathering" (Diamond, 1995a; Grossman & Pollack, 1984) is not only a salient factor in the healthy development of young boys and girls, but an important curative or transforming factor in the mental health of adult men. Contrary to past and popular belief, fatherhood is equally significant to many men as career achievement. Indeed, it appears to have a reverberating impact on their emotional capacities for balance, mental health and, physical well being. Barnett and Marshall (1991), have studied close to 200 married fathers living in the suburbs of Massachusetts. The only factor that significantly correlated with the physical health of the men was their having a good relationship with their children. Significantly, there was no correlation between the health of these men studied and their work or marital roles.

It appears that men's capacity to achieve a gender-sensitive empathic form of fathering provides the opportunity for personal transformation for two reasons. First, men can see and realize the positive impact their emotional commitment has on the well-being of their children—both girls and boys. They are able to give to their own children something that often they themselves did not completely receive from their fathers. This *altruistic transformation* often enhances men's self-esteem. In addition, men are aware that it often requires *identifying with their wives' caretaking capacities;* or, indeed, openly learning from their female partners, at times, how to nurture. In so doing, men are acknowledging the meaningfulness of women's relational skills and are internalizing this sense of maternal care giving in a manner that can dramatically undo earlier negative and more frightening feelings toward all things "feminine" and "maternal."

Fathering is a powerful emotional situation for men. Although historically, research has tended to focus on the absence or loss of the father, the presence of the father and the normative experience of fathering lies at the deepest emotional roots of men's being. As a result, parenting may affect men's functioning at work/career and men's work, in turn, affects fathering, child development and marital relationships.

PERSONAL TRANSFORMATIONS

By and large, the men in our study were not very positive about the role model that their own fathers had provided for them as parents. Primarily, they had aspirations to be better fathers to their own children, than their fathers had been to them. They did, however, feel that their own mothers had been good parents. They utilized that maternal nurturant experience as well as their identification with their wives' caretaking skills to make up for whatever "gaps" they felt existed in their own paternal self-image.

So, the response to our question as to whether these men thought they were the same kind of father to their children that their own father had been to them, or whether they felt more like their own father now (i.e., since becoming a father) was predominantly negative: "Definitely not," exclaimed one man. "No. I feel less like him, more conscious of the threat of being like him," answered another father who had felt quite hurt by his own father's parenting. "I don't know if my father was that great a father. I'd like to be a better father", he replied. (Grossman et al., 1980).

When we asked John, a man who we followed throughout the transition to parenthood, whether he felt more like his father since becoming one, his answer reflected the active psychological process of achieving a balance between accepting a legacy from the past while creating a new experience in the present: *"Well, in respect to being a father, I am not the same kind of father. But being a father, yes I feel more like him now than I ever did before. Cause it is different, it's sort of a mystical thing that I can't explain that . . . well . . . but it creates a sort of bond between my father and myself because for the first time I'm getting a feeling for what he must have felt while I was growing up."* By the end of his child's first year, John was saying that he enjoyed being an active co-parent with his wife. When asked whether there were differences between what a father and mother could do with an infant he replied: *"The relationship is obviously not the same. (My son) sees his mother, you know, and until yesterday she was breast feeding him. I wish I could, but couldn't have that type of relationship with him. When he looks at me he smiles but it is not same sort of smile he flashes to his mother."*

Indeed, John was able to admit that he was "jealous" of this special relationship, but it was just something he had to "accept." He was equally aware of how becoming a father had started to have profound affects on his own personality. Part of these changes in sense of self reverberated with an enhancement of self-esteem that accrues when a man spends time at home and dedicates himself to his child. In John's words: "I think I'm pleased with myself that I have lived up to the responsibility of being a good parent. I didn't know that about myself (before) and I definitely had questions about whether or not I would handle it." And when asked whether he would think of himself as a member of his family first or as an individual first he replied quite quickly: "Definitely I would say a member of my family first!"

When John's child was five, he reflected on the fact that slowly but surely he had become "more generally concerned with my family and the quality of the home life as opposed to how well I'm going to do in my profession." This man had gone from being "100% selfish" through a "balancing act" to having his role as a father become the most important thing in his life. Having achieved a personal transformation, he felt now that he was part of a larger community or life cycle beyond himself. Halfway through the life cycle, John considered himself fully transformed through the experience of fathering. Yet, what happens when men are less able to allow themselves the experience of becoming a father?

INHIBITIONS AND INTERRUPTIONS IN THE TRANSITION TO FATHERHOOD

To illustrate some of the inhibitions or psychological interruptions that may make it difficult or totally impede the possibility of becoming a father for certain men, I would like to present two brief clinical case vignettes: One that illustrates the possibility of achieving the psychological growth necessary to embrace fatherhood at any point in the life cycle (even several years after the physiological birth of the infant), and as such illustrates the distinction between merely being a father and what being Benedek called *fatherliness* (1959, 1970a). The second vignette highlights the a struggle with the intergenerational transmission of ambivalence about parenting in order to become a father.

Late Fathering

Doug was a successful business executive in his mid-fifties when he first sought psychological consultation. The ostensible reason for seeking treatment was the apparent impending dissolution of his 20-year marriage with his childhood sweetheart. Doug reported all of the pain that had become apparent in the last 3 years of the marriage, including a growing emotional isolation from his wife, and an inability to share his feelings with her. In addition, there had been a series of extra-marital affairs in order to deal with what Doug called a sense of "boredom" or "deadness" in the marriage. During the last affair, he was confronted by his wife and admitted everything—including his growing despair that the marriage was leading nowhere, and that he might need to leave. His wife was distraught by the possibility that he was being unfaithful to her, and the reality that he might seek divorce.

Doug was not reluctant to enter therapy, but questioned whether it could "really do me any good." He felt that his problems "went way back," and that his style of behavior, including the use of extra-marital affairs was something he had "just gotten used to."

As the therapist was receiving only a very shadowy sense of Doug's own relationship with his father, and, in turn, Doug's relationship with his now 10-year-old daughter, Rachel, he inquired first about the father–daughter pair. Doug quickly responded that he had never talked about Rachel in the treatment because he didn't think it had "anything to do with why I was here." But on further elaboration, it became clear that he was quite alienated from his daughter and felt that she was "my wife's child." Due to some perinatal difficulty, Rachel had required around-the-clock interventions as a young infant, which were mostly administered by Doug's wife—as he was often at work 60 or 70 hours a week. From then on, Doug explained, "I felt like I lost the opportunity to really be Rachel's father," as his wife became an active, autonomous and primary parent. "I didn't really know what to say to her," Doug explained, and as a result he often withdrew leaving her and her mother to "do their own thing."

As he spoke more about his estrangement in the relationship with his daughter Doug appeared sad, and the therapist pointed out this affective shift. Doug agreed, that perhaps for a long time he had hidden from himself how much he missed this father–child relationship. The therapist then inquired as to whether something might be being repeated here that Doug himself had experienced as a child with his own father.

The flood gates opened! Doug remembered how abandoned he had felt as a younger child, and then again as an adolescent when he had sought his father's support. Due to a series of business setbacks, and the abrupt onset of a psychiatric illness, his father was totally unavailable to him in anything but a cold, cognitive manner. Doug remembered how much he kept trying to "please him," but to no avail. When Doug's father died when Doug was in his early twenties, he remembered feeling only "relieved that I didn't have to try to get his love anymore."

Doug, who had already begun a trial separation from his wife prior to beginning treatment, began to arrange for "visitation" periods with his daughter. He realized that even though his contact with his wife would be minimal during this trial period, he wanted to maximize his connection with Rachel. He set up periods during the week and over the week-end in which they would do things by themselves, and even sometimes they would get together as a family.

Returning to the therapy several weeks later, Doug was beaming with pride. He explained, "I think I'm spending more time with Rachel, and more quality time than when I lived at home." Indeed, this did not seem like denial or distortion, but rather a true expression of the shift in the parenting relationship. "I don't have to be like my own father, do I?" Doug asked. And then, before waiting to see whether an answer was forthcoming, he replied for himself "No!, I don't." "Maybe I'm fooling myself," he said, "but I think divorce or not I'm creating a much closer relationship with Rachel, and I don't feel that will be lost."

Although the marital "sturm und drang" continued for long periods, Doug felt that he had worked through a very important piece of his personal experience concerning the earlier pain and disappointment with his own father; and that he had only now really become a father to his daughter for the first time, just before her tenth birthday. Just as Mahler has commented on the "psychological birth of the infant" (Mahler, Pine, & Bugman, 1975), there is an equally important point of time that we might the call the *psychological birth of the father*. Although optimally it will occur during the expectancy period, there is no reason that with psychotherapeutic intervention (especially one aimed at dealing with inhibition due to unconscious conflicts or deficits in father's own experience of parenting as a child) that such a capacity for "fatherliness" cannot be generated at any point in the parent–child life cycle.

The Reluctant Father

Jim was a successful, white, male, Protestant, attorney in his early 30's who had first come for therapeutic help several years before because of struggles with colleagues at work and the inability to maintain an emotional commitment with a woman. In the initial sessions, Jim described his family as a model 1950s American classic—somewhere between "Leave It To Beaver" and "Ozzie and Harriet." He reported a series of brief therapeutic encounters during college and graduate school in which he had sought out help to deal with his overly rigid self requirements for success, and his painful sense of failure in romantic relationships. Each time, and without exception, he experienced the therapist (both male and female treaters) as "misunderstanding me," and of being "of no use." What emerged later was that Jim had experienced an intense sense of dread in trying to "depend on" these treaters in the initial sessions, and eventually a terrible feeling of shame or humiliation in being unable to use the treatment offered to him. Over the course of the therapy, it became clear that Jim's parents—although well intentioned— had substituted rigid "rules for living" for a more empathic understanding of their child's specific needs. Jim's father would often pull away from his son when he was upset; and his mother would preach to Jim about what he should be doing, or how "silly" he had been to be so emotional.

Given such a childhood background, Jim had developed a number of psychodynamic defenses and a character structure through which he unconsciously distanced himself from most of his feelings—except those of anger. In addition, he avoided any dependent relationship on another person out of the likelihood that they might disappoint and/or abandon him—leading to a dangerous sense of embarrassment or shame.

Over time, Jim became trusting enough to share an unconscious fantasy. Although talking about his sense of failure and being doomed to boring work, he tentatively and uncharacteristically, shared the memory that when feeling scorned, incompetent, or ashamed as a child—all alone without support of parents or friends—Jim used to retreat to his room and fantasize about the future. *"A house would be burning down and no one would know how to save the occupants. Out of the blue Jim would arrive and without a glimmer of fear or hesitation thrust himself into the burning building carrying out the women and children into complete safety. Then he would be hailed as a hero and the "limelight" (as he described it) would be on him. Finally he would be "important," receive a medal and everyone would recognize his courage."* This "reparative fantasy"—a pastiche of boyhood Superman comics and Jim's father's wartime exploit stories—was the heroic and grandiose alternative to a life filled with an endless sense of "not measuring up," and being "a nobody."

Although Jim continued to complain that no one—including his therapist—understood or cared about him, with the aid of the uncritical holding environment of psychotherapy where his needs mattered, Jim became able to meet and sustain relationships with women whom he liked; and one whom he grew to love. Ambivalent all the while, he felt increasingly confident that he wished to make a permanent commitment, and married.

Soon after this, his father took ill and it seemed quite likely that he would be dying soon. Jim debated about whether or not he should return to make one last attempt at contact with this man who, "was never there for me," and, "so I'm not really losing anyone, anyway." Together, during this period, we worked through how painful it had been for Jim—over and over again—when his father abandoned him emotionally as he attempted to find support as a growing child. Due to his own perfectionism and isolation of affect, Jim's father, "always had to get things right"; and couldn't be bothered, "with children interfering with the gardening," he so loved. Perhaps, most painful, was Jim's final realization that these stereotypically masculine defensive traits—the avoidance of feelings and workaholic perfectionism—were the only male role models available to him in his predominantly female world. And that, therefore, to his horror in retrospect, he had identified with them, and made them his own. As Jim said, almost in tears: "I've become just like my dad."

Jim journeyed home and saw his father for what turned out to be the last time. Upon his return, after his father's death, and with tears in his eyes, Jim recounted the last discussion: a warm and friendly chat about baseball, but still devoid of a deeper meaning and connection that Jim had always longed for. Yet, for the first time, Jim acknowledged the fact that they had both had done the best they could, under the circumstances—and this recognition of the limitations of the human condition was a new and relieving experience for Jim. Now, the deeper interpersonal work on the intrapsychic defenses against parenting took place. Jim revealed that all his life he had "wanted somebody by his side" (usually a father or older brother figure); yet, often he felt in the treatment like telling the therapist to "Go Away", so that his need for parental support would not show.

Indeed, the pain of depending on a potentially helpful, later abandoning significant other (male or female) was almost annihilatory: "Needing someone like that is like being part of someone else's dream . . . They wake up and you disappear." It was only Jim's own childhood dream or fantasy of the invulnerable heroes that could soothe such deep anxieties and maintain connections.

Now, Jim began to speak about how he had fantasized for several years about having children, but felt it impossible. How could he risk being like his own father and emotionally abandoning his child in their time of need. "You really have to be dedicated to them all the time," he said. And Jim wasn't sure he'd have the emotional stamina and self-esteem security to achieve this seemingly daunting task. Most of all he worried that: "I won't be able to take their hand, help them stand up for themselves and let them know that *they're* important too."

Jim was afraid that what was now becoming his wife's pressing need to address child bearing would bully him into just doing, "what looks like the right thing," exactly as his own mother and father had done, to his detriment. He felt certain that the therapist would also have expectations of "mature behavior" and shame him into becoming a father. When it was clarified that no normative expectations were being held by the therapist, but that perhaps Jim was selling himself short in thinking that he had to fail at parenting, as his own father had, Jim began to cry, and then said:

> I see myself like in the picture of the student uprisings in Communist China, in Tianneman Square . . . Standing tall with my son by my side, facing the tanks and armies of totalitarianism. I am holding my son's hand and telling him: "This is important, you're important!"

Jim began to play with his nephews when they visited, and spoke of the joy it triggered. Stopping himself somewhat, he explained: "parenting won't just be fun," he acknowledged. The therapist agreed but suggested that it needn't be seen as an unbearable burden, either. Jim began to talk about the kind of father he'd like to be. The work continues, in progress.

CONCLUSION

Why is it that we live in an age where, finally, fathers' contributions to their childrens' development is recognized; but the salient role of being and becoming a nurturant caring father remains relatively unexamined in its centrality to men's own emotional health and development? The continued overemphasis by our society on the autonomous ('I') component of little boys and, later, adult mens' psychological makeup has not only taken its toll on intimate heterosexual relationships—just ask any woman her opinion of men's problems with intimacy! It has also too often impeded men from achieving a true sense of *emotional paternity:* One that balances the autonomy of self with the affiliative capacity of connections.

For indeed, true fathering is a balancing act: A balance between the *urge to achieve independently* and the equally pressing *need to be connected to meaningful others, beyond one's self.* It is a balance between men's often less than complete experience of nurturing caregiving from their own fathers, in the past, and their opportunity for achieving a different model of fathering for the next generation—and through this struggle to change, achieving a personal, psychological transformation for themselves. The journey to fatherhood is often a challenging one, at times fraught with impediments; ones that can, however, be overcome as men become more in touch with the inner world of feelings and often the shadowy unconscious repository of our childhood world of play and pain. The ultimate balance that fathering may offer men, therefore, is one between the day-to-day exigencies of adult life and the wellspring of inner life that paternal nurturance must—by its very existence—tap into. Perhaps a poem by the psychoanalyst, Donald Winnicott would be a fitting evocation of the inner balance that fathering can bring to men, when men can safely and positively come to fathering:

> Let down your tap root
> To the center of your soul
> Suck up the sap
> from the infinite source
> of your unconscious
> And
> Be evergreen
> (Winnicott, 1989, p. 17)

In "Turbulent Healing," Dr. Sachs focuses on the vital issues of counter-transference for new fathers. Blending personal experience, case studies and theoretical material, the author explores a new subject in some depth. Concerns regarding self-disclosure, patient and therapist sensitivity, and fragility are explored. Because of its innovative topic, and his own self-disclosure, this piece provides a particularly innovative component of the book.

27

Turbulent Healing: The Challenge of Doing Therapy During the Transition to Fatherhood

Brad Sachs

Shortly after finding out that my wife and I were expecting our third child, a new patient named Mark contacted me to begin therapy. A taciturn attorney who was almost exactly my age, he had called because he had separated from his wife 6 months before, and had vague feelings of loneliness and loss, as well as the sense that his life no longer had meaning.

He and his wife had not had any children, and while their breakup had, up until this point, been relatively amicable, he felt like he had little to show for the emotional investment of a 7-year marriage.

At one point early on, I asked him to outline for me a typical day in his life. He related that usually he woke up, took a run, went out to breakfast by himself and read the paper, went to work, had a business lunch at a restaurant, came back and finished work, went to the gym to work out or play racquetball, had dinner and drinks with a friend or two there, and then went back home to read until bed.

He did mention that, in his eyes, the increased amount of time and energy he now had for his practice was resulting in his doing better work, and some important new referrals rolling in: "It's like I really have nowhere else to go or anybody else to be with, so my clients are getting my full attention, and pretty damn good attention at that."

He said that he had just started dating, was surprised to find out how much he was "in demand," and that his first sexual encounters since having been married had been very exciting ones, even though he was somewhat ambivalent about pursuing them. One woman in particular had asked him to join her for a long weekend in Acapulco that she had won through high achievement at her job, and he was seriously considering the offer.

His parents lived in the area, and he reported that he had been stopping by there much more often than usual, for lunch or dinner if he didn't have other arrangements, and on weekends, and that he felt like they had been a strong source of support for him during this anxious and hurtful period of time.

During my first few meetings with Mark, I noticed that I was having a difficult time getting a handle on how I could be of some help. It wasn't that my mind was wandering: in fact, I felt extremely interested in and attentive to what he was saying about his life. It was as if I was actually *there* with him as he ran, worked, ate out, flirted with women, visited his parents, read himself to sleep.

Feeling a little stuck, I brought this case up in one of the consultation groups that I was a part of. After some discussion, one of my colleagues remarked, "You know, he sounds like he's gotta be in pain, but doesn't quite know how to express it, maybe because he's frightened of letting you and him in on how much of it there is."

"Pain," I asked myself, stunned. "Mark is in pain?" I was quiet for a moment. "Of course he's in pain," I reminded myself, "he came into my office pretty much announcing that that was why he was here . . . how could I not have known?" After all, I had worked with many people whose psychological "wires" were down, and yet could generally count on myself to stay in tune with them while gently teasing their subterranean ache to the surface. What was different about Mark and I?

The group leader encouraged me to talk more about the impact Mark was having on me, and what it was like to be with him. As I spoke, it became evident that he and I were at juxtaposed points in our lives, wherein what was painful to him felt simply enviable, if not delicious, to me.

I discussed with the group the ways in which my personal life, with two small children and another one already on the way, contrasted so drastically with his. He had "too much" free/alone time on his hands; I had almost none. He was served his food two or three times a day; my wife and I were lucky to sit for more than 5 minutes at a time during our frantic meals at home, and seemed to constantly be either loading or emptying a dishwasher.

He got to exercise twice a day, in a leisurely way; if I woke up very, very early, I had exactly 40 minutes to take a run, from out-of-bed to out-on-the-road to out-of-shower. He could make his work a priority: I felt constantly hamstrung between the demands of my patients, the demands of my family, and my often unfulfilled desire to write more. He was once again able to turn to his own parents to be parented; I was too busy parenting my children to get much parenting of my own. He read himself to sleep; I couldn't remember the last book I had been able to finish.

He was feeling the thrill of new romance and its attendant sexual passion; in my position, I was as likely to seduce, or be seduced by, another woman as I was to fly to the moon. He was going to Acapulco with an attractive, unattached woman; I was busy trying to find a sitter so that my wife and I could stumble out to see a movie every couple of weeks.

On and on I went as my therapeutic buddies sympathetically nodded their heads. Finally, feeling both spent and relieved, I was able to bring the focus back to Mark, and to go about setting up the treatment in a way that would lead him to feel healed, and able to move on. But it was only when I realized exactly how deprived and depleted I was feeling, and gave voice to the ways in which these feelings were impeding my capacity to resonate to his distress, that I was able to summon the energy, skill, and motivation to more fully care for him.

Therapist Fathers

There has been a great deal more clinical research and thought addressing the female therapist's transition into motherhood than the male therapist's transition into fatherhood. This is partially because, as long as a woman is having a child by birth rather than by adoption, the biology of expectancy makes it absolutely clear to her patients that this transition is taking place, whereas a man's expectancy is physiologically invisible.

This differential is also an outcome of the general belief that men are not to be taken seriously as caregivers for their children, however, and that their parental evolution is so trivial and circumscribed that it is unlikely to be worthy of any careful examination, particularly vis-à-vis their relationship with their patients.

After all, a "real man" is supposed to define himself and his self-worth by the work that he does, without allowing his personal life to intrude. Even if the work is psychotherapy, which relies by definition on a thoughtful examination of his patients' experiences as children, spouses, and parents, his *own* experiences in these roles are still supposed to fall dutifully into line and take their place behind his commitment to his career.

It is clear, however, that such an approach is shortsighted. Like it or not, a man's transition into parenthood is a profound experience, one that shakes the very foundations of his identity and that will leave him transformed as a man, and as a therapist. To ignore or minimize the impact of this transition on his therapeutic work limits his potential to resolve the concerns of those who come to him for help at this important stage in his life.

This chapter examines the impact of impending and early fatherhood on the psychotherapeutic work that men do. Because this topic has not been explored with much depth in the psychological literature, the findings are based on interviews with clinicians whose primary professional activity was psychotherapy, and who were either expectant or new fathers (fathers who had a youngest child 3 years old or less) at the time of the interview.

Although the patient's transferential response to the therapist's transition into fatherhood is significant in its own right, the focus here will be on the therapist's personal experience, and the countertransferential reactions that he may be likely to experience.

THE CHALLENGES

Readers of this volume probably do not need to be convinced that the transition into fatherhood is a complex and tumultuous time in a man's life. The new father will experience intense emotional lability, characterized by frequently alternating feelings of helplessness, rage, exhilaration, frustration, delight, sorrow, and passion. He may feel pleased and optimistic about his parenting skills one moment, demoralized and hopeless the next.

His marriage may feel like a roller-coaster, as the stress of new parenthood wallops the integrity of his bond with his mate, and battle lines are drawn in a number of different arenas, including child-rearing style, prioritizing of activities, scheduling of time, commitment to work, relationships with the grandparents, division of labor, and sexuality.

His concern with being a good provider will surge into prominence, and jumpstart heretofore hidden anxieties about the family's financial future. He will feel physically exhausted and emotionally depleted, at times as much in need of parenting as his offspring. And the presence of his new child will send him back on a reverberating journey into his own childhood, reawakening memories, struggles, and concerns that have lain dormant for decades, and that now clamor for recognition.

The ways in which this matrix of issues affects a therapist's relationships with his patients are of course multitudinous. Based on my discussions with the subjects of this study, however, I sorted these changes into several headings under which most of them could be categorized.

Neediness

Utilizing the support of my colleagues to process my experience with Mark enabled me to see how depleted I was feeling, and how needy I really was.

Every therapist I interviewed spoke to this same issue, and commented on how difficult it was to give to others during a period of time when you're not getting much for yourself. The extraordinary demands that are placed on new parents, and the gathering up of the emotional resources that are necessary to effectively care for their new families, take their toll on a therapist's capacity to steadfastly be there for his patients in the way that they may need and want him to be.

Sometimes, this became clear when a therapist realized how tempted he was to use the therapy to fulfill his own needs, possibly interfering with his fulfilling the needs of his patient. A therapist who had a 6-month old daughter commented:

> One of my patients is an older woman, a pediatric nurse, and she's constantly asking how the baby is doing, and frankly, it's so hard for me not to really open up to her, because she's very understanding, and probably would have some good advice for me based on her experience. The main reason she's in therapy, of course, is because she's never made her own life a priority, she's so busy "nursing" everybody else, her parents, her husband, her friends, and I know that her interest in me and the baby is probably calculated to take the focus off of herself, and slide into the caregiving role she's more comfortable with. But God, after another sleepless night, when I'm so

wiped out, part of me really would like to just switch roles, and have her listen to me, rather than the other way around.

Some therapists said that their feelings of being "psychologically malnourished" were expressed with a reduced feeling of tolerance and understanding with their more difficult patients. A psychologist with twin girls confided:

You'll pardon the expression, because I'm sure the better term is "borderline personalities," but I just don't feel like working with "assholes" anymore. I know these people are terribly hurt, terribly traumatized, and I'm sure they're not being malicious but are replicating with me whatever abuse or neglect they experienced long ago, but I'll tell you, I just don't have it in me anymore, I don't feel like sacrificing my time and my energy when I'm so unappreciated, when the work seems so unrewarding, and when I would just as soon be home taking care of my girls and making sure that they are inoculated against the kind of pain these people walk around with.

Another therapist explained:

I see patients in my home, which is really a mixed bag, but in any case, one night my daughter was running a very high fever, she was very little then, only a couple of months, and even though I knew my wife was taking good care of her, I just couldn't concentrate. It struck me as so ironic that that evening I had a client who kept focussing on how neglected her "inner child" felt, and all I could think about was my own, neglected "outer" child, my real-life child on the other side of the office wall, and how I'd rather be there holding and comforting her, than locked in with this patient.

And a psychologist who had a 2-year-old son remembered vividly:

Shortly after (Jason) was born, I took 2 weeks off from my practice. One patient, upon returning, really busted me up about this, telling me how irresponsible and unprofessional I was being to make myself so unavailable to my patients, and wondering how I could be so selfish and insensitive. Under normal circumstances, I would have simply heard him out, reflected back to him how abandoned and hurt he felt, and explored with him some of the other places in his life where he felt this way. But frankly, I was so pissed off at this reaction that I just got defensive, and started debating with him about how I was really being "very responsible" to take time off during a vulnerable time, that it wouldn't have been very professional to show up for work unless I could really do the work. This was a good point, I knew, but I also knew that he wasn't listening, and so we wasted most of the session arguing about whether or not I was being very professional, but really, what I resented was that he didn't understand that my fatherhood was a priority to me, and couldn't find within himself the capacity to put his own needs on hold, and value mine.

Most therapists spoke about the ways in which their sexual needs were unmet during the early stages of parenthood, and how that left them vulnerable to fantasizing about their female patients in a way that interfered with their ability to do good work. One noted:

I had this one patient who was really nice-looking, but whom I didn't feel all that attracted to. Until about 6 months into fatherhood, that is, I mean my wife and I were not doing all that well sexually, and all of a sudden, I was feeling very drawn to her, looking forward to seeing what she was wearing, thinking about her after sessions, and I knew that this wasn't a very good thing. I was able to get a handle on things by bringing it up in supervision, and with time, my infatuation sort of trailed off, but for a while there I thought I was a goner. Something about her being pretty and single and me feeling so burdened by marriage and parenthood, and so unattractive, made me very eager to fantasize about her.

Revivified Childhood Experiences

Having a child inevitably takes us back into our own childhoods. This haunting journey into the past can ultimately be a very healing one, enabling us to reveal and resolve conflicts and traumas that may have been influencing our lives without our having much awareness of this. At first, however, revisiting a history that is both unremembered but unforgettable is painful, for experiences that we may have chosen to repress, deny, or avoid begin to bubble up, and force us to give them a second look.

The disinterring of memories will significantly alter a therapist's relationship with his patients in many different ways. A social worker who was the father of an 18-month-old girl explained:

I used to run a therapy group for men who have abused their children, which most of the men were court-ordered into if they wanted to have visitation rights. I had been the group's therapist for more than 2 years, but shortly after my daughter was born, I had a terrible experience. One of the newer group members began to talk about how he had molested his own daughter, and I just got sick to my stomach. . .I almost told him to shut up, but somehow hung in there and was quiet. Shortly thereafter I started having some dreams about a babysitter that I had had, and went into therapy myself. I began to recall that she had done some very inappropriate things to me, things that border on sexual abuse, like washing my genitals over and over again when she gave me a bath, and inviting me into the bathroom when she was peeing . . . Something about having a daughter of my own, and dealing with these men, and WHAM!, I went right back to a place that I didn't even remember having ever been to. . .One of the things that came out of my being in therapy, though, was that I just lost my desire to run this group. . .it was like too much to handle, my own daughter, my own recovery from abuse, and these abusive men. . .

One clinician with two toddlers noted:

I remembered my mother as being kind of a "rage-aholic," she was always blowing up at my brothers and I. . .but since I left home, I obviously didn't see much of that anymore. However, one time I came home from work, and she had been babysitting for my sons, and she was really hollering at (the oldest), just blasting him for having crayoned on the walls. And I got all twisted up inside, because it was such a hideous memory of what things had been like for me long ago.

Anyway, the next week I was working with a family with two very challenging adolescents, and at one point the mother just blew up, telling them she was sick of them breaking curfews and drinking and missing school. . .and instead of seeing this as a possible breakthrough, and letting the family process this, seeing how her husband or children responded to her intensity, I jumped right in to rescue the kids, asking her to sit in the waiting room while I talked to them. In retrospect, it's like I wanted to exile her for being so much like my own mother was, and that glimpse of my mother that I saw when she was nailing my son was too much for me to take.

Increased Sense of Responsibility. Every man who makes the transition into fatherhood at some level feels more responsible than he ever has before for the fiscal needs of his family. Some of this is built into the socialization of males in this culture: they are instructed that their main role within the family is to provide financially, and provisioning for any other kind of needs is secondary.

Some of this is also a natural outcome of the actual circumstances associated with starting a family. For example, he may be in a marriage in which both he and his partner were wage-earners prior to childbirth, a situation that is a necessity for the vast majority of couples these days. If this was the case, his wife's temporary leave from work for pay before and/or after childbirth forces him to consider picking up the slack and carrying more fully the income-producing burden.

At the same time, however, having children changes the ways in which a man wants to spend his time. Although prior to fatherhood he (and his wife) may have been tolerant of, if not comfortable with, his relatively long hours, now he may find that he wants (and is wanted) to be home more, rather than less. He may desire to be more fully available to his wife and child during the period of time when both are so dependent on him, and/or he may desire to simply "be there" to witness the remarkable process of his children's growth and change.

All of these "logistical" issues in one way or another buffeted the therapists that I spoke with, and affected the ways in which they did their work. For example, I signed the lease for the office in which I began my private practice the same month that my first son was born. This 3-year legal commitment terrified me at first, and I found myself sometimes taking patients that, in retrospect, weren't all that well-suited to me, simply to keep the money coming in while referrals were fluctuating.

A colleague shared with me some difficulties that grew out of similar concerns:

> My first couple of years of parenthood, my wife wasn't working at all, and I was just so scared that we weren't going to make it financially. And I think it really impaired my judgement, I would just get so twitchy whenever a patient brought up terminating . . . it's like I didn't really give them room to leave, and then return if necessary, I was constantly questioning their "motives" in a way that probably wasn't very therapeutic. Now that things are a bit more settled, and I'm feeling a little more confident, I can see that I probably wasn't being all that competent if every time a patient wanted to finish up work, or take a break, I got so edgy . . .

Another therapist had the "opposite" problem, in that he was working in a different setting, but a problem that also grew out of the often conflicting pulls and tugs that new fathers experience:

> I was working at a mental health clinic at the time my daughter was born, and we were required to work two evenings a week, from noon to nine p.m. Well, I kind of enjoyed this prior to having her, but once she was born, I just wanted to be home as soon as possible at night . . .

it just didn't feel right having her go down without my being there to kiss her good night. So I would really discourage the patients who, due to their schedules, had to come in the evening, from coming. If they wanted to come weekly, I would suggest that maybe they could do with every other week, because the clinic's policy was pretty flexible in that we could just leave if we didn't have anyone scheduled. One time I felt awful, I learned that a patient whom I had been cutting back with, with some ambivalence, had had to be hospitalized . . . while I can't be sure this would've been prevented by more frequent appointments, the clinic director was appalled that this woman had been coming every other week when she was so shaky, and I kind of wonder if my impatience and reluctance to be there for her came across and really interfered with my doing what needed to be done.

Recommendations

In commenting on some possible solutions to the issues and concerns that have been described up until now, I'm reminded of the card I came across for couples who are expecting a child: "There are three rules for surviving the arrival of a new baby. . .Unfortunately, nobody knows what they are."

In some ways, of course, early parenthood by definition will be a turbulent, anxious time: this is a sign that real change is coming about, that real attachments are forming, that the parents, as well as the child, are evolving.

On the other hand, because the work that we do as therapists is so crucial, and so delicate, it does behoove us to explore the ways in which we can navigate the transition into fatherhood in a way that enhances, rather than limits, our capacities as therapists.

Finding Support

Although a positive personal therapy experience and consultation with skilled supervisors lay the foundation for effective therapeutic work at any stage of the clinician'sdevelopment, either or both may be particularly useful during the early stages of parenthood. That is because, as we have seen above, the internal and external stressors that adhere to the transition into fatherhood make it all the more challenging for a new father to disentangle his own issues from those of his patients.

Several of the therapists I interviewed were already in therapy and/or supervision when they became expectant fathers, and spoke enthusiastically about the support that they found there. Several others commenced therapy or study with a new supervisor shortly after becoming a father.

One therapist said, *"I had been in individual supervision for several years, but I decided to form a peer consultation group about a year into fatherhood, composed of other therapists who were kind of at my stage of life. I think it was not just wanting the perspective that other therapists provide, but also, maybe more so, the support that I got from my colleagues."*

In my personal life, while I had been in individual therapy prior to becoming a father, my wife and I found it very helpful to begin couples work with a different therapist to deal with the changes that had come about in our relationship since becoming parents. As the two of us adjusted to parenthood, and found that beginning a family could actually enhance rather than detract from our marriage, it gave me the confidence to help other couples to travel along the same intimacy-promoting pathways.

Although it would be hard to imagine the therapist in the throes of early parenthood who would not benefit from the support that good therapy or supervision provide, there are other forms of support that may be just as essential.

For example, men, raised as they are to be independent, and to not take the role of fatherhood in their lives very seriously, often have a difficult time connecting with other fathers around family issues. The prospect of opening up to another man about the spectrum of complicated feelings associated with parenthood may feel odd or scary. Yet men who deprive themselves of this kind of contact make it that much harder on themselves when it comes to negotiating the perplexing currents of family life.

I was extremely fortunate to have several close friends and colleagues, as well as a brother, who became fathers around the same time that I did, and the reciprocal sharing that we did among ourselves was one of the things that kept me grounded, and able to prevent my frequent feelings of bewilderment and demoralization from infiltrating my clinical work.

Another clinician remarked:

I'm part of a men's group, and we've all got kids, although most of theirs are older, and they're like the only guys I can really let my guard down with, and can reassure me that most of these things I'm wrestling with will work out just fine. . .it took me a while to open up and not feel like I had to be the group's therapist, but once I let go, it's been a tremendous source of relief and well-being.

Taking Care of Yourself and Your Family

It sounds so trite, yet it's so true: you can't give what you don't have, and if you're not taking good care of yourself, you'll have little to offer your patients. Because so much of a man's self-worth is tied in with his productivity on the job, it can become difficult for him to make family life at least as much of a priority as work life. But such prioritizing is an integral part of becoming the kind of person therapists may also be trying to empower their patients to become.

We might feel embarrassed, annoyed, or angry that such things as family illnesses and emergencies occur that prevent us from being available to our patients in the way that we, and they, might like us to be. But these are elements of real life, and the direct outcome of a commitment to one's wife and child(ren). How we handle them may have much more impact on our patients than any other aspect of the work that we do with them.

One therapist observed:

A patient was steamed with me for canceling at the last minute, due to my wanting to be with my daughter at the e.r. when she had to have a couple of stitches in her head. . .but he also said in a later session that he was very struck by how clearly I had made my fatherhood a priority, and realized that he had never left his job to deal with something in his daughter's life, as I had, and how maybe he needed to start reconsidering this.

Another interviewee remarked:

I practice what I preach, because that's important for my patients to note. . . If they hear me talking about the value of family life, but see me dropping everything to leap into action no matter what time they leave a message on my answering machine, then they know that my personal time, and my time with my family, can't be all that valuable, and they can't trust me. . .

A third commented:

"It may sound silly, but if I don't get a nap midday, I'm just out of it for my afternoon patients. . .I mean, I love my (9 month old) son, but

he's a lousy little sleeper, and my wife and I are still up once or twice
with him every night. . .and so I've made that nap a priority, and I'll
see to it that I get it by hook or by crook, I just put everything away
and shut down for those 30–40 minutes and it makes all the difference."

Self-Disclosure

One last issue that needs to be taken on is whether or not it is useful,
or necessary, for the therapist to share with his patients the fact that
he is about to become a father.

As noted above, female clinicians who are having children by birth
do not have the luxury of a choice in this matter, but the expectant
father's gestation is psychological, rather than biological, and thus
invisible to others.

Many feel that remaining behind the proverbial "cloak of anonymity"
is essential for therapeutic work to proceed. This ignores the reality
that most patients, in one way or another, are quite likely to learn about
their therapist's incipient or actual fatherhood, however. This will
either occur by chance (such as coincidentally seeing the therapist
and his offspring outside of the office, or a session cancelled by the
therapist due to a family matter) or by intent (such as by directly
wanting to know if the therapist is a parent, a common question at the
beginning stages of therapy, when the patient wants to know if his/her
clinician is "experienced" in family life, and can be "trusted").

Still, the therapists with whom I spoke all gave careful thought to
whether or not they would disclose with their patients their transition
into fatherhood. Some felt wary of the potential for self-indulgence,
the fear that they were sharing the news for their own gratification,
rather than because it was an important component of their relationship with their patients.

Others acknowledged some legitimate uneasiness and ambivalence
about becoming fathers in the first place, and were anxious that these
feelings might leak out when they told their patients what was up. A
few seemed to be somewhat "in denial" about the impact that fatherhood was going to have on their lives, and imagined (wrongly, as it
turns out) with some evident pride and bravado that since nothing
was going to change significantly, it was not an essential piece of
therapeutic business.

Some therapists were worried about their patients' reactions. They
anticipated that there might be anger, jealousy, rivalry, sadness, and a

host of other roiling emotions as their patients became aware that they, as therapists, would necessarily be shifting some of their energy away from their practice and toward their wives and babies.

Despite these concerns, almost every one of the therapists I interviewed chose to share the news of their transition into parenthood with most of their patients at some point along the way.

One interviewee pointed out that if patients do find out about their therapist's fatherhood without having been respectfully informed ahead of time, they are vulnerable to feelings of having been deceived and betrayed, and an atmosphere of mistrust may pervade the therapy to the extent that the opportunity for continued growth is diminished:

> Although I was pretty open with most of patients, I had decided not to share with a particular patient the fact that my wife and I were expecting, because I just wanted it to be a private matter. But one day I ran into her at the supermarket, while I was holding my baby, who was then two months old, in the front pack. She looked shocked, but didn't say anything. She canceled the following meeting, and seemed very walled off for the next two, wondering out loud if it was time to finish up. The session after, she blurted out, "I can't believe you were expecting a baby all this time, and didn't say a word about it."

> I tried to explore with her what the experience of seeing me with my baby had been like, knowing that it had probably kicked up some old feelings about other "secrets" that had been kept from her when she was a child. But unfortunately my own secretiveness seemed to have impacted on her so harshly that we weren't able to reconcile and examine it together. She decided to "take a break" from therapy, and hasn't ever called back.

> I know that this sense of betrayal that she walks around with probably would have come up anyway around something else, but I can't help wondering if having been straight with her from the get-go would have enabled her to trust me enough to do some more work, and get back to the real origins of her sensitivity to secrets.

Another therapist relayed an opposite experience:

> I decided to share with my patients the fact that my wife and I were going to receive a baby by adoption sometime in the next month or so, because I was planning on taking 2 weeks off to help out at home, and thought that they deserved to know where I was going to be. Mostly, I was glad that I did. Some of my patients responded very warmly and very enthusiastically and some seemed to ignore it. But

one in particular said, "You know, I'm so glad you told me, because I had the sense that you were a little preoccupied these last weeks, and now I know I'm not crazy." Maybe she had really picked up on something, maybe she hadn't, and was just imagining that she had . . . I'll never know, and I don't really need to. But the fact that I had inadvertently given her the opportunity to see herself as "intuitive" rather than "nuts" seems, in retrospect, to have been one of the most curative aspects of the therapy that we did.

In fact, all of the therapists I interviewed who disclosed felt generally positive about having shared the news with their patients (although several said that while they "as a rule" disclosed, they did have certain patients who were either so "damaged," or at such a precarious point in their own development, that they decided that the risks of disclosure far outweighed the risks of anonymity).

There was no question that the disclosure often stirred up often intense transferential reactions. But most found that these reactions provided "grist" for the therapeutic mill, and that staying on top of the clinical work at this crossroads often led to important insights and changes.

I have been fortunate to have shared the news of impending fatherhood three separate times in my own practice, and in each case my patients' reactions were revealing, as if I was able to have instant access to the results of a very effective projective test. Sometimes there was genuine joy, sometimes there was avoidance, sometimes there was annoyance, sometimes there was anger, sometimes a combination of these and other feelings, but in almost every case, the reaction, or apparent lack of reaction, pointed with precision to the hurt, vulnerable, stuck or changing points in patients' lives.

Paying attention to my own reluctance or eagerness to disclose my transition with a specific patient also was clinically useful, and led me to important perspectives on him or her (as well, of course, as myself).

For example, there was one patient whom I felt compelled to "protect" from the news of my second child's imminent birth, because she was currently experiencing fertility problems, and had thus far been unable to conceive. Although it certainly might have been difficult news for her to handle, I soon realized that she was promoting that same sense of "fragility" in her marriage, preventing her and her husband from connecting more intimately around some complicated but necessary matters. Becoming aware, both on my own and through my own experience in supervision, that my and my patients' responses were where the therapeutic "action" was enabled me to honor and explore, rather than fear and avoid, the disclosure and its emotional outcome.

Those interviewees who, as a rule, chose not to share the news did admit that they often felt preoccupied with their secret-keeping, and this, as much as the possibility of being found out, seemed to be the greatest risk:

> The hardest thing about trying to keep this aspect of my private life private is the constant internal debate I find myself engaged in during sessions. It's kind of distracting, really, particularly at points when one of my patients is questioning how much he or she can depend on me, and I'm fully aware that the answer may be "Not much, if my wife goes into labor in the next day or so."

So, although everybody needs to make his/her own personal decision, based on a careful assessment of what's best for them, as well as for each of their patients, it is clear, based on this initial study that therapists felt that the advantages of disclosing impending fatherhood generally outweighed the disadvantages, and that a decision to either disclose or not to disclose had its own attendant risks and benefits.

If a disclosure is made, the interviewees found it helpful to be prepared for patients' inevitable questions and concerns about their ability to concentrate. Sometimes, these came across straightforwardly, as in the case of patients who ask some version of, "How are you going to help me when you'll be so busy with the new baby?" Sometimes, patients' skepticism is embedded in a more veiled question, such as "Are you getting much sleep?," in which they are wondering, of course, if the therapist's care for his child is detracting from his ability to care for them.

Sometimes patients' idealization of the therapist emerges, borne by comments like, "Oh, you'll be a terrific father, I just know it."

Most therapists found that some direct reassurance was all that was necessary to quell these concerns. A statement that acknowledged the impact of fatherhood, testified to the difficulties "even for a therapist" so that patients didn't feel "less than" because they had or were having difficulties as parents, but that also highlighted the therapist's continued presence and availability, often did the trick: "Well, things are a little topsy-turvy, as you can imagine, but I'm feeling fine right now," or "I'm doing all right, but if for some reason or another I don't think I'll be able to adequately focus on our work, I'll be sure to let you know so that we can reschedule for a better time."

One therapist told me that he was very glad that he had been up front with his patients about his wife's pregnancy, because as it turned out his daughter was born with a defect in her heart that required several early surgical interventions. Having laid this foundation, he was able to be more clear when he explained that his availability might vary, and asked his patients to be tolerant of this for a little while until the dust cleared, or to accept a referral to another clinician if they were in too much distress.

He related that one patient's response was, "You seem to be taking such good care of yourself in the midst of this crisis . . . I wish I could do the same with all of the 'little things' that seem to bug me so."

OPPORTUNITIES

Although the focus of this chapter has been on some of the obvious and subtle challenges that awaited therapists as they made the transition into fatherhood, it should be emphasized that becoming a father is a tremendous opportunity for a therapist, too. Every clinician that I interviewed testified to this, celebrating the heightened sensitivity and empathy that accompanied the birth of their child.

One comment, which was echoed in similar ways by a number of others, was, *"I worked with kids and families before I became a father, but now that I'm a father myself, I can really see what my patients are up against. . .I'm a lot less cavalier, a lot less brusque, and a great deal more attentive to how complex family matters are."*

Another observation, which many therapists also spoke to in similar ways, was:

> I have to admit that (becoming a father) has really changed me. . .I'm a lot more open now, I seem to feel things more deeply, things matter to me more, like the environment, the future of our children's life here on earth. . .I don't take anything for granted anymore, and I realize that the work I'm doing as a therapist is absolutely crucial not only to the well-being of my patients, but to the well-being of my daughter, who will have to live in the world we all create for her. . .and so I take it all the more seriously, but enjoy it more, too.

CONCLUSION

No event will surpass fatherhood when it comes to changing the way that a man chooses to live his life. Despite the fact that it is a harbinger of fractious conflicts and unsettling difficulties, it is also one of the single most liberating and redemptive experiences life has to offer, the crucible in which our fullest, richest, and most resonant humanity is forged. Becoming fully conscious of the psychological power that erupts during this extraordinary stage in our lives is the first step towards harnessing it, and enabling us to more effectively inject hope, meaning, and vitality into the lives of the patients who have come to us to be healed.

ACKNOWLEDGMENT

The author would like to thank Dr. Thomas Burns for his friendship, insights, and support during the writing of this chapter, as well as the consultation group led by Dr. Haley Bohen.

References

Abelin, E. L. (1975). Some further observations and comments on the earliest role of the father. *International Journal of Psychoanalysis, 56,* 293–302.

Achenbach, T. M., Howell, C. T., Quay, H. C., & Conners, C. K. (1991). National survey of problems and competencies among four-to-sixteen-year-olds. *Monographs of the Society for Research in Child Development, 56*(3), 225.

Adams, P. L., Milner, J. R., & Schrepf, N. A. (1984). *Fatherless children.* New York: Wiley.

Anderson, G. C., Marks, E., & Wahlbag, V. (1986). Kangaroo care for premature infants. *American Journal of Nursing,* July, 807–809.

Andry, R. (1960). Faulty paternal and maternal-child relationships, affection, and delinquency. *British Journal of Delinquency,* 97, 329–340.

Antonucci, T. (1985). Social support: Theoretical advances, recent findings and pressing issues. In I. Sarason & B. Sarason (Eds.), *Social support: Theory, research and applications* (pp. 21–37). Boston: Marinus Nijhoff.

Arcana, J. (1983). *Every mother's son: The role of mothers in the making of men.* Garden City, NY: Doubleday.

Arnstein, H. S. (1972). The crisis of becoming a father. *Sexual Behavior, 2,* 42–47.

Atkins, R. (1982). Discovering daddy: The mother's role. In S. Cath, A. Gurwitt, & J. Ross (Eds.), *Father and child: Developmental and clinical perspectives.* Boston: Little Brown.

Bader, A. P. (1993). *Fathers' proficiency at recognizing their newborn by tactile, olfactory, and facial-visual cues.* Unpublished manuscript, Lehigh University, Department of Counseling Psychology, Bethlehem, PA.

Bader, A. P. & Greenberg, M. (1991). *The engrossment scale.* Unpublished manuscript, Lehigh University, Department of Counseling Psychology, Bethlehem, PA.

Baldwin, W. H., & Nord, C. W. (1984). Delayed childbearing in the U.S.: Facts and fictions. *Population Bulletin, 39,* 1–37.

350

Barnett, C., et al. (1970). Neonatal separation: The maternal side of interactional deprivation. *Pediatrics* 45(2):197–205.

Barnett, R. C., & Baruch, G. K. (1987). Determinants of fathers' participation in family work. *Journal of Marriage and the Family, 49,* 29–40.

Barnett, C. R., Leiderman, P. H., Grobstein, R., & Klaus, M. H. (1970). Neonatal Separation: The maternal side of interactional deprivation. *Pediatrics, 45,* 197–205.

Barnett, R. C., & Marshall, N. L. (1991). *Men, family role quality, job role quality and physical health.* Unpublished manuscript. Wellesley Center for Research on Women.

Barnett, R. C., Marshall, N. L., & Pleck, J. (1992.) Men's multiple roles and their relationship to men's psychological distress. *Journal of Marriage and the Family, 54,* 358–367.

Baruch, G. K., & Barnett, R. C. (1983). *Correlates of fathers' participation in family work: A technical report.* Wellesley, MA: Wellesley College Center for Research on Women, working paper # 106.

Belsky, J., Levine, M., & Fish, M. (1989). The developing family system. In M. Gunnar & E. Thelen (Eds.), *Minnesota Symposium on Child Psychology* (Vol. 22, pp. 119–166). Hillsdale, NJ. Erlbaum.

Benedek, T. (1959). Parenthood as a developmental phase: A contribution to the libido theory. *Journal of the American Psychoanalytic Association, 7,* 389–417.

Benedek, T. (1970a). Fatherhood and providing. In E. J. Anthony & T. Benedek (Eds.), *Parenthood* (pp. 167–183). Boston: Little, Brown.

Benedek, T. (1970b). Parenthood during the life cycle. In: E. J. Anthony & T. Benedek (Eds.), *Parenthood* (pp. 185–206). Boston: Little, Brown.

Benjamin, J. (1988). *The bonds of love.* New York: Pantheon.

Benjamin, J. (1991). Father and daughter: Identification with a difference, a contribution to gender heterodoxy. *Psychoanalytic Dialogues, 1,* 277–299.

Benson, L. (1968). *Fatherhood: A sociological perspective.* New York: Random House.

Betcher, W., & Pollack, W. (1993). *In a time of fallen heroes: The re-creation of masculinity.* New York: Macmillan.

Bibring, G. L. (1959). Some considerations of the psychological processes in pregnancy. *Psychoanalytic Study of the Child, 14,* 77–121.

Biller, H. B. (1971). *Father, child, and sex role.* Lexington, MA: Heath.

Biller, H. B. (1972). Include the father in pregnancy. *Medical aspects of human sexuality.* New York: Spectrum.

Biller, H. B. (1974). *Paternal deprivation: Family, school, sexuality, and society.* Lexington, MA: Heath.

Biller, H. B. (1993). *Fathers and families: Paternal factors in child development.* Westport, CT: Auburn House.

Biller, H., & Meredith, D. (1974). *Father power.* New York: David McKay.

Biller, H. B., & Solomon, R. S., (1986). *Child maltreatment and paternal deprivation: A manifesto for research, prevention and treatment.* Lexington, MA: Lexington Books, D.C. Heath.

Biller, H. B., & Trotter, R. J. (1994). *The father factor* New York: Simon & Schuster.

Biller, H., & Weiss, S., (1970). The Father-daughter relationship and the personality development of the female. *Journal of Genetic Psychology, 116,* 79–93.

Bills, B. J. (1980). Enhancement of paternal newborn affectional bonds. *Journal of Nurse Midwifery, 25,* 21–26.

Bion, W. R. (1959). *Splitting and projective identification.* Northvale, NJ: Aronson.

Bloom-Feshbach, J. (1979). *The beginnings of fatherhood.* Unpublished doctoral dissertation, Yale University.

Bloom, D. E. (1984). Delayed childbearing in the United States. *Population Research and Policy Review, 3,* 103–139.

Bloom, D. E., & Trussell, J. (1984). What are the determinants of delayed childbearing and permanent childlessness in the United States? *Demography, 21,* 591–611.

Blos, P., Jr. (1971), Review of parenthood. *Psychoanalytic Quarterly, 40,* 680–681.

Bly, R. (1990). *Iron John.* Reading, MA: Addison-Wesley.

Boehm, F. (1930). The femininity-complex in men. *International Journal of Psycho-Analysis, 11,* 444–469.

Booth, A., & Edwards, J. N. (1985). Age at marriage and marital instability. *Journal of Marriage and the Family, 47,* 67–75.

Bowlby, J. (1951). *Maternal care and mental health.* Geneva: WHO.

Bowlby, J. (1988). *A secure base.* New York: Basic Books.

Brassard, J. A. (1982). *Beyond family structure: Mother-child interaction and personal social networks.* Unpublished doctoral dissertation, Cornell University, Ithaca, NY.

Brazelton, T. B. (1969). *Infants and mothers.* New York: Delta.

Brazelton, T. B. (1992). *Touchpoints.* Reading: Addison-Wesley.

Brenner, P., & Greenberg, M. (1977, July). The impact of pregnancy on marriage. *Medical Aspects of Human Sexuality, 11,* 14–22.

Bronfenbrenner, U. (1989). Ecological systems theory. In R. Vasta (Ed.), *Six theories of child development* (Vol. 6, pp. 187–250). Greenwich, CT: JAI Press.

Brudal, L. F. (1984). Paternity Blues and the Father-Child Relationship. In J. D. Call, E. Galenson, & R. L. Tyson (Eds.), *Frontiers of infant psychiatry* (Volume 2, pp. 381–384).

Brunswick, R. M. (1940). The preoedipal phase of libidinal development. *Psychoanalytic Study of the Child, 9,* 293–319.

Burlingham, D. (1973). The Preoedipal infant-father relationship. *Psychoanalytic Study of the Child, 28,* 23–47.

Butler, M., Luther, D., & Frederick, E. (1988). Coaching: The labor companion, In F. H. Nichols & S. S. Humenick. (Eds.), *Childbirth education: Practice, research, and theory.* Philadelphia: W. B. Saunders.

Campbell, A., & Worthington, E. L., (1982). Teaching expectant fathers how to be better childbirth coaches. *MCN: The American Journal of Maternal-Child Nursing, 7,* 28.

Campbell, J. (1984, April). Our mythology has been wiped out by rapid change. *U.S. News and World Report.*

Carlson, E., & Stinson, K. (1982). Motherhood, marriage timing, and marital stability: A research note. *Social Forces, 61,* 258–267.

Carson, J. L., Burks, V., & Parke, R. D. (1993). Parent-child physical play: Determinants and consequences. In K. B. MacDonald (Ed.), *Parent-child play.* Albany, NY: State University of New York Press.

Cath, S. H. (1982). Vicissitudes of grandfatherhood: A miracle of revitalization. In S. H. Cath, A. R. Gurwitt, & J. M. Ross (Eds.), *Father and child: Clinical and developmental perspectives* (pp. 329–337). Boston: Little, Brown.

Cattell, R. & Scheier, I. (1976). *IPAT Anxiety Scale Questionnaire Self-Analysis Scale.* Champaign, IL: Institute for Personality and Ability Testing, Inc.

Cazenave, N. A. (1979). Middle-income black fathers: An analysis of the provider role. *Family Coordinator, 27,* 583–593.

Chapman, L. L. (1992). Expectant fathers' roles during labor and birth, *Journal of Gynecological Nursing, 21,* 114–120.

Chasseqget-Smirgel, J. (1970). Feminine guilt and the oedipus complex. In J. Chasseguet-Smirgel (Ed.), *Female sexuality* (pp. 93–134). Ann Arbor: Michigan University Press.

Chodorow, N. (1978). *The reproduction of mothering.* Berkeley, CA: University of California Press.

Chodorow, N. (1989). *Feminism and psychoanalytic theory* (p. 33). New Haven: Yale University Press.

Cochran, M. M., & Brassard, J. A. (1979). Child development and personal social networks. *Child Development, 50,* 601–616.

Cochran, M., Larner, M., Riley, D., Gunnarsson, L., & Henderson, C. R. (1990). *Extending families.* New York: Cambridge University Press.

Colarusso, C. A., & Nemiroff, R. A. (1982). The father in midlife: Crisis and the growth of paternal identity. In S. H. Cath, A. R. Gurwitt, & J. M. Ross, (Eds.), *Father and child: Clinical and developmental perspectives* (pp. 315–327). Boston: Little, Brown.

Colman, A. D., & Colman, L. L. (1971). *Pregnancy.* New York: Herder & Herder.

Comer, J. P. (1989). Black fathers. In S. H. Cath, A. R. Gurwitt, & L. Gunsberg (Eds.), *Fathers and their families* (pp. 365–383). Hillsdale, NJ: Analytic Press.

Conner, G., & Denson, V. (1990). Expectant fathers' response to pregnancy: Review of the literature and implications for research in high-risk pregnancy. *Journal of Perinatal and Neonatal Nursing, 4* (2), 33–42.

Cooney, T. M., Pedersen, F. A., Indelicato, S., & Palkovitz, R. (1993). Timing of fatherhood: Is "on-time" optimal? *Journal of Marriage and the Family, 55,* 205–215.

Consolvo, C. A. (1984). Nurturing the fathers of high risk newborns. *Neonatal Network, 2*(6), 27–30.

Corneau, G. (1991). *Absent fathers, lost sons.* Acton, MA: Shambala.

Cotterall, J. L. (1986). Work and community influences on the quality of child rearing. *Child Development, 57,* 362–374.

Covington, J. (1982). *Confessions of a single father* New York: Pilgrim Press.

Cowan, C. P., & Cowan, P. A. (1985, April). *Parents' work patterns, marital and parent–child relationships, and early child development.* Paper presented at the Meetings of the Society for Research in Child Development, Toronto, Canada.

Cowan, C. P., & Cowan, P. A. (1992). *When parents become partners.* New York: Basic Books.

Crnic, K. A., Greenberg, M. T., & Slough, N. M. (1983). Early stress and social support influences on mothers' and high-risk infants' functioning in late infancy. *Infant Mental Health Journal, 7,* 19–33.

Crockenberg, S. B. (1981). Infant irritability, mother responsiveness, and social influences on the security of infant-mother attachment. *Child Development, 52,* 857–865.

Crouter, A. C., Perry-Jenkins, M., Huston, T. L., & McHale, S. M. (1987). Processes underlying father involvement in dual career and single-career families. *Developmental Psychology, 23,* 431–440.

Cutrona, C. E., & Troutman, B. R. (1986). Social support, infant temperament, and parenting self-efficacy: A mediational model of postpartum depression. *Child Development, 57,* 1507–1518.

Daniels, P., & Weingarten, K. (1982). *Sooner or later: The timing of parenthood in adult lives.* New York: Norton.

Daniels, P., & Weingarten, K. (1988). The fatherhood cliché: The timing of parenthood in men's lives. In P. Bronstein & C. P. Cowan (Eds.), *Fatherhood today* (pp. 36–52). New York: Wiley.

DeFrain, J., & Eirick, R. (1981). Coping as divorced parents: A comparative study of fathers and mothers. *Family Relations, 30,* 265–274.

Degler, C. N. (1980). *At odds: Women and the family in America from the revolution to the present* (p. 75). New York: Oxford University Press.

De Leeuw, R., Colin, E. M., Dunnebier, E. A., & Mirmiran, M. (1991). Physiological effects of kangaroo care in very small pre-term infants. *Biological Neonatology, 59,* 149–155.

DeMaris, A., & Greif, G. L. (1992). The relationship between family structure and parent-child relationship problems in single father households. *Journal of Divorce & Remarriage, 18,* 55–77.

Demos, J. (1982). The changing faces of fatherhood: A new exploration in American family history. In S. H. Cath, A. R. Gurwitt, & J. M. Ross (Eds.). *Father and child: Developmental and clinical perspectives* (pp. 425–445). Boston: Little, Brown.

Deutscher, M. (1971). First pregnancy and family formation. In D. Milman & G. Goldman (Eds.), *Psychoanalytic Contributions to Community Psychology* (pp. 233–255). Springfield, IL: Charles C Thomas.

Deutscher, M. (1981). Identity transformations in the course of expectant fatherhood. *Contemporary Psychoanalysis, 17,* 158–171.

Diamond, M. J. (1986). Becoming a father: A psychoanalytic perspective on the forgotten parent. *Psychoanalytic Review, 73,* 445–468.

Diamond, M. J. (1992). Creativity needs in becoming a father. *Journal of Men's Studies, 1,* 41–45.

Diamond, M. J. (1995a). *Fathers and sons: Psychoanalytic perspectives on "good enough" fathering throughout the life cycle.* Unpublished manuscript, Los Angeles Institute for Psychoanalytic Studies.

Diamond, M. J. (in press). Someone to watch over me: The father as the original protector of the mother-infant dyad. *Psychoanalysis and Psychotherapy.*

Dickstein, S., & Parke, R. D. (1988). Social referencing in infancy: A glance at fathers and marriage. *Child Development, 59,* 506–511.

Dimen, M. (1991). Deconstructing difference: Gender, splitting, and transitional space. *Psychoanalytic Dialogues, 1*(3), 335–352.

Dinnerstein, D. (1976). *The mermaid and the minotaur.* New York: Harper and Row.

Ehrensaft, D. (1987). *Parenting together: Men and women sharing the care of their children.* New York: The Free Press.

Ehrensaft, D. (1994). Bringing in fathers: The reconstruction of mothering. In J. L. Shapiro, M. J. Diamond, & M. Greenberg (Eds.), *Becoming a father: Contemporary social, developmental, and clinical perspectives* (pp. 29–45). New York: Springer Publishing Co.

Eisler, M. J. (1921a). Womb and birth saving phantasies in dreams. *International Journal of Psychoanalysis, 2,* 65–67.

Eisler, M. J. (1921b). A man's unconscious phantasy of pregnancy in the guise of traumatic hysteria. *International Journal of Psychoanalysis, 2,* 255–286.

Elder, G. H. (1984). Families kin and the life course: A sociological perspective. In R. D. Parke (Ed.), *The family.* Chicago: University of Chicago Press.

Elder, G. H., & Hareven, T. K. (1993). Rising above life's disadvantage: From the Great Depression to war. In G. H. Elder, J. Modell, & R. D. Parke (Eds.), *Children in time and place* (pp. 47–72). New York: Cambridge University Press.

El Sherif, C., McGrath, G., & Smyrski, J. T. (1979). Coaching the coach. *Journal of Gynecological Nursing, 8,*87.

Elster, A., & Lamb, M. (Eds.), (1986). *Adolescent fatherhood.* Hillsdale, NJ: Lawrence Erlbaum.

Elster, A. B., & Panzarine, S. (1983). Teenage fathers: Stresses during gestation and early parenthood. *Clinical Pediatrics, 22,* 700–703.

Emerson, G. (1985). *Some American men.* New York: Simon and Schuster.

Entwisle, D., & Doering, S. (1981). *The first birth: A family turning point.* Baltimore: Johns Hopkins University Press.

Erikson, E. H. (1963). *Childhood and society.* New York: Norton.

Erikson, E. (1968). *Identity, youth and crisis.* New York: Norton.

Evans, W. N. (1951). Simulated pregnancy in a male. *Psychoanalytic Quarterly, 20,* 165–178.

Fairbairn, W. (1952). *The psychoanalytic studies of personality.* London: Tavistock.

Fast, I. (1984). *Gender identity.* Hillsdale, NJ: The Analytic Press.

Fedele, N. M., Golding, E. R., Grossman, F. K., & Pollack, W. S. (1988). The adult-to-parent transition: Psychological issues in adjustment to first parenthood. In G. Y. Michaels & W. A. Goldberg (Eds.), *Current theory and research on the transition to parenthood.* Cambridge: Cambridge University Press.

Fein, R. A. (1976). Men's entrance to parenthood. *The Family Coordinator, 25,* 341–348.

Feldman, S. S., Nash, S. C., & Aschenbrenner, B. G. (1983). Antecedents of fathering. *Child Development, 54,* 1628–1636.

Ferketich, S., & Mercer, R. (1989). Men's health status during pregnancy and early fatherhood. *Research in Nursing and Health, 12* (3), 137–148.

Finley, G. E., Janovetz, V. A., & Rogers, B. (1990). *University students' perceptions of parental acceptance-rejection as a function of parental age.* Poster presentation at The Conference of Human Development, Richmond, VA.

Fock, N. (1967). South American birth customs in theory and practice. In C. Ford (Ed.), *Cross-Cultural approaches: Readings in comparative research.* New Haven: Human Relations Area Files Press.

Foresight Audio Visual Limited. (1983). *Journey to attachment: The psychocial issues of prematurity* [film]. Toronto, Ontario.

Freeman, T. (1951). Pregnancy as a precipitant of mental illness in men. *British Journal of Medical Psychology, 24,* 49–54.

Freud, S. (1909). Analysis of a phobia in a five-year-old-boy. *Standard Edition, 10,* 1–149.

Freud, S. (1914). On narcissism: An introduction. *Standard Edition, 14,* 67–102.

Freud, W. E. (1981). To be in touch. *Journal of Child Psychotherapy, 7*(2), 141–143.

Freud, W. E. (1987). German introduction to Toronto film. Journey to Attachment: The Psychosocial Issues of Prematurity. Unpublished manuscript. Berlin, Germany.

Freud, W. E. (1991) Das "whose baby syndrome?:" Ein Beitrag zum psychodynamischen Verständnis der Perinatologie. In *Psychosomatische Gynokologie und Geburtshilfe, 1990/1991* (pp. 123–137). Berlin: Springer Verlag.

Freud, W. E. (1992a). Wie ich psychoanalytischer Forscher wurde. *Zwischenschritte, 11,* 86–89.

Freud, W. E. (1992b). Gedanken zur Prophylaxe der Frühgeburtlichkeit. *International Journal of Prenatal and Perinatal Studies, 4,* 819–329.

Freud, W. E. (1995). Premature fathers: Lone wolves? In J. L. Shapiro, M. J. Diamond, & M. Greenberg (Eds). *Becoming a Father: Contemporary social, developmental, and clinical perspectives* (pp. 220–228). New York: Springer Publishing Co.

Freud, W. E., Janssen, E. V., Lupke, H., & M. Nocker-Ribay P. (1993). Frankfurter Thesen: Recommendations put forward at conference on "The basil needs of prematures and their families."*International Journal of Prenatal and Perinatal Psychology, 5,* (3/4) 398–401.

Frodi, A. M., Lamb, M. E., Leavitt, L. A., & Donovan, W. L. (1978). Fathers' and mothers' responses to infant smiles and cries. *Infant Behavior and Development, 1,* 187–198.

Gaiter, J., & Johnson, A. (1984). Contact with intensive care infants: Fathers' sex type infant preference and frequency of visits. In J. Call, E. Calenson, & R. Tyson (Eds.), *Frontiers of infant psychiatry* (pp. 385–394). New York: Basic Books.

Garbarino, J., Guttman, E., & Seeley, J. W. (1988). *The Psychologically Battered Child.* San Francisco: Jossey-Bass.

Gelles, R. J., & Strauss, M. A. (1988). *Intimate Violence: The Definitive Study of the Causes and Consequences of Abuse in the American Family.* New York: Simon & Schuster.

Gerson, M. (1989). Tomorrow's fathers: The anticipation of fatherhood. In S. Cath, A. Gurwitt, L. Gunsberg (Eds.), *Fathers and their families.* Hillsdale: Analytic Press.

Gillespie, W. H. (1956). The general theory of sexual perversion. *International Journal of Psychoanalysis, 37,* 396–403.

Gilmore, D. D. (1990). *Manhood in the making.* New Haven, CT: Yale University Press.

Giveans, D., (1986). Speaking out. *Nurturing News,* 8(2). M. Greenberg (Ed.), Special issue entitled "The Birth of Fathers."

Glick, P. C., & Norton, A. J. (1979). Marrying, divorcing, and living together in the US today. *Population Bulletin,* 32(5).

Goldberg, W. A., & Easterbrooks, M. A. (1984). Role of marital quality in toddler development. *Developmental Psychology, 20,* 504–514.

Golding, W. (1962). *Lord of the flies.* New York: Putnam.

Goldman, J. D. G., & Goldman, R. J. (1983). Children's perceptions of parents and their roles: A cross-national study in Australia, England, North America, and Sweden. *Sex Roles, 9,* 791–812.

Goldner, V. (1991). Toward a critical relational theory of gender. *Psychoanalytic Dialogues,* 1(3), 249–272.

Gorski, P. A. (1979). Stages of the behavioral organization in the high risk neonate: Theoretical and clinical considerations. *Seminars in Perinatology* 3(1), 61–72.

Green, R. (1987). *The "sissy boy" syndrome and the development of homosexuality.* New Haven, CT: Yale University Press.

Greenberg, M. (1976). Greenberg first father engrossment survey. In O. G. Johnson (Ed.), *Tests and measurements in child development: A Handbook* (Vol. 2). San Francisco: Jossey-Bass.

Greenberg, M. (1985). *The birth of a father.* New York: Continuum.

Greenberg, M. (1987). Fathers: Falling in love with your newborn. In E. Shiff (Ed.), *Experts advise parents.* New York: Dell.

Greenberg, M., & Brenner, P. (1977). The newborn's impact on parents marital and sexual relationship. *Medical Aspects of Human Sexuality, 11*(8), 16–29.

Greenberg, M., & Brown, H., (1992, May). *Fathers and fathering.* Paper presented at American Orthopsychiatric Association Annual Meeting in New York City.

Greenberg, M., & Brown, H. (1995). Teen fathers: The search for the father. In J. L. Shapiro, M. J. Diamond, & M. Greenberg, (Eds.), *Becoming A father: Contemporary social, developmental, and clinical perspectives.* (pp. 151–164). New York: Springer Publishing Co.

Greenberg, M., & Morris, N. (1974). Engrossment: The newborn's impact upon the father. *American Journal of Orthopsychiatry, 44*(4), 520–531.

Greenson, R. (1968). Dis-identifying from mother: Its special importance for the boy. *International Journal of Psycho-Analysis, 49,* 370–374.

Greif, G. L. (1985a). *Single fathers.* New York: MacMillan/Lexington Books.

Greif, G. L. (1985b). Children and housework in the single father family. *Family Relations, 34,* 353–357.

Greif, G. L. (1987). A longitudinal examination of single custodial fathers: Implications for treatment. *American Journal of Family Therapy, 15,* 253–260.

Greif, G. L. (1990). The *daddy track and the single father.* New York: MacMillan/Lexington Books.

Greif, G. L., & DeMaris, A. (1990). Single fathers with custody. *Families in Society, 71,* 259–266.

Greif, G. L., & DeMaris, A. (1991). Single fathers who receive child support, *American Journal of Family Therapy, 19,* 167–176.

Griswold, R. (1993). *Fatherhood in America.* New York: Basic Books.

Grossman, E. (1987). Separate and together: Men's autonomy and affiliation in the transition to parenthood. In P. Berman & E. Pedersen (Eds.), *Men's transitions to parenthood* (pp. 24–39). Hillsdale, NJ: Erlbaum.

Grossman, F., Eichler, L., Winickoff, S., Anzalone, M., Gofseyeff, M., & Sargent, S. (1980). *Pregnancy, birth and parenthood.* San Francisco: Jossey-Bass.

Grossman, F. K., & Pollack, W. S. (1984, October). *Good-enough fathering: A longitudinal focus on fathers within a family system.* Paper presented at the Research Division of the National Council on Family Relations, Annual meeting, San Francisco.

Grossman, F. K., Pollack, W. S., & Golding, E. (1988). Fathers and children: Predicting the quality and quantity of fathering. *Developmental Psychology, 24*(1), 82–91.

Grossman, F. K., Pollack, W. S., Golding, E. R., & Fedele, N. M. (1987). Autonomy and affiliation in the transition to parenthood. *Family Relations, 36,* 263–269.

Gurwitt, A. R. (1976). Aspects of prospective fatherhood: A case report. *Psychoanalytic Study of the Child, 31,* 237–27.

Gurwitt, A. R. (1989). Flight from fatherhood. In S. Cath, A. Gurwitt, L.

Gunsberg (Eds.), *Fathers and their families* (pp. 167–188). Hillsdale, NJ: Analytic Press.

Hangsleben, K. L. (1983). Transition to Fatherhood. *Journal of Gynecological Nursing, 12,* 265–270.

Heaney, S. (1988). *Selected poems, 1960–1987.* New York: Farrar, Strauss, and Girouy.

Herzog, J. M. (1982a). On father hunger: The father's role in the modulation of aggressive drive and fantasy. In S. H. Cath, A. R. Gurwitt, & J. M. Ross (Eds.), *Father and child (pp. 163–174). Boston: Little, Brown.*

Herzog, J. M. (1982b). Patterns of expectant fatherhood: A study of the fathers of a group of premature infants. In S. H. Cath, A. R. Gurwitt, & J. M. Ross (Eds.), *Father and child: Developmental and clinical perspectives* (pp. 301–314). Boston: Little, Brown.

Herzog, R., & Sudia, C. E. (1973). Children in fatherless families. In B. M. Caldwell & H. N. Ricciuti (Eds.). *Review of child development research* (Vol. 3). Chicago: University of Chicago Press.

Hess, R. D., & Camara, K. A. (1979). Post-divorce family relationships as mediating factors in the consequences of divorce for children. *Journal of Social Issues, 35,* 79–96.

Hetherington, E. M., Cox, M., & Cox, R., (1982). Effects of divorce on parents and children. In M. E. Lamb (Ed.), *Nontraditional families.* Hillsdale, NJ: Lawrence Erlbaum Associates.

Hetherington, E., & Parke, R., (1979). *Child psychology: A contemporary viewpoint.* New York: McGraw Hill.

Hipgrave, T. (1982). Childrearing by lone fathers. In R. Chester, P. Diggory, & M. Sutherland (Eds.), *Changing patterns of child bearing and child rearing.* London: Academic.

Hite, S. (1981). *The Hite report on male sexuality.* New York: Knopf.

Hochschild, A. (1989). *The second shift. Working parents and the revolution at home.* New York: Viking.

Hoffman, M. L. (1977). Empathy, its development and prosocial implications. *Nebraska Symposium on Motivation.* Lincoln: University of Nebraska Press.

Holman, P. (1959). The etiology of maladjustment in children. *Journal of Mental Science, 99,* 654–688.

Holmes, D. L., Reich, J. N., & Pasternak, J. A. (1983). *The psychological development of infants born at risk.* Hillsdale, NJ: Erlbaum.

Howells, J. (1971). Fathering. In J. Howells (Ed.), *Modern perspectives in international child psychiatry* (pp. 125–156). New York: Brunner Mazel.

Humenick, S. S., & Bugen, L. A. (1987). Parenting roles: Expectation versus reality, *MCN, The American Journal of Maternal–Child Nursing* 12, 36–39.

Hurn, H. T. (1969), Synergic relations between the processes of fatherhood and psychoanalysis. *Journal of the American Psychoanalytic Association, 17,* 437–451.

Hyman, J. (1992). *The emotional reaction of new fathers to the feeding modality of their babies.* Unpublished doctoral dissertation, Institute for Clinical Social Work, Los Angeles, 1992.

Hyman, J. P. (1995). Shifting patterns of fathering in the first year of life: On intimacy between fathers and their babies. In J. L. Shapiro, M. J. Diamond, & M. Greenberg (Eds.), *Becoming a father: Contemporary social developmental, and clinical perspectives* (pp. 242–253). New York: Springer Publishing Co.

Isaacs, H. (1978). Bringing up the father question. *Daedalus, 88,* 189–203.

Jacobson, E. (1950). Development of the wish for a child in boys. *Psychoanaltic Study of the Child, 5,* 139–153.

Jaffe, D. S. (1968). The masculine envy of woman's procreative functions. *Journal of the American Psychoanalytic Association, 16,* 521–548.

Jarvis, W. (1962). Some effects of pregnancy and childbirth in men. *Journal of the American Psychoanalytic Association, 10,* 689–699.

Jessner, L., Weigert, E., & Foy, J. L. (1970). The development of parental attitudes during pregnancy. In E. J. Anthony & T. Benedek (Eds.), *Parenthood* (pp. 209–244). Boston: Little, Brown.

Jones, E. (1992). Psychology and childbirth. In *Papers on psychoanalysis* (pp. 384–388). Boston: Beacon Press.

Jones, E. (1961). The phantasy of the reversal of generations. In E. Jones (Ed.), *Papers on psycho-analysis* (pp. 407–412). Boston: Beacon Press. (Original work published 1913)

Jones, E. (1961). Psychology and childbirth. In *Papers on psycho-analysis* (pp. 384–388). Boston: Beacon Press. Original work published, 1942.

Jones, L. C., & Lenz, E. R. (1986). Father-newborn interaction: Effects of social competence and infant state. *Nursing Research, 35,* 149–153.

Jones, L. C., & Thomas, S. A. (1989). New fathers' blood pressure and heart rate: Relationships to interactions with their newborn infants. *Nursing Research, 38,* 237–241.

Jordan, P. L. (1995). The mother's role in promoting fathering behavior. In J. L. Shapiro, M. J. Diamond, & M. Greenberg (Eds.), *Becoming a father: Contemporary social, developmental, and clinical perspectives* (pp. 47–57). New York: Springer Publishing Co.

Josselyn, I. (1956). Cultural forces, motherliness and fatherliness. *American Journal of Orthopsychiatry, 26,* 264.

Juster, F. T. (1994). A note on recent changes in time use. In F. T. Juster & F. Stafford (Eds.), *Studies in the measurement of time allocation.* Ann Arbor, MI: Institute for Social Research.

Kaftal, E. (1991). On intimacy between men. *Psychoanalytic Dialogues, 1*(3), 305–328.

Kaitz, M., Good, A., Rokem, A. M., & Eidelman, A. I. (1988). Mothers' and fathers' recognition of their newborns' photographs during the postpartum period. *Developmental and Behavioral Pediatrics, 9,* 223–226.

Kalleberg, A. L., & Loscocco, K. A. (1983). Aging, values, and rewards:

Explaining age differences in job satisfaction. *American Sociological Review, 48,* 78–90.

Kaplan, D. M., & Mason, E. A. (1960). Maternal reactions to premature birth viewed as an acute emotional disorder. *American Journal of Orthopsychiatry, 30,* 539–552.

Keen, S. (1991). *Fire in the belly.* New York: Bantum.

Kennell, J. H., & Klaus, M. (1988). The perinatal paradigm: Is it time for a change. *Clinics in Perinatology 15*(4), 801–813.

Kemp, V., & Hatmaker, D. (1989). Stress and social support in high-risk pregnancy. *Research in Nursing and Health,* 12(4), 331–336.

Kernberg, O. (1975), *Borderline conditions and pathological narcissism.* New York: Jason Aronson.

Kestenberg, J. (1975). Parenthood as a developmental phase. *Journal of the American Psychoanalytic Association, 23,* 154–166.

Kimball, G. (1988). *50-50 parenting: Sharing family rewards and responsibilities.* Lexington, MA: Lexington.

Kipnis, A. (1991). *Knights without armor.* Los Angeles: Tarcher.

Klaus, M., & Kennell, J. (1982). *Parent-infant bonding.* St. Louis: C. V. Mosby Co.

Klaus, M. H., Kennell, J. H., Klaus, P. H. (1993). *Mothering the Mother: How a doula can help you have a shorter, easier and healthier birth.* Boston: Addison-Wesley.

Klein, G. (1976). *Psychoanalytic theory.* New York: International University Press.

Kohut, H. (1971), *The analysis of the self.* New York: International Universities Press.

Kotelchuck, M. (1976). The infant relationship to his father: Experimental evidence. In M. E. Lamb (Ed.), *The role of the father in child development* (pp. 379–344). New York: Wiley.

Kubie, L. (1974). The drive to become both sexes. *Psychoanalytic Quarterly, 43,* 349–426.

Lacoursiere, R. (1972a). Fatherhood and mental illness. *Psychiatry Quarterly, 46,* 109–124.

Lacoursiere, R. (1972b). The mental health of the prospective father. *Bulletin of the Menninger Clinic, 36,* 645–650.

Lamb, M. E. (1975). Fathers. *Human Development, 18,* 245–266.

Lamb, M. E. (1976). The role of the father: An overview. In M. E. Lamb (Ed.), *The role of the father in child development* (pp. 1–63). New York: Wiley.

Lamb, M., (1977). Father-infant and mother-infant interaction in the first year of life." *Child Development, 48,* 167–181.

Lamb, M. E. (1981a). The development of father-infant relationships. In M. E. Lamb (Ed.), *The role of the father in child development* (pp. 459–488). New York: Wiley.

Lamb, M. E. (1981b). Fathers and child development: An integrative overview. In M. E. Lamb (Ed.), *The role of the father in child development* (pp. 1–70). New York: Wiley.

Lamb, M. E. (1981c). *The role of the father in child development,* rev. ed. New York: Wiley.

Lamb, M. E. (1983). Fathers of exceptional children. In M. Seligman (Ed.), *The family with a handicapped child: Understanding and treatment.* New York: Grune and Stratton.

Lamb, M. E. (1984). Mothers, fathers and child care in a changing world. In J. D. Call, E. Galenson, & R. L. Tyson (Eds.), *Frontiers of infant psychiatry* (Vol. 2; pp. 343–362). New York: Basic Books.

Lamb, M. E. (1986). The changing roles of fathers. In M. E. Lamb (Ed.), *The father's role: Applied perspectives* (pp. 3–27). New York: Wiley.

Lamb, M. E., Pleck, J. H., Charnov, E. L., & Levine, J. A. (1985). Paternal behavior in humans. *American Zoologist, 25,* 883–894.

Lamb, M. E., Pleck, J. H., Charnov, E. L., & Levine, J. A. (1987). A biosocial perspective on paternal behavior and involvement. In J. B. Lancaster, J. Altmann, A. S. Rossi, & L. R. Sherrod (Eds.), *Parenting across life span: Biosocial dimensions* (pp. 111–142). Hawthorne, NY: Aldine.

Lamb, M. E., Pleck, J. H., & Levine, J. A. (1985). The role of the father in child development: The effects of increased paternal involvement. In B. S. Lahey & A. E. Kazdin (Eds.) *Advances in clinical child psychology* (Vol. 8). New York: Plenum.

Lamb, M., & Sagi, (Eds.) (1983). *Fatherhood and family policy,* Hillsdale, NJ: Erlbaum

Lansky, M. R. (1992). *Fathers who fail.* Hillsdale, NJ: Analytic Press.

Lawrence, G. (1985). *The mother's differential cathexis and treatment of the male and female preoedipal child.* Unpublished doctoral dissertation, The Wright Institute, Berkeley, California.

Leidenberg, D. (1967). *Expectant fathers.* Paper presented at American Orthopsychiatric Association Meeting, Washington, DC, March 1967.

Lemmer, C. (1987). Becoming a father: A review of nursing research on expectant fatherhood. *Maternal-Child Nursing Journal, 16*(3), 261–275.

Lennon, R., & Eisenberg, N. (1987). Gender and age differences in empathy and sympathy. In N. Eisenberg & J. Strayer (Eds.), *Empathy and its development* (pp. 195–217). Cambridge: Cambridge University Press.

Leonard, M., (1966). Fathers and daughters: The significance of fathering in the psychosexual development of the girl. *International Journal of Psychoanalysis, 47,* 325–334.

Leonard, S. (1976). How first-time fathers feel toward their newborns. *American Journal of Maternal Child Nursing, 1,* 361–365.

Lerner, H. (1974). Early origins of envy and devaluation of women: Implications for sex role stereotypes. *Bulletin of the Menninger Clinic, 38,* 538–553.

Lerner, H. (1979). Effects of the nursing mother-infant dyad on the family. *American Journal of Orthopsychiatry, 49*(2), 339–348.

Levant, R. F. (1988). Education for fatherhood. In P. Bronstein & C. Cowan

(Eds.), *Fatherhood today: Men's changing role in the family.* New York: Wiley Interscience.

Levant, R. F. (1990). Psychological services designed for men: A psycho-educational approach. *Psychotherapy, 27,* 309–315.

Levant, R. F., & Doyle, G. F. (1983). An evaluation of a parent education program for fathers of school-aged children. *Family Relations, 32,* 29–37.

Levant, R. F., & Kelly, J. (1989). *Between father and child.* New York: Viking/Penguin.

Levine, J. A. (1976). *And who will raise the children? New options for fathers (and mothers).* Philadelphia: Lippincott.

Levine, J. (1992, May). Discussion of M. Greenberg's, *A father's support group for juvenile offenders in detention centers in Southern California.* Paper presented at the Annual Meeting of the American Orthopsychiatric Association, New York.

Levinson, D. (1988). Family violence in cross-cultural perspective. In V. B. Van Hasselt, L. Morrison, A. S. Bellack, & M. Hersen (Eds.), *Handbook of family violence* New York: Plenum.

R. Levy, D. M. (1943). *Maternal overprotection.* New York: Columbia University Press.

Levy-Shiff, R., & Israelashvili, R. (1988). Antecedents of fathering: Some further exploration. *Developmental Psychology, 24,* 434–440.

Lichtenberg, J. D. & Slap, J. W. (1973). Notes on the Concept of Splitting and the Defense Mechanism of the Splitting of Representations. *Journal of the American Psychoanalytic Association, 21,* 772–787.

Lidz, T. (1963). *The family and human adaptation.* New York: International Universities Press.

Liebenberg, B. (1973). Expectant fathers. In P. M. Shereshefsky & L. J. Yarrow (Eds.), *Psychological aspects of a first pregnancy and early postnatal adaptation* (pp. 103–114). New York: Raven Press.

Loewald, H. W. (1951). Ego and reality. *International Journal of Psycho-Analysis, 32,* 10–18.

Lynd, R. S., & Lynd, H. M. (1929). *Middletown.* New York: Harcourt Brace.

Lynn, D. (1974). *The father: His role in development.* Monterey, CA: Brooks/Cole.

Maccoby, E. E. (1977, September). *Current changes in the family and their impact upon the socialization of children.* Paper presented to American Sociological Association, Chicago.

Maccoby, E., & Jacklin, C. (1974). *The psychology of sex differences.* Stanford, CA: Stanford University Press.

MacDonald, K., & Parke, R. D. (1986). Parent-child physical play: The effects of sex and age of children and parents. *Sex Roles, 7/8,* 367–378.

Mahler, M. S., Pine, P., & Bergman, A. (1975). *The psychological birth of the human infant* New York: Basic Books.

May, K. A. (1978a). Active involvement of expectant fathers in pregnancy: Some further considerations. *Journal of Gynecological Nursing 7,* 7–12.

May, K. (1978b). *Development of detachment and involvement styles during pregnancy by first-time expectant fathers.* Unpublished doctoral dissertation, University of California, San Francisco.

May, K. (1980). A typology of detachment and involvement styles adopted during pregnancy by first-time expectant fathers. *Western Journal of Nursing Research, 2*(2), 445–461.

May, K. A. (1982a). The father as observer. *MCN: The American Journal of Maternal-Child Nursing, 7,* 319–322.

May, K. (1982b). Three phases in the development of father involvement in pregnancy. *Nursing Research, 31*(6), 337–342.

May, K. (1982c). Factors contributing to first-time fathers' readiness for fatherhood: An exploratory study. *Family Relations, 31,* 352–361.

May, K. (1989). The father's role: Is it time to "fire the coach"? *Childbirth Educator, 19,* 30–35.

May, K. (1991). Psychosocial aspects of high-risk intrapartum care. In Mandeville, L., & Troiano, N. (Eds.), *High-risk intrapartum nursing.* Philadelphia: J.B. Lippincott.

May, K. (1993). *Impact of home-managed preterm labor on families.* Final report, Grant #R01 PN02377, National Institute for Nursing Research, National Institutes of Health, U.S. Department of Health and Human Services, Washington, D.C.

May, K. A. (1995). The impact of high-risk childbearing on expectant fathers. In J. L. Shapiro, M. J. Diamond, & M. Greenberg (Eds.), *Becoming a father: Contemporary social, developmental, and clinical perspectives* (pp. 78–89). New York: Springer Publishing Co.

May, K. (in press). Impact of maternal activity restriction for preterm labor on the expectant father. *Journal of Gynecological Nursing.*

May, K., & Sollid, D. (1984). Unanticipated cesarean birth: from the father's perspective. *Birth, 1*(2), 87–95.

May, R. (1986). Concerning a psychoanalytic view of maleness. *Psychoanalytic Review, 73,* 174–193.

McCorkel, R. J. (1964). Husbands and pregnancy: An exploratory study. Unpublished master's thesis. University of North Carolina, Chapel Hill (reported in Jessner, Weigert, & Foy, 1970).

McHale, S. M., & Huston, T. L. (1984). Men and women as parents: Sex-role orientations, employment, and parental roles with infants. *Child Development, 55,* 1349–1361.

Mead, M. (1935). *Sex and temperament in three primitive societies.* New York: Morrow.

Mendes, H. A. (1976). Single fatherhood. *Social Work, 21,* 308–312.

Mercer, R. (1990). *Parents at risk.* New York: Springer Publishing Co.

Mercer, R., & Ferketich, S. (1988). Stress and social support as predictors of anxiety and depression during pregnancy. *Advances in Nursing Science, 10*(2), 26–39.

Mercer, R., & Ferketich, S. (1990). Predictors of family functioning eight months following birth. *Nursing Research, 39*(2), 76–82.

Mercer, R., Ferketich, S., & DeJoseph, J. (1993). Predictors of partner relationships during pregnancy and infancy. *Research in Nursing and Health, 16,* 45–56.

Mercer, R., Ferketich, S., DeJoseph, J., May, K. & Sollid, D. (1988a). Effect of stress on family functioning during pregnancy. *Nursing Research, 37*(5), 268–275.

Mercer, R., Ferketich, S., May, K., DeJoseph, J., & Sollid, D. (1988b). Further exploration of maternal and paternal fetal attachment. *Research in Nursing and Health, 11*(2), 83–95.

Miles, M. S. (1992). The stress response of mothers and fathers of preterm infants. *Research in Nursing and Health, 15,* 261–269.

Mitscherlich, A. (1969). *Society without the father* (E. Mosbacher, trans.). New York: Harcourt, Brace & World.

Mussen, P. H., & Rutherford, E. (1963). Parent-child relations and parental personality in relation to young children's sex-role preferences. *Child Development, 34,* 589–607.

Nash, J. (1965). The father in contemporary culture and current psychological literature. *Child Development, 36,* 261–297.

Neville, B., & Parke, R. D. (1987). *Parental age and gender effects on parent-child play.* Unpublished manuscript, University of Illinois, Urbana-Champaign.

Neville, B., & Parke, R. D. (1993). *Waiting for paternity: Interpersonal and contextual implications of the timing of fatherhood.* Unpublished manuscript, University of Washington.

Nydegger, C. N. (1973). *Timing of fatherhood: Role perception and socialization.* Unpublished doctoral dissertation, The Pennsylvania State University, University Park, PA.

Ochberg, R. (1987). *Middle-aged sons and the meaning of work.* Ann Arbor, MI: U.M.I. Research Press.

O'Connell, M. (1991). Late expectations: Childbearing patterns of American women for the 1990's. *Current Population Reports,* Series P-23 No. 176.

Odent, M. (1992). *The nature of birth and breastfeeding.* London: Bergin and Garvey.

Osherson, S. (1987). *Finding our fathers: The unfinished business of manhood.* New York: Fawcett.

Osherson, S. (1992). The wounded father within. In C. Scull (Ed.), *Fathers, sons, and daughters: Exploring fatherhood, renewing the bond.* Los Angeles: Tarcher.

Osofsky, H. J. (1982). Expectant and new fatherhood as a development phase. *Bulletin of the Menninger Clinic, 46,* 209–230.

Osofsky, H. J., & Culp, R. (1989). Risk factors in the transition to fatherhood. In S. Cath, A. Gurwitt, & L. Gunsberg (Eds.), *Fathers and their families* (pp. 145–165). Hillsdale, NJ: Analytic Press.

Ostrovsky, E. (1959). *Father to the child.* New York: Putnam.

Parens, H. (1975). Parenthood as a developmental phase. *Journal of the American Psychoanalytic Association, 23,* 154–165.

Parke, R. (1981). *Fathers.* Cambridge MA: Harvard University Press.

Parke, R. D. (1988). Families in life-span perspective: A multilevel developmental approach. In E. M. Heatherington, R. M. Lerner, & M. Perlmutter (Eds.), *Child development in life-span perspective* (pp. 159–190). Hillsdale, NJ: Erlbaum.

Parke, R. D. (1990). In search of fathers: A narrative of an empirical journey. In I. E. Sigel & G. H. Brody (Eds.), *Methods of family research.* Hillsdale, NJ: Erlbaum.

Parke, R. D., Hymel, S., Power, T. G., & Tinsley, B. R. (1980). Fathers and risk: A hospital-based model of intervention. In D. B. Sawin, L. C. Hawkins, L. O. Walker, & J. H. Penticuff (Eds.), *Psychosocial risks in infant-environment transactions.* New York: Brunner-Mazel.

Parke, R. D., & O'Leary, S. E. (1976). Father-mother-infant interaction in the newborn period: Some findings, some observations, and some unresolved issues. In K. Riegel, & J. Meacham (Eds.), *The developing individual in a changing world, Vol. 2: Social and environmental issues.* The Hague, Netherlands: Mouton.

Parke, R. D., Power, T. G., & Gottman, J. (1979). Conceptualizing and quantifying influence patterns in the family triad. In M. E. Lamb, S. J. Suomi, & G. R. Stephenson (Eds.), *Social interaction analysis: Methodological issues.* Madison: University of Wisconsin Press.

Parke, R., & Sawin, D. (1975, April). *Infant characteristics and behavior as elicitors of maternal and paternal responsiveness in the newborn.* Paper presented at the Society for Research in Child Development, Denver.

Parke, R., & Sawin, D. (1976). The father's role in infancy: A re-evaluation. *The Family Coordinator, 25,* 365–371.

Parke, R. D., & Tinsley, B. J. (1981). Family interaction in infancy. In J. Osofsky (Ed.), *Handbook of infancy* (pp. 579–641). New York: Wiley.

Parker, H., & Parker, S. (1984). Cultural rules, rituals, and behavior regulation. *American Anthropologist, 86,* 584–600.

Parker, H., & Parker, S. (1986). Father daughter sexual child abuse: An emerging perspective. *American Journal of Orthopsychiatry, 56,* 531–549.

Payne, D. E., & Mussen, P. H. (1956). Parent-child relations and father identification among adolescent boys. *Journal of Abnormal and Social Psychology, 52,* 358–362.

Pedersen, E., Zaslow, N., Suwalsky, J., & Caine, R. (1980). Parent-infant and husband-wife interactions observed at five months. In E. Pedersen (Ed.), *The father-infant relationship* (pp. 65–91). New York: Praeger.

Pedersen, F. A. (1975, September). *Mother, father and infant as an interactive system.* Paper presented at the Annual Convention of the American Psychological Association, Chicago.

Pedersen, F. A. (Ed.). (1980). *The father-infant relationship: Observational studies in the family setting.* New York: Praeger.

Pedersen, F. A. (1981). Father influences viewed in family context. In M. E.

Lamb (Ed.), *The role of the father in child development* (pp. 295–317). New York: Wiley.

Peterson, G. H., Mehl, L. E., & Leiderman, P. H. (1969). The role of some birth-related variables in father attachment. *American Journal of Orthopsychiatry, 49*(2), 330–338.

Pleck, E. (1976). Two worlds in one: Work and family. *Journal of Social History, 10,* 178–195.

Pleck, J. H. (1981). *The myth of masculinity.* Cambridge, MA: MIT Press.

Pleck, J. H. (1983). Husband' paid work and family roles: Current research issues. In H. Lopata & J. H. Pleck (Eds.), *Research in the interweave of social roles: Families and jobs* (Vol. 3). Greenwich, CT: JAI Press.

Pleck, J. H. (1984). *Working wives and family well-being.* Beverly Hills, CA: Sage.

Pleck, J. H. (1985). *Working wives/Working husbands.* Beverly Hills: Sage.

Pleck, J. H. (1987). Healing the wounded father. In F. Abbott (Ed.), *New men, new minds: Breaking male tradition.* Freedom, CA: Crossing Press.

Pleck, J. H. (1995). The father wound: Implications for expectant fathers. In J. L. Shapiro, M. J. Diamond, & M. Greenberg (Eds.), *Becoming a father: Contemporary social, developmental, and clinical perspectives* (pp. 196–209). New York: Springer Publishing Co.

Pleck, J. (in press). Are 'Family supportive' employer policies relevant to men? In J. Hood (Ed.), *Work, family, and masculinities.* Newbury, CA: Sage.

Polatnick, M. (1973–1974). Why men don't rear children: A power analysis. *Berkeley Journal of Sociology, 18,* 44–86.

Pollack, W. S. (1982). *"I"ness and "We"ness: Parallel lines of development.* Unpublished doctoral dissertation, Boston University.

Pollack, W. S. (1983). Object-relations and self psychology: Researching children and their family systems. *The Psychologist-Psychoanalyst, 4,* 14.

Pollack, W. S. (1995). A delicate balance: Fatherhood and psychological transformation—A psychoanalytic perspective. In J. L. Shapiro, M. J. Diamond, & M. Greenberg (Eds.), *Becoming a father: Contemporary social, developmental, and clinical perspectives* (pp. 303–318). New York: Springer Publishing Co.

Pollack, W. S., & Grossman, F. K. (1985). Parent-child interaction. In L. L'Abate (Ed.), *The handbook of family psychology and therapy* (pp. 586–622). Homewood, IL: Dorsey.

Porter, R. H., Balogh, R. D., Cernoch, J. M., & Franchi, C. (1986). Recognition of kin through characteristic body odors. *Chemical Senses, 11,* 389–395.

Porter, R. H., Boyle, C., Hardister, T., & Balogh, R. D. (1989). Salience of neonates' facial features for recognition by family members. *Ethology and Sociobiology, 10,* 325–330.

Power, T. G., & Parke, R. D. (1982). Play as a context for early learning: Lab and home analyses. In I. E. Sigel & L. M. Laosa (Eds.), *The family as a learning environment.* New York: Plenum.

Power, T. G., & Parke, R. D. (1984). Social network factors and the transition to parenthood. *Sex Roles, 10,* 949–972.

Pruett, K. D. (1983a). Infants of primary nurturing Fathers. *The Psychoanalytic Study of the Child, 38,* 257–277.

Pruett, K. D. (1983b, April). *Two year follow up of infants of primary nurturing fathers in intact families.* Paper presented to Second World Congress on Infant psychiatry.

Pruett, K. D. (1985). Oedipal configurations in father raised children. *Psychoanalytic Study of the Child, 40,* 435–456.

Pruett, K. D. (1987). *The nurturing father.* New York: Warner Books.

Pruett, K. D. (1993). The paternal presence. Families in society. *The Journal of Contemporary Human Services, 74,* 46–50.

Pruett, K., & Litzenberger, M. (1992). Latency development in children of primary nurturing fathers: Eight-year follow-up. *Psychoanalytic Study of the Child, 47,* 85–101.

Radin, N. (1978, September). *Childrearing fathers in intact families with preschoolers.* Paper presented to American Psychological Association, Toronto.

Radin, N. (1981). The role of the father in cognitive, academic, and intellectual development. In M. E. Lamb (Ed.), *The role of the father in child development* (pp. 379–427). New York: Wiley.

Radin, N. (1982). Primary caregiving and role-sharing fathers. In M. E. Lamb (Ed.). *Nontraditional families: Parenting and child development.* Hillsdale, NJ: Erlbaum.

Radin, N., & Russell, G. (1983). Increased father participation and child development outcomes. In M. E. Lamb & A. Sagi (Eds.), *Fatherhood and family policy* (pp. 121–141). Hillsdale, NJ: Erlbaum.

Radin, N., & Sagi, A. (1982). Childbearing fathers in intact families in Israel and the U.S.A. *Merrill-Palmer Quarterly, 28,* 111–136.

Ragozin, A. S., Basham, R. B., Crnic, K. A., Greenberg, M. T., & Robinson, N. M. (1982). Effects of maternal age on parenting role. *Developmental Psychology, 18,* 627–634.

Raspberry, W. (1993). *Washington Post,* January 1993, p. A-21.

Redican, W. K. (1976). Adult male-infant interactions in nonhuman primates. In M. E. Lamb (Ed.), *The role of the father in child development* (pp. 345–385). New York: Wiley.

Redmond, M. A. (1985). Attitudes of adolescent males toward adolescent pregnancy and fatherhood. *Family Relations, 34,* 337–342.

Reiber, V. D. (1976). Is the nurturing role natural to fathers. *MCN, The American Journal of Maternal-Child Nursing, 1,* 366–371.

Reik, T. (1946). *Ritual.* New York: International Universities Press. Original work published 1919.

Rendina, I., & Dickerscheid, J. D. (1976). Father involvement with first-born infants. *Family Coordinator, 25,* 273–379.

Reppetti, R. L. (1989). Effects of daily workload on subsequent behavior during marital interaction: The roles of social withdrawal and spouse support. *Journal of Personality and Social Psychology, 57,* 651–659.

Richards, M. P. M., Dunn, J. F., & Antonis, B. (1977). Caretaking in the first year of life: The role of fathers' and mothers' social isolation. *Child: Care, Health and Development, 3,* 23–26.

Rice, A. (1982). *Cry to heaven.* New York: Knopf.

Richman, J. (1982). Men's experiences of pregnancy and childbirth. In L. M. McKee, & M. O'Brien (Eds.), *The father figure.* London: Tavistock.

Riley, D. A. (1985). *Father involvement in childrearing: Support from the personal social network.* Unpublished doctoral dissertation, Cornell University, Ithaca, NY.

Riley, D. A., & Cochran, M. M. (1985). Naturally occurring childrearing advice for fathers: Utilization of the personal social network. *Journal of Marriage and the Family, 47,* 275–286.

Rindfuss, R. R., & St. John, C. (1983). Social determinants of age at first birth. *Journal of Marriage and the Family, 45,* 553–565.

Ritvo, S. (1971). Late Adolescence. *Psychoanalytic study of the child. 26,* 241–263.

Robinson, B. (1988a). *Teenage fathers,* Lexington, MA: Lexington Books, D.C. Heath.

Robinson, B. (1988b). Teenage pregnancy from the father's perspective, *The American Journal of Orthopsychiatry, 58*(1), 46–51.

Rodman, H., & Safilios-Rothschild, C. (1983). Weak links in men's worker-earner roles: A descriptive model. *Research in the interweave of social roles: Families and jobs* (Vol. 3, pp. 239–250). Greenwich, CT: JAI Press.

Rose, G. J. (1961). Pregenital Aspects of Pregnancy Fantasies. *International Journal Psycho-Analysis, 42,* 544–549.

Rosenthal, K., & Keshet, H. F. (1981). *Fathers without partners: A study of fathers and the family after marital separation.* Totowa, NJ: Rowman & Littlefield.

Ross, J. M. (1975). The development of paternal identity: A critical review of the literature on generativity and nurturance in boys and men. *Journal of the American Psychoanalytic Association, 23,* 783–817.

Ross, J. (1979). Fathering: A review of some psychoanalytic contributions on paternity. *International Journal of Psychoanalysis, 60,* 317–378.

Ross, J. M. (1982a). The roots of fatherhood: Excursions into a lost literature. In S. H. Cath, A. R. Gurwitt, & J. M. Ross (Eds.), *Father and child: Developmental and clinical perspectives* (pp. 3–20). Boston: Little, Brown.

Ross, J. M. (1982b). In search of fathering: A review. In S. H. Cath, A. R. Gurwitt, & J. M. Ross (Eds.), *Father and child: Clinical and developmental perspectives* (pp. 21–32). Boston: Little, Brown.

Ross, J. M. (1985). The darker side of fatherhood: clinical and developmental ramifications of the Laius motif. *International Journal of Psychoanalytic Psychotherapy, 11,* 117–144.

Ross, J. M. (1986). Beyond the phallic illusion: Notes on man's heterosexuality. In Godel, G., Lane, F., Liebert, F. (Eds.), *The Psychology of Men* (pp. 49–71). New York: Basic Books.

Ross, J. M. (1990). The eye of the beholder: On the developmental dialogue of fathers and daughters. In R. A. Nemiroff & C. A. Colarusso (Eds.), *New dimensions in adult development* (pp. 47–70). New York: Basic Books.

Ross, M. (1993). *The expectant father's experience of high-risk pregnancy and antepartal hospitalization.* Unpublished master's thesis, University of British Columbia, Vancouver, Canada.

Rossi, A. (1977). A biosocial perspective on parenting. *Daedalus, 87,* 1–31.

Rotundo, E. A. (1982). *Manhood in America: The northern middle class, 1770–1920.* Unpublished doctoral dissertation, Brandeis University.

Rotundo, E. A. (1983). Body and soul: Changing ideals of American middle-class manhood, 1770–1920, *Journal of Social History, 16*(4), 23–38.

Rotundo, E. A. (1993). *American manhood: Transformations in masculinity from the revolution to the modern era.* New York: Harper Collins.

Rubin, Z. (1982). Fathers and sons: The search for reunion, *Psychology Today,* June, p. 23.

Russell, G. (1983). *The changing role of fathers?* St. Lucia, Queensland (Australia): University of Queensland Press.

Russell, G., & Radin, N. (1983). Increased paternal participation: The father's perspective. In M. E. Lamb (Ed.), *Fatherhood and family policy* (pp. 139–165). Hillsdale, NJ: Erlbaum.

Rutter, M. (1973). Why are London children so disturbed? *Proceedings of the Royal Society of Medicine, 66,* 1221–1225.

Rutter, M. (1979). Maternal Deprivation, 1972–1978: New Findings, new concepts, new approaches. *Child Development, 50,* 283–305.

Rutter, M., & Garmezey, N. (1983). Developmental psychopathology. In P. H. Mussen (Ed.), *Handbook of child psychology: Vol IV* (pp. 775–911). New York: Wiley.

Sagi, A. (1982). Antecedents and consequences of various degrees of paternal involvement in child rearing: The Israeli project. In M. E. Lamb (Ed.), *Nontraditional families: Parenting and child development.* Hillsdale, NJ: Erlbaum.

Schaefer, R. (1991). *Women and the maze of power and rage.* Annual lecture, Northern California Society for Psychoanalytic Psychology: May 4.

Schafer, R. (1968). *Aspects of internalization.* New York: International Universities Press.

Schwartz, A. E. (1993). Thoughts on the constructions of maternal representations. *Psychoanalytic Psychology, 10,* 331–344.

Scott-Heyes, G. (1982). The experience of perinatal paternity and its relation to pregnancy and childbirth. In N. Beail & J. McGuire (Eds.), *Fathers psychological perspectives.* London: Junction Books.

Scrocco, J. L. (1987). *Treasures of Chanukah.* Parsippany, NJ: Unicorn.

Sears, R., Maccoby, E. E., & Levin, H. (1957). *Patterns of child rearing.* Evanston, IL: Peterson.

Secunda, V. (1992). *Women and their fathers.* New York: Delacorte.

Shannon-Babitz, M. (1979). Addressing the needs of fathers during labor and delivery. *MCN: The American Journal of Maternal-Child Nursing, 4,* 378–383.

Shapiro, J. L. (1985). *The lost cord: Becoming a father in the age of feminism.* Unpublished manuscript, Santa Clara University, Santa Clara, CA.

Shapiro, J. L. (1987). *When men are pregnant: Needs and concerns of expectant fathers.* San Luis Obispo, CA: Impact Publishers.

Shapiro, J. L. (1993a). *The measure of a man: Becoming the father you wish your father had been.* New York: Delacorte.

Shapiro, J. L. (1993b). *When men are pregnant: Needs and concerns of expectant fathers.* New York: Delta. (Original work published 1987.)

Shor, J., & Sanville, J. (1978). *Illusion in loving.* New York: International Universities Press.

Sosa, R., Kennell, J. H., Klaus, M. H., Robertson, S., & Vrrutia, J. (1980). The effect of a supportive companion on perinatal problems, length of labor, and mother-infant interaction. *New England Journal of Medicine, 303,* 597–600.

Snarey, J. (1993). *How fathers care for the next generation: A four-decade study.* Cambridge, MA: Harvard University Press.

Stauber, M. (1979). Psychosomatische Aspekte in der Geburtshilfe. *Deutsches Ärzteblatt: Ärztliche Mitteilungen, 12,* 797–804.

Stechler, G., & Kaplan, S. (1980). The development of the self: A psychoanalytic perspective. *Psychoanalytic Study of the Child, 35,* 85–106.

Stening, W., & Roth, B. (1993). The kangaroo method for premature infants. In T. Blum (Ed.), *Prenatal perception, learning and bonding.* Berlin: Leonardo.

Stern, D. H. (1985). *The interpersonal world of the infant.* New York: Basic Books.

Stolz, L., Dowley, E. M., Chance, E., Stevenson, N. G., Faust, M. S., Johnson, L. C., Faust, W. L., Engvall, A., Ullman, L., Ryder, J. M., & Gowin, D. B. (1968). *Father relations of war-born children.* New York: Greenwood Press. (Original work published 1954)

Stoller, R. (1975). *Perversion: The erotic form of hatred.* Washington, DC: American Psychiatric Press.

Strecker, E. (1946). *Their mothers' sons.* Philadelphia: Lippincott.

Szalai, A. (Ed.). (1972). *The use of time: Daily activities of urban and suburban populations in twelve countries.* The Hague: Mouton.

Teachman, J. D., & Polonko, K. A. (1985). Timing of the transition to parenthood: A multidimensional birth-interval approach. *Journal of Marriage and the Family, 47,* 867–879.

Teichman, Y., & Lahav, Y. (1987). Expectant fathers: Emotional reactions, physical symptoms and coping styles. *British Journal of Medical Psychology, 60,* 225–232.

Tinsley, B. R., & Parke, R. D. (1984). Grandparents as support and socialization agents. In M. Lewis (Ed.), *Beyond the dyad.* New York: Plenum.

Tinsley, B. J., & Parke, R. D. (1988). The role of grandfathers in the context of the family. In P. Bronstein & C. P. Cowan (Eds.), *Fatherhood today.* New York: Wiley.

Tomlinson, P. A. (1987). Father involvement with first-born infants: Interpersonal and situational factors. *Pediatric Nursing, 13*(2), 101–105.

Towne, R. D., & Afterman, J. (1955). Psychosis in Males Related to Parenthood. *Bulletin of the Menninger Clinic, 19,* 19–26.

Trethowan, W. H. (1965). Sympathy pains. *Discovery, 26,* 30–34.

Trethowan, H., & Conlon, M. (1965). The couvade syndrome. *British Journal of Psychiatry, 111,* 57–56.

U.S. Department of Commerce Bureau of the Census (1989). Studies in marriage and the family. *Current Population Reports,* Series P-23, No. 162. Washington, DC: U.S. Government Printing Office.

U.S. Department of Commerce Bureau of the Census (1990). *Household and family characteristics; March 1990 and 1989.* Series P-20, No. 447, Washington, DC: U.S. Government Printing Office.

Van der Leeuw, P. J. (1958). The preoedipal phase of the male. *The Psychoanalytic Study of the Child, 13,* 352–374.

Vanden Heuvel, A. (1988). The timing of parenthood and intergenerational relations. *Journal of Marriage and the Family, 50,* 483–491.

Van Leeuwen, K. (1965). Pregnancy envy in the male. *International Journal of Psycho-Analysis 47,* 319–324.

Vinovskis, M. (1986). Young fathers and their childhood: Some historical and policy perspectives, In A. B. Elster & M. E. Lamb (Eds.), *Adolescent fatherhood* (pp. 171–192). Hillsdale, NJ: Erlbaum.

Volling, B. L., & Belsky, J. (1991). Multiple determinants of father involvement during infancy in dual-earner and single-earner families. *Journal of Marriage and the Family, 53,* 461–474.

Waletsky, L. (1979). Husbands' problems with breast-feeding. *American Journal of Orthopsychiatry, 49*(2), 349–352.

Walter, C. A. (1986). *The timing of motherhood.* Lexington, MA: Lexington Books.

Westney, O. E., Cole, O. J., & Mumford, J. L. (1986). Adolescent unwed prospective fathers: Readiness for fatherhood and behaviors toward the mother and the expected infant. *Adolescence, 21,* 901–911.

Wilkie, J. R. (1981). The trend toward delayed parenthood. *Journal of Marriage and the Family, 43,* 583–591.

Williams, E. (1993). We saved the baby: unfortunately the family is cracking up. *Independent,* June 29.

Winnicott, C., Shepard, R., & Davis, M. (1989). *D. W. Winnicott: Psychoanalytic explorations.* Cambridge: Harvard University Press.

Winnicott, D. W. (1958). Primary maternal preoccupation. In *Collected Papers: Through Paediatrics to Psycho-Analysis* (pp. 300–305). New York: Basic Books.

Winnicott, D. W. (1965). The theory of the parent-infant relationship. In D. W. Winnicott's *The maturational process and the facilitating environ-*

ment (pp. 37–55). New York: International Universities Press. (Original work published 1960.)

Winnicott, D. W. (1965). *Maturational processes and the facilitating environment.* Madison, Connecticut: International Universities Press.

Winnicott, D. W. (1971). *Playing and reality.* London: Tavistock.

Wolf, B. M. (1987). *Stress and social supports: Impact on parenting and child development in single parent and two-parent families.* Unpublished doctoral dissertation, Temple University, Philadelphia.

Wolson, P. (1995a). The vital role of adaptive grandiosity in artistic creativity. *Psychoanalytic Review, 82* (in press).

Wolson, P. W. (1995b). Some reflections on adaptive grandiosity in fatherhood. In J. L. Shapiro, M. J. Diamond, & M. Greenberg (Eds.), *Becoming a father: Contemporary social, developmental, and clinical perspectives* (pp. 272–278). New York: Springer Publishing Co.

Wonnell, E. B. (1971). The education of the expectant father for childbirth. *Nursing Clinics of North America, 6*(4), 591–603.

Yarrow, A. L. (1991). *Latecomers: Children of Parents Over 35.* New York: The Free Press.

Yogman, M. W. (1984). The father's role with preterm and full term infants. In J. D. Call, E. Galenson, & R. L. Tyson (Eds.), *Frontiers of infant psychiatry* (Vol. II-, pp. 363–374). New York: Basic Books.

Yogman, M. (1987). Father-infant play with pre-term and full term infants. In E. Pedersen & P. Berman (Eds.), *Men's transitions to parenthood: Longitudinal studies of early family experiences* (pp. 97–114). New York: Erlbaum.

Zarling, C. L., Hirsch, B. J., & Landry, S. (1988). Maternal social networks and mother-infant interactions in full-term and very low birth weight, preterm infants. *Child Development, 59,* 178–185.

Zaslow, M., Pedersen, F., Suwalsky, J., Rabinovich, B., & Cain, R. (1985). *Fathering during the infancy period: The implications of the mother's employment role.* Paper presented at the meetings of the Society for Research in Child Development, Toronto, April.

Zilboorg, G. (1931). Depressive reactions related to parenthood. *American Journal of Psychiatry, 10,* 927–962.

Index

Springer Publishing Company

GENDER ISSUES ACROSS THE LIFE CYCLE

Barbara Rubin Wainrib, EdD, Editor

This diverse and fascinating volume goes beyond simply helping to sharpen the existing models of male and female adult development. It probes the implications of those developmental and social shifts for clinicians struggling with day-to-day gender issues arising within the clinical context. The result is a richly conceived and well-executed exploration of issues that are basic to us all—as people and as practitioners.

> Gender
> Issues
> Across the
> Life Cycle
>
> *Barbara Rubin Wainrib*
> *Editor*

Partial Contents:

Who's Who and What's What: The Effects of Gender on Development in Adolescence, *W.J. Cosse* • Clinical Issues in the Treatment of Adolescent Girls, *A. Rubenstein* • The Worst of Both Worlds: Dilemmas of Contemporary Young Women, *N. McWilliams* • Gender Issues of the Young Adult Male, *M. Goodman* • The New Father Roles, *R.F. Levant* • The Thirty-Something Woman: To Career or Not to Career, *F. Denmark* • Thirty-Plus and Not Married, *F. Kaslow* • Motherhood in the Age of Reproductive Technology, *S. Mikesell* • Helping Men at Midlife: Can the Blind Ever See? *A.L. Kovacs* • Motherhood and Women's Gender Role Journeys: A Metaphor for Healing, Transition, and Transformation, *J.M. O'Neil and J. Eagan*

Behavioral Science Book Service Selection
1992   224pp   0-8261-7680-1   hardcover

536 Broadway, New York, NY 10012-3955 • (212) 431-4370 • Fax (212) 941-7842

Springer Publishing Company

THE EMPLOYED MOTHER AND THE FAMILY CONTEXT
Judith Frankel, PhD, Editor

This book examines the effect of maternal employment on all members of the family and addresses policy implications arising out of these effects. A number of different kinds of families, including Hispanic, African-American, adolescent, and working-class are included in the study.

Contents:

Springer Series: Focus on Women
1993   304pp   0-8261-7950-9   *hardcover*

536 Broadway, New York, NY 10012-3955 • (212) 431-4370 • Fax (212) 941-7842

Springer Publishing Company

BECOMING A MOTHER
Research on Maternal Role Identity From Rubin to the Present

Ramona T. Mercer, RN, PhD, FAAN

A comprehensive review of all the current knowledge on maternal role attainment since Reva Rubin's seminal work. Drawing from research in nursing, maternal child health, psychology, sociology, and social work, this book examines the psychological transition to motherhood from a contemporary, multidisciplinary perspective. Special circumstances such as preterm birth and single parenthood are discussed, as well as the effect of maternal employment, and maternal age (such as teens and older mothers).

Contents:

I: Anticipating Motherhood. Feminine Identity and Maternal Behavior • Cognitive Work During Pregnancy • Maternal Tasks During Pregnancy

II: Achieving The Maternal Identity. Physical and Psychological Recovery Postpartum • The Process of Becoming Acquainted With/Attached to the Infant • Work Toward Maternal Competence Early Postpartum • Integrating the Maternal Self • Preterm Birth • Transition to the Maternal Role Following the Birth of an Infant with Anomalies or Chronic Illness

III: The Mother in Social Context. Life Circumstances and Teenage, Older, and Single Mothers • Employment and the Maternal Role

Springer Series: Focus on Women
1995   352pp (est.)   0-8261-8970-9   hardcover

536 Broadway, New York, NY 10012-3955 • (212) 431-4370 • Fax (212) 941-7842